Major Figures of Contemporary Austrian Literature

MAJOR FIGURES OF CONTEMPORARY AUSTRIAN LITERATURE

edited by
Donald G. Daviau

PETER LANG

New York · Berne · Frankfurt am Main

Library of Congress Cataloging-in-Publication Data

Major Figures of Contemporary Austrian Literature.

   1. German literature – Austrian authors – History and criticism.   2. German literature – 20th century – History and criticism.   3. Authors, Austrian – 20th century – Biography.   I. Daviau, Donald G.
PT3818.M35   1987   830'.9'9436   86-15273
ISBN 0-8204-0418-7

CIP-Kurztitelaufnahme der Deutschen Bibliothek

Major Figures of Contemporary Austrian Literature /
ed. by Donald G. Daviau. – New York ; Berne ; Frankfurt am Main : Lang, 1987.
   ISBN 0-8204-0418-7

NE: Daviau, Donald G. [Hrsg.]

© Peter Lang Publishing, Inc., New York 1987

Printed by Weihert-Druck GmbH, Darmstadt (West Germany)

TABLE OF CONTENTS

Preface

The aim of this volume is to help make the major figures of the contemporary generation of writers in Austria accessible to an English-speaking audience. The idea for such an undertaking developed out of the widespread interest in Austrian literature that has grown perceptibly in the last decade. Not only in the United States, but also in England, Scotland, France, Germany, Italy, Japan, India, and Egypt attention to Austrian literature has been in a process of escalation. Numerous publications and symposia on Austrian literature in general, on individual writers, and even on the most basic question "What is Austrian Literature?" attest to the widespread scholarly activity in all of these countries. The award in 1982 of the Nobel Prize for Literature to Elias Canetti further enhanced the situation by attracting international attention to Austrian letters.

The appeal of Austrian literature is further demonstrated by the number of works that are currently becoming available in English translations. From the works of classical writers like Franz Grillparzer and Johann Nestroy to turn-of-the-century figures like Arthur Schnitzler, Hugo von Hofmannsthal, Karl Kraus, and Stefan Zweig and up to and including many of the contemporary authors discussed in this volume, Austrian literature is constantly becoming better represented in English versions. Similarly, secondary literature is growing apace particularly with the advent of journals like *Modern Austrian Literature* (USA), *Austriaca* (France) and *Studies in Modern Austrian Literature* (Scotland), which are devoted exclusively to the publication of research on Austrian literature. This enthusiasm for Austrian literature, as it emerges more and more clearly from the shadow of German literature, seems likely to continue to grow in the future because of the quality of the writing and because of the surprising array of authors, a number that seems disproportionately large for the size of the country.

This volume, which is planned as the first in a series, is intended to introduce the major contemporary Austrian authors and their writings. Because of space limitations not all of the authors who could have been included are represented. However, those omitted will appear in the following volume. The intention of the series is to move back in time with each volume, concluding with the generation of Franz Grillparzer, in the nineteenth century, the figure many writers feel represents the beginning of the uniquely Austrian literary tradition.

The methodological approach followed in the various essays is a straightforward discussion of the life and works of the writers. The contributors were asked to accomplish a difficult task, namely, to write an introductory essay for an English-speaking audience without any background in Austrian or German literature, while at the same time providing sufficient depth of analysis to make the essays of interest and utility even to specialists in the field. Readers should derive from this volume a knowledge of the major contemporary Austrian writers, an understanding of their major works and themes, a perception of the dominant literary trends currently in vogue, and finally an awareness of the general features that distinguish Austrian literature.

Since the age of Franz Grillparzer in the nineteenth century Austrian literature has proved to be a strong source of impetus to German letters, particularly during the *fin de siècle* and again in the period after World War II. The essays that follow will demonstrate that the intellectual and artistic forces emanating from Austria are once again as strong today as they have been at any time in the past one hundred and fifty years. They will also further contribute to an understanding of the uniqueness of Austrian literature and thus help to demonstrate and document its claim to a separate identity.

ACKNOWLEDGEMENTS

I would like to express my appreciation to all those who helped bring this volume to fruition. In addition to the contributors of the individual essays my thanks go to the anonymous readers for their many valuable suggestions. Specially I wish to thank Professors Harvey I. Dunkle and Richard H. Lawson for giving generously of their time in reading and improving the manuscript, Jean Weiss for preparing the name index, and Christie J. Hammond for secretarial assistance.

EDITORIAL NOTE

German titles are used throughout the book after being given in English following the first mention. If the work has been published in an English translation, the official translated title is presented in italics. If the English titles are not in italics, this indicates that the works in question have not been published in translation. Both German and English titles have been listed alphabetically in the index for the reader's convenience in locating discussions of specific works.

Introduction

Donald G. Daviau

Contemporary Austrian Literature finds itself in an exciting state which has existed virtually since the end of World War II. Blessed with an abundance of significant authors, including a Nobel Prize winner, Elias Canetti, Austria has been internationally recognized as a literary center in a way and to a degree it had not enjoyed since the flourishing of the *Jung-Wien* group—Hermann Bahr, Hugo von Hofmannsthal, Arthur Schnitzler, Richard Beer-Hofmann, Leopold von Andrian, and Felix Salten—at the turn of the century. In every respect Austrian literature (as well as its other arts) is currently enjoying a period of creativity that will eventually mark this era as one of the outstanding periods of Austrian literary and cultural history.

One important result of this international acclaim has been the steadily increasing recognition of Austrian literature as a unique and independent entity rather than as a sub-category of German literature as had long been the prevailing opinion among Germanists. Austria was established originally in 976 A.D. under the Babenbergs by decree of the German King Heinrich II, and this historical connection along with their shared language is cited as evidence for the interrelationship of the two nations and hence of their literary traditions. Moreover, since Austria was in effect established by Germany and since the language was German, the prevailing view became established that Austrian was subordinate to German literature and that all literature written in German was to be regarded as German literature. It has been suggested that despite the early political ties a specifically Austrian literary tradition can be traced from the Middle Ages to the present,[1] but whether one wishes to accept this extreme position or not, it is certainly more difficult to argue against the idea of a separate tradition after 1800. Among many other diverse reasons, which are too complex to argue in detail here, th Austrian Baroque tradition of the seventeenth century, which has continued to influence Austrian writers to the present day in a way not typical of German literature, represents a particularly important factor that has always distinguished Austrian literature from the German tradition.

The idea of identifying Austrian literature as a unique entity first arise in the eighteenth century in the writings of Johann Baptist Gabriel Mareck and Franz Sartori, who made the initial attempts to compile a distinctly Austrian literary history.[2] These efforts were continued in the nineteenth and twentieth centuries by J. W. Nagl, Jakob Zeidler and Eduard Castle, Josef Nadler, Adalbert Schmidt,

Hilde Spiel, and Herbert Zeman.[3] The question "What is Austrian Literature?" became one of the most hotly debated issues of postwar Austrian literature and has continued to serve as the subject of a large number of symposia, articles, and books.[4] Although the matter has not yet been satisfactorily resolved, and no consensus has been reached to date, nevertheless the idea of a separate Austrian literature has taken firm root. The weight of scholarly evidence to document this position continues to mount, and the acceptance of this view is so widespread today that it is unlikely to be reversed. Although the debate will probably continue for some time to come, it is overwhelmingly clear when viewed objectively that modern Austrian literature, whether viewed in aesthetic, cultural, social, or political terms, justifies consideration as an integral, independent tradition. The number of journals and symposia specifically devoted to Austrian literature continues to grow, more and more books have been published specifying Austrian literature in the titles, and universities outside of Austria are offering courses devoted exclusively to Austrian literature, which formerly had been subsumed under German literature.

While the evidence that the Austrian and German literary traditions developed differently can no longer be dismissed, it is still possible to debate the questions of when and precisely why they did so. From the late-eighteenth century Austrian authors like Alois Blumauer (1755-1798) and Franz Grillparzer (1791-1872), the greatest name in Austrian letters, began to regard themselves as Austrian, not German writers. There is in fact considerable scholarly sentiment for the idea of dating the separate Austrian tradition from the age of Grillparzer.[5] During the period from approximately 1750 to the present the progression of German literary history reveals a series of abrupt changes, as successive generations of writers from the Enlightenment to the present attempted new beginnings. By contrast Austrian literature during the same time span proceeds more or less in a continuous line, featuring an unbroken tradition that maintains contact with the strengths of the past even during periods of intense innovation, as took place among the generation of 1890 and again in the postwar period during the 1960s and 1970s. The stress on preserving the cultural heritage of Austria remained so strong that even the change from Monarchy to Republic in 1918 following World War I and the reduction of the country from a multinational country of fifty million to a state of approximately seven million people caused no appreciable effect on the literary development. Writers continued to produce works devoted to traditional themes, ignoring the fact that the Monarchy no longer existed. Claudio Magris in his volume *Der Habsburger Mythos in der österreichischen Literatur* (The Habsburg Myth in Austrian Literature) has demonstrated that the preservation of the Habsburg Myth was one of the main features of the continuity of Austrian literature as well as of its difference from German literature.[6] The writers of the so-called *Jung-Wien* group at the turn of the century all emphasized the importance of tradition in their writings and devoted some of their best efforts to transmitting the Austrian cultural heritage to the public. Hermann Bahr emphasized the uniqueness of the Austrian cultural tradition and devoted over forty years of his life to mediating literature and the other arts to the public in an attempt to elevate the arts in Austria to the level of those in other European countries. His aim was to achieve closer rapprochement of Austria with Western Europe through a reciprocal awareness of artistic and intellectual developments.

Bahr's good friend and colleague Hofmannsthal likewise stressed the Austrian cultural heritage as a national strength, and in 1915 inaugurated a series of volumes called *Österreichische Bibliothek* (Austrian Library), a collection of important literary monuments constituting the Austrian tradition. It was Hofmannsthal who in 1929 coined the term "conservative revolution" to emphasize the need for change but always within a context of preserving the best from the past. Many of his writings and activities follow the same principle, being reworkings of traditional themes in contemporary contexts to make the works relevant to present-day circumstances. Indeed the term "conservative revolution" appropriately characterizes all of Austrian literature, which features innovation and tradition running concurrently throughout its history. For that reason Austrian literature has never veered from its even course of development, for the anchor of tradition is ever-present to act as a balance and maintain the equilibrium.

Following the *Jung-Wien* era, the next generation of writers, including Raoul Auernheimer, Felix Braun, Hermann Broch, Ödön von Horváth, Rainer Maria Rilke, Joseph Roth, Franz Werfel, and Stefan Zweig, all continued to emphasize tradition, as did most of the Austrian writers of those years with the major exception of Franz Kafka. In times of political or social upheaval the tendency has always been to seek refuge in tradition. Like Hofmannsthal Zweig also inaugurated a book series entitled *Bibliotheca Mundi* (Library of the World). The motivating principle was the same – to emphasize the cultural heritage – with the only difference being that Zweig, the most cosmopolitan and also the most widely translated of all Austrian authors, stressed the European humanistic tradition rather than exclusively Austrian texts.

A major disruption in the continuity of the Austrian tradition was caused by the political events of the 1930s. The game of cat and mouse between Germany and Austria, which had been carried on since 1934 when a Nazi group assassinated Chancellor Dollfuss in Vienna in an attempted *Putsch,* ended abruptly when Hitler ordered the forced annexation (*Anschluß*) of Austria on 11 March 1938. The negative effects of Hitler's policies had already influenced the cultural scene since 1933 by causing the flight of many Jewish and other politically active writers. Those who did not move quickly enough or who believed the prevalent idea that Hitler was only a short-term phenomenon that would soon self-destruct, ended in suicide (Ernst Weiss), imprisonment (Auernheimer), or execution in a concentration camp (Jura Soyfer). Even those writers who remained in Austria faced the choice of producing works in accordance with the dictates of the Nazi policies or of going into "inner emigration" and withholding their writings for a more propitious cultural climate.

The writers who fled into exile produced a major cultural hiatus, for they formed a veritable "Who's Who" of Austrian literature at that time, as can be illustrated by this partial list: Raoul Auernheimer, Richard Beer-Hofmann, Felix Braun, Hermann Broch, Ferdinand Bruckner, Elias Canetti, Franz Czokor, Albert Drach, Erich Fried, Fritz Hochwälder, Ödön von Horváth, Ernst Lothar, Erwin Rieger, Joseph Roth, Felix Salten, Manès Sperber, Hilde Spiel, Friedrich Torberg, Johannes Urzidil, Berthold Viertel, Ernst Waldinger, Hans Weigel, Franz Werfel, Stefan Zweig, and Frank Zwillinger. It can be seen that a substantial part of the established generation of writers who would have been prominent on the literary scene during these years was forced into flight. The emigration represented an irreplaceable loss that had severe effects on the production of literature in Austria during this twelve-year period. The exiled writers also suffered severely from the loss of their homeland and of their normal audience. They faced extreme difficulties trying to adapt themselves and their writing to altered circumstances, in which they were forced to confront a new reality of the world and a new means of expression. Very few of these exiled writers ever learned English or any other language well enough to write in it. Some like Lothar, Werfel, and Zweig published in translation and even made the best-seller list in the United States, but for the majority the language and cultural barriers were insurmountable obstacles that were never overcome during the entire period of exile. Nevertheless, despite these difficulties almost the only literature that is remembered today from the seven-year period 1938–1945 was produced by the exiled writers.

Following the end of the war in 1945, the revival of literature and the other arts became an immediate urgent task in Austria as a means of helping reunite the country during the chaotic period of reconstruction. Austria had been absolved of any responsibility for the war by the Allied governments, so there was no particular need for writers to wrestle with the problems of war guilt,

which became such a major theme in Germany. As a result there was no movement among Austrian writers toward political activism, and only a few works
confronting the issues of the war and war guilt appeared in Austria.[7] Indeed,
the postwar course of literature in Austria ran virtually opposite to that followed in Germany, for instead of beginning again at "ground point zero" Austrian writers, critics, and literary editors made a conscious decision to reestablish
the tradition that had been interrupted by the annexation with Germany in
1938. Partly this step can be seen as a means of avoiding a confrontation with
the immediate past, but also and more importantly it reflected the tendency of
Austria to gather strength from its cultural heritage. Thus, writers like Richard
Billinger, Christine Busta, Heimito von Doderer, Albert Paris Gütersloh, Rudolf
Henz, Fritz von Herzmanovsky-Orlando, Alexander Lernet-Holenia, Max Mell,
and George Saiko who immediately came to the fore after the war, belonged to
the older generation that had its roots in the prewar era. It was not a case of
beginning anew for these authors, who had remained in Austria, but of returning
to public view. In almost all cases they published their most important books
after the war. For example, Doderer's *Die Dämonen* (1956, begun 1931, *The
Demons*) is considered to be the most important novel of the 1950s, and Gütersloh's *Sonne und Mond* (1962, begun 1935, Sun and Moon) that of the 1960s.
Neither novel deals with the war, but like Saiko's *Auf dem Floß* (1948, On the
Raft) and *Der Mann im Schilf* (1955, The Man in the Reeds) they treat the
interwar years. Even those writers like Felix Braun, Ernst Lothar, Friedrich
Torberg, Berthold Viertel, and Hans Weigel, who returned from exile, brought
no new influences or techniques, for throughout their period of exile they had
continued to write in their previously established manner. A number of other
writers like Raoul Auernheimer, Hermann Broch, Elias Canetti, Franz Theodor
Czokor, Erich Fried, and Fritz Hochwälder remained in exile but contributed to
the postwar literary scene by continuing to write about Austria and by publishing their books and having their plays performed there. The works of Ödön von
Horváth, who died in exile in Paris in 1938, enjoyed a renaissance, as did those
of Fritz von Herzmanovsky-Orlando, Franz Kafka, Robert Musil, and Joseph
Roth. Hochwälder's *Das heilige Experiment* (1947, *The Strong are Lonely*), one
of the most frequently performed plays of the postwar era in Austria, was a
traditionally constructed five-act work employing the Aristotelian technique of
nineteenth-century drama. Hochwälder, in fact, serves as a good example of the
way Austrian writers remain rooted in the Austrian tradition. Although he
essentially began his literary career in exile in Switzerland, where he still resides,
Hochwälder nevertheless stresses that he continues the theater tradition of the
Vienna Burgtheater and of the popular folk comedy of Johann Nestroy and

Ferdinand Raimund.[8]

By reestablishing the continuity of the literary tradition the new young authors were given an identifiable framework in which to create while they were adapting to a changed world and were absorbing the literary developments of countries like France, England, and the United States, from which they had been cut off for over seven years. Rediscovered Kafka and French Surrealism represented particularly strong influences. Brecht, however, who so strongly influenced German playwrights with his concept of epic theater, was ignored, indeed, boycotted in Austria because of the Communist political message of his writing.

Viktor Suchy called Ilse Aichinger's *Die größere Hoffnung* (1947, *Herod's Children*), the first important Austrian postwar novel.[9] It was published through the influence of Hans Weigel, who in effect served as godfather to the new generation of writers. These young poets were led by Ingeborg Bachmann and Paul Celan, who were among the first postwar Austrian authors to gain acceptance in Germany, thus preparing the way for their recognition in their own country. This new generation, which includes all of the figures represented in this volume along with many other deserving authors who could not be included for lack of space, had no roots in the prewar years but began their careers after 1945. Whereas they began to write in the climate of reestablished tradition, they came to form the basis of the reaction against it in the late 1950s and 1960s.

A major factor in this revival of tradition was the great resurgence of national pride during the postwar era, a period which afforded Austrians a unique opportunity to liberate themselves from identification with Germany and to stress to the world their independent national identity. In short, when postwar literature found its voice again, it was an Austrian voice. It is an almost typical Austrian irony that the idea of Austria began to be publicized when the country was essentially only a shadow of its former greatness in both size and power. The way had been prepared for this step of establishing the uniqueness of Austria partly by the excellent public relations work carried out ironically enough by patriotic exiled writers in their host countries. Through their efforts Austria gained an identity in foreign countries that had not existed earlier. In the United States, for example, devoted Austrians like Raoul Auernheimer, Ernst Lothar, and Franz Werfel, among many others, emphasized through the *Austro-American Tribune* as well as in numerous lectures, articles, and books the differences between Austria and Germany.[10] They particularly stressed the necessity for the Allies to treat Austria differently from Germany after the war. This advice was followed by the Allied Governments, which had from

1938 accepted the notion of a forcibly annexed Austria fostered by the media. As a result Austria for the first time received full recognition abroad as an independent country and not as a geographical province of Germany.

The Allied four-power occupation of Austria, which remained in effect until the signing of the peace treaty in 1955, also contributed to the revival of tradition, for during the denazification period after the war the older writers and those who were in exile were immediately sanctioned as politically reliable individuals to help restore the country. Austrians were understandably anxious to disavow any association with the war guilt of Germany. Indeed, the Austrian reaction against Germany was so strong that as early as 1946 the cry was raised by more temperate voices to overcome the past and to restore harmonious relations with Germany. For example, in August 1945 the journal *Der Turm* (The Tower) in an effort to counteract the postwar attitude of repudiating Germany, republished Hofmannsthal's essay "Der Preuße und der Österreicher" (The Prussian and the Austrian), an attempt at a typology characterizing the two distinct types, along with a plea for "humanity."[11]

The recovery of Austrian literature along traditional lines occurred also in the other arts. Almost immediately reconstruction began on Vienna's landmark buildings such as the Opera, the Burgtheater, and above all on St. Stephan's Cathedral, the central landmark of Austria, in an attempt to restore the most important visual aspects of cultural heritage. An emphasis on the interrelationship of the arts was a prominent feature of the postwar period both in Vienna and in the "Forum Stadtpark" in Graz, where writers and visual artists associated closely.

Literary periodicals played a central role after the war in reviving tradition, in bolstering national pride, in introducing new authors, and in fostering an awareness of foreign trends. All of the journals pursued the same goal of re-activating cultural life, and although they were all short-lived for lack of support, they made a significant and influential contribution to intellectual life by their number and by their basically conservative editorial stance. The most important publications were *Plan*, Literatur, Kunst, Kultur (1945-1947), a journal that had first been published by Otto Basil in 1938 before its prohibition by the Nazis,[12] and *Der Turm*. Monatsschrift für österreichische Kultur (1945-1946), the very name of which emphasized emblematically its intended unifying role.[13] Others in no particular order of importance include: *Österreichische Rundschau* (1945-1946); *Austria, Die Welt im Spiegel Österreichs,* Zeitschrift für Kultur und Geistesleben (1946); *Das Silberboot,* Zeitschrift für Literatur (1946); *Österreichisches Tagebuch,* Wochenschrift für Kultur, Politik, Wirtschaft (1946); *Wiener literarisches Echo,* Kritische Vierteljahresschrift für Dichtung und Geistesgeschichte (1948-1949); *Europäische Rund-schau* (1946); *Wort und Tat,* Internationale Monatsschrift (1946-1947); and *Wort und Wahrheit,* Monatsschrift für Religion und Kultur (1946).

The introductory essay in *Plan* by Basil, "Zum Wiederbeginn" ("On Beginning Again"), conveys in general the purpose of all these journals:

> Our journal . . . would like to become the focus of all those forces which in the artistic and cultural life of our homeland foster the solidification of the idea of a democratic-republican state and the revival of a spiritual Austrian identity of European measure and world format. The motto is: work, activity, positive achievement . . . We summon the young people to join together and help us . . . .[14]

Plan was representative in its progressive attitude, its interdisciplinary approach, including coverage of the other arts in addition to literature, in its affirmation of Austria while featuring a European outlook, and in its warning against a revival of Naziism. Basil had his roots in Expressionism and was partial to French Surrealism. All of the contributing editors to *Plan* shared an enthusiasm for Karl Kraus, who is featured both by reprinted excerpts from his works and by essays about him. None of the *Jung-Wien* writers is represented, but such Kraus favorites as Altenberg, Raimund, and Nestroy are mentioned. Thus nineteenth-century as well as postwar writers, the traditional and the experimental, were included side by side, as the journal looked backward and forward, home and abroad, simultaneously. Later *Wort in der Zeit,* edited by Rudolf Henz, followed the same policy of establishing literary connections between the old and new Austria, as does also the present-day *Literatur und Kritik,* founded by Henz and edited for some ten years by Jeannie Ebner, who was succeeded in April 1979 by the current editor, Kurt Klinger, when she resigned to devote full time to her own writing.

Not surprisingly, politics were a major concern in the first few years of the chaotic postwar period, especially fear about the danger of reinfection by the disease of Naziism. However, the rather rapid return of economic and political stability led in the course of the 1950s to a turn away from any form of politics (the contrary of the situation in Germany). There was an outcry to become skeptical of all ideological thinking, not to be duped again. An essay that has been recognized to be of programmatic significance in this regard is Ilse Aichinger's "Aufruf zum Mißtrauen" (Call to Mistrust), in which she admonishes her contemporaries to remain vigilantly self-critical not only against outside ideas, but also against their own thoughts and feelings:

You must mistrust yourself! Yes? Did you understand? We must mistrust ourselves. The clarity of our intentions, the depth of our thoughts, the goodness of our deeds! We must mistrust our own truthfulness. Are there not lies within us again? Our own voice! Is it not icy wth lack of love? Our own love! Is it not sullied by selfishness? Our own honor! Is it not bankrupt from pride? [15]

Such a call for scrupulous honesty and truthfulness with oneself as with others is not directed simply at the political context of the time. Rather this essay fits into the direct line running from the normal skepticism that is generally regarded as a basic Austrian characteristic to the language skepticism of the young postwar generation of writers. It should be noted that Aichinger's statement was published in an issue of *Plan* intended for young people. It is evident that her call touched a responsive chord, for the appeal was later repeated by others. For example, Herbert Eisenreich entitled his essay on the Austrian literary tradition "Das schöpferische Mißtrauen" (1962, Creative Mistrust), and Otto Breicha and Gerhard Fritsch entitled their anthology *Aufforderung zum Mißtrauen. Literatur, Bildende Kunst, Musik in Österreich seit 1945* (1967, Summons to Mistrust. Literature, Visual Arts, Music in Austria since 1945).

But beyond the call to remain alert and personally responsible for one's actions, the overall political tenor of Austrian literature was conciliatory; by emphasizing tradition the attempt was made to overcome the seven years of the *Anschluß* with Germany and the ravages of the war almost as if they had not existed. There was essentially no "Schutt- und Trümmerliteratur" ("literature of the ruins") and little "Heimkehrerliteratur" ("literature of the returning soldier"). There was also no movement toward political activism among writers, and no equivalent of the "Gruppe 47" ("Group 47"), the influential organization of writers founded in Germany in 1947. Because of the political circumstances that prevailed, there was no necessity in Austria for the writers to remind their readers of their implication in the war, to prod their consciences lest they forget the inhumanity that had transpired, as Heinrich Böll, Günter Grass, and Peter Weiss, among others, were doing in Germany.

A position paper by the critic Edwin Rollett in 1945 entitled *Österreichische Gegenwartsliteratur. Aufgabe, Lage, Forderung* (Austrian Contemporary Literature: Task, Situation, Challenge), the first major critical statement of the postwar era, provides a good survey of the literary scene and of the intellectual concerns of the time. Rollett stressed the need for cooperation between writers and particularly for greater communication between authors in Vienna and those in the provinces in order to create a unified Austria:

> Are the individual zones and provinces going to develop in different
> directions intellectually and arbitrarily, instead of finally finding their
> way together again? Of all questions this is the most important, the
> decisive one. For it bears directly on the intellectual conditions of all
> of Austria.[16]

Rollett wished to overcome the notion that Viennese literature alone represented Austrian literature. He also stressed the need for public support of
writers, for if Austria was to remain a cultural nation, the country could not
rest on past laurels:

> The feeling that we are a cultural nation at any rate is the best way not
> to remain one. Culture is obligation, culture demands attention, inner
> commitment, and the engagement of spirit and soul, not only pleasure
> and enjoyment . . . The latter course leads to the avoidance of the great
> and the fostering of the insignificant.[17]

This particular recommendation found active response from the governmental
and cultural agencies in Austria, which have vigorously supported the arts.
Every author in this volume has been awarded a variety of prizes and stipends
in recognition of their excellence.

Rollett also emphasized the necessity for cultural mediation. Austria must
be "weltoffen" ("open to the world"), by which he means not only to be
receptive to the intellectual accomplishments of other countries, but also to
show other nations what Austria is and can achieve. Finally, he pleaded for
responsibility of the press and freedom of speech without bureaucratic censor-
ship. Rollett's suggestions provided a sensible plan for the future, but except
for the receptivity of young writers to foreign influences – French, English,
and American – for the most part his ideas met with little response. Particularly
the idea of breaking down the barriers between Vienna and the provinces found
no echo, and the situation today remains as problematical as it always has
been in Austria. The antagonism between the P.E.N. Club in Vienna and the
"Forum Stadtpark" in Graz is as strong today as ever.[18] Because of their difficulties gaining acceptance with their Viennese colleagues, the Graz writers in
1973 formed their own independent anti-P.E.N. organization, the "Grazer
Autorenversammlung" (Graz Writers' Association) under H. C. Artmann. A gulf
now exists not only between Vienna and the provinces, but also between the

older and younger generations of writers.

Because of the importance of the theater and opera in Austria, these institutions were reopened as quickly as possible with the aid of the occupation forces, for both the Austrian and the Allied governments recognized their significance for helping to restore the country to normality. Ernst Lothar, who had worked under Max Reinhardt in the Theater in der Josefstadt and who had also made a name for himself as a director in the Burgtheater in the 1930s, returned to Vienna from exile in the United States on 25 May 1946 in the uniform of a U. S. Army officer (he had become a citizen of the United States). He was charged with the task of "promoting the interests of the American Theater and American music in Austria through the medium of his office and of working equally for the rehabilitation of artistic life in Austria."[19] The latter part of his mandate resulted in his responsibility for reestablishing and supervising more than twenty-five theaters in Vienna as well as the Salzburg Festival. Lothar had begun his literary career under the influence of Schnitzler, whom he greatly admired all his life, and, as can be seen by his later novels, *Unter anderer Sonne* (1944, Beneath Another Sun), *Der Engel mit der Posaune* (1947, The Angel with the Trumpet), and *Die Rückkehr* (1948, The Return), his heart and his art were solidly rooted in the Austrian tradition. His novel *Der Engel mit der Posaune* bears a motto from Grillparzer which shows Lothar's attachment to his country: "If the Austrians knew better what Austria is, they would be better Austrians; if the world knew better what Austria is, the world would be better."[20]

Another major organizer and catalyst in the postwar development was Hans Weigel, who returned immediately after the war from exile in Switzerland and played an important role in fostering young writers, even though he himself is a traditionalist. It was Weigel who in 1948 coined the witticism that Austrian literature then consisted of two authors: Lernet and Holenia (a play on the name of the established writer Alexander Lernet-Holenia), and he set about with determination and seemingly limitless enthusiasm and energy to rejuvenate the literary scene. As he states: "I looked for young Austrian literature and found a generation"[21] It was he who gathered the new writers around him, encouraged them, helped them to get into print, and introduced them to the public. Weigel published five anthologies of lyric poetry, *Stimmen der Gegenwart* (1951-1956, Voices of the Present), as a means of gathering and publicizing the new young poets. Also beginning in 1951 he published twelve volumes of "Junge österreichische Autoren" (Young Austrian Authors), as well as a volume entitled *Die gute neue Zeit* (The Good New Time), containing twenty-four narrative selections from Schnitzler to the present.

For all his efforts on behalf of the young writers, Weigel himself remained in the mainstream of the Austrian tradition, as evidenced by the volume *Flucht vor der Größe* (1960, Flight from Greatness), dedicated to Adalbert Stifter and containing essays on six prominent Austrian writers and composers of the nineteenth century: Schubert, Raimund, Nestroy, Grillparzer, Stifter, and Johann Strauss. This work fits into the general trend of the 1950s to re-discover and reaffirm the Austrian cultural tradition. In his introduction Weigel debates but does not answer the question of when Austrian literature begins, whether in the Middle Ages or with Grillparzer around 1800. For the general theme of the essays he traces the "Austrian 'fate' of not being recognized . . . of being misunderstood, greatness in flight from itself."[22] Weigel's aim with this book – to spread information about Austrian cultural history both within Austria and in other countries – fits the trend of cultural mediation urged by Rollett.

Weigel has direct connections to the past through his books *Johann Nestroy* (1967) and *Karl Kraus oder Die Macht der Ohnmacht* (1968, Karl Kraus or the Power of Weakness). He attempted to emulate Kraus both in his social criticism and above all in his concern for the purification of language. His volume *Die Leiden der jungen Wörter* (1975, The Sorrows of Young Words), modeled on Kraus's *Die Sprache* (The Language) and dedicated to Kraus, is directed against the misuse and abuse of language. At the same time this work fits into the trend of language skepticism and precision of expression that characterize the writing of the 1960s.

Probably the strongest and most forceful voice urging a return to the past was that of Lernet-Holenia, who took an unequivocal stand on this issue in an article entitled "Gruß des Dichters" (The Poet's Greeting) in *Der Turm* on 17 October 1945:

> Indeed, we only need to resume at the point when the dreams of a mad-man interrupted us; in fact we do not need to look ahead but only back. To state it with complete clarity, there is no necessity for us to flirt with the future and undertake nebulous projects; we are, in our best and most valuable aspects, our past. We only have to remind ourselves that we are our past – and it will become our future.

The attempt to revitalize the Austrian tradition after 1945 must be judged completely successful, perhaps from the standpoint of the young writers even too successful, for they were at first completely overshadowed by the powerful thrust toward reestablishing the links with the past. The polyhistorical baroque novels of Doderer, the most prominent writer of this era, and those of Saiko and Gütersloh reestablished the novel form in the preeminent fashion of Broch, Musil, Roth, and Stifter and made it appear as if time had stood still as far as narrative technique of the novel was concerned. Doderer's *Die Strudelhof-stiege* (1951, The Strudelhof Stairway) may be regarded as the last attempt to use the novel form to create a total world, to achieve universality, and above all to project the optimism of "eine heile Welt" ("an harmonious world"). These novelists along with Eisenreich and Fritsch all display a traditional concern with Austria and the Austrian idea, a theme that has dominated literature from Grillparzer to Bernhard and Handke, among others on the contemporary scene.[23] As the critic Walter Weiss has stated:

> A universally understood order as past and future, as renewal (restoration), as hope and certainty, supported by the ultimately unshakable conviction about its continuation – that is the common factor that unites Eisenreich, Doderer, and Gütersloh with past representative Austrian authors like Broch and Hofmannsthal, Stifter, and Grillparzer.[24]

An aggressive attack on the apathy of the public toward the new generation of writers was voiced by Milo Dor in an introductory essay in his lyric anthology *Die Verbannten* (1962, The Banished). Under the title "Dieses Buch ist eine Kriegserklärung" ("This Book is a Declaration of War") Dor excoriates all classes of people from professors to dunces for their bad taste and for their preference for a good meal or drink to a good book. He states that the anthology could have been called "The Survivors," for those represented in it grew up during the war and had overcome the past. It could also have been called "The Friends," because despite rejection, they still displayed "their unrequited love for a city that rejected them." But it was entitled "The Banished," because this generation was scattered over Europe and even those in Vienna were in "inner emigration." They were known in Germany but not in their own country. The anthology was intended to bear witness that they were there.[25]

Tradition stifled innovation initially, but eventually the young writers who first began to publish after the war reacted against tradition and struggled to integrate modern aesthetic and linguistic theories into literature and art. The period of Modernism, which had dominated the arts since approximately 1880, began to be supplanted by Postmodernism with its skepticism toward language, toward all ideologies, and toward all qualitative judgments. The turning point was H. C. Artmann's dialect volume *med ana schwoazzn dintn* (1958, with black ink), which was followed by the works of the "Wiener Gruppe" (Vienna

Group): Oswald Wiener, Friedrich Achleitner, Konrad Bayer, and Gerhard Rühm. The breakthrough was assisted by Doderer, who thus became a key figure of this transitional postwar period. While his own novels represented a solid link to the past, including the baroque tradition, at the same time like Ferdinand von Saar toward his young contemporaries at the turn of the century, Doderer was supportive of the new experimental directions of the young writers. He was one of the few established writers to accept and publicize the "Wiener Gruppe." In an essay, "Drei Dichter entdecken den Dialekt" (Three Poets Discover Dialect), he pointed out that Artmann, Rühm, and Achleitner were "poets in dialect" not "dialect poets." They caused one to think of Karl Kraus, not of the regional dialect author Franz Stelzhammer.[26] Doderer tried to give additional support to the young writers by inviting them to publish some of their works in the newspaper *Wiener Kurier* in the weekly space made available to him. When the editors refused to print the submissions, Doderer resigned in protest.[27]

Another younger writer of this transitional type is Gerhard Fritsch, who began his career as an exponent of the Austrian tradition with his highly regarded novel *Moos auf den Steinen* (1956, Moss on the Stones) but subsequently joined the reaction against the very tradition glorified in his novel. The shift was not sudden, for *Moos auf den Steinen* already contained criticism of the falsity and superficiality of the postwar restoration movement. The stress on the Austrian past in the 1950s had become a popular fad, even to the point of redecorating homes in the old style, and such trivialization of the surface without the substance of the older tradition aroused a countermovement by Fritsch and other writers, particularly those of the "Wiener Gruppe." This reaction, which has become known as *Anti-Heimatdichtung* (anti-regional literature) may be seen as a call for truthfulness and for overcoming the discrepancy between literature and reality. The aim of the anti-regional writers, such as the poets Achleitner, Artmann, Rühm, and Alfred Gesswein, along with the novelists Thomas Bernhard, Gerhard Fritsch, Franz Innerhofer, and Gert Jonke, was to destroy the idyllic myth of regional literature, to expose the hollowness and falsity of the pastoral "heile Welt" (harmonious world) and the notion of the provinces as the source of wholesomeness, decency, and integrity as opposed to the decadence and corruption of Vienna.[28] Peter Turrini pursues the same aim in his hard-hitting satiric dramas.

In all cases *Anti-Heimatdichtung* acknowledges the existence of tradition by trying to repudiate it. Indeed, initially both publishers and the public failed to recognize the attack on traditional values represented by such literature and accepted it at face value. *Moos auf den Steinen* was such a case in point as was also Artmann's *med ana schwoazzn dintn,* which owed not only its popular success, but also its Austrian publisher to this kind of error. The public was initially confused into thinking that the dialect poetry of the "Wiener Gruppe" represented a form of standard regional literature in the manner of Joseph Weinheber.[29]

The use of dialect by the members of the "Wiener Gruppe," consisting of a blend of normal dialect and colloquial speech, was an innovation, and yet the use of dialect itself represented a revival that placed these writers squarely in the Austrian tradition. The group was also united with tradition in the aim of experimenting with language, of exploring the playful possibilities of sounds and nonsense syllables, and with visual arrangements of letters and words, a technique that again has precedent in the Baroque period. Language was treated as an independent entity, as if it had lost its referential relationship to corresponding signifiers outside of itself. For the "Wiener Gruppe," for poets like Friederike Mayröcker and Ernst Jandl, and for authors like Bachmann, Bernhard, Frischmuth, Handke, and Jonke, language itself became the total subject matter, the "message" as well as the medium. Poetic experimentation and simple playfulness were carried to the point of dissecting, of deconstructing language to explore its range and limits and to try to determine to what degree language and reality coincide. By experimenting with new combinations and recombinations of words and letters in such "concrete poetry," these writers hoped to break out of clichéd linguistic patterns to produce new perceptions, to strive for a new definition of reality, and at the very least to show the complexities and dangers inherent in language.

The use of dialect provided another dimension to the various linguistic possibilities. While Fritz Mauthner, Karl Kraus, and even more importantly Wittgenstein had served as important influences in the examination of the roots of language, the "Wiener Gruppe" transcended its models. Kraus had used jargon and dialect but remained a devoted follower of language:

I am only one	Ich bin nur einer von
of the epigones,	den Epigonen,
who remain at home	die in dem alten Haus der
in the old house of language.	Sprache wohnen.[31]

Unlike Hofmannsthal and Rilke, Kraus never succumbed to the prevailing language skepticism and had never lamented the inadequacies of language but only those of the people using it. Wittgenstein similarly had no desire to abolish language or to see it disintegrate into meaninglessness: "Only the sentence has meaning; only in the context of the sentence does a name [word] have meaning."[32]

The danger of such postmodernist experimentation involving the deconstruction of language is the limitation of communication that results. Paul Celan, for example, in attempting to separate language from its referential character, to introduce his own code of meanings which did not remain constant from poem to poem, produced works that are extremely difficult to penetrate. Other poets have achieved outstanding humorous effects, but the cognition is highly specialized, depending as it does on the element of surprise, and rarely amounts to more, say, than the impact of a verbal witticism or aperçu. Attractive and pleasurable as the results can sometimes be, the resemblance to art for art's sake, to Dadaism, is close, as is also the risk of falling into mannerism. The next step for such experimental writers after the shock or novelty has lost its impact has to be either silence or retreat to more conventional language usage. The turning point came in 1964 with the suicide of Konrad Bayer, which effectively dissolved the "Wiener Gruppe." All of the major experimental authors, such as Artmann, Handke, Jandl, and Mayröcker have grown noticeably more conservative with the years. Today only Jandl continues to make major use of such forms.

The "Wiener Gruppe," the most original and imaginative Austrian literary force of the late 1950s, though short-lived, continued its influence on the literary scene through the writers of the "Forum Stadtpark" in Graz, who succeeded it as the primary new force of the 1960s. The same skeptical attitude toward language and the same anti-regionalist tendencies characterize the authors Wolfgang Bauer, Barbara Frischmuth, Peter Handke, Franz Innerhofer, Gert Jonke, Gerhard Roth, Michael Scharang, and Peter Turrini, who joined together around the poet Alfred Kolleritsch, founder of the "Forum Stadtpark" and editor of the influential journal *manuscripte*. In effect, Kolleritsch played essentially the same role in Graz in the 1960s and 1970s as Weigel had done in the 1950s in Vienna. The "Forum," a small donated building located in the city park, provided a meeting place and a hall for readings, lectures, and performances. The Graz writers still form one of the liveliest centers of Austrian letters and now attract widespread attention with an annual event called the "Steirischer Herbst" (Styrian Fall), a festival of all of the arts.

Although the Graz writers followed the lead and the impetus of the "Wiener Gruppe," there was only minimal interaction between the two groups even though for the most part they pursued shared interests and values. Language remained the primary concern, but the approach to the problem was substantially different. For with the exception of Handke, who more than any of the other writers represents postmodernism[33] in his early experimental poetry and plays exploring language as a series of open relationships rather than of fixed meanings, the Graz writers were less interested in exploring the possibilities inherent in the words themselves or in visual arrangements of words than in delving into language as a means of examining the epistemological process itself, the manner in which individuals learn, and hence the way that people are molded and manipulated by the language they acquire. Handke in *Kaspar* (1967) and *Die Unvernünftigen sterben aus* (1973, *They Are Dying Out*), Frischmuth in *Die Klosterschule* (1968, The Convent School), Bauer in *Change* (1969), and Jonke in *Geometrischer Heimatroman* (1969, Geometric Regional Novel),[34] and Innerhofer in *Schöne Tage* (1974, *Beautiful Days*), show how people are trained to think — one might say brainwashed — and how language is used to inculcate ideas as a means of controlling and dominating people. Other "Sprechstücke" ("Speaking Plays") by Handke like *Publikumsbeschimpfung* (1966, Offending the Audience) and *Das Mündel will Vormund sein* (1969, *My Foot, My Tutor*), which is pure pantomime, likewise try to bring about new perceptions by breaking down expectations and stereotypes to make people aware of the degree to which language is ritualized and taken for granted and at the same time of the dangers inherent in it.

This approach to the problem of language is not aesthetically oriented as are the linguistic experiments found in the "concrete poetry" of the "Wiener Gruppe," which at times resemble *l'art pour l'art*, but derives from a moral concern over the misuse of language. The members of the Graz group traveled more widely than the concrete poets in Vienna and had been more involved with the German literary scene, particularly the German "Gruppe 47," which played such an influential role in the immediate postwar years. The involvement with language by the Graz writers grew out of its debasement by Nazi phraseology, which destroyed any connection between the word and its meaning. The reaction of the young writers was to strip language of all embellishment, to eliminate all mythological and metaphorical overtones in order to render a meaning as precisely and unambiguously as possible. In this form of language skepticism they echo the concern for truthfulness of expression described by Hofmannsthal in "Ein Brief" (1902, "A Letter" [of Lord Chandos]) as well as the social-critical approach of Kraus, who demanded that a person and his/her language be identical. The latter particularly used language as an index of character and reduced people to their words as a means of exposing their true nature.[35] Like Kraus, Handke and the other Graz writers view language as the basic reality, and like Kraus, by examining language they are engaging in social criticism. Handke's view that human beings are reduced to role-playing by learning the "script" of language and hence the part that society mandates also relates him closely to earlier writers like Bahr, Schnitzler, and Hofmannsthal, who placed heavy stress on the Baroque idea of life as a theater and people as puppets in the hands of a higher power. While in the earlier view this was a positive rather than a negative view, the advent of Hitler and other dictators showed the dangerous misuse to which language could be put.

Writers rarely stay committed to one theme for very long, and concern over the problem of language showed signs of weakening as Austrian literature approached the 1980s. The change is not surprising, for writers actually have no other choice available to them: they must either accept the fact that an imperfect language with all of its limitations is their only means of expression or they must fall silent. Hence literature moved ahead but with a changed focus. Emphasis on the writing process per se, attempts to achieve strict precision of meaning and objectivity, and efforts at language criticism as practiced by Bachmann, Bernhard, Celan, Frischmuth, Handke, Jandl, Mayröcker, Rosei, and Schutting, gave way during the 1970s to a return to subjectivity and feeling, as literature entered a new phase that has been labeled "Die neue Empfindsamkeit" (The New Sensitivity).[36] This new development featured a turn to autobiography and a preoccupation with self. No longer was it deemed necessary to avoid feelings, to strive for cold, concrete descriptions. Instead there was a return to subjectivity, to warmth, and to introspection. In addition to a subjective examination of the reactions of the individual to reality or to a probing of one's inner consciousness, an increasing interest in the interaction of people is evident. Frischmuth, whose writings may be considered representative of the trends of the last decade, illustrates how literature has proceeded from concern with language in *Die Klosterschule* to subjective works involving fantasy and humor blended with autobiographical elements and expressions of social concern and criticism. This mixture of autobiography, social themes such as feminism, the environment, the problem of the "guest workers," fantasy, and humor are found in the works of almost all the authors represented here. Bernhard, Canetti, Handke, Innerhofer, Frischmuth, Jonke, Rosei, and Roth have all produced autobiographical works, if not outright autobiographies.

As will be seen in the following essays on the individual authors, a similarity of themes emerges despite the heterogeneity of forms: the individual's search for reality, the best means to represent reality, introspection and self-examination, the father-son conflict, the examination of one's father as a means of achieving one's own identity, feminism, the child, anti-regionalism, anti-homeland, and finally the Austrian tradition. Fantasy and mythological literature has also returned to accompany the fantasy painters. The early postmodernistic phase of most of those writers, in which they renounced their predecessors' examination of society and social values, their search for life's purpose and meaning, and their aspiration for transcendence restricted them for the most part to exploring language per se and life in terms of its linguistic expression. Depth was sacrificed for surface, and moral seriousness for playful freedom. However, even the idea of viewing life in relative terms, on which Postmodernist thinking is based, was not as novel as Handke and Jandl, among others, had initially thought. The notion that all of life remains in constant flux and that consequently all of life's values can be viewed only in relative terms remains one of the great innovations of the turn-of-the-century writers.[37] Hence the interconnectedness of the generations remains intact. The similarities will become more and more evident as this postwar generation of writers, having gained maturity and the success of worldwide reputations, no longer feels that it has to attract attention merely by being interesting or controversial with shock tactics, experimental extremes, and plain offensive rudeness. Now that they are firmly established and have found their own voices, they can afford to be themselves and openly acknowledge their attachment to the tradition of earlier writers. For example, Handke and Bernhard, who were among the most outspoken authors against their homeland, have now both rediscovered the Austrian past as have most of the other authors represented here.[38]

It is one of the notable aspects of contemporary Austrian literature that an unusually large proportion of the significant writers are women.[39] Unlike the adverse situation in the eighteenth and nineteenth centuries, when a male-dominated society looked askance at "women writers" who for the most part experienced great difficulty in developing to their true potential, contemporary women authors suffer no such obstacles. Today women who write are regarded simply as writers completely coequal with their male counterparts. They follow the same trends, compete on the same terms, and reap the same rewards and recognition. Perhaps, because they have received equal treatment at least as writers, there has been no strident feminism evident in their works. The leading voice in this respect is Frischmuth, who may be considered as a model to feminists because of her sensible moderate approach to the entire complex of problems associated with feminism and feminist aesthetics, none of which lends itself to facile solutions.

The atmosphere in recent years in Austria has become much calmer, but the literary scene is no less vibrant and the literature no less vital for the absence of radical trends or the posture of *épater le bourgeois* of early Bauer, Bernhard, Handke, and Turrini. Experiments in form and technique—Handke, for example, has made several films—continue but in a more subdued fashion. The diversity

is so great at present that no particular trend or tendency can be said to dominate, but the drift toward conservatism in both theme and form is very pronounced. Austrian literature has always evidenced a tendency to stay within
its own borders, and contemporary writers fit that pattern very well even though
a number of the writers have traveled much more than earlier writers used to
do, particularly to the United States, which prior generations rarely visited.
Whatever the new literary direction may turn out to be in the future, the likelihood is strong that Austrian literature, which shows no signs of diminishing
in productivity or prominence, will continue to be characterized by the contrasting features of innovation and tradition, as it has been throughout its rich
and eventful history in the twentieth century.

Notes

1. Kurt Adel, *Geist und Wirklichkeit. Vom Werden der österreichischen
   Dichtung* (Wien: Österreichische Verlagsanstalt, 1967).
2. Cf. Kurt Adel, "Die Anfänge der österreichischen Geschichtschreibung,"
   Österreich in Geschichte und Literatur, Vol. 1, No. 6 (1969), 352-364;
   also Herbert Zeman, "Die österreichische Literatur und ihre literarge-
   schichtliche Darstellung vom ausgehenden 18. bis zum frühen 19. Jahrhundert," in *Die österreichische Literatur: Ihr Profil an der Wende vom
   18. zum 19. Jahrhundert (1750-1830),* ed. Herbert Zeman, 2 (Graz:
   Akademische Druck- und Verlagsanstalt, 1979), pp. 563-586.
3. Jakob W. Nagl, Jakob Zeidler, Eduard Castle, *Deutsch-österreichische
   Literaturgeschichte,* 4 vols. (Wien: J. Fromme, 1899-1937); Josef Nadler,
   Literaturgeschichte Österreichs (Salzburg: Otto Müller Verlag, 1951);
   Adalbert Schmidt, *Dichtung und Dichter Österreichs im 19. und 20.
   Jahrhundert,* 2 vols. (Salzburg, Stuttgart: Bergland-Buch, 1964); Hilde
   Spiel, ed., *Die zeitgenössische Literatur Österreichs. Autoren, Werke,
   Tendenzen seit 1945* (Zürich und München: Kindler Verlag, 1976); Herbert Zeman, ed., *Die österreichische Literatur. Ihr Profil an der Wende
   vom 18. zum 19. Jahrhundert (1750-1830),* 2 vols., *op. cit.;* also *Die
   österreichische Literatur. Ihr Profil im 19. Jahrhundert (1830-1880)*
   (Graz: Akademische Druck- und Verlagsanstalt, 1982). Two further
   volumes are currently in progress tracing Austrian literary development
   from 1880 to 1980.
4. The December 1984 issue of *Modern Austrian Literature* contains an
   extensive bibliography (over 400 entries) of books and articles dealing

with efforts to characterize Austrian literature. Two volumes, both the results of symposia, provide a representative sampling of the diversity of opinions and approaches to this question: Karl Konrad Pohlheim, *Literatur aus Österreich–österreichische Literatur* (Bonn: Bouvier Verlag Herbert Grundmann, 1981); Karl Bartsch, ed., *Für und wider eine österreichische Literatur* (Königstein/Ts.: Athenäum, 1982).

5. Günther Nenning, for example, believes that "there is an Austrian literature that begins at the time of Emperor Franz with Grillparzer as the first great figure." "Grillparzers Schnoferl oder Poesie als Weltanschauung. Über Literatur und Politik in Österreich," in Karl Bartsch, ed., *Für und wider eine österreichische Literatur,* p. 34. See also Donald G. Daviau, "Preface," in *Modern Austrian Literature,* Vol. 17, Nos. 3/4 (December 1984), i-vi. (Special Issue "Perspectives on the Question of Austrian Literature.")

6. The Habsburgs succeeded the Babenbergs in 1247 and ruled continuously until 1918. Although the Austrian critic Walter Weiss has persuasively argued against Magris's theory, it continues to find advocates. Weiss concludes his repudiation with the emphatic statement: "Austrian literature is not a captive of the Habsburg myth. . . ." "Österreichische Literatur–eine Gefangene des hapsburgischen Mythos?" in *Deutsche Vierteljahresschrift,* Jg. 43, Heft 2 (Juni 1969), 333-345. Despite his negative view of Magris's idea, Weiss is one of the strongest proponents of a separate Austrian tradition.

7. For an enumeration and discussion of the novels dealing with "Lost Austria" and World War II see Roland Heger, *Der österreichische Roman des 20. Jahrhunderts,* I (Wien: Wilhelm Braumüller, 1971), pp. 184-227.

8. Fritz Hochwälder, "Über mein Theater," in *Im Wechsel der Zeit.* Autobiographische Skizzen und Essays (Graz: Verlag Styria, 1980), pp. 81-102.

9. Viktor Suchy, *Literatur in Österreich 1945-1970* (Wien: Jahoda und Siegle, 1971), pp. 21-22.

10. Representative unpublished lectures of this type, which Auernheimer delivered to many American groups, include "I Was an Austrian," "Austria–a Symbol," "Thoughts About Austria," "There Was a Country Named Austria," "How to Get Along With Austrians," and "Vienna– Not in Germany."

11.   The Austrian Character: The German Character
        more humanity   more efficiency
        unlimited individualism   unlimited authoritarianism
        traditional outlook   topical outlook

The Austrian Character:	The German Character:
acts according to propriety	acts according to rules
irony about the self	self-confidence
apparently immature	apparently masculine
takes life easily	systematizes life
bashful, vain, witty	self-righteous, presumptuous, pedantic
pleasure-seeking	place-hunting
predominance of private sphere	predominance of business
irony to the point of self-negation	open self-exaggeration

Der Turm, Jg. 1. Heft 1 (1945–1946), p. 5.

12. See Ruth Gross, *"Plan" and the Austrian Rebirth* (Columbia, South Carolina: Camden House Press, 1982).

13. "For it is not only buildings, indeed, not even only art works, which this war has transformed into ruins: it is a part of our hearts. . . . Thus "Der Turm" was not chosen at random as the symbol of this journal . . .; as a representative of the Austrian spirit it projects far abroad into the history and culture of Europe. The great buildings of Vienna are imperishable witnesses for the victory of the free human spirit over depravity, destruction, and barbarism." (*Der Turm*, Vol. 1, No. 1 (August 1945), 1.

14. Otto Basil, "Zum Wiederbeginn," in *Plan*, Vol. I, No. 1 (1945), 1–2.

15. Ilse Aichinger, "Aufruf zum Mißtrauen," in *Plan*, Vol. II (1945–1946), 588.

16. Edwin Rollett, *Österreichischer Gegenwartsliteratur. Aufgabe, Lage, Forderung.* (Wien: "Neues Österreich," 1946), p. 32.

17   Ibid., p. 26.

18. Cf. Hilde Spiel, *Die zeitgenössische Literatur Österreichs* (München: Kindler Verlag, 1976), pp. 111–122. A. Leslie Willson, editor of *Dimension*, also called attention to this split in his preface to a special issue devoted to the avant-garde writers excluded by the P.E.N. Club: "In Austria itself, the pioneering authors represented in this issue of *Dimension* . . . drew tight ranks in 1972 against the Austrian P.E.N. Club, in reaction to the Club's long-maintained refusal to admit them into membership." *Dimension*, Vol. VIII, Nos. 1 and 2 (1975), 9.

19. Ernst Lothar, *Das Wunder des Überlebens* (Wien: Paul Zsolnay, 1961), p. 227.

20. Ernst Lothar, *Der Engel mit der Posaune* (Wien: Paul Zsolnay, 1963). Preface. This novel was first published in English in 1944 and in German

in 1947.

21. Cf. Hans Weigel, "Es begann mit Ilse Aichinger," in Otto Breicha and Gerhard Frisch, eds., *Aufforderung zum Mißtrauen*, p. 28.

22. Hans Weigel, *Flucht vor der Größe* (Wien: Morawa & Co., 1960), p. 13.

23. Concerning Bernhard and Austria see Christa Strebel-Zeller, *Die Verpflichtung der Tiefe des eigenen Abgrunds in Thomas Bernhards Prosa* (Zürich: Juris Druck, 1975), pp. 77-85; Josef Donnenberg, "Thomas Bernhard und Österreich," *Österreich in Geschichte und Literatur,* Vol. 14, No. 5 (May 1970), 237-251; A. P. Diereck, "Thomas Bernhard's Austria: Neurosis, Symbol or Expedient?", in *Modern Austrian Literature,* Vol. 12, No. 1 (March 1979), 73-93. For Handke and Austria see Norbert Gabriel, *Peter Handke und Österreich* (Bonn: Bouvier Verlag Herbert Grundmann, 1983).

24. Walter Weiss, "Thematisierung der 'Ordnung' in der österreichischen Literatur," in *Dauer im Wandel.* Aspekte österreichischer Kulturentwicklung, eds. Walter Strolz and Oscar Schmitz (Wien: Herder, 1975), p. 30.

25. Milo Dor, *Die Verbannten* (Graz: Stiasny, 1962), p. 8.

26. Heimito von Doderer, "Drei Dichter entdecken den Dialekt," in *Die Wiederkehr der Drachen* (München: Biederstein Verlag, 1970), pp. 237-238.

27. Gerhard Rühm, ed., *Die Wiener Gruppe* (Reinbek bei Hamburg: Rowohlt, 1967), p. 26.

28. For a discussion of the "Anti-Heimat" movement see Peter Pabisch, *Anti-Heimatdichtung im Dialekt* (Wien: A. Schendl, 1978), p. 24; Wendelin Schmidt-Dengler, "Die antagonistische Natur. Zum Konzept der anti-Idylle in der neueren deutschen Prosa," in *Literatur und Kritik,* Vol. 40 (November 1969), 577-585.

29. Peter Pabisch, *Anti-Heimatdichtung im Dialekt,* p. 24.

30. For a discussion of "concrete poetry" see Liselotte Gumpel, "Concrete Poetry from East and West Germany" (New Haven and London: Yale University Press, 1976). For an overall discussion of "Austrian Poetry: 1945-1980" see the special issue of *The Literary Review,* Vol. 25, No. 2 (Winter 1982), edited and introduced by Beth Bjorklund. In addition to English translations of much poetry this volume also contains interviews with several authors.

31. Karl Kraus, *Worte in Versen* (München: Kösel Verlag, 1959), p. 59.

32. Ludwig Wittgenstein, *Tractatus Logico Philosophicus,* 3.31 (New York: The Humanities Press, 1963), p. 24.

33. Cf. Jerome Klinkowitz and James Knowlton, *Peter Handke and the*

Postmodern Transformation (Columbia: University of Missouri Press, 1983).

34. See Johannes Vazulik, "G. F. Jonke's Geometrischer Heimatroman," in *Modern Austrian Literature,* Vol. 10, No. 2 (June 1977), 1-7.

35. Cf. Donald G. Daviau, "Language and Morality in Karl Kraus's *Die letzten Tage der Menschheit,*" *Modern Language Quarterly,* Vol. XXII (March 1961), 46-54.

36. Cf. the special issue of *Modern Austrian Literature,* Vol. 13, No. 1 (1980) entitled "Metamorphose des Erzählens: Zeitgenössische österreichische Prosa." Cf. also the sequel to this volume: *Studien zur österreichischen Erzählliteratur der Gegenwart,* edited by Herbert Zeman, *Amsterdamer Beiträge zur neuen Germanistik,* Band 14 (1982).

37. Cf. Donald G. Daviau, "Das junge und das jüngste Wien," in *Österreichische Gegenwart. Die moderne Literatur und ihr Verhältnis zur Tradition,* edited by Wolfgang Paulsen (Bern und München: Francke Verlag, 1980), pp. 81-114.

38. Cf., for example, Norbert Gabriel, *Peter Handke und Österreich* (Bonn: Bouvier, 1983) and Gerald A. Fetz, "Thomas Bernhard und die österreichische Tradition," in *Österreichische Gegenwart. Die moderne Literatur und ihr Verhältnis zur Tradition,* edited by Wolfgang Paulsen (Bern und München: Francke Verlag, 1980), pp. 189-205. Cf. also Gerald A. Fetz, "The Works of Thomas Bernhard: 'Austrian Literature?'" in *Modern Austrian Literature,* Vol. 17, Nos. 3/4 (1984), 171-192. (Special Issue: Perspectives on the Question of Austrian Literature).

39. Cf. the special issue of *Modern Austrian Literature* devoted to Austrian women writers: Vol. 12, Nos. 3/4 (December 1979). Included are articles on such contemporary authors as Erika Mitterer, Rose Ausländer, Christine Lavant, Marlen Haushofer, Doris Mühringer, Christine Busta, and Hilde Spiel.

Ilse Aichinger

Joanna M. Ratych

"My language is one which is partial to foreign words"[1] – these are the opening words of Ilse Aichinger's story "Meine Sprache und ich" (ms 219)[2] (1978, My Language and I), which was initially published in 1968 and which a decade later provided the title for a collection of her short stories. This sentence, or more precisely the notion of the "foreign word," is inextricably connected with all of her writing. What is meant here is the alienated word, the word which makes waves, which somehow forces itself upon the reader and unnerves him because it is formed in a context in which its conventional meaning no longer yields any sense.

A skeptical attitude toward the possibilities of linguistic expression has not been a novelty for quite some time, certainly not since Hofmannsthal wrote his Lord Chandos letter, "Ein Brief" (1902), and Wittgenstein repudiated the logic of language. Many writers of the present century have reached the conclusion that the conventional structure of language and stale meanings do much more to hinder than to help a person orient himself to reality. The individual who asks questions and wants answers is reassured by being fed a collection of erroneous certainties. As a result he is prevented from coming to grips with the world in a creative way. "Werld would be better than world," Aichinger contends in one of her prose texts, "not as useful, not as clever. Aerth would be better than earth. But now it's this way. Normandy is called Normandy and nothing else. The rest too" (sW 34). These observations are to be found in *Schlechte Wörter* (Bad Words), a collection which among other things contains her most recent prose works. The book thus represents the latest phase of a development that began some thirty years ago with the publication of her novel *Die größere Hoffnung* (1948, *Herod's Children*).

In this novel, her only one to date, all the episodes revolve about a single theme: the attempt to cross a border from one country into another. The main character, a half-Jewish girl by the name of Ellen, finds herself caught in a kind of no-man's land between pursuers and pursued as a consequence of her having two "wrong" grandparents. Her mother was expelled from the country because she was a Jew, and her Aryan father is in the service of the oppressor. Therefore Ellen lives with her grandmother, who ultimately frees herself from the atmosphere of relentless threats by committing suicide. The girl tries to attach herself to a group of Jewish children. However, they are somewhat

reluctant to let her join in their games, for she is after all not one of them.
When the children are shipped to a death camp the girl is deprived of the only
human beings to whom she can still relate. The knowledge that her situation
is fairly hopeless is intensified: Ellen is not allowed to emigrate to America;
an attempt to flee across the border fails; it is no longer possible for her to
disown her "wrong" grandparents, for she has made a deliberate decision to wear
the star. When she hides in a train carrying munitions, the border she wants to
cross is no longer a political one: "I wanted to cross the border – to my grandmother –" (GH 145), she says later by way of explanation. In the chaos and
confusion that mark the last days of the war, in the inferno of a blazing city
being torn to shreds by shellfire the promise of an untroubled and unconcerned
existence rises before her mind's eye: "How simple, being paralyzed. Becoming
insensitive to the mystery and wiping away pain like foam off the top of a
glass" (GH 185). But on her way "to the bridges" she is killed by an exploding
shell.

It is not difficult to draw certain parallels between the plot of the novel
Die größere Hoffnung and the life of its author. Ilse Aichinger was born in
Vienna on 1 November 1921 and, like Ellen, she had two "wrong" maternal
grandparents residing in Linz, with whom Ilse and her twin sister Helga spent
the years of their childhood. In 1942 her grandmother was sent to a concentration camp from which she never returned. Helga was able to emigrate to England, but Ilse stayed with her mother in Vienna. The latter was no longer allowed to be a practicing physician; instead she had to work in a factory. After
the liberation of Austria Ilse Aichinger took up the study of medicine. She
left the university after five semesters, having reached the decision that being
a writer was much more important to her than being a doctor. In 1947 she
met Brigitte Fischer, who was instrumental in getting Aichinger's novel accepted
almost immediately by the Viennese publishing house of Bermann-Fischer.
The firm employed her as a reader for a time and has remained her publisher
to this day. She married the German poet and dramatist Günter Eich in 1953.
After the death of her husband in 1972 Aichinger decided to remain with her
two children, Clemens and Mirjam, and her mother in Groß-Gmain, a community that straddles the border between Austria and Germany. She is a member
of Group 47 and the Academy of Arts in Berlin, and she has been the recipient
of numerous literary prizes, including the Kafka Prize awarded to her in 1983.[3]

Although comparisons can be made between the fate of Ellen and the life
of her creator, the novel is neither historical nor autobiographical. The events
of the era and their effect on the personal life of the protagonist do of course
furnish the background for the plot; however the confrontation with the histori-

cal period in question takes place exclusively in the realm of literature and aesthetics. And, one might well add, this is the only time that concrete events and a determinable span of time are recognizable in any of Aichinger's works, although here too a tendency toward abstraction is already perceivable.

Instead of forcing a plot that develops along causal lines into a chronological time structure, Aichinger divides her novel into individual segments, each of which emphasizes a definite experiential situation. The characters do not have a profile. They seem to be leading a phantom-like existence. Ellen herself is sketched in fairly bare outlines. P. Haas Stanley[4] takes Aichinger to task because Ellen is "not a real person" and similarly holds it against the author that she "fails to develop the character of the girl-protagonist in 'Mirror Story'" ("Spiegelgeschichte," mS 46), one of her best-known works. As observations Stanley's remarks are correct; as criticisms they may be off target, for it seems very likely that Aichinger did not set out to fashion "real persons." Even in the later works her characters remain no more than anonymous participants in the plot. An external experience changes into an internal vision without warning, and the scene of the plot or action is transformed just as suddenly from the immaterial to the material world. The result is that the reader often gets lost in the dense network of thematic relationships. Thus the initially very realistic scene, in which the driver of a hearse tries to rescue the persecuted children by taking them across the frontier in his black coach, is unexpectedly transmuted into a dream vision. Three figures climb aboard in succession: the legendary Viennese bard Augustine, who defied death by singing in a pesthole; Columbus, who discovered a strange continent;[5] and little King David, who bested Goliath (and whose star serves as Ellen's inspiration). When the coachman awakens the children with a despairing: "We're not going to get across the border," they merely reply: "We're already across" (GH 56). The increasing certainty of being captured is offset by the possibility of gaining a freedom against which no earthly power can prevail.

The chapter entitled "In the Service of a Foreign Power" (GH 56) points to Aichinger's later work, for it is here that her relation to language is formulated. The Jewish children have aroused suspicion because they are learning English even though all frontiers are closed. A voice on the radio warns against listening to a foreign transmitter, but all that the old English teacher can say is:

Which one of you is not a foreigner? Jews, Germans, Americans, we're all foreigners here. We can say "Good morning" or "It's getting light," "How are you?," "There's a thunderstorm coming," and that's all we can say, almost all. Only haltingly do we speak our language. But I am going to

help you to learn it [German] all over again, the way a foreigner learns
a foreign language, cautiously, warily, the way you turn on a light in a
dark house and move on again (GH 63).

And a little further on we read: "'Secret language. Chinese and Hebrew, what
the poplars say and the fish conceal, German and English, living and dying,
it is all secret.' 'And the foreign transmitter?' 'Each of you can hear it if you
are quiet enough,' said the old man" (GH 68).

Utilizing as his starting point Aichinger's article "The Vision of Alienation,"[6]
in which she laments the lost "Vision of Childhood," R. Watt argues convincingly that in *Die größere Hoffnung* Aichinger showed exemplary skill in creating
a childlike optics. The events of the novel are depicted not from the vantage
point of the narrator but from that of the girl Ellen:

In every instance what happens is transposed from the plane of the real
world and of clear consciousness to that of dreaming and playing or
vice versa, without the slightest interruption in the narrative flow which
might hint at such a transposition. For children subjective and objective
reality, dreaming and being awake are one, and the narrative technique
compels the reader to take part in this experience.[7]

W. Eggers rather persuasively advances the argument that in its totality one
can regard Aichinger's work as being determined by the perspective of childhood: "It seems to be one of Ilse Aichinger's premises that this quasi-childlike
thinking brings us closer to the truth of the world or lets us penetrate it more
deeply than the scientific thinking which made possible its physical conquest."[8]
Building on this statement, Eggers is able to equate Aichinger's method of
representation with a technique in which there is conscious utilization of a
child's mode of vision. In this way the author can achieve the greatest possible
freedom of expression within the strictures imposed by our earthly existence.

Captivity and freedom are also the major themes of Aichinger's well-known
short story "Der Gefesselte" (mS 7) ("The Bound Man"), from which the first
anthology of her tales to be published in Germany derived its title: a man
wakes up and discovers that he is bound hand and foot with a thin rope. Because
he eventually learns to exploit whatever room to maneuver his fetters allow
him, he is actually able to move more freely and more securely than those
who are not bound. The man becomes the stellar attraction of a traveling circus
and never allows himself to be untied, for "what good would his leaps be without his bonds, what good would he himself be without them?" (mS 14). Some

distrustful villagers, not believing he has single-handedly killed a wolf that has been ravaging the countryside, demand a repeat performance. The moment he enters the wolf's cage the wife of the circus owner cuts the rope: "He pushed the woman back, but his movements were already without direction" (mS 19). He shoots the wolf and flees.

Like Ellen the bound man is in an intermediate realm between captivity and freedom: "They probably didn't have enough time to tie the ropes properly, because for someone who wasn't supposed to move at all, the ropes were too loose, and for someone who was supposed to move, they were somewhat too tight" (mS 11). A circus with its tamed beasts and its clowns and rope-dancers is really no different from a collection of beings subsisting on the edges of existence and related to "the children at the edge" (vR 8). Ellen's decision for the star and therefore for a life of persecution, for "the greater risk" (GH 103) and "the greater adventure" (GH 81) is re-echoed in the bound man's decision for his fetters: "By staying completely inside them, he also became free of them, and because they did not lock him in, they lent him wings and guided his jumps" (mS 10).

The freedom of the individual to develop within the limitations of empirical reality can lead to truly great accomplishments. These accomplishments, however, are achieved not because others wish it so, not because they have an effect on others, but because they are done for their own sake. Hence, every great accomplishment is unique and cannot be repeated, even if a skeptical public demands otherwise: "The bound man explained that a fight of this kind is not properly part of a circus act" (mS 18).

In the world as conceived by Aichinger every repetitious act inevitably leads to rigidity and to the loss of the potential for creativity. For in falling back on the known a vivid imagination is replaced by routine, by a deadly adherence to the tried and true, to the straight and narrow. A person destroys his creative powers through repetition and, like Emily in the dialogue entitled "Möwen" (ZkS 17) ('Seagulls"), is transformed into a shell of his former self, emptied of all substance. So too in the three stories comprising "Seegeister" (mS 64) ("Sea Spirits") the characters are shackled to the accoutrements of their dehumanized existence. In the first story a man who counterbalances his own insubstantiality with the illusion of power over a particular machine becomes part of this machine. In the second a woman who hides herself behind sunglasses because she is afraid of making contact with her fellow humans on an existential level, now has to wear her glasses all the time if she is to remain an entity. In the last of these stories three girls, who by their merciless behavior cause the death of the sailor on a small steamer, are doomed to be its passengers for all eternity. Because the ultimate actions of the man, the woman, and the girls are perpetually repetitive, any solution via death is automatically precluded. To die means that one has lived, and in the instances adduced here there is no authentic living. Aichinger herself seems to furnish a confirmation of this interpretation in her "Spiegelgeschichte" (mS 46) (Mirror Story). Here the central figure, at the point of death, traces her life all the way back to the day she was born. In this moment of revelation in which future, present, and past coincide and are experienced as an integral whole, the meaning of life is brought home in a flash. Ellen has a similar experience on her final journey to the bridges: "Now someone was shouting far ahead of her: 'Run faster, run even faster. Don't stop any more or you'll fall, don't think any more or you'll forget. Wait till you catch up with yourself!'" (GH 187).

Even the boy in "Das Plakat" (mS 27) (The Poster) senses somehow that authentic existence can be achieved only in a living and dying that are subject to the element of time. It becomes his overriding wish to revise the words addressed to him by the sickly man whose job is to put up the posters: "You will not die" (mS 27), so that for at least one fleeting instant he can relish what it means to have lived. The boy condemned to a timeless existence finds himself, as it were, "behind death's back"[9]—from this position he must cross the frontier into the realm of temporality in order to make the real world his own.

There is a pronounced similarity in theme between the works just discussed and a number of dialogues contemporaneous with them. For good reason Aichinger developed the form of the literary dialogue as an especially convenient vehicle for conveying her perspective on the truth of things. This form responds rather marvelously to her predilection for abstraction and dialectical configuration. In the dialogues the tension between timelessness and temporality is proffered in variant guises, of which, however, only a few can be singled out here. The problem is posed with exceptional lucidity in "Französische Botschaft" (ZkS 9) (French Embassy): someone leads a girl into temptation by offering to transform her into a statue on a church pillar, thus enabling her to escape from time into the rigidity of petrifaction. In a dialogue called "Erstes Semester" (ZkS 44) (First Semester) things are not much different. The janitor of a boarding house for foreign students offers a woman security and warmth, provided that she agrees to remain within the confines of the day on which she crosses the threshold into timelessness. She will have to do the same things and attend the same classes over and over again, summer will always be far off and Christmas always close without ever arriving (ZkS 47).

Here too the smashing of clocks connotes rigidity and "loss of ethical responsibility,"[10] for accountability can exist only in a world that recognizes time. The girl and the woman student return to the realm of time and thus to the fulfillment of their earthly obligations. But, contrary to the opinion of some critics, it is not the threshold of death on which the student turns her back, for in Aichinger's conception of things rigidity and death are mutually exclusive. A contented existence far removed from all sense of responsibility can on the other hand terminate in rigidity and a loss of substance. That is why—if we return to Aichinger's novel for a reinforcement of our assertion— Ellen does not succumb to the enticements of a life in contentment, but instead chooses to pursue the path to the bridges.

The theme is taken up again in Aichinger's later prose. "Preserve its voyage from comfort," is the benediction pronounced by the father over his ship in the short story "Eliza, Eliza" (mS 124). The lifeless but talking heroine of "Die Puppe" (mS 89) (The Doll) complains: "I am as warm as I am cold, I am deprived of pain, of dangers, of the sufferings of the saints" (mS 92). The rodent narrator of "Die Maus" (mS 94) ("The Mouse") is happy because it is undetectably safe in its little hole, but what this signifies is that life will go on in the world above and pass the mouse by. Just like Emily in the dialogue "Möwen" (ZkS 17), the mouse is destined to lead a vicarious and inconsequential existence: "I hear the ice cracking with as much concern as unconcern" (mS 95).

The radio play "Knöpfe" (M 43) (Buttons) can also be grouped with those works stressing the theme of rigidity and removal from time. Female workers prefer the warmth and apparent security of the button factory to the freedom of the outside world with its attendant perils and risks. In time they become the buttons that they make. The various scenes of the play take place in locations and stretches of time still readily identifiable despite the basic irrationalism of the plot. In a time frame comprising a number of successive days there is a confrontation between the world of the factories and that of the docks. A worker called Ann is caught between these two forces and ultimately decides in favor of rain, of cold, of proximity to the sea. She makes her choice upon comprehending the connection between the disappearance of one of the sorters and the production of a new type of button named after the missing employee.

In two subsequent radio plays, "Auckland" (A 113) and "Gare Maritime" (sW 83) Aichinger again pursues the theme of rigidity, of imprisonment within the clichés that dominate our speaking and our thinking. Here she deals with the power of *stories* ("Auckland") and of *history* ("Gare Maritime") to determine our lives. In both instances the net result of such a determination is a rigidified system of concepts, which must be demolished if our view of reality is to become free of distortion. Thus in "Auckland" the stories told by several narrators are continually varied, because none of them seems to have a very good recollection of events. In fact, it becomes increasingly uncertain whether these stories actually took place or not. In any case no agreement on a clear-cut version is reached, for no sooner are incidents established as certain than they are rendered questionable. The striking absence of any punctuation in both radio plays would seem to indicate that any and every attempt at determination of communication should be abandoned: "Or did I hear nothing Was no one sitting behind me Were there no deckchairs there striped the bluish white ones (resolutely) Not so How quickly your witnesses get lost on you Just now you still had them absolutely certain merely had to turn around to touch them" (A 126).

The radio play "Gare Maritime" (sW 83) is a work that lacks any basis of reality. One might even say the play is an end game. Not only do the main characters, Joe and Joan, seem to exist simultaneously in various forms, they also appear to belong to diverse historical epochs. Joan has a clear recollection of the Crusades and of the Dauphin to whom she gave help as Joan of Arc. The visitors to the maritime museum in which Joe and Joan have taken refuge from their persecutors regard the two protagonists as doll-like objects made of plaster, wood, and bone. But in the quiet conversations that Joe and Joan have together and in their warm concern for each other they reveal themselves as far more human than the "real" humans who come to gaze at them. As with other Aichinger figures, the flight into rigidity offers Joan a way of escaping from human sorrow and sufferings. Because she has the uncanny ability to hold her breath indefinitely, Joan could easily withdraw from the present moment into one of her historical forms of existence. But she chooses to breathe because she wants the spiritual values she embodies to survive. The attendant, who regards Joe and Joan as a threat to the well-ordered symmetry of his museum, proceeds to destroy them. For the wrong reasons he does what is right and proper: "O yes yes Joan I think we're making progress" (sW 127) are Joe's last words. The ossified trappings of the myth have to be destroyed so that the idea can "breathe" again. The title "Gare Maritime" (Maritime Station) refers to the location of the museum next to a port basin, into which the demolished statues are to be thrown. At the same time the title has to do with the proximity of the sea, from which (as in "Buttons") there issues the promise of spiritual renewal and revitalization — in other words the promise of a return akin to that in Aichinger's dialogue "Wiederkehr" (ZwS 62) (Return).

In the little piece "Zu keiner Stunde" (ZkS 13) (At No Hour), the title scene of her collection of dialogues, Aichinger sets *prospects* (Aussichten) against *view* (*Aussicht*), sets the blind striving of a student of shipbuilding oriented to utilitarian goals against the world view of a dwarf.[11] Every afternoon between the hours of three and four the latter compares the green color of his cap to the various shadings of green he can discern from his dormer window. Within the spatial confines of an attic and a time limit of sixty minutes a limit-less number of connections between green and green are revealed to the dwarf: "There's no end to it" (ZkS 15).

In a certain sense this dialogue typifies all of Aichinger's subsequent work. For with a growing passion she has directed her efforts at devising whole systems of personal references that she then incorporates in her plays and prose pieces. In every case the end result of this sort of concentration on subjective associa-tions, of which the reader can have little or no inkling, is a body of work so hermetically sealed that it has affected the reception of her books. Not unlike the lady in the story "Das Fenstertheater" (mS 61) (The Window Theater), the insecure reader cannot comprehend the nature of the reality that the written word aims to depict. In this particular story a woman is intently observing an old man from her window. He is standing by his window in the house opposite and giving a very strange and puzzling pantomimic performance, the meaning of which the woman is unable to figure out. In her perplexity she summons the police and follows them into the old man's house. When the police force their way into his apartment it is soon ascertained that the old man's perform-ance at the window was not directed at the woman across the way but was actually for the benefit of a child one floor above the woman. The reader, too, would like to be in a position to follow the literary custodians of law and order into the dwelling of the author. Although they have a variety of keys, not one of them may fit the lock in question, and Aichinger's doors are not so easy to break down.

It should not come as a surprise that in their attempts to interpret Aichinger critics have come up with some rather divergent results. A good example of this is the title story of a collection of short prose works, *Eliza, Eliza.* In this tale there is a lady who owns a large golden fan. It needs airing and so she has it placed out on the street in front of her house. A family takes up residence on the fan. One of the two daughters of the family, called Eliza by the other members, does not take part in their efforts to change the fan into a ship. The owner of the fan, who has been observing these activities from a window, eventually goes out into the street and starts a conversation with Eliza. At close range it becomes manifest that what the lady sensed as she looked out her window is fact: the family is made out of paper: "If you took a good look, then you soon gained the impression that they were also flatter. . . . Their arms lacked the proper curvature, the backs the proper width, and it might even be that they were fashioned from newspapers. . . ." (mS 123).

In the course of the conversation the lady conjures up a storm tide which is supposed to have an impact on Eliza. But there is no reaction from the girl: ". . . her features were faint, no more than an outline or so it seemed, and black streaks, somewhat blurry, ran across her temples, as if the news report to which she owed her life could be recognized. 'Midday storm wreaks—' the lady was actually reading . . ." (ms 125). When it starts to snow the lady tries to pull the fan up a hill overlooking the town. But a whirlwind comes along and swoops it up into the air. It glides toward the coast. The lady manages to rescue herself by securing a place on the fan, where the family greets her as its daughter Eliza. In the meantime the girl has shriveled to the size of a newspaper page and is fluttering toward the water. "Stale news," the father says behind her in his calm voice, "an old newspaper, which we used for practice" (mS 129).

Whereas R. Lübbren favors a surrealistic interpretation postulating the overcoming of the memory of a catastrophe as the main impact of the story,[12] M. Fleming talks of an allegory of the artist's world, in which the central character represents the author and Eliza her "erstwhile self, with whom she trades roles at the end."[13] D. Lorenz on the other hand, views "Eliza, Eliza" as an escape from stagnation: "Subordination to the past, acceptance of one's own destiny, affirmation of a future in flux."[14] W. Lautenschlager interprets the work as a process of self-discovery: "It would appear that the woman, reminded of a childhood trauma by an old newspaper, lapses into a daydream. The intuitive, irrational processes of the daydream, however, help her gain an awareness of self that reason alone could never have fostered."[15]

Typical of the stories in this volume, and especially of the first-person narratives, is the restrained, "undercooled" tone in which the raw materials of consciousness, the bits and pieces fueling our thought processes, are expressed through the monologue. P. Haas Stanley's[16] contention that Aichinger's subdued way of expressing things and of asking questions is tantamount to a kind of resignation—here our critic is taking her cue from W. Hildesheimer[17]—seems as mistaken as her "urge to shake each of these narrators vigorously in an effort to revitalize her [the narrator]" seems misdirected. In fact, the neutrality of the author's language produces an effective contrast to those bold flights of fancy that hit the reader fairly hard.

A similar phenomenon is revealed in the titles. Banal headings like "Holzfahrscheine" (mS 100) (Permits to Transport Timber), "Bauernregel" (mS 175) (Rule for Peasants), and "Fünf Vorschläge" (mS 190) (Five Proposals) prepare the reader in no way for the fantastic events depicted in these stories. Titles like

"Eliza, Eliza" (mS 120), "Herodes" (ms 142), and "Nur Josua" (mS 188) (Only Joshua) seem to belie the assertion of Alldridge that "One remarkable feature of her language is her general avoidance of proper names."[18] At the same time these names do not fulfill the expectations that they arouse in the reader, for they are "foreign words" (*Fremdwörter*) and are employed differently from the way convention requires: "I thought that perhaps a whiff of air would force its way among the old names and finally shred them" ("Die Schwestern Jouet," A 94, The Jouet Sisters). Apart from the fact that Herod (mS 142) and Noah (GH 66) both wear green dressing gowns, there is no common bond between them or with their biblical namesakes. Likewise Ajax ("Ajax," mS 124), the Emperor Ferdinand, and Little Edison ("Fünf Vorschläge," mS 190) do not adhere to the roles prescribed by myth and history. In this way they satisfy Aichinger's requirement that nothing should be predetermined by a particular meaning. And in the anthology *Schlechte Wörter* geographical names like Dover, Albany, St. Ives, and Wisconsin, just to mention a few, are transmuted into locales with an infinity of possible points of reference. They thus evince the progressive broadening of Aichinger's associative horizons.

In the tale "Der Querbalken" (mS 161, The Crossbeam) the narrator would like to set up house on a crossbeam and feel thoroughly at home there.[19] Hence he tries first of all to determine whether the crossbeam can provide the necessary protection and support. However, the many individuals who are asked "What is a crossbeam?" answer the question either unsatisfactorily or not at all. The hope of getting the right answer is of course based on a misconstruction, since each and every reply accords with the perspective of the person questioned and not with that of the questioner. According to Hildesheimer, the unanswered question becomes "the abstract hero of the story" (1180). It is the only thing certain for the wandering narrator, the world having failed to provide him with the guarantee that his intentions and his actions are the right ones.

The reader encounters the theme of security through the environment as early as *Die größere Hoffnung;* Ellen cannot cross the frontier, because no one wants to become surety for her. And the sailors in the dialogue "Return," who are convinced of their safety because they have bought life buoys, all perish. In the absence of surety the individual is compelled to issue his own visa, just as Ellen does when the consul is obliged to refuse his signature. And so the narrator is left with the freedom to take the "greater risk" and to make himself at home on the precarious crossbeam without any guarantee of security.

Various commentators (Eggers, Haas Stanley, Hildesheimer, Schafroth[20]) have emphasized with some accuracy a certain spiritual affinity between Aichinger and the writers of the absurd. Doubtlessly she shares with them the feeling of being a stranger in a questionable world, a world from which no answers are forthcoming and whose reality human reason is unable to penetrate sufficiently. A very skeptical attitude toward the possibility of comprehending the human condition and an immense doubt about the potential of language to formulate validly the metaphysics of our existence on the planet earth — these things are to be found already in *Die größere Hoffnung,* when Aichinger has the clerk say: "What I have perceived I have established, and what I have established has toppled over. Nothing have I let grow, nothing have I concealed" (GH 141).

These words do not connote the outright rejection of language as a means of expressing thought processes. To a far greater extent Aichinger's skepticism seems to be directed at the determinative and communicative possibilities of language. Consequently her dialogues are not real conversations between people, but rather dialectical monologues, in which diverse aspects of a problem are discussed and resolved in the Socratic manner. This is especially true of her short dramatic pieces. In her later prose fiction, however, matters are no longer brought to a resolution, because " the existing usages of the language will not allow a determination—we are dealing with possibilities" (sW 7).

In surveying Aichinger's prose works in their totality, one is struck by the predominance (since about 1960) of a first-person narration in which the individual is always trying to get his bearings in a silent world. He gropes, he asks questions, he seeks the outer limits of this world. He does these things most intensely in the latest collection of Aichinger's prose, *Schlechte Wörter.* Some of the texts appearing in this book, e.g., "Der Gast" (sW 25, The Guest) and "Ambros" (sW 131) might still be labeled short stories, but most of them dispense with a plot susceptible to synopsis. In his treatment of *Schlechte Wörter* H. Politzer asserts: "The only thing Aichinger has left is her breath, a vigorous breath and despite the brevity of her sentences, which are fragments chopped up and then made paratactical again, a long-lasting breath. You can depend on this breath; it rises and falls like the tides. What it carries are the fragments of a world, the flotsam and jetsam of stranded vocabularies."[21]

"Now I don't use the better words any more" (sW 7), Aichinger herself says in the first prose piece of her collection. Because the so-called "better words" have a meaning which has become fixed and frozen as a result of overusage and convention, only the "bad words" can still vitalize language. Every sudden and unexpected occurrence in life, no matter how trivial, brings with it uncertainty, forcing the individual to adjust his outlook on the world. The sugary milkstains on the easy chairs, perhaps deposited there by children "before they find their dead fathers" ["Flecken," sW 13 (Stains)], illuminate in a flash the threat lurking behind harmless occurrences and unexpectedly bringing chaos into a calm and spotless world. In this respect one feels compelled to recall the broken cup of Donna Catarina in Günter Eich's radio play *Die Brandung* (The Surf at Setúbal).

Aichinger has a fondness for conversational situations. These she has developed into meditative monologue that has become a hallmark of her prose fiction. Her predilection has also served her well in the writing of radio plays; it could be a major reason why she likes this form. These works, which take the word *play* at face value, operate on a number of levels simultaneously. Their structure is acausal and the fantasy world they depict is often practically inaccessible. Small wonder then that the hermetic structure of the radio plays makes the reader (or listener) rack his brains far more than does the rest of Aichinger's *oeuvre*. In these anti-rational fictions, in which even the continuity of time is suspended, there is only a fixed Now and an alternation of fantastic locales. W. Weber speaks of a "hovering present, in which the oldest element is as new as the newest is old; in which the dream is as real as the reality is dreamed, in which delusion is as accurate as what is accurate is wrong."[22] Her radio plays give Aichinger a better chance to unfold the potentialities of her highly creative imagination: a crocodile is dreaming in the river of the north, and a woman is knitting an olive-colored western sea with a black border ("Visit to the Parsonage"/"Besuch im Pfarrhaus," A 7). Eleven sea cows leave eleven umbrellas behind on a beach; Simplizius opens one of them and is whisked away, umbrella and all, to the land of Never-See-You-Again "Nachmittag in Ostende," (A 35) "Die Schwestern Jouet" (A 73), like the short story of the same title (mS 209), plays on word associations and highlights the problems and possibilities of the creative individual.

"I have also become cautious when it comes to forming connections" (sW 8), Aichinger states in *Schlechte Wörter*. The resoluteness displayed by the dwarf at the attic window, in comparing the shadings of green visible in the world outside to the green of his cap, has yielded to a sense of uncertainty. This feeling stems from the insight that the phenomena perceivable in the world around us cannot function by themselves as points of reference and orientation. In the interval Aichinger has outgrown even the constricted range of vision that takes in only what is green (to stay with Aichinger's metaphor). What remains solely is the asking of questions, but not the sort of question posed in "Crossbeam," where there was still the chance of an answer. "I'm just asking" one of her pieces ends, "You don't have to give a reply, you don't have to answer me. you can't anyway" ("Privas," sW 41).

Although the search for solutions has to remain open-ended in a world in which all is uncertainty, the questions must never cease being asked. Not looking for the answers is what brings on rigidity. And so the question *as question* qualifies as a way of keeping our lines of communication open to the world: "Why do we contemplate our moments . . .Why do we esteem them highly or think little of them, why do we or do we not have them stolen from us? And how? How do you live through a moment that is still ahead of you and yet already lost for all time? Not to speak of the moments gained, which are behind us. How do we unlearn to say recently and later, just now and right away?" (sW 36). Aichinger has in fact come close to perfecting the monologue composed of associative questions as a variant of the dialectical monologue, and with the recession of her epic impulses she has been placing more and more emphasis on this form.

In 1947 Ilse Aichinger dedicated to her friends Brigitte and Gottfried Bermann-Fischer a poem to which she had prefixed the title "Um diese Zeit" (At This Time): "I am letting myself be chased/by the hunting horns,/from my hiding-places/over to the dawn/beneath the snow,/to the yellowing grass.// With my hands/I am already reaching/the vows of the children,/which are swiftly drawing me up,/(I am) getting myself/the angular moon//."[23] This same poem can be found in the anthology *Verschenkter Rat* (Advice Dispensed Gratis) under the heading "Winterrichtung" (vR 38, Direction of Winter) and instead of the phrase "vows of the *children*" we now have "vows of the *aged.*" The new title indicates the direction in which Aichinger's literary intentions have developed in the intervening years. She is heading toward winter, toward the "dawn beneath the snow." For this is not the only poem concerning winter in the book. "Winterantwort" (Winter's Answer, vR 8), "Winterfrüh" (Winter Morning, vR 23), and "Winteranfang" (Winter's Beginning, vR 32) are some of the titles that catch the eye as it glances over the table of contents.

Yet Aichinger's winter lyrics can hardly be put in the category of emotional poetry. If anything their images are quite prosaic: "The grotto rides on the hills/are now closed,/the turnips long out of the ground,/the children gone" (vR 14). Invariably familiar concepts put in their appearance—one of her favorite words, as A. Hildebrand has pointed out, is "snow."[24] In an early dialogue, "Erstes Semester" (ZkS 44, First Semester), the snow is used as a symbol of liberation, of the removal of barriers and frontiers. When the student returns to life, "it starts to snow in big, watery flakes" (ZkS 49). Likewise in the even earlier story "Angel in the Night" ("Engel in der Nacht," mS 38) the driving snow erases the boundaries between life and death.

The change from children to the aged, conditioned by the new title "Winterrichtung," is less radical than it might seem to the uninitiated reader. In

Aichinger's scheme of things children and old people are equated with one another as peripheral figures in the game of life—in this respect one could think of the "Fenstertheater" (mS 61)—so that even an orientation to the "vows of the aged" can lead the speaker of the poem to the "dawn beneath the snow." One might bring in the poem "Winter's Answer" (vR 8) as a demonstration of this point. "Is it not a dark forest—that we have entered?" the poem asks at its conclusion. The answer is positive: "No, grandmother, it isn't dark,/ I know it, I lived for a long time/among the children at the edge,/and it is also not a forest" (VR 8). The stay with the children at the edge of existence, the "perspective of childhood," has familiarized the speaker with life on the periphery. The "dark forest" is merely a cliché that has to be demolished. By breaking down the symbol of existential fear into its component parts and negating these individually, Aichinger deprives the "dark forest" of its magical powers of suggestion.

The modest volume bringing together the poems Aichinger wrote between 1958 and 1978 (for individual dates see Lorenz's monograph)[25] allows us at long last to survey as a whole a body of poetry previously scattered and in some cases difficult to find. For the most part her poems are short, without rhyme and without a second stanza. Both from a thematic and linguistic standpoint they do not differ radically from her prose. And like her prose they are characterized by simple expressions and open beginnings: "For what would I do/if the hunters did not exist,/my dreams" (vR 7). Frequently, too, the posing of questions is a constituent of her poetry: "Who is on the trail of the rocks,/who is lining the grasses,/who is blocking off the squares/beyond the streets?" (vR 13). Another striking feature of Aichinger's poetry is the frequent use of the imperative mood which is of course ideally apt for dispensing advice: "First of all you must believe/that the day will come/when the sun rises./ But if you don't believe it,/say yes./Secondly/you must believe/and with all your might,/that the night will come,/when the moon appears./But if you don't believe it,/say yes/or nod your head complaisantly,/that too they'll accept" (vR 82, "Zeitlicher Rat," [Timely Advice]).

Because of the highly stratified nature and the estranged language of her work it comes as no surprise that the critics are far from a consensus on the most rewarding methodological approach to Aichinger. The biggest bone of contention is the area of code and symbol. According to Lorenz, Ilse Aichinger "...did not object to the term 'encoding' ['Chiffrierung'], provided it was not taken to mean that the author herself was the arbiter of a code but that the codes found in the text were received as such with the author merely functioning as a transmitting medium, without having logically constructed them for any definite purpose."[26] In their attempts to decipher Aichinger's work Fleming and Lautenschlager do not hesitate to utilize codes and existential constructs. On the other hand Eggers, along with Hildesheimer and Schafroth, rejects any symbol fixation and proposes a method which excludes any element of anticipation and in which the word is simply taken "at its word."[27]

There is no doubt that in her earlier works Aichinger made heavy use of images, symbols, and codes. But as her skeptical attitude to language as a medium of communication has increased, so has her introspective recording of thought processes. Her dread of the hermetic effect of repetition is evinced most tellingly in her aversion to traditional verbal significations. The consequence is an alienation of concepts, a recourse to the "Fremdwort," and the creation of a kind of secret language which makes it extremely difficult for the reader to accept words at their face value, or, to borrow Eggers's felicitous expression, to take words "at their word."

The previously discussed variant elucidations of the story "Eliza, Eliza," make it clear that a generally acceptable interpretative approach to the later prose fiction is a virtual impossibility. With unlimited freedom to form any kind of associations she wants to, Aichinger makes light of the chains that bind mortal man to empirical realities. So-called realities are subjected to an estrangement process which makes them part and parcel of that other reality, the highly personalized world view of Ilse Aichinger. And that is why we so often come up against unwonted and remarkable concepts, against such things as a green donkey, a short-necked giraffe, a father made of straw, and a language that has lost its lilac shawl. Aichinger synthesizes the most diverse notions into new and very novel configurations. Their spatial and temporal dimensions defy the known world, far beyond which they enjoy a life all their own. Transmuted into words, her concepts and images achieve their effect through the incongruities of semantic content.

It would seem that Aichinger has never left the spiritual realm of the "children at the edge." The inhabitants of this realm possess the privilege of enunciating the foreign word (*Fremdwort*) as well as the privilege of remaining silent. "I have concealed nothing" (GH 141), the clerk explains in *Die größere Hoffnung,* and the author herself expressed the need for remaining silent at one of the annual gatherings of Group 47. A report of this session informs us: "Heissenbüttel's poetry, she [Aichinger] says, gives us merely a rough translation of reality. And then she advises— and seems to sense how far she is going with this piece of advice: 'What it needs is to be concealed once more.'"[28] H. Politzer begins his discussion of *Schlechte Wörter* with a description of a caricature printed in the *New Yorker,* in which a group of intellectuals, suddenly confronted with a horrendous monster in their midst, cope with the problem by talking about it. In contrast to their way of dealing with the issue, Politzer continues, Ilse Aichinger keeps the monster a secret by putting it into words.[29]

The only course open to the reader who wants to tame the monster with Aichinger is to learn to listen for what has been kept secret. It is good to recall the words of the old teacher: "'Secret language. Chinese and Hebrew, what the poplars say and the fish conceal, German and English, living and dying, it is all secret.' 'And the foreign transmitter?' 'Each one of you can hear it if you are quiet enough.'"

Notes

My sincere thanks to Ralph Ley who translated this article for me.

1. The original of "foreign words" is *Fremdwörter*. The German adjective *fremd* has a very strong double connotation: it can mean both "foreign" and "strange."

2. The following abbreviations of Ilse Aichinger's works are used in the body of this article:

   GH: *Die größere Hoffnung* (Frankfurt: Fischer Taschenbuch, 1974).
   ZkS: *Zu keiner Stunde.*
   H: *Hörspiele.*
   mS: *Meine Sprache und ich.*
   A: *Auckland.*
   sW: *Schlechte Wörter.*
   vR: *Verschenkter Rat.*

3. Cf. Wendelin Schmidt-Dengler, "Laudatio anläßlich des Kafka-Preises 1982," and Aichinger's acceptance speech, "Die Zumutung des Atems," both in *Literatur und Kritik,* 177/178 (1983), 419–423.

4. Patricia Haas Stanley, "Ilse Aichinger's Absurd 'I,'" *German Studies Review,* 2 (1979), 334.

5. Cf. the following from Aichinger's review of a work by Ernst Schnabel in "Die Sicht der Entfremdung," *Frankfurter Hefte,* 9 (1954), 47: "He [Schnabel] knows . . . that it is the mission of today's Columbus not to familiarize us with a strange world, but to render unfamiliar the world that we know all too well."

6. Ibid., p. 46f.

7. Roderick H. Watt, "Ilse Aichingers Roman 'Die größere Hoffnung,'" *Studia Neophilologica,* 50 (1978), 243.

8. Werner Eggers, "Ilse Aichinger," *Deutsche Literatur seit 1945,* ed. Dietrich Weber (Stuttgart: Kröner, 1970), p. 235.

9. Hans Egon Holthusen, "Im Rücken des Todes. Ilse Aichinger: Zu keiner Stunde," *Süddeutsche Zeitung,* Easter 1957.

10. Theodore Ziolkowski, *Strukturen des modernen Romans* (München: List, 1972), p. 188.

11. A similar confrontation of "Aussicht" with "Aussichten" occurs in "Where I Live" ("Wo ich wohne," mS 76), a short story in which a student of shipbuilding again plays a role. Cf. Ralf R. Nicolai, "Ilse Aichingers Kritik des modernen Bewußtseins," *Literatur und Kritik,* 153 (1981), 175-179.

12. Rainer Lübbren, "Die Sprache der Bilder. Zu Ilse Aichingers Erzählung 'Eliza, Eliza,'" *Neue Rundschau,* 76 (1965), 626-636.

13. Marianna E. Fleming, "Ilse Aichinger: 'Die Sicht der Entfremdung,'" Diss. University of Maryland, 1974, p. 170.

14. Dagmar C.G. Lorenz, *Ilse Aichinger* (Königstein/Ts.: Athenäum, 1981), p. 135.

15. Wayne Lautenschlager, "Images and Narrative Techniques in the Prose of Ilse Aichinger," Diss. Washington University, 1976, p. 139.

16. Haas Stanley, p. 338.

17. Wolfgang Hildesheimer, "Ilse Aichinger: 'Der Querbalken,'" *Merkur,* 17 (1963), 1179-1181.

18. James C. Alldridge, *Ilse Aichinger* (London: Wolff, 1969), p. 7.

19. The dative "Ich wollte mich auf *einem* Querbalken niederlassen" suggests that the narrator wishes to settle there permanently, a point overlooked by most interpreters.

20. Heinz Schafroth, Introduction to *Meine Sprache und ich* (Frankfurt: Fischer, 1976).

21. Heinz Politzer, "Ilse Aichingers todernste Ironien," *Merkur* 5 (1976), 486.

22. Werner Weber, "Ilse Aichinger," *Schriftsteller der Gegenwart,* ed. Klaus Nonnenmann (Olten und Freiburg: Walter, 1963), p. 15.

23. Brigitte B. Fischer, *Sie schrieben mir* (Zürich und Stuttgart: Classen, 1978), p. 198 f.

24. Alexander Hildebrand, "Zu Ilse Aichingers Gedichten," *Literatur und Kritik,* 23 (1968), 166.

25. Lorenz, pp. 214-252.

26. Ibid., p. 39.

27. Eggers, p. 234.

28. Joachim Kaiser, "Mißverständnisse," *Almanach der Gruppe 47,* ed. Hans Werner Richter (Reinbek bei Hamburg: Rowohlt, 1962), p. 45.
29. Politzer, p. 486.

Works by Ilse Aichinger

Die größere Hoffnung. Wien: Bermann-Fischer, 1948.
Die größere Hoffnung. Frankfurt: Fischer, 1974.
Rede unter dem Galgen. Wien: Jungbrunnen, 1952.
Der Gefesselte. Frankfurt: Fischer, 1953.
Zu keiner Stunde. Frankfurt: Fischer, 1957.
Besuch im Pfarrhaus. Frankfurt: Fischer, 1961.
Hörspiele. Ed. Ernst Schnabel. Frankfurt: Fischer, 1961.
Wo ich wohne. Frankfurt: Fischer, 1963.
Eliza, Eliza. Frankfurt: Fischer, 1965.
Auckland. Vier Hörspiele. Frankfurt: Fischer, 1969.
Nachricht vom Tag. Frankfurt: Fischer, 1970.
Dialoge, Erzählungen, Gedichte. Stuttgart: Reclam, 1971.
Schlechte Wörter. Frankfurt: Fischer, 1976.
Meine Sprache und ich. Frankfurt: Fischer, 1978.
Verschenkter Rat. Gedichte. Frankfurt: Fischer, 1978.

Works by Ilse Aichinger in English Translation

Schaeffer, Cornelia, trans. *Herod's Children* (Die größere Hoffnung). New York: Atheneum, 1963.
Mosbacher, Eric, trans. *The Bound Man and Other Stories.* Freeport, New York: Books for Libraries Press, 1956. Reprinted 1971.
Holroyd-Reece, Gitta, trans. "Mirror Story." *Austria Today,* 4 (1981), 44-47.

Secondary Works in English

Alldridge, James C. ed. "Introduction," *Ilse Aichinger.* Oxford/New York: Pergamon, 1966.

Alldridge, James C. ed. "Introduction," *Ilse Aichinger.* London: Wolff, 1969.

Bedwell, Carol B. "Who Is the Bound Man? Towards an Interpretation of Ilse Aichinger's 'Der Gefesselte.'" *German Quarterly,* 38 (1965), 30-37.

Bedwell, Carol B. "The Ambivalent Image in Aichinger's 'Spiegelgeschichte.'" *Revue des langues vivantes,* 33 (1967), 363-368.

Haas Stanley, Patricia. "Ilse Aichinger's Absurd 'I,'" *German Studies Review,* 2 (1979), 331-350.

Lautenschlager, Wayne. "Images and Narrative Techniques in the Prose of Ilse Aichinger," Diss. Washington University 1976.

Livingstone, Rodney. "German Literature from 1945." *Periods in German Literature,* ed. J. M. Ritchie. London: Wolff, 1966, pp. 283-303.

Secondary Works in German

Eggers, Werner. "Ilse Aichinger," *Deutsche Literatur seit 1945,* ed. Dietrich Weber (Stuttgart: Kröner, 1970), pp. 252-270.

Fleming, Marianna E. "Ilse Aichinger: 'Die Sicht der Entfremdung,'" Diss. University of Maryland 1974.

Friedrichs, Antje. "Untersuchungen zur Prosa Ilse Aichingers." Diss. Wilhelms-Universität Münster 1970.

Hildebrand, Alexander. "Zu Ilse Aichingers Gedichten." *Literatur und Kritik,* 23 (1968), 161-167.

Kleiber, Carine. *Ilse Aichinger. Leben und Werk.* Bern/Frankfurt am Main: Peter Lang, 1984.

Lorenz, Dagmar C.G. *Ilse Aichinger.* Königstein/Ts.: Athenäum, 1981.

Lübbren, Rainer. "Die Sprache der Bilder. Zu Ilse Aichingers Erzählung 'Eliza, Eliza.'" *Neue Rundschau,* 76 (1965), 626-636.

Oldemeyer, Ernst. "Zeitlichkeit und Glück. Gedanken zu Texten von Ilse Aichinger." *Geistesgeschichtliche Perspektiven.* Bonn: Bouvier, 1969, pp. 281-307.

Watt, Roderick H. "Ilse Aichingers Roman 'Die größere Hoffnung,'" *Studia Neophilologica,* 50 (1978), 233-251.

Weber, Werner. "Ilse Aichinger." *Schriftsteller der Gegenwart,* ed. Klaus Non-
    nenmann. Olten und Freiburg: Walter, 1961, pp. 11–17.

H. C. Artmann

Peter Pabisch

Once praised as "der Erzpoet,"[1] the prodigal German poet, H. C. Artmann, has participated in various literary trends while always retaining his own creative individualism and not bowing to any rules of a group or school. Hans Carl Artmann is rarely omitted from the list of the foremost writers in Austrian and German literature after World War II by experts in the field, be they critics or connoisseurs. To pinpoint Artmann's qualities as a writer, one does not refer to his unique style, his cohesive power of narration, nor to a preferred genre, but rather to the way this poet dazzles and startles his readers by his variety of styles, his puns, his far-fetched metaphors, his manneristic notions, in short, his eccentricities.

Now in his mid-sixties the author can look back on a colorful existence shaped by a stubbornly independent life style and a correspondingly eventful life. Born in 1921, the only child of a poor craftsman's family in or near Vienna, the author first became acquainted with literature through an uncle, who introduced him to a Viennese public library.[2] Supposedly Artmann first wrote detective stories for his schoolmates. World War II interrupted his literary activities — or at least any products thereof were lost. Immediately following the war and his return from the army, he stayed with the German actor Herbert Stettner for a few weeks, enjoying his host's large private library and discovering the works of several German symbolists and expressionists. Accordingly, his earliest poems bear some resemblance to Rilke or even the French symbolists.[3] On his return to Vienna he studied other world literature and encountered such exotic delights, as he considered them, as Japanese *haikus* or Ramón Gómez de la Serna's *greguerías,* forms which he subsequently adopted.[4]

This technique of imitation was expanded over the years to a masterly skill. No one could accuse him, though, of mere borrowing; he always lends a personal touch to his versions, even in translations. As original literature he has written Persian quatrains, baroque epigrams and adventure stories, a book of dreams, horror and monster stories, ballads, seafaring tales, fictitious diaries, aphorisms, love poems, novellas, and harlequin plays.[5] Also in translations (he has done many from various languages) his creative fervor dominates and not just loyalty to the original texts. Thus, in his own way, he served Calderón de la Barca, Molière, Edward Lear, Carlo Goldoni, H. P. Lovecraft, and especially François Villon.[6] From the latter Artmann translated the famous *balads,* thereby trying to capture the colloquial Parisian jargon of the poet in his own Viennese jargon, which in itself is rich in metaphors unknown to standard German. In doing so Artmann wove a new texture, so to speak, which is truly original.

To understand Artmann's literary art, one has to recognize the intentions of modern art itself, as they were stipulated by Pablo Picasso, for example, back in 1908 when he and Braque proclaimed the rules for Cubism. Realistic depiction of scenes no longer sufficed for them; rather fantasy and creativity drawn from psychological insights—mainly the world of dreams and imagination—was to be the basis for art. Artmann shares his themes with modern art, as it was reborn after World War II, as, for example, in Vienna's "Fantastic Art" movement.[7] Artmann himself was a member of Vienna's *art-club* in the late 1940s and early 1950s, initially the only writer in the group. If one knows the paintings of Ernst Fuchs, Friedensreich Hundertwasser, Wolfgang Hutter, and Albert Paris Gütersloh, among others, Artmann's often dreamlike sequences can be better understood. He does not depict scenes in descriptive fashion but rather through linguistic effects and dreamlike metaphors—his special strength. Essentially he is fascinated by language itself, and by what it is able to evoke. Not *what* language says is important but *how* it says things. As is typical of "Fantastic Art," also known as "Fantastic Realism," Artmann's technique is reminiscent of the way known features of human life can be seen only psychologically. Artmann also alludes to popular literature, to the Bible, and to historical events, through this psychological technique. To a large degree his trademark is his own name, which he frequently inserts in his works. He does this playfully, in accord with the humorous element found in all of his writings. This feature can be so entertaining that it borders on the frivolous at times, as some of his titles can demonstrate: *Im Schatten der Burenwurst* (1983, In the Shadow of a Polish Sausage), *how much, schatzi?* (1971, = original English title), *Die Sonne war ein grünes Ei* (1982, The Sun Was a Green Egg) or *Das Prahlen des Dschungels im Urwald* (1983, The Primeval Forest of the Jungle Shows Off).[8] It is for this originality that his entertaining public readings are very popular and well attended. Also because of his originality he enjoys a popularity unmatched by any of his colleagues, most of whom are themselves enthusiastic fans and members of Artmann's audience.

Another even more important influence upon Artmann has been language philosophy and the general language skepticism, well known in Austrian writing as far back as Hugo von Hofmannsthal's famous *Ein Brief* (1902, Letter of Lord Chandos), and deepened after the experience of two world wars, particularly after the misuses of the language in the Third Reich. In the view of Artmann and his fellow authors language had become empty and meaningless, new ways of communication had to be found. Whereas many authors chose a somewhat conservative route to find new paths of expression, Artmann and some of his disciples turned to radical means, which were softened in Artmann's case by his humorous tendencies, so that his radicalism was often overlooked.

In the 1950s, while still residing in Vienna, Artmann met Konrad Bayer, Gerhard Rühm, Friedrich Achleitner, and Oswald Wiener, all extreme opponents of tradition and of the establishment. They have become known as the *Vienna Group* (Wiener Gruppe) which was dissolved in 1964 when Bayer for unknown reasons committed suicide. Artmann never appreciated a group climate—it inhibited his individualism—but he did collaborate with the other four authors. There are photographs documenting their appearance together in various lecture readings.

Their works were as unusual as they were puzzling and also, at times, offensive. We find meaningless phonetic dadaistic variations, nonsensical lists of words, distorted approximations of rhyme, computer poetry of no substance, graffiti language—anything and everything to annoy and agitate a traditional readership—and surprisingly with the utmost success, as various newspaper reports and critical articles of the time can attest. Their furor brought several successful innovations which were adopted in modern German literature. In Artmann's case this was dialect poetry, which he introduced to tremendous popular attention and enjoyment.

Artmann first rose to unexpected stardom in 1958 when a friend with some influence on Vienna's literary scene, Friedrich Polakovics,[9] read from and soon thereafter published a first manuscript in dialect, entitled *med ana schwoazzn dintn* (with black ink).[10] The book became a best seller, but not for the reasons intended. It is a harsh criticism of the Viennese worker's ugly jargon with its rude and offensive expressions, but instead of viewing the work as a criticism of their language and life style people enjoyed the poems as an expression of Artmann's black humor. What Artmann meant to be a serious indictment of people who had tacitly endured Hitler's rule, was mistaken by his readers as a good-natured parody. Artmann was celebrated as a popular dialect poet. At the moment of his triumph and thereafter, almost no one took notice of Artmann's varied publications in standard German, such as *Der Schlüssel des heiligen Patrick* (1959, The Key of St. Patrick), a creative translation of Irish prayers, his baroque poems in the manner of Andreas Gryphius, or his Hussar stories à la Grimmelshausen. His dialect poetry made people classify him as their "Heimatdichter," a folkloristic author, which he neither wanted to be nor accurately represented. Still his name appeared on Austria's literary map, as it were, overnight. For the moment this brought him and his friends not only popularity, but also financial success and thus represented the breakthrough that he and the others had been long awaiting. So he went along with the glory, while contemplating the best way to return to his actual mission of writing innovative literary art.

This change, when it did occur, was caused by need, not by virtue. In his marital obligations, as in his writing, Artmann has remained independent. His marriages have rarely been legal ones, and, according to some claims, he has fathered six children with as many women. So as abruptly as his popularity had begun, it ended in 1961 when Artmann decided to leave Austria because of an alimony case.

Even though his popularity ebbed and he was involved in domestic troubles, his literary productivity never ceased. As the bibliography at the end of this article illustrates, his most active phase as a writer occurred in the 1960s and early 1970s with works written in standard German. Major collections of his poetry, prose, and drama were published by Gerald Bisinger, Peter O. Chotjewicz, and Klaus Reichert.[11] Actually his production has remained undiminished to this day—he averages one book publication per year. To assist the reception of his writings, Artmann makes personal appearances on radio and television, slipping into many masks according to the occasion. He has been awarded a number of literary prizes[12] and still enjoys being the center of attention among his friends, who are delighted by his spur-of-the-moment utterances, not seldom occurring when Artmann is in alcoholic good spirits.

In the 1970s, after having roamed through half of Europe for a decade, he returned to Austria to live in Salzburg. In 1973 he became the president of the Austrian Anti-P.E.N. Club, founded by members of the progressive *Grazer Autorenversammlung*,[13] to which all the survivors of the former *Vienna Group* also belonged at this time. In the 1980s he has moved more closely toward Vienna, namely, to the rural "Waldviertel," which he claims as his ancestral home.

When we turn to his works per se, some examples may suffice to show the surreal character of Artmann's work and to illustrate some of the author's more significant techniques on which his reputation is largely based. Some reference will be made to the literary trends that the author followed or disregarded. Although it represents only some two percent of his entire oeuvre, greater attention will be paid to Artmann's dialect poetry, mainly because of its influence on the subsequent German literary movement of dialect poetry, labeled now as the "New Dialect Wave."

First a sample from his prose in standard German, a story in *Die Sonne war ein grünes Ei* (1982). Certain nonexistent English words were coined purposely in the translation in an attempt to approximate the German original as closely as possible:

All living beings had been created, only man was missing. The Great Spirit had a little daughter, he carried her around in the chest pocket of his suit, he took her along wherever he went. As she grew up and became taller she sat on his shoulder; she no longer fit into the vest pocket of his suit. The daughter lived on the shoulder of her father, they were inseparable.

One day, while the Great Spirit rested and slept on a meadow in the woods, the girl stepped off his shoulder and ran across the meadow. She saw a bull following a cow. She saw a stag following a doe. She saw a ram following a ewe. She saw a boar following a sow. She saw a hare following a haress. She saw a grasshopper following a grasshopperess. She saw a firebug following a firebugess. When the girl saw next that all the females were being mounted, a lustful feeling overcame her—and she said: "I am the daughter of the Great Spirit, why is no one following me!"

She returned to her father who was still asleep. She looked at him and thought: "If I were to find a man like him, he could follow me and I would be served well." She took clay and moistened it with her saliva. She formed an image of the Great Spirit, shaping a face, hands, feet; she formed all the parts of the body. When she was done she wondered: "How can I bring him alive?" She began to sing a magic song, she formulated new words and sounds, she invented dancing, but she did not succeed in making the clay man live.

Meanwhile the Great Spirit had awakened, he stretched himself and rubbed his eyes. When his daughter noticed him, she became frightened, she hid behind the clay image, she was embarrassed in front of her father. The Great Spirit saw the image his daughter had made, he realized instantly what she desired. He thought: "My daughter is grown up now, why should she not have a man?"

He took out his pocket knife, he made a small cut into his thumb, blood poured out. The blood he smeared onto the mouth and the penis of the clay man. The penis stiffened and the mouth opened in order to talk. The Great Spirit turned around and went back quietly into the woods. He thought: "It feels as if my left shoulder were missing."

When the living clay man saw the girl, he said: "Why did you create me in the image of your father?" The girl replied: "Please, Adam, ask me a more difficult question!"

Thereafter they became man and wife, and all mankind springs from them. (*Die Sonne war ein grünes Ei,* pp. 97-98.)

Artmann's story toys with the biblical view of Creation by offering another version, in which man was created in the image of the Great Spirit according to the wish of a woman. Artmann borrows from the Bible and alters what he takes to suit his own literary purposes. He does this with the firm intention of voicing his opposition to something he does not believe in. He and other writers of the new era are strict atheists. Yet if this conclusion seems too serious for this story, it points to Artmann's humorous, lighthearted way of rebelling. The result is still a radically changed version of the biblical one. Generally Artmann's countermodels reflect events, trends and views of our era. His work shows opposition to the usual intellectual notions of German-Austrian society: that these countries are the lands of poets and thinkers (*Dichter und Denker*) and that man is always guided by his nobler inclinations and never by his basic drives. In the story the girl's Elektra complex emerges as the animalistic desire to have a man for herself in the image of her own father, whether he is the Great Spirit or not. All the discoveries of modern psychology since Freud are represented in Artmann's work and in that of his generation of writers. Yet even in his most blatant attacks on the establishment Artmann remains genial, both in his writing and personally. Pleasant stories with friendly parodistic sarcasm, like the one above, have guaranteed him an impressive flock of admirers and followers. The story is not at all provocative or hateful in content; rather it amuses, possibly provoking a smile on the face of even the most outraged reader who would object to it on religious grounds.

Further examples of such antithetical plots abound in Artmann's work, notably in a booklet entitled *allerleirausch* (1968), a parody of *Allerleirauh,*[14] a collection of traditional German children's songs edited by Hans Magnus Enzensberger. In his attack Artmann writes countersongs mocking the idyllic bourgeois heritage as it was corrupted during the Hitler era and after. Having lived through World War II, Artmann and his fellow writers miss no opportunity to attack any form of militarism, the false notions of fatherland, honor, and especially of German supremacy. One document reveals this directly; ten years after the war Artmann judged his countrymen in his "Declaration against the Restoration of an Austrian Army" (1955), in which he explains why he believes that Austria – "as the only truly cultural nation on earth"[15] – should do without an army. Together with some of his artist friends he carried posters through Vienna to demonstrate his rejection of such a return to militarism, only to discover that the demonstration was largely ignored or ridiculed, while police dispersed the group.

Maybe in order not to look foolish again Artmann henceforth refrained from publishing anything as political as this Declaration. He returned to literature where he contributed to political criticism in his own way as an author and possibly to greater effect. For example, in his short play *Kein Pfeffer für Czermak*[16] (1969, No Pepper for Mr. Czermak), a Viennese storekeeper, Herr Gschweidl, who sells flour, salt, and pepper, also tyrannizes his customers, imposing on them his personal etiquette and mores. Gschweidl refuses to sell pepper to young Czermak, an admirer of his niece, because Czermak is an artist, and as such very impoverished. Thus, according to Czermak, he is worthless. After the war Austrian society had little time for considering the arts at all, let alone the innovative ones; the government also had other problems, restoring an economy still suffering from the destruction of war. Gschweidl's opportunism was quite in tune with the Austrian mindset of the time. The only art scene Austria supported was one that strengthened tourism and increased its profitability, such as the Viennese music scene, first and foremost the Vienna State Opera, which received three-quarters of Austria's small cultural budget. The modern art scene was not supported until after the 1960s, when it gained more popular appeal. In the 1960s Austrians were still conservative in their taste for art and literature; the majority embraced Michelangelo and Goethe, Waldmüller and Grillparzer, but cursed Picasso and Brecht. The generations born during the Wilhelmine and post-Wilhelmine eras that witnessed so many political changes in the first half of this century—from monarchy to the First Democratic Republic to Austrofascism to the Third Reich and to the Second and present Democratic Republic of Austria—had political attitudes that were rather confused and anything but fixed. Many of these Austrians became hedonistic opportunists, living for the moment.

Artmann's Herr Gschweidl is just such a self-centered "homo austriacus." Viennese cabaret artists Carl Merz and Helmut Qualtinger, friends of Artmann, adopted Herr Gschweidl and transformed him into their famous "Herr Karl." Portrayed by Qualtinger, a very popular, almost three-hundred-pound actor, "Herr Karl" explains to his fellow Austrians in a one-act monologue how he survived many political regimes while retaining his self-esteem and decent views: "I am a good person, but the young people would need a new Hitler so they'd know what discipline means. . . ." These and similar statements made self-righteous "Herr Karl" a dramatic parody of postwar moral standards; the figure was adopted by admirers worldwide and can be found in America in the television figure Archie Bunker. The character's popularity stems from

its being played so that the audience was free to identify with or react in opposition to it. The dramatic presentation of "Herr Karl" allowed audiences to
recognize their own Viennese features, particularly because "Herr Karl" speaks
in Viennese dialect. His popularity increased further when he was portrayed on
television.

Artmann as well as Rühm and Achleitner enjoyed similar success with their
dialect poetry; it too mocks society by mirroring it indirectly. The artist assumes
the mask of what he wants to eradicate. Rühm and Achleitner must be mentioned here because they gave Artmann the idea of writing in dialect. In 1959,
a year after his own best seller *med ana schwoazzn dintn* had appeared, Artmann
published a second dialect volume, *hosn rosn baa*[17] (1959, pants roses bones),
in coauthorship with Rühm and Achleitner: but in both works Artmann's
skills outshine those of his friends. The wealth of his vocabulary, the Viennese
jargon of his home district "Ottakring," the dissonant harmony by means of
which he associates words, metaphors, and thoughts, his ability to pinpoint
correctly people's sinister emotions and related psychological features, made
him a star in the literary firmament of the late 1950s. Journalist Otto F. Beer
celebrated him in a Viennese daily newspaper with the rare praise of "Habemus
poetam!"[18] To this day Artmann has been able to retain his foremost position
in the entire German-speaking world.

One poem from *hosn rosn baa* that exemplifies Artmann's sarcastic yet
entertaining effects is "de pflostara," superbly translated into colloquial English
by Winter Laite:

The Street Crew[19]
imagine
the other day I'm walkin'
all alone
down the Stättermeiergasse
there's the road crew
tearin' up the street
I go on over
and watch 'em for a while
I says to 'em
that s'posed to be work?
I'm a shoemaker
and makin' shoes used to be
like diggin' gold
now it's just like shovelin' shit

but what you're doin' there
that ain't even shit
why, ev'r dog pisses on it!
ah, man
one o' them stands up slow
y'know
a guy like that with a bound up knee
and slaps me twice in the face
I thought
my backbone 'd bust
and I hear the angels singin'!!

what else can i tell you?
after all
them road crews
ain't got no shame and no religion
in public in the middle of the street
they slap a fellow twice!

As a rule it is difficult to convey an impression of the uniqueness of these dialect poems in English. The entertaining effect lies in the choice of the poetic self (*das poetische Ich*) represented by a typical lower-class Viennese who likes to needle (*stänkern*) others and then enjoys recounting the actions taken against him, self-righteously protesting his innocence. The subject of the poem is unassuming, yet the surrounding tension created by the poet makes it exciting. The action swings between emotional extremes, from calm to brutal, from harmless to warlike.

"The Street Crew" is also interesting from a sociohistorical point of view. It sheds light on the life style of the underprivileged classes as they existed in Vienna 1850 to 1950; foreign workers swelled the population of the city from the time of its emergence as a metropolitan center to the end of the First World War. Many of these Czechs, Hungarians, Yugoslavians, and even Germans from rural areas stayed on when their work was finished, their various accents coloring the standard German idiom. By 1950 most of these people were deceased or old; their children and grandchildren, born in Vienna, spoke a more unified dialect. These people lived in the poor districts of Vienna, where Artmann grew up. Perhaps he occasionally served as an interpreter during his childhood, because in his German version of this poem two dialect models are offered: one, that of a Czech immigrant speaking with a heavy accent and faulty grammar, and the other–to which our English translation pertains–the modern jargon of the Viennese worker. The first lines of each model are as follows:

JARGON WITH CZECH ACCENT	USUAL JARGON	TRANSLATION INTO ENGLISH
ŠTELN S INEN FOR	SCHDÖN S INA FUA	IMAGINE

Ingeniously, Artmann borrowed a letter proper only to Czech–namely "Š." with the diacritical mark reflecting the sound "sh." Artmann's ability to reconstruct various accents and idioms is phenomenal, particularly if we recall that he also wrote Baroque poems and biblical passages from the Irish at the same time he was working on his dialect poems.

The appellation "Volksdichter" (people's poet) was bestowed on him in error when *med ana schwoazzn dintn* was bought even by those people about whom Artmann had written. Better-educated Viennese mentioned Artmann in the same breath with Joseph Weinheber,[20] not recognizing that Artmann had been playing with language and had unintentionally found a treasure. This may sound unbelievable, but at the time Artmann, Rühm, and Achleitner were anything but popular, so that they had no idea about the positive consequences their dialect writing would bring. Many German regions throughout the entire German-speaking realm, even German-speaking regions within other language areas, adopted Artmann's achievement for their own purposes. As mentioned, a dialect wave evolved, making up for the loss of serious dialect poetry in German-speaking countries during the Hitler era, when dialect had been misused as a folkloristic trapping for the political machine. The decline of dialect poetry and of dialect literature generally may have started earlier when nationalistic tendencies called for the more uniform standard language in literature. This may also explain the lack of development of dialect in other countries. But following Artmann's success dialect poetry became fashionable in other European languages as well as in German. Artmann made it clear that in order to obtain any verisimilitude with the figures depicted, the author would have to adopt their language. In recent years close to fifty renowned writers have utilized their respective German dialects in hundreds of book publications. However, to claim that this resurgence of popularity was Artmann's doing alone would be as incorrect as to overlook his major contribution to this revival.

Why then did Artmann not enjoy his role as "Volksdichter?" Obviously because he did not start out writing on behalf of this segment of society, but against it. This is what the audience had misunderstood and why Artmann subsequently avoided the crowds and moved away from the use of dialect in his writing. Artmann's dialect phase sheds light on the important stage in his literary career after the rather frustrating time he spent in search of ways to be creative. Not only did his generation implement previously unfamiliar artistic modes, but they also reasserted the irrevocable right of the artist to be as original in his creations as he wished, a notion inherited from turn-of-the-century artists. Artmann and his fellow writers and artists found protection for their experimental art in Austria's renewed democratic constitution. They needed this protection; at times the Viennese of the 1950s reacted more vehemently to the unusual pre-dialect and dialect products of the young writers than to the trials of the mass murderers of the Hitler era. This reaction to artistic novelty was one of the targets of Merz and Qualtinger's "Herr Karl," who represents this sort of Viennese. With other texts like "Herr Karl" Artmann contributed to this criticism of his society.

Accustomed to sarcasm and irony in their folkloristic dialect songs, the Viennese praised *med ana schwoazzn dintn* and its poet. People learned his poems by heart. Artmann appeared in the media. In 1959 the City of Vienna even gave him an apartment. The Viennese Tramway Association made a dialect magazine available in each streetcar, and this *Straßenbahnzeitung* quickly gained popularity; the magazine was written almost entirely in dialect and was published for many years. A group of quasi-poets (*Dichterlinge*) emerged from nowhere, pathetically trying to copy Artmann's work. These false disciples from every walk of life were not the talented representatives of the more recent dialect wave. They were imitators without any literary skills who called themselves Artmann fans. Artmann soon was so disgusted with his fame as a dialect poet that he decided to abandon the dialect scene once and for all.

1960 saw the end of an era during which Artmann had worked on many short dramas, dadaistic outpourings, and nonsensical word sequences, all works more simply ignored than rejected. As fast as his fame had arisen from nowhere, it faded again, and Artmann disappeared from the scene.

The two examples of Artmann's work that we have already considered attest to Artmann's imaginative powers, particularly his ability to display the picturesque wealth of language. The vividness of *The Sun Was a Green Egg* and the dramatic tension in "The Street Crew" show how Artmann inclines to the use of contrasts and sharp delineations in his work. It is no wonder that he has collaborated with famous artists such as Uwe Bremer or Ernst Fuchs, who have contributed drawings and woodcuts to illustrate his poems.

From the epigrams Artmann published in 1959 one sample gives further proof of the metaphorical richness of his language:

> Bei mavors and apoll/bei venuß auff dem linnen/
> sucht ich so manches jahr den lorbeer zu gewinnen/
> doch nun im tiefen grab gnügt mir/dem augenlosen/
> ein bündlein voll ade mit tau und herbstzeitlosen . . .[21]

Freely rendered the poem reads:

> With Mars and Apollo/with Venus on the bedsheet/
> I tried to obtain the laurel for many a year/
> but now in my deep grave I/the eyeless—am satisfied/
> with a farewell bouquet of dew and meadow saffrons . . .

The poem offers more than one insight into Artmann's personality as an author. First of all, it shows how Artmann studies even older literature and captures its typical features; at first sight this seems to be a typical Baroque poem, complete with allegorical figures from Greek mythology. Yet the poem actually camouflages an existentialist *Weltanschauung* of our times. Mavors, the god of war, represents man's daily struggles; Venus symbolizes earthly life and love; and Apollo, the god of intellect and language, is the writer's herald to describe life and its essence. Art is the very form of existence that gives meaning to life, which otherwise ends in a despairing fashion, as represented by the eyeless skull of the dead. Artmann unites his pictorial and linguistic talents to portray his concern in the exotic nutshell of an epigram.

In another poem-like motto to *The Sun Was a Green Egg* that is supposedly from Rasmussen's *The Netsilik Eskimos,* he literally explains how his literature originates:

> So many thoughts arise in my head
> of long-known things; old thoughts,
> but becoming altogether new when
> one has to put them into words. (p. 5)

Putting thoughts into words, not simply describing things, is a key concern of Artmann and the authors around him. Their entire era was ruled by their notion that one must care for words and consider their associative power. Words create, they are not slaves of description, and they have a life of their own.

Although Artmann himself was not an ideologist of the era, he attempted to follow its discoveries. His friends in the Vienna Group attacked traditional literature. They aimed at questioning every word as it might have gone through changes of meaning during the previous Hitler era. Artmann experimented with all new forms; among his works are poems entitled *Verbarien* (1966) containing nonsensical sequences of words and sentences that suggest a very loose associative context. For example, several of the words might allude to a theme such as sex, trivia, brutality, and the like. Yet they are rather frugal even for Artmann, and perhaps therefore unpopular.

During these early years of Artmann's creativity the philosophies of Martin Heidegger and Ludwig Wittgenstein made their first impact upon the young generation, which began to recognize that the world had entered a new era, as signaled by the discoveries and innovations in technology and the sciences, as well as by the new political configurations in world affairs with the two superpowers rapidly emerging. Heidegger's existentialism especially was accepted and spread worldwide in part because modern means of transportation enabled writers to meet their international colleagues. So it happened that the concretists Decío Pignatari (Brazil) and Eugen Gomringer (Switzerland) met in Switzerland to establish the international concretist movement, which was soon joined by authors from twenty-three nations, among them the members of the Vienna Group and poets such as Ernst Jandl and Friederike Mayröcker. Their semantic experimentation and their rejection of traditional literary forms earned their era, the period of the 1950s and 1960s, the sobriquet: "die große Differenz"[22] (the great distinction). Indeed, its contrast to the work of the avant-garde, of "Neue Sachlichkeit" (the new matter-of-factness), is extreme; only in movements such as dadaism and surrealism had there been similar extremes. Ernst Jandl and Gerhard Rühm repeatedly stressed their regard for earlier practitioners of these movements such as Jean Arp, Kurt Schwitters, and Raoul Hausmann, to name just a few.

Just as Heidegger's *Sein und Zeit* (*Being and Time*) was becoming better known to a wider intellectual readership, Wittgenstein's views first confronted this postwar generation via his early work, the *Tractatus logico-philosophicus.* Thus the dooming seventh principal clause penetrated many of the new works of these young authors: one must not utter what cannot be expressed! This may have led to the concern for language displayed by the young authors. It is from this striving for an adequate new language that we must understand the era of the "große Differenz," which Artmann witnessed and to which he contributed his own sensitivity and genius. He went along to try the experiment yet never bowed to ideologies. With Peter Handke's early works in the later 1960s this era of language purification and alternation reached its apex in

German literature – and also its conclusion.

Already with works such as *das suchen nach dem gestrigen tag* (1964, in search of yesterday), *Grünverschlossene Botschaft* (1967, A Message Sealed in Green) or *Frankenstein in Sussex* (1968) Artmann had changed to prose in the more traditional sense, albeit with surrealistic and manneristic content. The political events of the late 1960s brought about a return to activism, to engaged literature; the oil crisis of the early seventies signified the end of years of economic tranquility in Germany and Austria. Literature became sensitive and increasingly more introverted, thus lending itself to the traditional distinction between prose and lyrics. In actual fact the difference between older and new literature was now so insignificant that it was labeled the "kleine Differenz," implying that there was still a difference and not simply a complete return to old literary shores.

Artmann's own lyrical production accords with this change, so much so that his parodistic vein emerges when he composes such lighthearted rhymes as the following:

> ON THE VOLCANO ARTMANN ends,
> the jungle far behind him fades,
> he quietly the rim ascends,
> his lionhearted softness bends,
> a master of all trades.
>
> the leaden lava downhill flows,
> for fauna and for plants no chance,
> through lonesome rocks the fierce wind blows,
> all matter – dashing down it goes,
> swings scarfs and hats in dance.
>
> from sulphur vapor cheeks are green
> there start to melt his rubber soles,
> and fire gushes to be seen,
> he marks the magma's glowing screen,
> stands as on warming coals.
>
> it seems a fiery build, this isle,
> the ground on gases shakes,
> no vulture, hawk, no eagle's style,
> no buzzard's nest here all the while,
> just flames, that's all it wakes.[23]

The scene is a splendid revelation of Artmann's spiritual state, as in his mid-fifties he looks back on the jungle of his younger years. His present life, though, does not lack excitement, and his acquisition of many skills has made him a literary master of all trades. *Aus meiner Botanisiertrommel* (From My Collecting Box), the book of poetry that contains the above poem, was published in 1975. Artmann, who so typically appears in this poem by name, could look back on a period of satisfactory production since his success in 1958. In this poem his lyrical qualities are summarized once more. Again we are presented with his ability to adapt his energetic fantasy to any style. He never seems to be at a loss for new ideas. It is a moving scene, a colorful, breathtaking landscape on a strange volcanic island full of danger, amidst which the poet receives his inspiration. Finally, there is his language, rich in the elements of good poetry: assonance, alliteration, exotic creations, metaphors, oxymorons (e.g., "his lionhearted softness"), and an overall texture that makes for entertaining reading. The notion in this poem that Artmann would end under awkward circumstances on the volcano, where no other life exists, is symbolic of his solitude in matters of art. Though he may have left the jungle of his youth, he is still in need of the fervid stimulus that he portrays here in abundance.

Scholars to date have generally avoided dealing with Artmann's work. Possibly it is too elusive, too unpredictable for them, perhaps even too crazy. So far only three theoretical books have been written on Artmann's work; a few occasional articles round out this list (see bibliography). All generally concur in admiring Artmann's virtuosity, his talent of adopting older literary models and recasting them in his own fashion, and also in admiring his vast store of unusual vocabulary and idioms.

In the literary world there is full agreement that H. C. Artmann's contribution to German writing has been exceptional. His strongest talent lies in his lyrics, although we must acknowledge his production in other genres, particularly his stories. Whether he likes it or not, his fame springs from the Villon-like dialect poetry of *med ana schwoazzn dintn*, "dark ink" that marks the inception of a whole new era in German letters with an unmistakable Austrian tinge.

Notes

1. Expression used by Artmann expert Ruediger von Schmeidel, a free-lance writer whom I interviewed in Berlin in May 1984.
2. Gerald Bisinger, *Über H. C. Artmann* (Frankfurt: Suhrkamp, 1972), p. 181.
3. To be found in *"A lilywhite letter from lincolnshire"* (Frankfurt: Suhrkamp, 1969).

4. Artmann's haikus are introduced for the first time in *Lesezirkel: Wiener Zeitung Literaturmagazin, Nummer 3*—under "38 haikus" (Vienna: February 1984), p. 4. His greguerías are assembled in *Das im Walde verlorene Totem: Prosadichtungen 1949-53* (Salzburg: Residenz, 1970).

5. In H. C. Artmann's *die fahrt zur insel nantucket: theater* (Neuwied: Luchterhand, 1969).

6. *baladn, François Villon* (Frankfurt: Insel, 1968).

7. See, for example, Alessandra Comini's work *The Fantastic Art of Vienna* (New York: Ballantine Books, 1978).

8. For detailed information of these and subsequent works by Artmann refer to the attached bibliography.

9. Friedrich Polakovics was a strong Artmann supporter in the late 1950s, when as editor for the lyrics section of the educational *neue wege* he published several of Artmann's poems.

10. *med ana schwoazzn dintn* had six editions by 1969.

11. Gerald Bisinger, *ein lilienweißer brief aus lincolnshire,* 1969; Peter O. Chotjewicz, *die fahrt zur insel nantucket: theater,* 1969; Klaus Reichert, *The Best of H. C. Artmann,* 1970 (despite the English title, this work is written in German).

12. Artmann received the Austrian State Prize for Literature in 1960 and 1974, the Prize for Literature of the City of Vienna in 1977, a special Austrian Prize for his achievements for Austrian Literature in 1981, as well as some regional literary prizes.

13. The separation of P.E.N. and Anti-P.E.N. marked a protest against the distribution of grant monies by the authorities, who seemed to favor the older authors. The situation has been remedied over the past decade; moreover Artmann no longer presides over the revolutionary camp.

14. Hans Magnus Enzensberger, *Allerleirauh: viele schöne Kinderreime* (Frankfurt: Suhrkamp, 1961, 2nd edition, 1968).

15. H. C. Artmann, "Manifest," in: Gerhard Rühm, *Die Wiener Gruppe* (Reinbek: Rowohlt, 1967), pp. 18-20.

16. H. C. Artmann, "Kein Pfeffer für Czermak," in: *Die fahrt zur insel nantucket,* pp. 31-72.

17. *hosn rosn baa* was published by Frick-Verlag in Vienna, 1959, a publishing house that has ceased to exist.

18. Otto F. Beer, "Lyrik aus Breitensee," review in the daily newspaper *Neues Österreich,* 27. April 1958.

19. H. C. Artmann, "de pflostara," translated by Winter Laite, in *Dimension,* XII, 3 (1979).

20. In his foreword to *med ana schwoazzn dintn* F. Polakovics took issue with this claim that Artmann could be compared to Weinheber.
21. H. C. Artmann, *Von denen Husaren* . . / *Epigrammata*, p. 105. My translation.
22. I would like to thank Alexander von Bormann, Professor of German in Amsterdam, for his information on the most recent literary theory; he introduced me to this term. Interview at Laren, Holland, June 1984.
23. H. C. Artmann, *Aus meiner Botanisiertrommel*, p. 29. My translation.

Primary Literature

a. Poetry:

med ana schwoazzn dintn (Salzburg: O. Müller, 1958).

Hosn rosn baa, with Gerhard Rühm and Friedrich Achleitner (Vienna: W. Frick, 1959).

Von denen Husaren und anderen Seil-Tänzern / Epigrammata (München: Piper, 1959).

Der Schlüssel des Heiligen Patrick (Salzburg: O. Müller, 1959).

das suchen nach dem gestrigen tag (Olten: Walter, 1964).

verbarium: gedichte (Olten: Walter, 1966).

Grünverschlossene Botschaft: 90 Träume (Salzburg: Residenz, 1967).

Allerleirausch: neue schöne kinderreime (Berlin: Rainer, 1968).

Das im Walde verlorene Totem: Prosadichtungen – 1949-53 (Salzburg: Residenz, 1970).

ein lilienweißer brief aus lincolnshire: Gedichte aus 21 jahren (Frankfurt: Suhrkamp, 1975).

Gedichte über die Liebe und über die Lasterhaftigkeit (Frankfurt: Suhrkamp, 1975).

Aus meiner Botanisiertrommel: Balladen und Naturgedichte (Salzburg: Residenz, 1975).

das prahlen des urwaldes im dschungel (Berlin: Rainer, 1983).

b. Prose:

Von denen Husaren und anderen Seiltänzern (München: Piper, 1959).

Frankenstein in Sussex. Fleiß und Industrie (Frankfurt: Suhrkamp, 1968).

Die Anfangsbuchstaben der Flagge: Geschichten (Salzburg: Residenz, 1969).

Mein Erbteil von Vater und Mutter (Hamburg: Merlin, 1969).

how much, schatzi? (Frankfurt: S. Fischer, 1971).
*Der aeronautische Sindtbart. Seltsame luftreise von niedercalifornien
     nach crain* (Salzburg: Residenz, 1972).
Von der Wiener Seite: Geschichten (Berlin: Literarisches Colloquium,
     1972).
Under der Bedeckung eines Hutes: Montagen und Sequenzen (Salzburg:
     Residenz, 1972).
Ompül (Zürich: Artemis, 1974).
Nachrichten aus Nord und Süd (Salzburg: Residenz, 1978).
Grammatik der Rosen: Gesammelte Prosa (Salzburg: Residenz, 1979).
*Die Sonne war ein grünes Ei: Von der Erschaffung der Welt und ihren
     Dingen* (Salzburg: Residenz, 1982).
Im Schatten der Burenwurst: Skizzen aus Wien (Salzburg: Residenz,
     1983).

c. Theater:
   die fahrt zur insel nantucket: theater (Neuwied: Luchterhand, 1969).

d. Mixed Genres:
   The Best of H. C. Artmann (Frankfurt: Suhrkamp, 1970).

Secondary Literature

Note: All works in English as well as major works in German are listed here.
Friedrich Polakovics, preface to *med ana schwoazzn dintn* (Salzburg: O. Müller,
     1958), pp. 9-16.
Gerhard Rühm, *Die Wiener Gruppe* (Reinbek: Rowohlt, 1967).
J. C. Alldridge, "H. C. Artmann and the English Nonsense Tradition," *Affinities*
     (London, 1971), pp. 168-183.
Gerald Bisinger, *Über H. C. Artmann* (Frankfurt: Suhrkamp, 1972).
Peter Pabisch, *H. C. Artmann: Ein Versuch über die literarische Alogik* (Vienna:
     Schendl, 1978).
Peter Pabisch and Alfred Rodríguez, "H. C. Artmann's adaptation of Ramón
     Gómez de la Serna's Greguería," *World Literature Today,* 53 (1979),
     231-234.
Peter Pabisch, "Sensitivität und Kalkül in der jüngsten Prosa H. C. Artmanns,"
     Modern Austrian Literature, Vol. 13, No. 1 (1980), 129-147.
Josef Donnenberg, ed., *Pose, Possen und Poesie: zum Werk Hans Carl Artmanns*

(Stuttgart: Akademischer Verlag, 1981).

Peter Pabisch, "H. C. Artmann," *Encyclopedia of World Literature in the 20th Century* (New York: F. Ungar, 1981).

Wolfgang Bauer

Jürgen Koppensteiner

In an article written for the *Almanac for Literature and Art 1981* of a prestigious Salzburg publishing house, Wolfgang Bauer, after attempting to define art, concludes that it is inexplicable. He goes on to say that critics who describe or interpret it belong to a higher order of parasites that suck their sustenance from the body of art. He concedes, however, that it is the noise made by their sucking that attracts the public's attention to art.[1]

Whatever one may think of Bauer's analogy, it is certain that the critics' "noise" has helped him achieve the celebrity status that he enjoys today. In 1978, *text und kritik,* a noted German literary journal, devoted an issue to Bauer, and in 1981 Gerhard Melzer published the first comprehensive scholarly work on him.[2] Wolfgang Bauer is an established writer, even though he does not enjoy universal esteem, and there is no consensus on his literary rank. Some critics would like to dismiss him as a peripheral figure on the Austrian literary scene, but some theatergoers, convinced that he is Austria's best playwright, have dubbed him "Magic Wolfi." Others disqualify him with labels like "so-called poet," "impudent Styrian author," and "trash dramatist." In any case Wolfgang Bauer has become the *enfant terrible* of the Austrian bourgeoisie. His name often provokes violent reactions on the part of otherwise peaceloving and good-natured Austrians, even from those who are not interested in literature. After the telecast of a Bauer play a few years ago, the TV station was deluged with phone calls from angry viewers, one of whom recommended the extermination of that "pest" and "vermin," Wolfgang Bauer.[3]

What literary crime had Bauer committed to bring such a judgment down on his head? A brief review of his career and writings up to now may serve to answer that question.

Born in Graz in 1941 the son of a *Gymnasium* teacher, Bauer began to write while still young. His first creative activity was in Graz's "Forum Stadtpark," a cultural center that also publishes *manuskripte,* one of the best literary journals in German. Bauer initially studied law, then, finding that too unimaginative, took up French and geography. However, since the freedom of student life had afforded him the time to write, he decided against a teaching career and went to Vienna to study drama. He associated more with artists than with academics, and so it was not surprising when, after a few semesters, he returned to Graz to try to establish himself as a playwright.

Bauer's early works are in the tradition of the theater of the absurd. In *Der Schweinetransport* (1962, Shipment of Hogs) Ionesco's rhinoceros are replaced by foul-smelling pigs. Some of the themes central to these early plays are: the disjuncture of self and world, the obliteration of the border between reality and fiction, and the conflict between nature and civilization. The plays are barely accessible and only partially performable, especially the so-called microdramas (1962–1964), which, although only one and a half pages long, require technically impossible stage sets. Scenes take place in a swimming pool full of floating noodles (*Franz Xaver Gabelsberger. Erfinder der Schnellschrift* [Franz Xaver Gabelsberger. Inventor of Shorthand]), in a DC6 (*Die drei Muske-tiere* [The Three Musketeers]), in a crowded stadium, and in a factory holding a thousand workers (*Rasputin*). In one (*Richard Wagner*) the stage directions require 10,000 Apaches; in another (*Haydn*) storm conditions and waves three feet high on Lake Neusiedl, and in yet another (*Ramses*) a fire that fills the theater.

Analogous to a pianist's finger exercises, these early works now interest only literary scholars. In his monograph Gerhard Melzer traces lines of develop-ment between Bauer's early "absurd" plays and the later "realistic" ones.[4] This connection. although not discernible at first glance, can be found in *Party for Six*, a play performed in 1967 but receiving little attention until after 1968. It drew negative reviews from most critics, and the theater public felt cheated when the play did not deliver what its title had promised.

The entire action of *Party for Six* takes place in a vestibule which is dark most of the time. In the first act the audience sees the host, a young man, receiving his guests and frequently coming out of the living room (behind the set, hence invisible) to get drinks from the bar. When the door to the living room is open, light is seen coming from there, and the sound of stereo music and glasses clinking is heard.

Nor does the audience see the party in the second act, the action of which consists largely of guests making their way to and from the bathroom. Accord-ing to the stage directions, the flushing of the toilet is the central sound in this act. A kind of dramatic conflict does develop when two young men make passes at the same girl. One of them is so drunk that he soon falls asleep and does not even react when the other pours wine on him.

All hope of getting at least a glimpse of the party vanish in the third act. Now the vestibule is fully lit. As there are no longer any coats on the coat rack, the party is apparently over. A rooster crows every thirty seconds for four minutes before the curtain falls. The fourth and final act is very short: two girls straighten up the apartment.

Party for Six certainly does not fulfill one's expectations of what an evening at the theater should be. The first impression is that it is just a hoax. Not only does it fail to live up to its title, but it is also a play without a recognizable plot. Why, then, not disregard it completely?

In many respects *Party for Six* is a key to Bauer's works. As Gerhard Melzer has demonstrated, it forms a bridge between the early and later dramas. With its four acts, it has all the marks of a conventional play. Despite the absence of plot in the usual sense, it has at least the beginning of dramatic tension. To the unbiased spectator or reader, the action appears to take place on a realistic level. The initiated easily recognize the Graz milieu and dialect. A number of elements, however, make one wonder about the author's intentions. The play's English title and its subtitle, "Volksstück," for example, should arouse suspicion. Never would a *Volksstück* have an English title. And all moderately educated German-speaking theatergoers know that a *Volksstück* is an easily understandable play that usually has a rural setting. It is often sentimental, contains folksongs, and is rife with situation comedy, none of which applies to *Party for Six*. Both its title and subtitle, therefore, help produce, as Melzer recognizes, "a tension arising from expectations aroused and then left unfulfilled."[5]

Contradiction permeates the entire play. A further example is the use of dialect by the characters. This is certainly appropriate in a *Volksstück* but the people in *Party for Six,* students who live in a city, do not at all resemble those found in a *Volksstück.* Nor are the contradictions limited to title and language. There is clearly a discrepancy between the conventional composition (four acts) and the lack of content in the "story" presented. These contradictions combine with other elements to evoke feelings of insecurity in those who watch the play.

Although it is not immediately apparent, Bauer used contradiction here for a specific purpose. Far from writing a "realistic" play, he sets out in *Party for Six* to undermine, even destroy, our conception of what is "realistic" and "surrealistic." He wants to confront and comment on the question of reality in the theater. Although the veracity of detail makes this play ring true, Bauer is demonstrating in it that the theater cannot present total reality but only a slice of life. It is precisely his shaking up of the conventional principles of selection that makes this play interesting. Its point is that everything that "really" happens either may – or may not – be presented on stage.

Now it is clear why, instead of the party itself, Bauer gives us only what is incidental to it – opening doors, fixing drinks, going to the bathroom – events a conventional drama omits, and which, striking the viewer as extraneous,

irritate him. In order to grasp the meaning of this play he would have to penetrate its realistic surface level, a difficult task. That is no doubt the reason
why *Party for Six* has been largely disregarded and widely misunderstood.

Magic Afternoon, which premièred in Hanover in 1968, appears to present
no such difficulties. While *Party for Six* had only an outer garment of realism,
here verisimilitude seems to abound. The stage directions, calling for a dis-
orderly, smoke-filled room, leave little doubt about time or place of action.
Contributing to the illusion of reality are the colloquial Austrian language,
references to personalities and locations of the Austrian cultural scene, and
the use of what Melzer calls "musical signals,"[6] namely the records (one of
Bauer's most important props) played on the stereo in the course of the afternoon. In addition there is complete congruence of presented time with time
of presentation. The performance is supposed to last precisely two hours and
fifteen minutes, the exact time it would take in "real life" to perform the
thirty-odd actions in it. These include making lemonade (four to five minutes)
and going to the bathroom, an important element in this play also.

As *Magic Afternoon* begins, two young people, Birgit and Charly, who are
students, or at least belong to the student milieu, are so bored that they begin
to scuffle. When they leave the stage they are replaced by Monika and Joe,
friends of theirs who are in a similar mood, but rambunctious to the point
that he breaks her nose. While Joe takes Monika to the hospital, Birgit and
Charly return, their aggressiveness undiminished. An argument ensues which,
after Joe comes back, turns into a brutal fight. Then the men smoke pot and,
while they are high, threaten Birgit and even attack her. She in turn fatally
stabs Joe with a kitchen knife, after which she feels animated enough to seduce
a benumbed and frightened Charly. She then exits rather abruptly, and the
play ends as Charly rolls Joe's body in a rug.

Magic Afternoon made Wolfgang Bauer famous overnight. In the 1969–1970
theater season it was among the six plays most frequently presented in German-
speaking countries. Translated into many languages, it has been performed
throughout the world. At the time of this writing, its most recent première
was in Israel in 1981.[7] With *Magic Afternoon,* in the success of which he is
still basking, Bauer established himself both as a literary star and as "the wild
man from Graz," a reputation he has still not been able to shed.

Much of the success of *Magic Afternoon* has been attributed to Bauer's
having captured in it the spirit of the youth culture of the 1960s. The characters' rejection of the adult world, their permanent boredom and the isolation
of their subculture recall the revolts of students and other youth of the 1960s.
Furthermore, this play has entertainment value. It satisfies human curiosity

about offensive, shocking behavior and the breaking of taboos. *Magic Afternoon* allowed viewers to feel comfortable about being indignant, because Bauer does not permit development of sympathy for his characters. When the final curtain falls, the viewer has a pleasurable feeling of gloating. He now "knows" that young people do indeed act as grossly as he had imagined and he feels satisfaction when these good-for-nothings seal their own fate by committing acts of violence.

Was *Magic Afternoon* a mirror reflecting reality, however distorted? On the contrary, as Melzer has pointed out, there are many indications that Bauer did not intend to present concrete reality in it.[8] At first this play seems to have nothing in common with Bauer's earlier ones, yet there definitely is a connection. In previous works Bauer basically wanted to show that the world is out of kilter: alienated from nature, man lives separated from it; an authentic natural life is no longer viable; a person experiences the world as "artificial," as "mediated."[9] This is also the presupposition in *Magic Afternoon*. The reality experienced by the characters is a mediated culture, which they find burdensome. They would like to escape from it, to suspend the reality in which they live and to find a "natural" reality. This is exemplified in the "book battle": as Birgit and Charly throw books at each other, they cuss out the authors whom, as representatives of culture, they hold responsible for their unhappiness. Other opportunities for escaping from pressure are offered by music and the theater, records, and the use of alcohol and drugs. The latter make their reality dwindle down to a globe that Charly takes from a shelf and throws at Joe with the words: "The world . . . is really . . . all . . . fucked up. . . ."[10] They try to bury reality by flushing the globe down the toilet. When they are unsuccessful Charly concludes: "The world will go on forever."[11] Although Joe and Charly fail to destroy reality, Birgit, by resorting to force, attains a "new, radical immediacy."[12] She overcomes alienation but her newly won freedom results only in a confrontation with death. (She stabs Joe.) No, *Magic Afternoon* does not claim to present a definite, "actual" reality. Rather, like Bauer's early works, it must be seen as a study of cultural alienation. In this case the 1960s provide a concrete historical background.

Up to its abrupt, melodramatic ending *Magic Afternoon* is a somewhat static play, moved forward mostly by the moods of its characters. In sharp contrast is *Change* (1969), considered by many to be Bauer's first major work, because it has not only a larger cast and scope of action but also a structured plot. Far from limiting the action to one room, *Change* provides a series of different scenes: the kitchen at the Councilor's house, a boutique, a sleazy bar, the gay salon of a wealthy art patron, a hospital ward, and two artists' studios. As in the other plays, the toilet is present throughout, at least acoustically.

The plot of *Change* had already been outlined in *Magic Afternoon,* when Charly tells Birgit a story which he finds amusing and out of which he would like to make a play. In it an established artist dreams up a plan: he will take a young provincial umbrella maker, turn him into a famous painter, then suddenly he will withdraw his support, driving his protégé to despair and suicide. Put into effect, the plan succeeds to the extent that the umbrella maker does become a painter. He has, however, no desire to kill himself. Instead it is the initiator of the scheme who commits suicide.[13]

What happens in *Change* is quite similar – and more turbulent. Fery, a painter frustrated by failure, attempts to be a conceptual artist. He wants to support Blasi, a country bumpkin locksmith who is a moderately talented amateur painter, and to build him up to be a star. At the height of Blasi's career, Fery will let him fall and watch him being driven to suicide out of despair. Fery considers this type of manipulation to be "total art." Invigorated by the scheme he proceeds to put it into operation, planning to keep a running account in the form of a journal of all the stages he envisions Blasi going through. But Blasi upsets Fery's calculations in every respect. All too quickly the "art work" allows the erstwhile locksmith an unanticipated independence. First, Blasi the macho steals Fery's girlfriend, Guggi. She accompanies him on a nocturnal burglary trip and gets pregnant by him. Blasi then turns his attention to Guggi's mother, a former opera singer who is starved for affection. When Guggi catches them on the kitchen floor, she calls her father, a former Court Councilor, who, tormented by jealousy, has a stroke and dies on the spot. Shortly thereafter, Blasi marries the widow of the late Court Councilor.

This is all too much for Fery. At the wedding reception he becomes obstreperous and is asked to leave. That leads to fighting, stopped only when a policeman is called to the scene. After threatening the policeman with a knife, Fery is shot, wounded and taken to the hospital. The wedding guests go to visit him there. Guggi, who is already in advanced pregnancy, and, like the others, very drunk, provokes Fery with her gibes. He hits her, whereupon her (their) child is born – and dies. At the end, Blasi gives a reconciliation party at which, under his direction, change-dance games are played. Blasi requires of his guests total change, not just an exchange of clothing. Each participant must slip into the skin of another. Fery becomes Blasi and vice versa. When Fery hears words he had previously spoken coming from Blasi's lips, it undoes him. Hurrying to the bathroom, he hangs himself.

Did Bauer wish to present a segment of concrete reality in *Change?* Critics saw the play as a "macabre panorama of the times,"[14] a "description of the state of contemporary affairs,"[15] even a "moral picture of the present day."[16] These interpretations of it as naturalistic, a mirror of the times, aroused in the public the same indignation and defense mechanisms that *Magic Afternoon* had provoked. Again Bauer was accused of composing "low class sex sketches."[17] At the same time, brisk ticket sales testified to his play's satisfying an appetite for indecency and scandal. When *Change* was shown on TV, the public reacted with questions and comments. Concerned viewers asked whether the characters portrayed in it were "real." Others, seeing a direct connection between Bauer's play and juvenile delinquency, feared that it would draw young people to drugs and depravity.[18]

Some critics, however, soon recognized that *Change* had a second dimension. Botho Strauß wrote in 1969: "The more realistically natural events are imitated on stage in Bauer's plays, the more the illusion that looms over their naturalness is intensified."[19] Strauß speaks of an ostensibly mimetic presentation of reality, which, in his view, has motives different from those of literary naturalism. Referring to *Change,* Strauß maintains that in Bauer's plays we are compelled to understand that even external realistic events are forms of art.[20] Melzer uses this idea as a basis for his interpretation of the play, which, he believes, presents at best a distorted image of reality. Writing of the improbable quality of the play, Melzer avers that the quasi-surrealistic impression it creates is precisely the result of the realistic presentation of everything in it.[21]

In *Change,* as in *Magic Afternoon,* Bauer thematicizes the artificiality and mediacy of life. It makes good sense to ground this criticism on the art and culture industry, because artists play roles dictated to them by society. Fery clearly recognizes this and feels uncomfortable in his role as an artist. He suffers from his somewhat falsified identity and would like to enter into a "direct and immediate relation to reality."[22] His manipulation of Blasi can be seen as an attempt to reject the role society has dealt him and an as advance toward an "autonomy responsible only to itself."[23] His failure and subsequent suicide result not only from his having to play the role he had planned for Blasi but also from the realization that in doing so he has fallen into the very trap he was trying to un-spring.

Blasi, on the other hand, does not seek actual creative immediacy. He adjusts easily to the role of the artist as "prescribed" by society. For him, simulation is an integral part of being an artist. To advertise his "fame," he wears gaudy clothes and, when certain that removing them is another way to strengthen his position as artist, he stages a striptease at a reception for a dignitary.

It is evident from a secondary episode that, in *Change,* Bauer is not dealing

with the mediacy of the artistic life alone. Although he has nothing to do
with artists, Mitterndorfer, Fery's neighbor in the hospital ward, also lives a
life of role-playing. He simulates, apparently with some success, an illness
that enables him to prolong his hospital stay indefinitely, thereby keeping
himself in an artificial reality containing certain parallels with the life of the
artist.

Artificiality and the mediacy of life are also the topic of Bauer's next play,
Film und Frau (1971, Film and Woman). At the beginning this one-act play
is reminiscent of *Party for Six* and *Magic Afternoon.* Four young people, not
knowing what else to do, kill time talking about the movies and movie stars.
After Senta, the only woman, reads the movie program aloud, two of the men
decide to go see "Shakespeare the Sadist," a pornographic film. Senta stays
home with the third man, Bruno. The stage now becomes a movie theater
where the porno film is being shown. The audience does not see the film itself
but what happens in it is acted out on the stage behind a scrim. The protagonists
are Senta and Bruno, who, as Shakespeare, tears off Senta's clothes, binds,
gags and beats her, then gleefully puts out his cigarette on her skin. Using a
megaphone, he shouts his sonnets into her ear. While he cuts off her hair, she
is forced to read the sonnets to him. All this is preliminary to an "unparalleled
act of intercourse"[24] which is to climax with a "gigantic orgasm"[25] on the
desk. The film ends when Shakespeare cuts off Senta's head and throws it in
the wastebasket.

After this masochistic torture scene the play returns to its real-world point
of departure. The two men return from the movies and relate the events that
have just been shown on the stage. When Senta is bored as the men play cards,
the "real events" are once again fused into a film, this time a western, in which
Bruno, after an argument, guns down the other men. Meanwhile Senta, his
beloved, has readied the horses for flight. As the music swells to a crescendo
there are pledges of love and farewells, followed by the words "The End"
on the screen to signal that both the film and the play are over.

Although the audience is unaware of it, the word "film" in the title of
the play refers not only to its film scenes but also to its cinematic form, a
movie script containing forty-nine scenes with four-to-five-second blackouts
between them. Mentioned in the stage directions are the MGM lion and such
techniques as slow motion and fast forward.

When we consider *Film und Frau* within the context of Bauer's total production, it is clear that here too he presents problems of alienated identity,
self-realizaton and immediacy, albeit with somewhat different emphases. In
Change Fery uses manipulation as a means of abandoning his role and attaining

individual immediacy. This is not the case with the protagonists of *Film und Frau*. Although reality makes them suffer too — their boredom is symptomatic — their escaping from it does not result in self-realization. Throughout the play they remain in a world of dreams. Their "dream of a better, freer, more experiential life," as Melzer puts it, degenerates into "merely a substitute for life."[26] These people have no individual autonomy; they are prisoners of the artificial world of movies and music. Bruno, for example, is quite stupid, illiterate, and ineffectual as a lover. At the movies he experiences what reality denies him; in the role of the sadist he is both a fearsome stud and writer of sonnets. A critic has accurately described Bruno's plight: "The more miserable reality is, the more desperate are one's dreams and compensations."[27]

Bruno's return to reality after the film is a sobering experience. Although the viewer is not told what Senta and Bruno did when the others went to the movies, he can guess. Bruno's embarrassment when asked about it reveals that he was not entirely successful in his approaches to Senta. While the others revel in the details of the porno film and one of them makes love to Senta, who readily makes herself available to him, Bruno sits on a desk looking at a porno magazine — and begins to masturbate.

Later the events repeat themselves with slight variations. Senta feels isolated because of the men's indifference toward her. She experiences as boredom the depersonalization illustrated in an exaggerated way by the porno film. Reacting to this, she fantasizes that she is the sweetheart of a western hero. Just as Bruno wants to resemble Shakespeare, Senta wants to be loved by a brave man. Both of them suffer because of the discrepancy between their private misery and the utopia they glimpse in the movies. What each considers to be self-realization is exposed by Bauer as being but a substitute for fulfillment.

Film und Frau received generally positive reviews, but Bauer's next play, *Silvester oder Das Massaker im Hotel Sacher* (New Year's Eve or The Massacre in the Sacher Hotel), which premièred in Vienna in 1971, was rejected by critics and public alike and had only one performance. Bauer was attacked for his lack of imagination and was accused of copying himself. The renowned Viennese critic, Hilde Spiel, went so far as to ask in a review: "Must we bid good-bye to Wolfgang Bauer?"[28] Many of those who considered him a brilliant dramatist could not conceal their disappointment. Others, confirmed in their opinion that he was, at best, a third-rate writer of boulevard plays, took spiteful pleasure in his apparent failure. The literary career of Bauer, who was barely thirty years old, seemed to have reached a dead end.

How can this sudden fall from fame be explained? Bauer doubtless felt pressured to repeat the successes of *Magic Afternoon* and *Change*. "People expect something of me," he said.[29] In an interview in the news magazine *Der Spiegel* he alluded to a longstanding fear that his imagination would fail him: "The nonchalance I previously had when, as a literary desperado, I simply wrote down what came to mind, that kind of spontaneity is gone."[30]

There may well be symbolic meaning in the idea that Wolfram Bersenegger, the protagonist of *Massaker,* is a writer with nothing to write about. Suffering from the pressure of success, he has not produced anything in years, yet has promised to deliver his new play to a theater manager at midnight on January first. He hits upon the idea of making a play out of a New Year's party that he is giving at the elegant Sacher Hotel in Vienna. Besides the theater manager, the guests include an author, an actor, all sorts of bon vivants, playboys and bunnies, a group of activists who stage a happening, and a psychopath called Robespierre, who is the former lover of the present Mrs. Bersenegger. Bersenegger confides to his friend that all the guests have been invited because of what they can contribute to his scheme. With a hidden tape recorder he plans to record the conversations during the party. At midnight he will present the tape—his new play—to the theater manager.

The party comes off as a kind of "chance drama" reminiscent of *Magic Afternoon.* The guests chatter, laugh, drink, telephone, take bubble baths, and go to the bathroom frequently; they undress, exchange clothes, dress again, and some play sex games in the background. Meanwhile, the actors do a scene from *Romeo and Juliet.* Then the happening-people stage the My Lai Massacre, as part of which they wreck the furniture and spray red paint all around. The guests join in "at first hesitatingly, then with increasing gaiety" (say the stage directions),[31] helping to totally demolish the party room. To celebrate the end of the old year, the psychopath recites a crazy monologue. At midnight the radio plays "The Blue Danube"—an Austrian tradition—and, as the guests embrace, Robespierre takes a pistol and shoots himself. The theater manager has his play.

The opening—and only—stage performance of *Massaker* ended on a festive note. To the waltz beat that the actors danced to, the audience added a concert of boos and whistles. And reproaches were heaped upon Bauer. There seemed now to be no doubt that his imagination had dried up. The milieu and characters of the play echoed those of *Magic Afternoon* and *Change.* It was even suggested that the whole play was based on tapes Bauer had recorded at parties. Of course, Wolfram Bersenegger was taken for Wolfgang Bauer. The latter took the negative criticism calmly, objecting only to the autobiographical interpretation of the play. He wanted to show, he said in an interview, "the emptiness that occurs in time in a writer."[32] Also, "I wanted to destroy my so-called image. This writer," he maintains, "is my image; he is not me."[33]

In retrospect we wonder whether Bauer's efforts to rid himself of his image in *Massaker* were successful. We do know enough about his plays to refute the frequently expressed opinion that his intention was to present a slice of reality, the Viennese cultural and social scene. To be sure, the names of artists frequently pop up (Karajan, Hundertwasser, Gütersloh, etc.), and several Viennese celebrities are recognizable. But Bauer wants these to be understood only as prototypes. As Melzer puts it, this play, like the others, deals with "the transformation of reality into fiction."[34] In *Massaker* the characters of the culture industry all have a mediated, indirect relationship to life. On this evening they do not see themselves as actors but merely guests. Like their counterparts in *Change,* they are not even conscious of role playing, hence that does not have to be simulated for Bersenegger's taped drama. It is nonetheless evident that the party guests are role players without recognizable individuality and that their behavior is a series of clichés. Two women, Stella and Sybill, exemplify this. Completely controlled by a consumer-oriented society, they submit to the dictates of fashion as decreed by various women's magazines. When during the play they change clothes, they are simply changing into another theater costume. Their clothes, determined entirely by the role the wearers are playing in life, have nothing to do with their personalities. The theater manager is another role player. At the party he impresses the guests by delivering dramatic-aesthetic opinions, each of which contradicts the others. Changing one's position is part of a theater manager's "game." Lying and telling tales of bizarre adventures, as a writer character in this play does, is acceptable behavior in the culture industry.

It is grotesquely ironic that the only one able to recognize the lack of identity in the others and to refuse to condone it is the psychopath. This is first revealed when he rejects the name Robespierre, foisted upon him by the others, apparently to label him once and for all as the insane outsider. He in turn pokes fun at them for role playing. His suicide finally brings to an end the "obscene game with reality which transforms life as well as art into a lie."[35] His death suspends the struggle between appearances and reality, the essence of the play, and can therefore be understood as his reaching the highest, as well as final, stage of authenticity.

Gespenster (Ghosts), Bauer's next play, received much attention when it was performed during the 1975 "Styrian Autumn," an annual avant-garde arts festival that has gained international renown. The telecast of *Gespenster* brought forth, among other things, a week-long letter-writing campaign. Once again Bauer was accused of everything from "impudence," "primitive smut," and "pornography" to "degenerate art."

Ghosts' cast of characters looks as though it were borrowed from *Magic Afternoon, Change,* and *Massaker.* It consists of intellectuals, the unproductive writer, his friend, and their wives and girlfriends. Living almost in seclusion in a sort of subculture, they bore one another, drink and change partners so frequently that they are not always sure who belongs to whom. Their conversations are full of colloquialisms and obscenities that make those of previous plays pale by comparison. All imaginable sexual activities are verbally presented, and Bauer does not hesitate to break all taboos. Not surprisingly, it was the language more than the action on stage that shocked and angered the audience. Other elements from previous plays are also present: the writer's chaotic household, the gross violence and brutality, and the unclad ladies flitting across the stage.

The plot line of *Ghosts* is scanty and downright nonsensical. As it begins, the newly divorced wife of the writer is piling her possessions in the middle of the floor. The dialogue consists of an argument between another couple, this one still married. A young lady, obviously associated with the two couples in more than a platonic way, is part of this closed society. A further addition to the group is Magda, a sensitive, vulnerable Swiss girl who yearns for companionship but whose dialect marks her as an outsider. Unbeknownst to her, she is manipulated by the group: she is humiliated in her role as a maid, given too much to drink, beaten up, and raped. She is driven to insanity and, when her paranoia becomes apparent, put into a straight jacket and taken to a mental hospital. The evening ends as the two men send out for two girls to come to the house – their wives have gone out bar-hopping together.

Whereas *Massaker* portrayed roles played by people in the culture industry as providing at least a substitute identity, *Ghosts* expresses the view that role playing is futile – it simply does not work. Recognizing this, the writer and his friend create for themselves a "game of life," the rules of which, known only to them, can be changed or dispensed with at will. This game puts them in a peculiar state of suspension – they can assume or discard roles according to their needs. Living in a state of tension between accommodation and refusal, they are not total dissidents. They readily accept money from bourgeois institutions (television and academia), which they despise and reject. Their work means nothing to them. "Academe turns me off, man," says one.[36] Their life goals are ambiguous and contradictory. They seem to be free and mobile. Whenever a problem arises, they can switch roles. At any time they can distance themselves from any role they happen to be playing through the use of alcohol, to which they turn at the slightest threat to their sense of reality. Finally they "freeze," as Hellmuth Karasek puts it, in a position of suspension.[37]

At first glance, the title of *Ghosts* seems unrelated to its content. Originally Bauer had planned to rework Ibsen's play of the same name, in such a way that during the performance the characters would gradually lose their identity. Later he confesses his inability to carry it off, saying: "Ibsen's play is just too good to be used in that way."[38] Yet use of its title here can be justified by the presence of a few of its motifs and by the sinister, uncanny impression created by the characters. Their nihilism, instability and dehumanization do indeed turn them into ghosts.

The première of Bauer's next play, *Magnetküsse* (Magnetic Kisses), in Vienna's *Akademietheater* in 1976 did not provoke the expected scandal. Instead there was general confusion as to what Bauer might have intended with this mystery drama. *Die Presse,* a Vienna newspaper, reported on the opening with the headline: "The question remains: What is it?"[39] A prominent German scholar admitted in the theater program (of all places!) that he did not understand the play either. No wonder then that theatergoers suspected that the whole thing was just a bad joke. The report in *profil* magazine was cryptic: "Bauer's play *Magnetic Kisses,* in which the characters beat each other up, sleep together, perform surgery, murder, smoke pot, and are born, and in which the telephone rings eleven times—all that is very puzzling."[40]

That this concoction is not easily digestible, not even by experts, may be attributed to the play's having evolved from a paranoid episode experienced by Bauer after taking some bad LSD. In an interview for the San Francisco *Chronicle* on the occasion of the American première of *Magnetic Kisses,* he said: "After three months in that mental state, I came to this play."[41]

The plot, not easy to recount, is of little significance. Ernst Ziak, a writer of detective stories, murders his pregnant girlfriend, Iris, because he suspects her of holding time constant by means of a magnet in her stomach. The difficulty in reconstructing the events arises from the viewer's failure to realize until the end of the play that Ziak is insane. One recognizes only then that the first ten scenes present one single moment from the perspective of the protagonist. In the eleventh and last scene, Ernst is sleeping on his bed, Iris's body, covered with blood, is on the table. After the telephone rings ten times, Ernst awakens. According to the stage directions, he laughs, goes to the phone, calls his psychiatrist and gives an enthusiastic account of a "perfect operation." The psychiatrist alerts the police or the rescue squad—sirens are heard in the background—but before they arrive to take him away, Ernst pours oil on the furnishings in the room and sets them on fire.

The final scene is the only "real" one and it is only from its perspective that the first ten scenes make sense. Only now is it clear why the atmosphere and time in the first ten remain constant (the clock is stopped at 3:15). Only now do we understand why the telephone rings at the end of every scene. Only now are we aware that the time in the first ten scenes is that of a dream in which Ernst, in a series of nightmares, experiences the prehistory of the murder. That the events are reflections of Ziak's insanity, hence beyond the realm of logic, explains the scurrilous, seemingly incomprehensible figures like the Norwegian musicologist-pyromaniac who has a full beard on half his face. Another example is "El Monstre," a young man of enormous girth who prattles in heavy dialect and, like other characters in the play, is compulsive about taking showers.

Knowing that we are dealing with Ernst Ziak's visions of horror makes it easier to understand the superimposition and transformation of roles and all those elements grouped by critics under the heading of "trivial Freudian symbolism."[42] The Norwegian pyromaniac, for example, also appears as a policeman investigating alleged arson in Ziak's apartment. Ziak's estranged wife, Olga, becomes a nurse and serves as midwife to Iris, who, we learn at the same time, is "not at all pregnant."[43] The "baby" is Ziak's father, who comes on stage in diapers with a pacifier in his mouth and, ready for his birth, lies down in the cradle beside Iris. Before this, Iris had shot Ziak. Now dead, yet not dead, he is present at the delivery. Olga is later transformed into a man with a full beard and a "penis approximately twenty-eight inches long."[44] That does not prevent her from making passes at her late husband. In the ninth scene, Ziak is transformed into a small child wearing a sailor suit. A friend of Iris's tells him a story about a prince whose girlfriend swallowed a magnet, thus eliminating the passing of time for the prince, who was happy until he began having dreams of deceit and murder. While listening to the story, Ziak falls asleep. His father appears again, this time as a doctor, and punctures Iris's stomach to remove the magnet. The stage directions call for Iris, "a pregnant queen," to step majestically out on the roof and start to disrobe.[45]

The plot of *Magnetic Kisses* is too chaotic to recount here. Everything remains impenetrable; the viewer never has a moment of certainty. Distorted to the point of grotesqueness, the characters create a mysterious and threatening effect. But gradually the audience understands Ziak's state of mind. He obviously suffers from delusions of jealousy and persecution. He accuses his girlfriend of infidelity and of leading a conspiracy that is threatening him. The images in his mind center around Iris's pregnancy, a topic continually reintroduced and often surrealistically distorted until it reaches a grotesque climax in the birth scene. The baby's being identical to Ziak's father can be interpreted as follows: just as Ziak was once dependent on his father, a child would create new dependencies and duties for which he (Ziak) does not feel prepared and from which he shirks. That is why images of his girlfriend's baby overlap images of his father. Although Ziak wants to relate to a woman, he is afraid of the consequences of such a relationship and seeks refuge in insanity.[46]

In *Magnetic Kisses* Bauer has given a new twist to an old theme. Seeking authenticity and individual autonomy, the protagonists of his earlier plays flee into the ecstasies of drugs or alcohol or into the illusionary world of the movies. None of these possibilities exists for Ernst Ziak, whose struggle for freedom leads to insanity.

Bauer's play *Memory Hotel*, written in 1979-1980 and performed in Graz, is in many ways reminiscent of *Magnetic Kisses*. Once again the opening left critics and theatergoers baffled. But the two plays have more in common than their effect upon the audience. The protagonists of both are writers of detective stories and both have a disturbed sense of perception. *Memory Hotel*'s Toni is merely a psychiatrically disturbed hypochondriac, while Ziak is obviously paranoid. The plays are also similar in form. The action in both occurs within the mind of the protagonist. All but one scene in *Magnetic Kisses* were mental projections; in *Memory Hotel* Toni's attempts to recall the recent past permeate and overshadow the action, making it no less difficult to summarize.

Toni, a millionaire, has been told by his wife and her physician-lover, who want to inherit his money, that he has terminal cancer. Toni's unexpected decision is to use his remaining time and money to take a trip to Jamaica with his lover and an artist friend. Checking into a hotel, he meets all kinds of questionable characters. A real estate agent and his highfalutin wife who collects magic mushrooms are interested in Toni's money. They are joined by his girlfriend and the artist in many unsuccessful schemes to trick him out of his money. When Toni persists in refusing to sign any papers, they decide to rob him. There ensues a massacre of which Toni is the sole survivor. Covered with blood, he awakens in his bed just as his wife and her lover arrive. They come, of course, out of fear that he will squander his money, leaving nothing for them. Firmly resolved to force him to sign a will entitling them to his millions, they must first ascertain where the money is. Although Toni has fallen into a semicoma, they try to make him recall the events of the past few days. Unable to endure the pressure they are putting on him, Toni jumps into the ocean, to be immediately killed by a shark.

At this point the action slips into the surreal. In the final scene, designated as "hypothetical," Toni reappears, carrying his own corpse and that of the shark. Convinced that he has "overcome death through death,"[47] he tells them:

"I'll internalize all of you,"[48] whereupon they disappear. Toni then turns to a waiter and asks: "Is breakfast ready?"[49]

In context, this banal statement is charged with meaning. It may, in fact, be the key to understanding the play. It can be interpreted as an indication of renewed life or as a possibility for happiness, both of which were denied to Bauer's other protagonists. Here for the first time he expresses the hope that man may actually succeed in liberating himself.[50]

But Bauer's attempt in *Memory Hotel* to fuse the present with flashbacks from the past is not wholly successful. On stage the play seems to be a chaotic sequence of "happenings." We tend to agree with those critics who say that it should be read before being seen. Multiplicity of levels, rapid dialogue, associative and fragmented language all contribute to the confusion.

One critic dismissed *Memory Hotel* as an "unprocessed, overdone tangle of ideas."[51] The philosophical ideas upon which it is based lie buried beneath the chaos of the action and have to be uncovered with much care by the interpreter. Once this is done, it becomes clear that *Memory Hotel* remains true to Bauer's basic theme and overriding concern: the struggle for human liberation.

Not surprisingly, this is also true of his play *Woher kommen wir? Was sind wir? Wohin gehen wir?* (1981, translated as *Singapore Sling*). With some of the stage directions resembling the earlier microdramas, *Singapore Sling* too has striking parallels with the theater of the absurd. True, this time Bauer does not require a DC6 or the like on the stage, but there is something definitely absurd about the props and the stage setting. Gauguin, for instance, appears on stage carrying a shopping bag filled with human ears, which he politely offers to his friend Van Gogh (who seems to be hard of hearing). Also in the vein of the absurd a lady seriously considers ice skating in a bathtub.

As the German title of the play suggests, *Singapore Sling* like earlier plays by Bauer is concerned with basic questions of human existence and a search for a meaningful, authentic life. Three couples who are invisible to each other are locked into an imaginary hotel room in Singapore. They want to escape the war that has broken out in Europe and that is broadcast live to that distant part of the world. As soon as they open the window of their room they hear the battle noise. Thus their hotel room becomes a beleaguered paradise, a symbolic place. Not only do the couples want to flee from themselves and from each other, they also want to escape a reality they can no longer endure. As happens frequently with Bauer's heroes, their attempts are futile. In the end God appears in the guise of Van Gogh and chases them away. They offer resistance, they huddle together refusing to become individuals, but a marabou with a giant beak drags them to their death, which simultaneously is their birth. Appropriately then when the play ends, the crying of babies accompanies the death knells.

Again *Singapore Sling* leaves us with more questions than answers. The protagonists are tormented by their inability to establish any relationships. Just as the three couples in the hotel room do not take notice of each other and behave like puppets, we all suffer from a lack of communication. Only in the most perilous situation, in the face of death are we ready to shed our cloak of artificiality and become human.

If we want to see Bauer's most recent work to date, *Ein fröhlicher Morgen beim Friseur* (1983, A Happy Morning in the Barber Shop) as applied philosophy, we might consider it a failure. However, if we are willing to accept the play as a "wild celebration of nonsense"[52] it becomes thoroughly enjoyable. In doing so we need not speculate about the meaning of the neo-Gothic cathedral that the hero of the play gets implanted or rather cemented into his skull by his barber. Nor do we need to philosophize about the train conductor who is transformed into a stewed pear. Also we will not be shocked to find all characters regressing into babbling infantilism when the play closes. *Ein fröhlicher Morgen* can best be understood as a parable for the senselessness of the world, for the inexplicable chaos and the infinite madness of our time.

Now that Bauer's plays have been around for more than twenty-five years, it is time to make an assessment. There seem to be two distinct phases in Bauer's output so far. Critics have always considered his realistic plays as worthwhile and have filed the others under "irrelevant deviations." In any case, only the realistic plays have been successful. *Magic Afternoon* was performed in fifty theaters, while *Magnetic Kisses, Memory Hotel,* and *Ein fröhlicher Morgen beim Friseur* had only one stage performance apiece. (English versions of *Magnetic Kisses* and *Singapore Sling* were produced in San Francisco.) Bauer himself objects to this division of his oeuvre and rightly so. As this essay has tried to show, his plays contain a clearly recognizable continuity of ideas and techniques. If read in chronological order they almost have the effect of a drama cycle. With the same or similar settings they are without exception based on the same philosophical presuppositions: modern man, desiring directness, immediacy, and naturalness, suffers from alienation in a characterless society. At times Bauer's message is presented realistically; at other times the same message is shrouded in surrealism.

Bauer's celebrity results in part from a widespread misunderstanding. In *Magic Afternoon,* by offering access to the youth subculture, so exotic and yet so close, he filled a vacuum in the theater market. His plays satisfied the curiosity of adults and were considered sensational. Although it is known that

Bauer did not necessarily intend to present concrete reality in *Magic Afternoon* and *Change,* this fact has been purposely ignored by the public.

To a certain extent Bauer is responsible for his "false" reception. He let himself be carried along by his success; not only did he stay with the same topic, he limited himself to the same situations with similar plot lines and even similar language. The same small clique of unconventional literati and intelligentsia continues to appear, growing older in each play. What was first perceived as sensational became tedious with time.

The theatergoing public did not want to accept Bauer's later "deviations" from the realism of *Magic Afternoon.* This was because, in his later plays, he made it extremely difficult to follow the interpenetration of reality and fiction, the mixture of actuality and phantasmagoria, dream-vision, delusion, and de-generating memories. Writing about the première of *Magnetic Kisses,* Bauer admitted: "I myself do not know any more which moment is real nor when time stands still or goes forward."[53] In spite of having some brilliant ideas about the theater, Bauer has been only minimally successful in translating them to the stage.

Another weakness of Bauer's plays is that their "message," buried under the turbulent action and language, barely gets through to the audience. Many of his plays require detailed program notes and some a thorough reading before viewing.

Despite all that, Bauer's seriousness as a dramatist, which has often been questioned, cannot be denied. Whatever one thinks of him or his work, it would be shortsighted to ignore him. Whether we like it or not, Bauer is one of the major German-speaking exponents of the contemporary theater scene—and one whose international reputation is still growing.

Notes

1. See "Manche Künstler sind Dichter," in *Zeitgenössische Literatur. Literatur für Zeitgenossen. Almanach für Literatur und Kunst 1981.* (Salzburg und Wien: Residenz, 1981), p. 30.
2. *text + kritik,* 59 (1978). Gerhard Melzer, *Wolfgang Bauer. Eine Einführung in das Gesamtwerk* (Königstein/Ts.: Athenäum, 1981).
3. Hansjörg Spies, "Gehört Wolfi Bauer wie ein Borkenkäfer vergast?" *Kleine Zeitung* (Graz), 20 October 1975.
4. See Melzer, pp. 7-19.
5. Melzer, p. 54.

6. Melzer, p. 11.
7. (*Austria Today*, 7, No. 4 (1981), 56.
8. See Melzer, pp. 89–100.
9. For the terminology and some interpretations I am indebted to Melzer.
10. The quote is taken from the English translation and adaptation of *Magic Afternoon* by Herb Greer in Wolfgang Bauer, *Change and Other Plays* (New York: Hill and Wang, 1973), p. 199.
11. My translation of German original ("Die Welt is ewig."). *Magic Afternoon* in Wolfgang Bauer, *Die Sumpftänzer. Dramen, Prosa, Lyrik aus zwei Jahrzehnten* (Köln: Kiepenheuer und Witsch, 1978), p. 240. Subsequent quotes from and references to Bauer's plays will be taken from this edition unless otherwise noted.
12. Melzer, p. 99.
13. See *Magic Afternoon*, p. 235.
14. Friedrich Torberg, "Österreichischer Januskopf. Oder: Ein Horvath unserer Tage—Neues Stück von Wolfgang Bauer," *Die Welt*, 13 October 1969.
15. Hans Fenz, "Wolfi Bauers Sittengemälde 'Change,'" *Die Wahrheit* (Graz), 20 June 1970.
16. Ibid.
17. Othmar Herbrich, "Mit pornographischer Akribie," *Volkszeitung* (Klagenfurt), 2 April 1971.
18. See letters to the editor in *Neue Illustrierte Wochenschau*, 25 April 1971.
19. "Melodrama und Mikropsychologie: Wolfgang Bauers 'Change,'" *Theater heute*, 10, Heft 11 (1969), 39;
20. Ibid.
21 Melzer, p. 102.
22 Melzer, p. 106.
23. Melzer, p. 107.
24. *Film und Frau*, in Wolfgang Bauer, *Gespenster. Silvester oder Das Massaker im Hotel Sacher. Film und Frau. Drei Stücke. Nachwort von Hubert Fichte* (Köln: Kiepenheuer und Witsch, 1974), p. 137. Quotes from and references to these three plays will be taken from this edition.
25. *Film und Frau*, p. 137.
26. Melzer, p. 109.
27. Benjamin Henrichs, "Lustmörder Shakespeare," *Süddeutsche Zeitung*, 19 April 1971.
28. "Abschied von Wolfgang Bauer?", *Frankfurter Allgemeine Zeitung*, 27 September 1971.

29   "Happening aus Not," *Der Spiegel,* 25, Heft 39 (1971), 190.

30.   Ibid.

31.   *Silvester oder Das Massaker im Hotel Sacher,* p. 118.

32.   Wolfgang Bauer, quoted by Hilde Schmölzer, *Das böse Wien. Gespräche mit österreichischen Künstlern. Mit einem biographischen Anhang* (München: Nymphenburger Verlagshandlung, 1973), p. 48.

33.   Ibid.

34.   Melzer, p. 114.

35.   Ibid., p. 121.

36.   *Gespenster,* p. 9.

37.   "Der Bauer im Bauer," *Der Spiegel,* 28, Heft 24 (1974), 130.

38.   Thomas Thieringer, "Verlorene Rollen. Ein Gespräch mit dem Dramatiker Wolfgang Bauer," *Süddeutsche Zeitung,* 5 June 1974.

39.   Piero Rismondo, "Die Frage bleibt: Was war's?", *Die Presse,* 2 April 1976.

40.   "Die Maske des Wolfi Bauer," *profil,* 7, Heft 15 (1976), 37.

41.   Bernard Weiner, "How Bad LSD Led to a Play," *San Francisco Chronicle,* 22 March, 1979.

42.   Paul Kruntorad, "Bauers Alpträume," *Theater heute,* 17, Heft 5 (1976), 16.

43.   *Magnetküsse,* p. 362.

44.   Ibid., p. 370.

45.   Ibid., p. 373.

46.   See Melzer, p. 135.

47.   *Memory Hotel,* in Wolfgang Bauer, *Woher kommen wir? Wohin gehen wir? Dramen und Prosa mit bisher unveröffentlichten und neuen Stücken* (München: Heyne, 1982), p. 485.

48.   The original reads: "Kommt her alle, Ihr Würmer! Ich werde euch jetzt alle erinnern! . . . ich denke euch nicht nur, ich erinnere euch in alle Ewigkeit, hahaha . . . kommt schon!" (*Memory Hotel,* p. 485).

49   "Ist das Frühstück schon da?" (*Memory Hotel,* p. 487).

50.   See Melzer, p. 143.

51.   "Traum, Trauma und Chaos," *Wiener Zeitung,* 24. Juni 1980.

52.   See "Theatertip," *Kleine Zeitung* (Graz), 10. Dezember 1983.

53.   Manfred Mixner, "Gespräch mit Wolfgang Bauer," *text + kritik,* 59 (1978), 11.

I gratefully acknowledge the assistance of Jane Schwartz (University of Northern Iowa) and Beth Bjorklund (University of Virginia) in translating portions of this article from the original German.

Primary Works in German

Ein fröhlicher Morgen beim Friseur. Text. Materialien. Fotos. Ed. Gerhard
   Melzer and Michael Muhr. Graz: Droschl, 1983.
*Gespenster. Silvester oder Das Massaker im Hotel Sacher. Film und Frau. Drei
   Stücke.* Köln: Kiepenheuer und Witsch, 1974.
Das Herz. Gedichte. Salzburg: Residenz, 1981.
Die Sumpftänzer. Dramen, Prosa, Lyrik aus zwei Jahrzehnten. Köln: Kiepen-
   heuer und Witsch, 1978.
*Woher kommen wir? Wohin gehen wir? Dramen und Prosa mit bisher unver-
   öffentlichten und neuen Stücken.* München: Heyne, 1982.

Works Translated into English

Change and Other Plays. New York: Hill and Wang, 1973.
Microdramas. Translated by Rosemarie Waldrop. *Dimension,* 5, 1 (1972),
   106-131.

Secondary Literature in English

Esslin, Martin. "Introduction. The Absurdity of the Real." In *Wolfgang Bauer,
   Change and Other Plays.* New York: Hill and Wang, 1973, pp. vii-xii.
Haberland, Paul M. "Duality, the Artist, and Wolfgang Bauer." *Modern Austrian
   Literature,* Vol. 11, No. 2 (1978), 73-86.
Rorrison, Hugh. "The 'Grazer Gruppe,' Peter Handke and Wolfgang Bauer." In
   Modern Austrian Writing. Literature and Society after 1945. Ed. Alan
   Best and Hans Wolfschütz. London: Oswald Wolff; Totowa, New Jersey:
   Barnes and Noble, 1980, pp. 252-266.

Major Secondary Literature in German

Bauer, Roger. "Die Poeten der Wiener Gruppe und die Herren Vettern aus
   Steiermark." In *Laßt sie koaxen, Die kritischen Frösch' in Preußen und
   Sachsen! Zwei Jahrhunderte Literatur in Österreich.* Wien: Europaverlag,
   1977, pp. 219-234.
Böhm, Gotthard. "Wolfgang Bauer: 'Die Wölt is nämlich unhamlich schiach.'" In
   Die zeitgenössische Literatur Österreichs. Ed. Hilde Spiel. Zürich und Mün-

chen: Kindler, 1976, pp. 614-619.

Fichte, Hubert. "Grazer Vaudau—Wolfgang Bauers theatralische Typenlehre." In Wolfgang Bauer, *Gespenster. Silvester oder Das Massaker im Hotel Sacher. Film und Frau. Drei Stücke.* Köln: Kiepenheuer und Witsch, 1974. Pp. 145-151.

Friedrich, Regine. "Wolfgang Bauer. Dichter." In *Wie die Grazer auszogen, die Literatur zu erobern. Texte, Porträts, Analysen und Dokumente junger österreichischer Autoren.* Ed. Peter Laemmle and Jörg Drews. München: edition text + kritik, 1975, pp. 76-87.

Melzer, Gerhard. "Der große Schnitt. Zu Wolfgang Bauers Stück *Ein fröhlicher Morgen beim Friseur.*" In Wolfgang Bauer, *Ein fröhlicher Morgen beim Friseur. Text. Materialien. Fotos.* Eds. Gerhard Melzer and Michael Muhr. Graz: Droschl, 1983, pp. 34-42.

Melzer, Gerhard. *Wolfgang Bauer. Eine Einführung in das Gesamtwerk.* Königstein/Ts.: Athenäum, 1981.

Nyssen, Ute. "Zu einigen Stücken Wolfgang Bauers." In Wolfgang Bauer, *Die Sumpftänzer. Dramen, Prosa, Lyrik aus zwei Jahrzehnten.* Köln: Kiepenheuer und Witsch, 1978, pp. 395-402.

Sauerland, Karol. "Das österreichische Drama in jüngster Zeit." *Literatur und Kritik,* 96/97 (1975), 341-353.

text + kritik, Wolfgang Bauer, 59 (1978).

Theobald, Erika E. "Das österreichische Drama der Gegenwart." *Modern Austrian Literature,* Vol. 4, No. 1 (1971), 7-22.

Thomas Bernhard

Gudrun Brokoph-Mauch

Thomas Bernhard, the grandson of the Austrian writer Johann Freumbichler, was born 10 February 1931 out of wedlock as the son of a peasant. He grew up in Southern Bavaria and lived there until he entered a boarding school in Salzburg in 1943. In 1946 he exchanged school for a two-year apprenticeship in a grocery store in a poverty-stricken district of Salzburg. There he contracted a lung disease that sent him to several hospitals and lung sanatoriums for the following three years. During that time his grandfather and his mother died (1949 and 1950), severing both his most rewarding and his most difficult relationship up to this point in his life. At the sanatorium Grafenberg he started to write his first prose out of a lack of anything else to do. After his recovery, however, he did not immediately launch into a writing career but pursued his longstanding interest in music. Thus he enrolled at the music academy in Vienna in 1951 and a year later at the Mozarteum in Salzburg, from where he graduated in 1956 with a thesis on Artaud and Brecht. With no family to support him Bernhard worked in Vienna as a laborer as well as an attendant for a seventy-year-old insane woman and in Salzburg as a courtroom reporter and free-lance writer. In 1965 he purchased a farm in Ohlsdorf, Austria, where he has been living ever since.

Bernhard's literary career began with some poems written at the age of sixteen and the publication of a short prose piece, "Vor eines Dichters Grab" (At a Poet's Grave) in the *Salzburger Volksblatt* in 1950. In 1959 he wrote a ballet sketch, *Die Rosen der Einöde* (The Roses of Solitude), and a year later created several short plays that were performed in Maria Saal in Kärnten. His fame as a prose writer was established with his first novel *Frost* (1963) and as a playwright with *Ein Fest für Boris* (1970, A Party for Boris).

Twenty-one years ago Thomas Bernhard published his first novel, *Frost,* which brought him as much criticism as praise, both tinged with pathos.[1] He was misunderstood as a dilettante linguist and psychologist;[2] further it was said that the narcissistic quality of his naggings served merely as "confirmation literature" for a circle of elite readers who gloried in their intellectual and social isolation.[3] Still "the unbelievably controlled dynamics" of his language[4] and his unerring search for truth[5] were soon recognized, for they captivated and moved readers. Also for a long time critics could not agree whether his novels were new or anachronistic. But with the publication of *Kalkwerk* (1970, *Lime*

Works) scholars concluded: "Here was a writer who, regardless of whether he was modern or not, could write."[6]

Thomas Bernhard is not only a master of prose; he also belongs to the German avant-garde in drama. Yet as a young man he wrote sentimental religious lyrics. Their biblical references, ecstatic mysticism, and intense yearning for salvation surprise us today. Indeed, the very titles convey the melancholy and spirituality of these early poems: "November Sacrifice," "Putrefaction," "Sadness," "Black Hills," "Death and Thymian," "Death." Death and mourning provide the dominant vocabulary:

> Behind the trees there is another world,
> a grass that does not taste of mourning, a black sun,
> a moon of the dead,
> a nightingale, which does not stop lamenting
> about bread and wine
> and milk in large jugs
> in the night of the prisoners (EH, 27).*

The images of death and mourning originate in uncertainty about the existence of God, a doubt that wounds the faith of the young poet:

> I die before the sun and
> before the wind and before the children who fight about the dog I die
> on a morning which will not become a poem
> only sad and green and endless
> in this morning . . . (EH, 62).

In other poems Bernhard speaks of the "uncertainty of the dim Gods" (EH, 69), and he sees God "as a drowning God with open mouth above the world" (EH, 70).

Bernhard's "Nine Psalms" bear witness to his swaying between loss of faith and confession of faith, his despair and his hope, his yearning for death and his longing for life:

> You, however, are the unending rain of sadness,
> the unending rain of forsakenness,
> the rain of the stars.
> The rain of the weak
> which makes my eyes powerless (EH, 73).

Contrasting with this litany of resignation are passages in which his will to resurrect God in his writing creates Him with his own words:

> I will fill my hands with earth
> and speak my words,
> the words which will become stone on my tongue
> to rebuild God,
> the great God,
> the one and only God . . . (EH, 74).

When death replaces religion,[7] the author turns from poetry to prose, the form in which he would make his fame. Yet, as he says, "The most terrible thing for me is to write prose. . . . And from that moment on, when I became aware of that, I swore that I would write prose" (DT, 154). When Bernhard says he writes prose against his nature, he also characterizes the most prominent gesture of his works: repulsion from and destruction of the aesthetic forms, philosophical assumptions, and social practices of the consciousness that ignore the finality of death and despair. For this "disappointed metaphysicist"[8] is now fixed on one goal: namely, to demonstrate in an unmistakable and "relentless" way that everything is ridiculous in the face of death.[9] From his first volume of prose, the short narratives *Ereignisse* (1963-1969, Incidents), up to his last prose work, *Beton* (1982, Concrete), he is on the track of death and truth;[10] and he searches with a decisiveness that does not shrink from linguistic excess when he attempts to prove that life is "an amnesis of death" and every quest for knowledge actually "a method of death,"[11] which is therefore evil and void.

In 1968 Bernhard remarked, "Death is my theme because life is my theme,"[12] a statement that applies unmistakably to the tales in *Ereignisse*. The themes of guilt, fear, disgust, sickness, crime, insanity, and death anticipate themes in the later writings. But the horror of the earlier works is dimmed somewhat by the dream-logic that perhaps protects the reader through its apparent fictionality, as in "Der Kassierer" (The Cashier) in the volume *Ereignisse*. Notice the pattern of escalation, catastrophe, and anticlimax (the revelation that it is all a dream):

> The cashier in an iron work marries a woman eight or nine years older than he. Shortly after the wedding the quarrels begin. There is an enormous hostility with which both fall asleep and wake up. Finally the woman becomes very ill, which may have something to do with her childlessness,

with her hands, at home she writes everything on calendar pages: "I want
to go away," for example, or "It is beautiful outside." She hates it when
people pity her. Finally she feels pain in her legs and becomes completely
stiff. She has to be pushed in a wheelchair. She waits at the window.
When her husband comes home, he has to push her around outside.
Always the same stretch. Further and further. She threatens with clenched
fists. She is more and more hungry for new houses, new trees, new people.
She looks out of her winter cape through the trees of the alley. One
evening, pushing her in front of him close to the edge of the road, he
turns the wheelchair over and tosses it into the abyss. She cannot scream.
The metal chair bursts into splinters. This event he dreams. But he will
do something like that with her, he thinks.[13]

The actual event, the "Ereignis," is retracted at the very moment it happens
by the statement that it is a dream. Thus the impulse to murder is satisfied
momentarily, and indeed the mounting tension finds an explosive release in the
description of the murder; but the statement, "This event he dreams," deflates
the effect. Of course, the positioning of this sentence allows for both the fulfillment of the reader's secret identification with the husband's pent-up feelings
of hate, the wish that his wife were dead, while at the moment of its satisfaction the necessary defense mechanism or "emergency break" takes hold.
However, the last sentence does allude to the possible actualization of the
dream and maintains a certain tension to the very end.

Bernhard's later works forsake this method of dream "framing."[14] Although
the *Ereignisse* already contain the material for the fables of the later works,
their objective and epigrammatic style sets them apart as a distinct literary form.

The novel *Frost* (1963) is the first prose work that structurally leads to a
new form. It is "literature of the most harsh, hostile, and hurting kind."[15]
The content may at best be sketched, for the largest part of the book consists
of reflective monologues that can hardly be narrated here. A young medical
student travels to Weng, a small mountain village in the Austrian Alps, in order
to observe the painter Strauch, who seems to be insane. He is assigned to this
task by his superior, who is also Strauch's brother. The nameless narrator's
observations about the painter and the surroundings are written in the form
of diary notes and letters. These diary entries mirror on the one hand the progressive mental decay of the painter and on the other the progressive loss of
identity of the narrator as he drowns in the painter's flow of egomaniacal
suicidal speech. The letters of the medical student to Strauch's brother demonstrate in style and language this gradual mental rape of the young man by

the elder.

The condition of the mind and the condition of the world mirror each other. The village Weng is painted in the colors of disgust; it is a vestibule of Hell, a place dominated by death. The inhabitants are sick and feebleminded alcoholics. They have lice and gonorrhea and suffer from what Bernhard simply calls the "land plague" (F, 172). Excesses of drunkenness, arson, injury, murder, and accidental death (often caused by the brain-dissolving frost of a hostile nature) are a constant threat to everyday existence, which is meaningless anyway. Over the entire landscape hovers a suffocating odor of slaughterhouses and corpses, the ubiquitous "world stench," and through it all the dogs bark and howl. Relentlessly Bernhard dismantles here the postcard idyll of the Austrian tourist business and hits at a vulnerable but until now protected spot in his fellow Austrians. The "stupidity in shirt sleeves" that he portrays (F, 172) negates the picture of the wholesome simple country people of Adalbert Stifter and Peter Rosegger. Thus this "wasteland" is not confined to one region. No, it represents the world's condition as Bernhard sees it. It is equally one-sided to categorize Bernhard as a "Heimatdichter" (provincial writer)[16] as it is to call him a social and cultural critic. Donnenberg has demonstrated convincingly that Bernhard does not fit nicely into either category in spite of his polemical tendencies.[17]

The figure of the painter recalls Büchner's Lenz and the medical student Hans Castorp just as the entire snow and mountain landscape refers to the mythic associations of Thomas Mann's *Der Zauberberg* (*Magic Mountain*).[18] Like Hans Castorp the narrator faces disease and death as "punishment" (F, 346); and this confrontation incites his consciousness and his destructive self-reflection. When he abruptly ends his stay at Weng after twenty-six days, leaving the painter to his suicidal end, he who was originally described as lacking in sensitivity and imagination is deeply scarred. He has to pay for his "expeditions into the jungles of solitude" (F, 20) and his spying on another man's suffering with the loss of his own spiritual security.

The novel *Frost* lays the philosophical, material, and stylistic basis for Bernhard's following work to such a degree that the author has been said to be writing with "maniacal tenacity" on a single novel.[19] Although the horror does lose its pictorial explicitness, it increases its effect through abstraction. Repetition takes the place of variation. The action narrows more and more and merely serves to launch the endless monologues behind which looms a gaping emptiness. The theme of disease is intensified in *Amras* (1965) and in *Verstörung* (1967, *Gargoyles*), but in the later novels it remains more in the background. While in *Frost* the specific cause of the painter's physical illness remains unclear, it is already a "literary symptom"[20] of an equally undefinable mental illness and further of the condition of the world. In *Amras* the "mental confusion" has a clear and fitting "objective correlative"[21] in epilepsy, while in *Verstörung* the author goes as far as to establish a distinct hierarchy of the various diseases, beginning with physical sepsis and ending with highly spiritual insanity. Each disease correlates with the social rank and intellectual capacity of the individual and is located in a landscape divided into high, middle, and low regions.

The Prince, whose monologue fills up the last third of the novel, lives on top of a mountain and suffers from the highest degree of sensitivity and mental confusion. Its cause lies in the act of thinking which, as for the painter Strauch in *Frost*, is "an amoral blank space, thinking without a real function" (F, 339). "Diseases lead man on the shortest path to himself" (V, 228), says Bernhard in *Verstörung*, but the goal is always insanity or death. In *Korrektur* (1975, *Correction*) this theme is expressly connected with the narrator's search for identity. But in the last analysis all diseases are for Bernhard a symptom of the one "sickness unto death," which like suicide has its seed in the womb.

The knowledge that the highly sensitive and intellectual gain in their condition of confusion and permanent mental excitement is of a special kind: "A great vision is constructed out of a very small observation" (F, 296). Here the visionary often loses himself in the solipsistic swirls of thought and reflection. The protagonist or narrator in other words is confined within his own cerebral mechanism, a universe in his own head. His is not cognition of the world because there is nothing out there to be understood. Furthermore, the borders between inside and outside are nebulous, shifting, and not clearly definable, corresponding to the narrative perspective that switches back and forth between personal and projected thoughts. The mental condition of other persons cannot be judged objectively. Consequently, the reader does not gain any insight into personal or universal relationships; instead, he is confronted only with the "brain on printed paper" (F, 343), with a novel as interior monologue. Nevertheless, the reader will come to accept that these terrifying fantasies of insanity mirror the unbearable condition of the world as it is experienced by other splintered and solipsistic souls.

The novel *Kalkwerk* (*Lime Works*), published in 1970, is also indebted to *Frost,* but its form is developed and its content streamlined in such a sophisticated way that it sets a standard of literary craftsmanship and philosophical insight against which other works will be judged.[22] New for Bernhard is the perspective of a narrator who stands completely apart from the event refracted through two other reporters. The result is an extreme indirectness—an "event twice removed"—combined with precision of language and effect alternately bringing the reader into close contact with the object of narration through speech and distancing him through the presence of the intermediary narrator: "We are simultaneously inside and outside":[23] ". . . Konrad and his crippled wife have lived in the lime works for several years, I think, Höller thinks, Konrad supposedly said to Fro" (K, 122). This technique of narrative framing demonstrates how complicated it is to arrive at the authenticity of any statement; it also represents the isolation of the inhabitant of the lime works from nature, society, and tradition. The tension of "bipolarity"[24] between experiencing and narrating narrator, which was already veiled in *Frost,* is completely absent here in order to bring into the foreground the "fictionality of the narrative form."[25]

Again the plot is reduced to a minimum. After years of traveling around in the world Konrad has bought the longed-for lime works into which he and his crippled wife withdraw from the world. There he wants to write a scientific study on hearing that he carries in his head completely finished. After five and a half years of mutual torment and constant irritation preventing the composition of the study Konrad murders his wife. The whole novel is a single cry of anguish about the inability to actualize one's thoughts. The language absorbs the frustrations and aggressions that build up in Konrad and transmits them to the reader in the endless, circular sentences, which become sheer torture in their constant repetitions. In this way the reader is forced to participate directly in Konrad's verbal torture of his wife and the mental and emotional exhaustion of both, for neither has any means of escape.

Already in his earlier novels the place sought out as a protective refuge changed gradually into a hostile and death-inducing prison: Weng in *Frost,* Hochgobernsitz in *Verstörung,* the tower in *Amras* (1965), the shack in *Watten* (1969). However, nowhere did Bernhard succeed so completely and so convincingly in the evocation of this phenomenon as in *Kalkwerk.* Konrad's goal of writing down his research proves fatal for him, his wife, and his work: "Our goal was the lime works, our goal was death through the lime works" (K, 225).

The comical grotesque, which is present more allusively in *Frost* and more substantially in *Watten,* is realized fully in *Kalkwerk.* It responds to the abyss that opens once ideology and religion are rejected; it points to the ever-present danger of violence and downfall and as a style achieves the opposite of comic relief: anxiety.

The lament about the difficulty of transforming knowledge into language that *Frost* voices is central to the narrative of the *Kalkwerk.* Thus, paradoxically, the description of the impossibility of language to say what it means becomes itself a successful and complete work of literary art.[26] But despite this triumph it is clear that the author has reached the last stage of the separation of the writer from his audience that had begun in Romanticism; for Bernhard no longer concerns himself with the loneliness, suppression, and desires of the artist for understanding and social acceptance but instead attacks his readers hatefully and finally turns away from them indifferently.[27] The meaning of writing for Bernhard as well as his fictional creations no longer lies in a dialogue with the world but only in the actualization of their own personality. We are witness to an amazing event: literature succeeds here by including its own destruction.[28]

The latest novel, *Korrektur,* continues the premises of *Frost* while adding something that enlarges the basic thesis: "Research, realization, completion, destruction, eradication. In every case and in every matter in this sequence . . ." (Ko, 358). Nowhere else can one find realization and completion in Bernhard's works. Up to this novel science and research have always directly led to destruction and eradication. This is precisely the main theme of *Kalkwerk.* But in *Korrektur* the author for the first time has constructed "an architectural piece of art" and only then does he "correct," i.e., destroy it. The novel concerns a type of protagonist who has become typical for Bernhard ever since *Amras, Ungenach, Verstörung,* and *Watten:* namely, a man from a wealthy family, a gentleman scholar who refuses to maintain the family estate. He invests his huge inheritance in a cone-shaped house for his beloved sister who dies a mysterious death shortly after its completion.[29] He himself commits suicide after he has tried in vain to write down the planning and construction of the cone.

The work moves back and forth between the two poles already alluded to above: on the one hand, affirmation of existence through the building of the cone that opposes the hostile world into which man is thrown ("geworfen")[30] with its own realm, "so that we can say after a while, *we live in our world not in the existing world,* namely, a world which does not concern us and which wants to destroy and eradicate us" (Ko, 237). On the other hand there is the knowledge of inevitable failure, a knowledge that leads to suicide, as expressed in *Frost:* 'Life is a trial which one loses regardless of what one does" (F, 233).

Bernhard's basic premise that the goal of all science is death has not changed. But the question of whether Pascal's totalizing belief that "death makes everything infamous" (F, 315) applies here, or whether the author strikes a more conciliatory note this time must be asked at least. For even if there is no meaningful way to live in Bernhard's works, are there not degrees of meaninglessness? Death has perhaps two faces. The reader has known the one face since the beginning and immediately recognized it in the title: suicide as a correction of life. For the first time though Bernhard allows for a second kind of death, namely, death at a moment of intense happiness and fulfillment through the experience of dwelling ("wohnen") in the perfect place. However, since the symbolic form of this living space suggests the tomb (the relationship to the pyramid[31] and to the pole in the tombs of the Etruscans[32] is evident), it is difficult to say how far the relationship of happiness and death, of perfect building and mausoleum can be taken seriously; must it instead be understood as a bitter irony? Roithamer constructs the cone after the philosophy of space of the twentieth century,[33] which tries to overcome existentialism by actualizing Heidegger's theory of the unity of building, dwelling, and thinking. Yet the death of Roithamer's sister parodies the philosophy of the protective place that assumes naively that the existential situation of modern man can be overcome architecturally.[34]

Just as futile is Roithamer's attempt to create his own center in a world without metaphysical principles. After all his focus reveals itself as a place of death. This essential absence of a true philosophical center is mirrored in language and in style. The rotating, circular motion of the sentences seems to suck up bits and pieces of information and swirl them along. Indeed, all sentences and groups of sentences in the first third of the novel, for example, start with "Höller's attic room" and return to it eventually. Höller's attic room as center of these syntactical spirals functions as a grotesque attempt to make up for the "middle," the focus, of missing meaning. The result of rhetorical strain is, of course, that nothingness becomes not covered up but painfully evident. Maier understands the intentions and effects of this style, which is already present in the earlier works, as an expression of a "dissatisfaction with the world plan (world center)."[35] Bernhard's language lacks an anchor, it has nothing to tell. As Spinner observes, one cannot "dwell" ("wohnen") in it any longer.[36]

The construction of the cone reveals very clearly a dialectic that is basic to Bernhard's work: the opposition to tradition coupled with a love for the past. As Gamper says, the aggression against tradition—in this case the family residence Altensam—functions, in reality, as a "utopia projected backwards,"[37] it originates in the frustrated understanding that, although the past is truly valuable, it cannot be experienced truthfully in the present.[38] In *Korrektur* Roithamer tries to escape this destructive dilemma by creating a new place for the idealized past that his sister embodies. The irony of this attempted rescue of tradition lies in the symbolic representation of the cone as tomb, as we have seen.

In *Korrektur* and especially in *Kalkwerk* the reader must not forget that everything said is quoted (G, 22).[39] This means that the closeness between narrator and story, typical in the diary and epistolary novel, is defamiliarized through the reflection of quotation. Once more then Bernhard constructs the scaffold of a traditional fiction only to tear it down before the reader's eyes. Moreover, the first person narrator no longer intends to tell a story but only wants to take "notes" and to "inspect and order" the "scraps of paper" of the other narrator. Bernhard acknowledges this process in his autobiographical television sketch *Drei Tage* (1971, Three Days), in which he admits that he is a "destroyer of stories" (DT, 151).

Just as Bernhard's novel appeared to dissolve itself, leaving the reader to wonder what would happen next, the author took a sudden turn in his prose. He turned to autobiography and hence to telling a story. The five prose works, *Die Ursache* (1975, The Cause), *Der Keller* (1976, The Cellar), *Der Atem* (1978, The Breath), *Die Kälte* (1981, The Cold), and *Das Kind* (1982, The Child), form a novel in series about the life of the man Thomas Bernhard. These five works divide the most important phases of Bernhard's youth into five chronological stages. The author wants the reader to interpret the experiences in these five works as the "cause" of his special way of living, thinking, and writing.

With this series Bernhard joins in a movement in contemporary Austrian literature which, apparently tired of the concreteness, objectivity, and emotional coldness of the 1960s and early 1970s, views the autobiographical novel as a chance to return to subjectivity as a medium for discovering and researching one's own personality. Bernhard even goes a step further than his colleagues; he writes a real autobiography not an autobiographical novel. He says "I" without the least bit of disguise. So far it seems safe to say that this autobiographical quintet shows Bernhard again experimenting with a new form of expression, an attempt very much like his discovery of the theater in 1970 and of film in 1973.

After the aggressive, radical declaration of cognitive and metaphysical bankruptcy in *Korrektur*, Bernhard paused understandably for a time of self-reflection. He seemed to wish for a way out of the dead-end road along which he had traveled further and further in each new novel. In an early poem, "Biography of Pain" ("Biographie des Schmerzes"), Bernhard wrote tellingly: "The place I slept in yesterday is closed today. In front of the entrance the chairs are stacked one upon the other, and none whom I ask about me has seen me."[40]

Nevertheless, in his autobiography he opens the dwelling place of his youth; he sets up the chairs in a very distinct pattern. His research into the "cause of my misfortune"[41] concentrates mainly on the geography of Salzburg, the home of his parents, and the state of his youth, the "deadly soil," the "deadly region" (Ur, 69), and only secondarily does it focus on catastrophic occurrences there: his adolescent stay in the boarding school during and after the bombing of Salzburg in *Die Ursache*, his apprenticeship in a grocery store in the slums of the city in *Der Keller*, his struggle with death in the Municipal Hospital in *Der Atem*, his experience of isolation at the sanatorium Grafenberg in *Die Kälte*. These "constellations of severe misfortune," to use a phrase of Ingeborg Bachmann, end temporarily in Grafenberg (At, 237), and the reader is left waiting for the continuation of this autobiography.

Of course no autobiography is written spontaneously; some intention determines the selection, composition, and interpretation of the historical material. For this reason Bernhard limits his research of the "Ursachen" (causes) to the occurrences in his life that can lend authenticity to his depictions of sickness, insanity, and death in fiction. The causality imposed on the relationships and events of life changes the chronicle into a work of art. The will to poetic creation the urge to place detail into a totality, is as strong here as the will to truth in his fiction. As André Maurois observed, memory itself is an artist, making a work of art out of everyone's life.[42]

This aesthetic arrangement of historical material makes the locations and events translucent; that is, facts become metaphors. For example, attendance in the *Gymnasium* (equivalent to high school and two years of college) is interpreted as the adult world's betrayal of the child. The school, under its brutal directors, is an inferno; it exemplifies all oppressive political and religious ideology, contemporary and historical. The director's blow to the head of a pupil, the slap of a face, do damage to the souls of the boys as much as the bombs to the city; for they all symbolize the destructive fury in human nature. Driven to a type of narcosis for refuge, a talented pupil daily plays his violin in the narrow, evil-smelling shoe closet. His playing stimulates and accompanies his meditations about suicide, thoughts that are the result of this oppressive education. Bernhard's frequent condemnations of the Salzburg Festival as a paradigm of cultural decadence and the desire for intoxication, escape, and adolescent masturbation come to mind here.[43]

In the second part of the autobiography the cellar also becomes a metaphor. Obviously it contrasts with the hypocritical façade of bourgeois life. But the metaphor of the cellar refers to yet another realm of interpretation lying in the Pascal quotation at the beginning of *Der Atem*: "Since mankind was incapable of overcoming death, poverty, and ignorance, it decided not to think of them in order to be happy." However, Bernhard does not allow his reader any diversion from the unresolved problems of existence. He turns off the electric light in our modern cellars, to use a metaphor of Bachelard,[44] and leads us mercilessly down the cellar steps with a flickering candle in his hand, not just in this autobiography but in all of his works beginning with his first novel. Only by directly confronting sickness, vice, squalor, and death, the madness and horror beneath reason, can he conceive of a new beginning, if indeed it is at all possible. The stay in the "Scherzhauserfeldsiedlung" is a necessary stage during which the apprentice passes from adolescence to adulthood, ending the escapism of his meditations on suicide and making contact with his inner nature before starting a new life: "I had my life again. Suddenly I had it completely in my hand" (Ke, 16), Bernhard's autobiography is truly a biography of pain because this search for his lost ego does not lead him back to society but rather to a lung disease, the well-known "literary symptom" for "the sickness unto death" in his works. The search leads him away from social intercourse and brings him closer to the edge of human existence.

Again in *Der Atem* the factual yields symbolic meaning. The death chamber, which only Bernhard survives in this work, is the last scene in the theater farce of life. Everyone leaves the stage in a different manner, but the significance of these various ways of dying is not clear. In any case death does not pause; it knows no social distinctions here, in contrast to *Der Italiener* (1971) in which different social classes die differently. In *Der Atem* everyone is thrown into the same tin coffin after the corpse has spent two hours under a sheet with a number on his big toe.

In the foreground is the accusation against the conditions of Bernhard's youth: the political dilemma of the war period, the social chaos of the postwar era, the callousness of those who think themselves charitable in the hospitals. The immediate family is introduced: the daily life of three generations in the most inadequate living space—parents, grandparents, brothers, sisters, and one uncle, all of whom have been led into this tiny apartment at the end of the war to experience fright and horror: "My home was hell" (Ke, 94). The author, though, expressly denies the reader more details of these horrible conditions. Just exactly how unbearable his life with his mother, stepfather, half brothers, and sisters must have been we can only guess. He does not even elaborate the difficult relationship with his mother, a bond tainted with suspicion and mutual dislike. Its elucidation would help us understand why his female characters are always either passed over or portrayed unsympathetically; and perhaps it would clue us as to why there are no normal erotic relationships in his works.

This gap of information is finally closed in his last autobiographical volume, *Das Kind* (1982, The Child), which reads like an afterthought: instead of continuing the series in chronological sequence, *Das Kind* prefaces it with the hitherto undisclosed early childhood of the author. The book opens with the first bicycle ride of the eight-year-old and closes with the application of the adolescent to the Salzburg boarding school, which serves as a bridge to *Die Ursache*. It is the most intimate volume of the quintet describing in detail his illegitimate birth, his difficult life with his mother, his warm and loving friendship with his grandfather, and his misery and torment as an unsuccessful pupil in grammar school. Because his mother was ill prepared to raise such a precocious child, she turned to frequent corporal punishment in her helplessness and to yelling at him and cursing him. As much as he feared the leather strap on his skin, nothing would wound him as deeply as her "diabolical words": "You are the cause of my unhappiness. The devil shall take you. You have destroyed my life. It's all your fault! You are my death! You are nothing! I am ashamed of you . . . ! (Ki, 38). His close resemblance to his father, the man who had deserted her at a young age, was a constant reminder for her of her greatest disappointment. Therefore her instinctive love for her child was obstructed by her hatred of his father and her beatings, harsh words, and lamentations were not so much directed toward the child but toward the father. His mother's life was further complicated by her constant struggle against poverty and entrapment in her father's (the author's beloved grandfather) provocative, anachronistic, revolutionary mental escapades while she longed for normality and harmony.

All the while the child loved his mother but through the unfortunate circumstances of his birth and the economic and emotional pressures on his family was denied the comfort of motherly love and affection. His salvation was his grandfather who would always be his ally in difficult situations and essentially rescued him from the destructive forces around him. "We understood each other. A few steps with him, and I was rescued" (Ki, 79). He is his mentor who teaches him how to think, to ask questions, and to find answers. As a writer and as an eccentric he becomes influential for Bernhard's profession.

Bernhard's noticeable preoccupation with death in his works seems to go back to his childhood visits to the graveyard in Seekirchen (one of the several places of residence of the restless family). "The dead were already then my dearest friends, I approached them without reservations. For hours I would sit on the edge of a grave pondering being and its opposite" (Ki, 70-71). By offering valuable insight into a disturbing childhood this last autobiographical volume solicits deeper understanding for the author's predisposition toward isolation, insanity, self-destruction, and death in his writings.

Like his novels the autobiographic quintet is filled with voluminous reflections and lengthy commentaries that keep the reader in a constant tension between fascination and irritation. Their compulsive exaggerations rob the historical events of their authenticity. The result is a primarily apologetic tone that stands in the way of a true search for the self. Still it cannot be denied that these commentaries draw the reader into their magic circle; they largely make up the tension and emotional appeal of these works, not so much through content as style, particularly in the circular sentences, which absorb more material here than in the novels. This artificial style, imbued with a power of persuasion, intensifies the subjectivity of Bernhard's confrontation with life and overpowers the readers through its combination of absolute terms and syntactical breathlessness, forcing him into the author's perspective - at least as long as he is reading. This narrative strategy satisfies a compulsion to justify oneself, typical in autobiography, and at the same time it addresses the aesthetic and emotional needs of the reader.

Compared with his novels and short stories, Bernhard's autobiography appears conservative in form. The chronological-causal order of the phases of his life in the four volumes releases the reader from the usual labor of piecing a life story together like a puzzle from shreds of quotations and reports of other narrators. Rather, a linear story is told here by an author who has consistently called himself a "destroyer of stories" (DT, 151).

The tracing of his artistic development is very sketchy in this autobiography, probably because Bernhard decided late to become a writer. However, as compensation the five volumes serve up much of the intellectual and factual matter of his works, making them more accessible but without changing them into autobiographical writings. For the historical events and emotional turmoils have been filtered through a process of abstraction and reconfiguration in the individual works. As a result they are not easily recognizable. The confusion, terror, and deadly experiences of the author's youth have been rendered in the novels as general confusion, fright, and death in the form of an apocalyptic vision, which has dissolved the historical moment with its claim of absolute truth.

Bernhard's prose does not consist exclusively of novels and autobiography; it also includes shorter forms: the short stories in the volumes *An der Baumgrenze* (1969, At the Timber Line) and *Midland in Stilfs* (1969-1970, Midland at Stilfs) and the short novels *Amras* (1965), *Ungenach* (1968), *Watten* (1969), and *Ja* (1978, Yes). In the collection *Der Stimmenimitator* (1978, The Voice Imitator) he returns to the "short short story" of his first work, *Ereignisse*. Although very similar in content - insanity, suicide, murder, fatal accidents, mysterious deaths, macabre occurrences, and contradictions of a great variety - these works are very dissimilar in style and meaning. While the *Ereignisse* are characterized by sentences consisting of short main clauses in the present tense, which produce rapidly mounting tension and direct emotional impact, the stories in *Der Stimmenimitator* display long periods abounding in relative and dependent clauses as well as the indirect speech of the novels. This syntax requires great mental concentration from the reader and consequently does not yield the intense identification with the narrated event as happens in *Ereignisse*. Rather, one is led to a detached, intellectual observation of the story's development and direction and often of its paradoxical or ironical turn at the end.

The structure of the stories is often that of the anecdote – short narration of a single event that aims from the very first sentence at the goal, at the "Pointe" at the end – while the character of the story is taken from a news item in a local paper. Thus the title "Voice Imitator" refers not only to one of the stories in the volume about an artist who imitates the voices of celebrities, while he cannot imitate his own voice, but also to the peculiar ability of the author to invoke the voices of the newspapers in their columns about catastrophes. Bernhard is very successful in his attempt to bring out the ludicrous, the illogical, and the contradictory in journalistic style, which typically uses naive language, introduces immaterial detail, and misplaces the focus of the report. The piece "Too Much" illustrates this technique well: "A family father, who had been praised and liked for decades because of his so-called *extraordinary family sense,* and who on a Saturday afternoon – to be sure while the weather was extremely humid – murdered four of his six children, defended himself in front of the judge with the argument that the children had suddenly been *too much* for him" (St, 49).

In contrast to the man in *Der Stimmenimitator* Bernhard not only succeeds in imitating other voices but also seems to have little difficulty in imitating his own voice. The degree to which *Der Stimmenimitator* seems to be a summary of the characters, events, localities, and topics of his previous writings is striking, and the "voice" in this volume rings a familiar tune in the reader's ear with its occasional note of self-irony.

The discussion of the short novel *Beton* (1982, *Concrete*) will conclude our consideration of Bernhard's prose writings. It harks back to the *Kalkwerk* (*Lime Works*) of ten years earlier. Again we have a protagonist who is possessed by the single wish to write down a work of great importance to him, this time a thesis on Mendelssohn, and again is incapable of doing so because of his neurotic sensitivity toward the smallest inner and outer distractions. Although he never does write his Mendelssohn abstract in the course of this book, and it is doubtful that he ever will, his preoccupation with this and similar projects in the past serves as a justification for his life style, which is as expensive as it is absurd:

"I attacked Schönberg in order to justify myself, Reger, Joachim and even Bach, only to justify myself, as I now attack Mendelssohn for the same reason" (B, 70), he admits, only to come to the conclusion that neither he nor anyone else needs justification, because no one asked to be born.

The theme of the writer whose creativity is stifled because of an excessive degree of perfectionism is combined also in this work with the theme of extreme isolation. Robert lives alone in his country house in Peiskam communicating on a regular basis only with his housekeeper and on an irregular basis with his sister, who imposes upon him at her own will and convenience. And again, as we have seen in previous works, the main character is incapable of freeing himself from the intrusion of another human being on his mind to the degree that the preoccupation turns into obsession. Thus the novel opens with Robert's attempt to resume his normal, carefully orchestrated routine of living through yet another unproductive day after one of those spontaneous visits by his sister, only to find his thoughts totally dominated by her personality, her thoughts and opinions, and her way of life. The contrast between brother and sister that emerges gradually in the usual gyrations of language, the protestations and accusations against each and everyone, could not be starker: she is the picture of health and vitality with a sheer insatiable appetite for life's mundane gifts and adventures, a charming and skillful manipulator of people, a successful businesswoman, in short the guest of honor at the banquet of life, while he—a chronically ailing neurasthenic, hypersensitive man who depends on heavy medication for his mere survival, shunning human contact and the pursuit of ordinary tasks and pleasures—merely nibbles at the crumbs that fall off the table. While the sister is a familiar figure in Bernhard's works, she does not normally appear as such an independent and vital personality, but is usually crippled, tied to a wheelchair or otherwise totally subservient to her brother and dependent on him. Here the roles are almost reversed, for although not dependent upon her financially or physically he is preoccupied with her with that envious fascination of the unsuccessful toward the successful, whereas she on the other hand prods and nudges her little brother toward a more fruitful life.

In the end, unable to free himself from her spell over him, he journeys to Palma, Mallorca, where he recalls the sad fate of a woman he had met there two years ago and who had since committed suicide. Her grave, a slab of concrete, gives this novel its title. Anna Härtl's fate with its progressive stages of misfortune only accidentally forms a contrast to the success story of Rudolf's sister. It is of no consequence to the narrator, who merely uses her story to fill his own empty life and the empty pages that should be filled with the story of Mendelssohn and is an inadequate substitute for the project in his mind. And — as is typical for Bernhard — death has won the day again and has succeeded in making everything else seem insignificant and irrelevant.

If one disregards here the very early theater and ballet sketches,[45] then *Ein Fest für Boris* is Bernhard's first play. He has since written a great number of others, which repeat the themes, images, and motifs of this one as well as of his novels and short stories. Not surprisingly, the main characteristics of Bernhard's dramas are closely related to those of his prose writings: endlessly long monologues, scarcity of action, the joining of two partners in conversation, one of whom talks almost without interruption while the other — inferior in appearance but intellectually often superior — is silent.

Thus the relationship between the "Good Woman," the main character in *Ein Fest für Boris,* and Johanna, her nurse, servant, and companion, is characterized by mutual dependence and mutual hatred, by the overt tyranny of the one and the subversive rebellion of the other; and this relationship is typical of most others in Bernhard's plays. Also typical is the main character's obsession with one problem throughout the play — a familiar occurrence in the novels, too. In this case the "Good Woman," rich, capricious, and tyrannical, is obsessed with only one event in her life: the car accident in which her husband was killed and she lost both of her legs. The mutual dependence of two persons who torment one another and the obsession with one unresolved problem are also found in *Der Präsident* (1975, *The President*) and *Der Weltverbesserer* (1979, The World Reformer). Both complexes are metaphors for the torturous coexistence of human beings and the absorption of each individual in his own condition.

The play *Ein Fest für Boris* centers on a birthday banquet for Boris, a cripple and glutton. He celebrates among his former friends from the asylum where he lived before the "Good Woman" rescued and married him. The "Good Woman" plays the sympathetic benefactor: she listens to the cripple's scurrilous and frightening dreams and fantasies, the complaints about the poor treatment of the inmates. Soon their tales turn into war cries and the feast into a rebellious chaos during which Boris collapses quietly and dies. The play ends with the "Good Woman's" "terrible laughter" (B, 107).

Comedy or tragedy? They are interchangeable for Bernhard simply because death lies in ambush at the end of almost every play, robbing tragedy of its dignity and comedy of its final serenity. As he says:

> We continuously develop
> a tragedy

or a comedy
when we develop the tragedy
we really develop only a comedy
and vice versa (M, 18).

Also in the later plays Death concludes the masquerade that is life, as in *Die Jagdgesellschaft* (1974, The Hunting Party). In the play *Minetti* (1976) Bernhard combines death with art. An eccentric and possibly mad actor claims to have been asked by a director to perform *Lear* after thirty years retirement. Yet he commits suicide in the ongoing war between artist and audience.

Art is the central theme in several plays. In *Minetti* the artist struggles with his "intellectual object" against the "intellectual garbage" (M, 26) in society. He wants to suppress the common stupidity under the "intellectual cap" (M, 26), but he is not strong enough. In the end he is destroyed by his public. The other plays—*Der Ignorant und der Wahnsinnige* (1972, The Ignorant and the Mad), the comedy *Die Macht der Gewohnheit* (1974, The Force of Habit), and the satire *Die Berühmten* (1976, The Famous) deal with the ineffectiveness of today's art and its inability to influence society. Bernhard sees several reasons for this. In *Minetti* the trouble is the public's desire for the perfection and harmony of classical literature, in which one can be protected from assuming responsibility for a perplexing and disturbing reality: Minetti refuses to be part of this "shamelessness" (M, 48). He declines every offer and resists all pressure to perform classical roles with the exception of *Lear*, a role which is his fate and which drives him to insanity. As a result he is chased from the theater and lives in depravity. *Die Berühmten,* on the other hand, provides a contrast to Minetti's protest, for it is the protagonists' ambition to imitate and possibly surpass those "classical" stars of the theater, opera, and concert hall whom society has placed on a pedestal. The public rewards these efforts with money and the comforts of an opulent lifestyle. Bernhard calls this ambition to be the public's favorite at any cost "the insolence of the artist."

Of a different nature is Bernhard's criticism of art and the artist in *Der Ignorant und der Wahnsinnige.* Here he attacks the reduction of art to mechanical virtuosity, which in its inexhaustible exertion to reach the perfection of form has forgotten human content and descended to the level of empty mechanism. Such striving for artificial perfection also transforms the performing artist, in this case a soprano, into a machine, a "Koleraturmaschine."

While the performing artist's obsession for perfection in *Der Ignorant und der Wahnsinnige* is treated in a morbidly serious way, it is caricatured in the play *Die Macht der Gewohnheit.* The circus director Caribaldi has been practicing the "Forellenquintet" daily for twenty-two years. His single goal in life is to be able to perform the quintet once with absolute perfection. But he never succeeds because he is dependent both on circumstances—the instruments that break down—and on the cooperation and ability of the other performers, who periodically sabotage his efforts. Then too his own failing health undermines his performance. Bernhard borrows the characters and situations from the *commedia dell' arte;* these comical elements are successfully combined with a fundamental skepticism.[46] Caribaldi's wish to make "perfect music" does not originate from the true joy of playing an instrument well but rather from a sincere revulsion against it: "But we must play!" he exclaims (Gew, 42), just as we must live life, which is equally unloved. The performance of art appears as a discipline, a therapy, even a diversion from life.

The idea that the talent and the genius are essentially a kind of disease or deformation of human nature runs like a red thread through this play: "The extraordinary is always crippled. That which happens in it a deformation" (Ber, 35). This idea of course is not new but a variation of the well-known equation of genius and illness by writers since German Romanticism: but this definition of the creative mind as a sick deviation from the healthy norm is just another way for Bernhard to express his disappointment with art and culture.

Bernhard's cultural pessimism does not end with art and the performing artists but includes also philosophy and the philosophers. In his comedy *Immanuel Kant* (1979), for instance, the philosopher is portrayed as a lunatic traveling on a luxury liner from Königsberg to the United States in order to undergo an eye operation and to receive an honorary degree from Columbia University. In reality he is taken into custody by employees of an insane asylum as soon as the ship lands.

Two themes supply the targets for Bernhard's mockery in the play: first, Kant's eye problem, which prevents him from seeing the "thing itself"—in this case the artificial kneecap of the millionairess—an attack on the basic premise of Kant's philosophy; second, his constant companion, the parrot, who repeats Kant's own thoughts and themes on command. Obviously the parrot plays the role of the epigones who accepted and repeated Kant's philosophy thoughtlessly, without constructive skepticism. Bernhard also finds humor and satire in the fact that Kant's presence in the twentieth century is accepted as perfectly natural by his fellow voyagers. That he is not questioned by anyone shows that a madman appears perfectly normal among lunatics.

Among Bernhard's political plays, *Die Jagdgesellschaft, Der Präsident,* and *Vor dem Ruhestand* (1979, *Eve of Retirement*), the latter is the most significant.

It offers a provocative challenge to the remaining secret obsession of postwar Germany with the ideology of National Socialism, its longing for the glorious past and its belief in the return of the Golden Age, the utopian millennium. Every year for the past forty years Rudolf and Vera Höller celebrate Himmler's birthday as a ritual that transcends a past historical moment to the higher order of eternal cosmic forces. Accidental occurrences and incidents that repeat themselves annually on that day give Himmler's birthday as well as the entire National Socialist ideology a "supernatural legitimation."[47] Robert and Vera have created a symbolic universe with their Nazism, which they must protect and defend against Germany's postwar reality, denigrated as "heretical," "decadent," and "destroyed," as well as against their crippled sister Clara, a Socialist and subversive rebel to their belief. They subdue her spoken and unspoken revolt with repeated threats of institutionalization and annihilation, diminishing her by calling her perverse and crazy, and incorporating her into their universe by assigning her a role in it. She has to play the KZ-victim during their ritualistic birthday celebration. By bestowing ontological status on social roles through the process of reification,[48] all individual responsibility for past and present inhuman acts can be abandoned as inherent in the "office" held: "I only did my duty . . . I am not to be blamed for anything" (R, 62). Their toast to "the idea, to this one idea" (R, 99) unites them all with Nazi sympathizers in Germany and gives this private celebration a collective dimension.

"Reduction," "scarcity," "artificiality" (IW, 65) – these three terms characterize Bernhard's plays. One can hardly find rounded individuals. The persons are named only according to their professions and their roles in the drama; personal names are rare. Plots are reduced to a few compulsive gestures, such as the repetitious trying on of hat and gloves by the "Good Woman" or the singing and arm raising exercises of the diva. The language, which often consists only of a few provocations, half sentences, and exclamations, has lost its power to communicate: "Language is a mathematical instrument of ideas/The poet/Rhetorician and philosopher/play and compose grammatically" (Ber, 48).

The artificiality inherent in the stage is carried to such an extreme that the term "head theater" ("Kopftheater") has become commonplace among the critics. Bernhard's characters are not real people but figures out of the mind of the writer who manipulates them like puppets on a string:

> As you know
> it is a
> puppet show
> not people act here

puppets
everything moves
unnaturally here (IW, 47)

The structural principle is musical; it corresponds with the serial form of composition of the "Second Viennese School," which like Bernhard's writing is characterized by reduction, scarcity, and artificiality.[49] The musical structure follows
either the classical sonata form in three movements, as in the *Jagdgesellschaft,*
or rests upon the disharmony of two contrary semantic and linguistic elements,
as in *Der Ignorant und der Wahnsinnige.* Besides music the other sources of
inspiration for Bernhard's peculiar style are the natural sciences and mathe-
matics: "art is a mathematical art" (Gew, 153). But still death alone delivers
the only truly "exact work" (Jagd, 68).

Ever since the publication of his first novel Thomas Bernhard has written
with an undiminished and indeed astonishing productivity. His works give the
impression that he is trying anxiously to create order in a chaotic world. His
carefully constructed sentences, mammoth in length, proceed breathlessly
yet seem in their very length and complexity to forestall conclusion out of
fear that the end might bring on the chaos just beyond language and thought.
His novels are without plots, and his dramas are without action. However,
both are rich in emotions, mostly hostile and aggressive. Both undertake to
dismantle traditional forms; they are "anti-novels" and "anti-plays" with a
peculiar power to fascinate. Bernhard's endless complaints about the corruption
of the Austrian character, culture, and politics, his despair over the human
condition, his interest in the deformities of mind and body, and his love affair
with death have been called by the distinguished critic Jean Améry the pathol-
ogy of the "morbus austriacus," a widespread disease of the Austrian writers'
soul.[50] Trakl, Kafka, Roth, Weiss, Weininger, and Hofmannsthal were all similarly infected. But they found ways either to sublimate their morbidity or
convert it into something greater than itself. In Thomas Bernhard this disease
breaks out furiously; it is released, perhaps disciplined, only in the acrobatics
of language and syntax. Two sentences, both in the same essay by Bernhard,
establish the limits and possibilities of his work: "Death makes everything
unbearable," and "Death makes everything possible."[51]

Notes

1. Anneliese Botond, "Schlußbemerkung," *Über Thomas Bernhard,* edited

by A. B. Botond (Frankfurt: Suhrkamp, 1970), p. 139.

2. Marcel Reich-Ranicki, "Konfessionen eines Besessenen," Ibid., pp. 94–99.

3. Jens Tismar, "Thomas Bernhards Erzählerfiguren," Ibid., pp. 76–77.

4. Hartmut Zelinski, "Thomas Bernhards Amras und Novalis," Ibid., p. 31.

5. Karl Heinz Bohrer, "Es gibt keinen Schlußstrich," Ibid., pp. 114–115.

6. A. Botond, "Schlußbemerkung," Ibid., p. 139.

7. Peter Lämmle, "Stimmt die 'partielle Wahrheit' noch? Notizen eines abtrünnigen Thomas Bernhard Lesers," *Text und Kritik*, 43, (July 1974), 48.

8. Ibid., p. 49.

9. Thomas Bernhard, "Rede," *Über Thomas Bernhard*, p. 71.

10. Title of a speech by Thomas Bernhard, *Neues Forum*, pp. 173, 347–349.

11. Ibid., p. 347.

12. Ibid., p. 349.

13. Walter Schönau, "Thomas Bernhards 'Ereignisse' oder die Wiederkehr des Verdrängten," *Wissen aus Erfahrungen, Festschrift für Hermann Meyer* (Tübingen: Niemeyer, 1976), p. 831.

14. Ibid.

15. Urs Jenny, "Österreichische Agonie," *Über Thomas Bernhard*, p. 108.

16. Marcel Reich-Ranicki, "Konfessionen eines Besessenen," p. 95.

17. Josef Donnenberg, "Zeitkritik bei Thomas Bernhard," *Zeit- und Gesellschaftskritik in der österreichischen Literatur des 19. und 20. Jahrhunderts*, edited by the Institut für Österreichkunde (Wien: Hirt, 1973), p. 138.

18. Erwin Koller, "Beobachtungen eines Zauberberg-Lesers zu Thomas Bernhards Roman 'Frost,'" *Amsterdamer Beiträge zur neueren Germanistik*, 2, (1973), 122.

19. Wolfgang Maier, "Die Abstraktion vor ihrem Hintergrund gesehen," *Über Thomas Bernhard*, p. 22.

20. Koller, p. 120.

21. Ibid.

22. Bernhard Sorg, *Thomas Bernhard* (Frankfurt: Suhrkamp, 1977), p. 154.

23. Günter Blöcker, "Rede auf den Preisträger," *Deutsche Akademie für Sprache und Dichtung* (Jahrbuch, 1970), p. 81.

24. Franz Stanzel, *Typische Formen des Romans* (Göttingen: Vandenhoeck, 1969), p. 33.

25. Sorg, p. 148.

26. Ibid.

27. Ibid., pp. 150–151.

28. Ibid, p. 154.

29. George Steiner and Jean Améry have proved that this course of life corresponds to Wittgenstein's biography, and they have interpreted *Korrektur* accordingly as a "Schlüsselroman." See George Steiner, "Thomas Bernhard: Korrektur," *Times Literary Supplement* (London, 13 February 1976), p. 158 and Jean Améry, "Morbus Austriacus, Bemerkungen zu Thomas Bernhards 'Die Ursache' and 'Korrektur,'" *Merkur* Nr. 332 (January 1976), 91–94.

30. Bernhard uses Heidegger's terms here intentionally when he calls Roithamer's mother "die Frau mit dem guten Wurf" (the woman with the good throw), *Korrektur*, p. 246.

31. Sorg, p. 180.

32. O. W. Vacano, "Die Etrusker in der Welt der Antike," *Rowohlts deutsche Enzyklopädie,* Vol. 54 (1957), 85; quoted from Otto Bollnow, *Mensch und Raum* (Stuttgart: Kohlhammer, 1963), p. 61.

33. See Otto Bollnow, *Mensch und Raum;* Gaston Bachelard, *Die Poetik des Raumes,* translated by Kurt Leonhard (München: Hanser, 1960); Martin Heidegger, "Bauen, Wohnen, Denken," M. H. *Vorträge und Aufsätze* (Pfullingen: Neske, 1954).

34. "Das ewige Schweigen dieser unendlichen Räume macht mich schaudern." Pascal ("The eternal silence of these infinite spaces makes me shudder").

35. Wolfgang Maier, "Die Abstraktion vor ihrem Hintergrund gesehen," A. Botond, *Über Thomas Bernhard*, p. 18.

36. Kaspar H. Spinner, "Prosaanalysen. Aus Thomas Bernhards 'Watten,'" *Literatur und Kritik*, 90 (1974), 613.

37. Herbert Gamper, "'Eine durchinstrumentierte Partitur Wahnsinn,'" A. Botond, *Über Thomas Bernhard*, p. 131.

38. Ibid.

39. See Uwe Schweikert, "Im Grunde ist alles, was gesagt wird, zitiert," *Text und Kritik*, 43 (July 1974), 1–8.

40. Thomas Bernhard, *Auf der Erde und in der Hölle, Gedichte* (Salzburg: Otto Müller, 1957), p. 60.

41. Thomas Bernhard, "Unsterblichkeit ist unmöglich," *Neues Forum*, Vol. 15, (1968), 96.

42. Quoted from James Olney, *Metaphors of Self, The Meaning of Autobiography* (Princeton: Princeton University Press, 1972), p. 263.

43. Anton Krättle, "Eine Algebra des Untergangs. Über Thomas Bernhard, 'Die Ursache' und 'Korrektur,'" *Schweizer Monatshefte*, 55 (1975/1976), 822.

44.   Gaston Bachelard, *The Poetics of Space,* translated by Maria Jolas (New York: Orion Press, 1964), p. 19.

45.   Herbert Gamper, *Thomas Bernhard* (München: Deutscher Taschenbuchverlag, 1977), pp. 179-181.

46.   F. N. Mennemeier, "Nachhall des absurden Dramas," in *Modernes Deutsches Drama* 2 (München, 1975), p. 318.

47.   Joseph Federico, "Millenarianism, Legitimation, and the National Socialist Universe in Thomas Bernhard's 'Vor dem Ruhestand,'" *Germanic Review,* Vol. 59, No. 4 (1984), 145.

48.   Ibid., p. 143.

49.   Herbert Gamper, p. 85.

50.   Jean Améry, "Morbus Austriacus," in *Merkur,* 332 (January 1976), 92.

51.   Thomas Bernhard, "Unsterblichkeit ist unmöglich," in *Neues Forum,* Vol. 15 (1968), 94.

*Abbreviations of Bernhard's Works Cited

EH   = *Auf der Erde und in der Hölle.* Gedichte (Salzburg: Otto Müller, 1957).

Er   = *Ereignisse. Prosa* (Berlin, 1969).

DT   = Drei Tage, *Der Italiener* (Salzburg: Residenz Verlag, 1971).

F   = *Frost* (Frankfurt: Insel, 1963).

V   = *Verstörung* (Frankfurt: Suhrkamp, 1967).

K   = *Das Kalkwerk* (Frankfurt: Suhrkamp, 1970).

G   = *Gehen* (Frankfurt: Suhrkamp, 1971).

Ko   = *Korrektur* (Frankfurt: Suhrkamp, 1975).

Ur   = *Die Ursache. Eine Andeutung* (Salzburg: Residenz, 1975).

Ke   = *Der Keller. Eine Entziehung* (Salzburg: Residenz, 1976).

At   = *Der Atem. Eine Entscheidung* (Salzburg: Residenz, 1978).

St   = *Der Stimmenimitator* (Salzburg: Residenz, 1978).

B   = *Ein Fest für Boris* (Frankfurt: Suhrkamp, 1970).

M   = *Minetti* (Frankfurt: Suhrkamp, 1977).

Gew = *Die Macht der Gewohnheit* (Frankfurt: Suhrkamp, 1974).

Ber = *Die Berühmten* (Frankfurt: Suhrkamp, 1976).

IW   = *Der Ignorant und der Wahnsinnige* (Frankfurt: Suhrkamp, 1974).

B   = *Beton* (Frankfurt: Suhrkamp, 1982).

Ki   = *Das Kind* (Salzburg: Residenz, 1982).

All quotations in English have been translated by me.

Bibliography

Auf der Erde und in der Hölle. Gedichte (Salzburg: Otto Müller, 1957).

In hora mortis. Gedichte (Salzburg: Otto Müller, 1958).

Frost. Roman (Frankfurt: Insel, 1963; Suhrkamp, 1972).

Amras. Erzählung (Frankfurt: Suhrkamp, 1965).

Prosa (Frankfurt: Suhrkamp, 1965).

Ein Fest für Boris. Stück (Frankfurt: Suhrkamp, 1968).

Ungenach. Erzählung (Frankfurt: Suhrkamp, 1968).

Ereignisse (Berlin: Literarisches Colloquium, 1969).

An der Baumgrenze (Salzburg: Residenz, 1969).

Watten. Ein Nachlaß (Frankfurt: Suhrkamp, 1969).

Verstörung. Roman (Frankfurt: Suhrkamp, 1970).

Das Kalkwerk. Roman (Frankfurt: Suhrkamp, 1970).

Der Italiener. Eine Filmgeschichte (Salzburg: Residenz, 1971).

Midland in Stilfs. Drei Erzählungen (Frankfurt: Suhrkamp, 1971).

Gehen (Frankfurt: Suhrkamp, 1971).

Der Ignorant und der Wahnsinnige. Stück (Frankfurt: Suhrkamp, 1972).

Die Jagdgesellschaft. Stück (Frankfurt: Suhrkamp, 1974).

Die Macht der Gewohnheit. Stück (Frankfurt: Suhrkamp, 1974).

Korrektur. Roman (Frankfurt: Suhrkamp, 1975).

Der Präsident. Stück (Frankfurt: Suhrkamp, 1975).

Die Ursache. Eine Andeutung (Salzburg: Residenz, 1975).

Die Berühmten (Frankfurt: Suhrkamp, 1975).

Der Kulterer: eine Filmgeschichte (Frankfurt: Suhrkamp, 1976).

Der Keller. Eine Entziehung (Salzburg: Residenz, 1976).

Minetti (Frankfurt: Suhrkamp, 1977).

Der Atem. Eine Entscheidung (Salzburg: Residenz, 1978).

Der Stimmenimitator (Salzburg: Residenz, 1978).

Ja (Frankfurt: Suhrkamp, 1978).

Immanuel Kant. Komödie (Frankfurt: Suhrkamp, 1978).

Die Erzählungen (Frankfurt: Suhrkamp, 1979).

Vor dem Ruhestand: eine Komödie von deutscher Seele (Frankfurt: Suhrkamp, 1979).

Der Weltverbesserer (Frankfurt: Suhrkamp, 1979).

Die Billigesser (Frankfurt: Suhrkamp, 1980).

Spectaculum 32: fünf moderne Theaterstücke (Berlin: Suhrkamp, 1980).

Die Kälte. Eine Isolation (Salzburg: Residenz, 1981).

Über allen Gipfeln ist Ruh: ein deutscher Dichtertag um 1980: Komödie (Frank-

furt: Suhrkamp, 1981).
Am Ziel (Frankfurt: Suhrkamp, 1981).
Ave Vergil (Frankfurt: Suhrkamp, 1981).
Beton (Frankfurt: Suhrkamp, 1982).
Das Kind (Salzburg: Residenz, 1982).

Thomas Bernhard Works in English Translation

Gargoyles (*Verstörung*), translated by Richard and Clara Winston (New York: Knopf, 1970).
The Lime Works (*Das Kalkwerk*), translated by Sophie Wilkins (New York: Knopf, 1973).
The Force of Habit, Comedy (*Die Macht der Gewohnheit*), translated by Neville and Stephen Plaice (London: Heinemann Educational for the National Theatre, 1976).
Correction (*Korrektur*), translated by Sophie Wilkins (New York: Knopf, 1979).
The President (*Der Präsident*) and *Eve of Retirement* (Vor dem Ruhestand): Plays and Other Writings, translated by Gitta Honegger (New York: Performing Arts Journal Publications, 1982).
Concrete (*Beton*), translated by David McLintock (New York: Knopf, 1984).

Secondary Works in German

Über Thomas Bernhard, edited by Anneliese Botond (Frankfurt: Suhrkamp, 1970).
Bernhard Sorg, *Thomas Bernhard* (Frankfurt: Suhrkamp, 1977).
Herbert Gamper, *Thomas Bernhard* (München: Deutscher Taschenbuchverlag, 1977).
Special Thomas Bernhard Issue of *Text und Kritik,* Vol. 43 (July 1974).
Special Thomas Bernhard Issue of *Österreich in Geschichte und Literatur,* Vol. 4 (1979).

Secondary Works in English

D. A. Craig, "The Novels of Thomas Bernhard—a Report," in *German Life and Letters,* Vol. 25, No. 4 (1972), 343-353.

A. P. Dierick, "Thomas Bernhard's Austrian Neurosis: Symbol or Expedient?" in *Modern Austrian Literature*, Vol. 12, No. 1 (1979), 73-93.

Hans Wolfschütz, "Thomas Bernhard: The Mask of Death," in *Modern Austrian Writing. Literature and Society after 1945*, ed. by A. Best and H. Wolfschütz (London: Wolf; Totowa, N.J.: Barnes and Noble, 1980), pp. 214-235.

Noel L. Thomas, "The Structure of a Nightmare. Autobiography and Art in Thomas Bernhard's 'Der Keller,'" in *Quinquereme*, Vol. 6 (1983), 155-166.

D. L. McLintock, "Tense and Narrative Perspective in Two Works of Thomas Bernhard," in *Oxford German Studies*, 11 (1980), 1-26.

Charles A. Carpenter, "The Plays of Bernhard, Bauer and Handke. A List of Major Critical Studies," in *Modern Drama*, Vol. 23, No. 4 (January 1981), 484-491.

Joseph A. Federico, "Millenarianism, Legitimation, and the National Socialist Universe in Thomas Bernhard's 'Vor dem Ruhestand,'" in *Germanic Review*, Vol. 59, No. 4 (1984), 142-148.

Gerald A. Fetz, "The Works of Thomas Bernhard: 'Austrian Literature?'" in *Modern Austrian Literature*, Vol. 17, Nos. 3/4 (1984), 171-192.

John Updike, "Thomas Bernhard's 'Concrete,'" in *The New Yorker* (February 4, 1985), 97-101.

Robert F. Gross, Jr., "'The Greatest Uncertainty': The Perils of Performance in Thomas Bernhard's 'Der Ignorant und der Wahnsinnige,'" in *Modern Drama*, Vol. 21, No. 4 (January 1981), 385-392.

Francis M. Sharp, "Literature as Self-Reflection: Thomas Bernhard and Peter Handke," in *World Literature Today*, Vol. 55, No. 4 (Autumn 1981), 603-607.

Kathleen Thorpe, "The Autobiographical Works of Thomas Bernhard," in *Acta Germanica*, Vol. 13 (1980), 189-200.

Martin Esslin, "A Drama of Disease and Derision. The Plays of Thomas Bernhard," in *Modern Drama*, Vol. 23, No. 4 (January 1981), 367-384.

Robert Godwin-Jones, "The Terrible Idyll: Thomas Bernhard's 'Das Kalkwerk,'" in *Germanic Notes*, Vol. 13, No. 1 (1982), 8-10.

Gitta Honegger, "Wittgenstein's Children. The Writings of Thomas Bernhard," in *Theater*, Vol. 15, No. 1 (Winter 1983), 58-67.

Elias Canetti—Poet and Intellectual

Dagmar Barnouw

Canetti, Susan Sontag writes, "is both literally and by his own ambitions, a writer in exile."[1] Her recent enthusiastic review essay in the *New York Review of Books* is very welcome, because it provides a forceful introduction to an important European writer whose impact in this country has been very slight so far. Like many observations in her essay, however, her stylization of Canetti as a writer in exile is misleading. Canetti has been difficult to place, and partly for this reason recognition of his importance has come late; but he has not been subjected to the profound disruption of language and culture that exile has meant for so many writers. When he left Vienna in 1938 for London, where he has lived and written in German ever since, he went in a sense back to a language and a culture that had been important to him in his youth. He was born in Rustschuk, Bulgaria in 1905 into a large and lively sephardic family of merchants, who spoke Ladino, but from an early age he was very much aware of other languages spoken around him in his town of many nationalities. Preparing the child for the move to England in 1911 (to escape the tyrannical presence of his grandfather), his beloved and completely trusted father told the little boy: "In England everybody is honest . . . if a man promises you something, he will do it, there is no need for him to shake hands on it."[2] The child, then, is promised a different usage of language, of the speech-act: language is no longer separated from action: rather, it serves to communicate and influence action.

England, even though he lived there for only two years, proved to be extraordinarily important for the child, because he started going to school and he learned to read. In England began the lifelong process of taking possession of the many worlds accessible in books, mediated by teachers. Canetti has been emphatically grateful to both, receiving what they had to give with a passionate urgent curiosity. Learning meant a concrete immersion, a feeling of physical involvement in the world between the covers of the book. The theme of transformation central to all his texts can be traced back to the child's somatic sense of changing: becoming smaller to fit himself between the bookcovers and into the pictures illustrating the stories and larger, more powerful, according to the expansive properties of the stories themselves.

England, as Canetti writes in the first volume of his autobiography *Die gerettete Zunge* (1977, *The Tongue Set Free*) is the country associated for him with books and with talking about them, sharing them, with the father's gentle reasoning. When he says that everything that he experienced later had already happened in Rustschuk, he is referring to the archetypical constellation of social relations, of passions and power, envy and desire, as the sensitive imaginative child observed them in the volatility and explosion of tempers in his family. Rustschuk was also particularly fascinating for its variety of sounds—one could hear eight different languages in one day, Canetti remembers—of tastes, smells, and images. The isolating reality of power, the immediacy of human diversity, the magically spontaneous interconnections of language were experienced by the child early and with surprising involvement. In England those frightening magical speech-acts receded; there language was not used mainly to manipulate and dominate, but to explore, to share, to gain access. Yet, like bad magic, a curse uttered by the grandfather punishing the disobedience of his son follows the small family to England: in October 1912, hardly settled in their new surroundings, his father dies suddenly of heart failure, caused, so his mother tells the children, by news about another crisis in the Balkans, signaling war that he dreaded and hated. The child had just been given a book about Napoleon with the admonition to read it "the right way," that is, critically; there had been no time to discuss it with his father: "Of all of Napoleon's victims, my father to me was the greatest, the most horrible,"[3] Canetti writes, remembering this traumatic event that proved to be of central importance for the direction of his work.

Having just gained a sense of language—English—as an opening, sharing activity, the boy was taken out of this nurturing environment by his mother, forced to learn German quickly during some months they spent in Lausanne, sufficiently well to survive in a school in Vienna where the mother had decided to live. The father's death had caused a deep-rooted hatred of destructive power in the child, affirmed by the mother's consistent and highly articulate denunciation of war, and the misuse of language was intimately connected with this complex of emotional and intellectual reactions. In Bulgaria the parents had spoken German as *their* language, reminding them of the happy time they had spent together in Vienna, constituting the realm of their privacy and intimacy, inaccessible to the demands of a complex intense family and a tyrannical patriarch, his grandfather, who had imposed a deeply resented business career on Canetti's father. When his mother now forces the boy to learn the language at any cost—and she comes across as a brilliant and remarkably cruel teacher— she also admits him to that intellectual and emotional intimacy and privacy so coveted by the child. It is not, as some critics have remarked, a magic concept of language with which the child operates; it is, rather, a surprisingly rational, social one: language, once more, is understood by the child as a supremely human activity in that it facilitates social intercourse, makes possible access to the other. The child is not interested in building his own worlds with language: from a very early age Canetti has been intent on understanding the world of the other and has seen himself, the needs of his own growing and developing self, in terms of the needs of the other.

In 1916 his mother moves her sons to Zürich. The boy is deeply impressed by a country that has managed to stave off the tidal waves of irrationality that he had seen overwhelming the crowds in the streets of Vienna at the outbreak of the war. Zürich was a paradise for the adolescent; he was left alone and given the peace and space to develop, to learn. From 1921 to 1924 he lived and went to school in Frankfurt because his mother thought the situation in Zürich too idyllic, too protected. He never forgot or forgave this violation, but he realized that what he saw and heard during this time of inflation, of mass unemployment and starvation, became, like his father's early inexplicable death, the major material force directing his work. From 1924 he lived mainly in Vienna, interrupted by visits to Berlin in 1928 and 1929. There he came into contact with artists like George Grosz and Isaak Babel and the influential leftist publishing house Malik for which he translated several of Upton Sinclair's novels. In 1929 he completed his studies with a dissertation in chemistry but decided to devote himself to writing henceforth.

In England where he arrived in January 1939, he continued to write in German, and the relative isolation—in terms of an audience—in which he worked did not differ from the situation in Vienna. He had a small circle of friends, admirers of his work,[4] and English was not really a foreign language to him. After the war he chose to stay in England, and he explained his decision to go on writing in German:

> The language of my mind will continue to be German, because I am Jewish. Whatever remains of that country, ravaged in every sense, I will protect in myself as a Jew. It is also *their* fate that is mine; but I bear a universal human inheritance. I want to give back to their language what I owe to it. I want my contribution to add to the reason for being grateful to them for something once again.[5]

Given the long period of time during which he did not publish anything, this certainty that he would find readers, that his "contribution" would be recognized, that his texts would indeed add to the reason for being "grateful" to the German language and German culture, is remarkable. Working on the social psychological analysis of power and crowds, he sees himself in a tradition of successful poetic communication. He had been sure of the importance of that activity as well as of his share in it from an early age: the fourteen-year-old dedicated a long badly written drama to his mother who "loved the poets" and considered reading the center of her life, signing it "in spe poeta clarus"; and with characteristic tenacity, passion, and patience he was to become just that. Poetic language for Canetti does not signify the writer's inevitable existence in exile, as it did for Walter Benjamin. It means, rather, a complex of intellectual, imaginative verbal energies distinguished from ordinary discourse, yet also connected with it, dependent on it and of very great importance to it. Canetti's trust in the concrete effectiveness of poetic language is as anachronistic (unzeitgemäß), as is his belief in the social responsibility of the poet,[6] especially as it is combined with his demand that poetic language be accessible, that it be willing to accommodate questions. Poetic language for him is emphatically not a privileged medium and yet central to all cultural and social activities. The reasons for this enlightened belief in the essential communicability of human affairs, mental and physical, in the importance of the rational dimension of social intercourse in any form, for this amazing abstinence from ideology in any shade or substance seems to be related to his early exposure to many different languages, cultures, and temperaments, a circumstance that saved him from ever feeling like an exile. In collaboration with his mother, for he almost always collaborated with her even when she seemed most forceful and tyrannical, even cruel, because she offered him reasons, he *chose* German as his language and never forgot the act of choosing nor the implications of this act: language, communication is a man-made achievement, not an a priori given, magically sustained phenomenon.

Canetti's precise and intense involvement with three languages — the Ladino spoken in his family, English and German — corresponds to the *locus* of his writing; between the conventional literary genres as well as between different fields in the social sciences. By the late thirties he had become known to a small important and influential circle of writers, critics, and poets in Vienna and in Berlin.[7] His first and only novel *Die Blendung*[8] (*Auto-da-Fé*) published in 1935 but completed in the fall of 1931, is an interesting counterpart to Heinrich Mann's *Der Untertan* (written in 1914 but not published until after the war had ended) in its "prophetic" extrapolation from existing aggressive verbal and nonverbal behavior. By looking at available evidence Mann anticipated the language of survival as it was used during the war; Canetti anticipated the language of total repression as it was to be used under Hitler's totalitarian regime.

The main difference between these novels, which are strikingly similar in essential ways, for instance, in the handling of speech patterns in the fictional constructs of a social reality, lies in their reception: Mann's novel found many enthusiastic readers, whose response signaled a hoped-for cultural rebirth at the beginning of the Weimar Republic.[9] Canetti's novel, harsher, more extreme, and also more ambivalent in its indictment of his contemporaries, that is, Hitler's audience, than Mann's had been of the Emperor's subjects, came too late and too early to be effective. After the war *Die Blendung* returned to Germany via England and France where the response had been enthusiastic from small well-informed audiences.[10]

The novel and two early dramas written about the same time, *Die Hochzeit* (1932, The Wedding) and *Komödie der Eitelkeit* (1934, Comedy of Vanity)[11] record a confusing variety of what Canetti calls "acoustic masks," a character's speech habits that outline his individual functions and interactions in a group as distinctly as would a visual mask. Demands on the concentration of the reader/listener/spectator are high and exhausting. Canetti, who considers himself to be essentially a dramatist in all of his writings, developed the concept of the acoustic mask under the influence of Karl Kraus, the Viennese social and literary critic, writer of aphorisms, philosopher of language, poet, and journalist. For almost forty years (1899-1936) Kraus singlehandedly edited and from 1912 wrote *Die Fackel* (The Torch), the highly influential journal against what Kraus called "Journaille," a corrupted press that reflected and reinforced the general social verbal hypocrisy and physical cruelty. Above all he wanted his readers to doubt the official interpretation of their social reality, the conventions of language. Taking language "at its word," his judgments implicit in the "acoustic quotations," as Canetti calls them,[12] whether recorded in *Die Fackel* or flung out to the audiences crowding his immensely popular lectures, were irresistibly right: the world in which we live is seething with stupidity, greed, and cruelty and so is the corrupted language of daily life: "The fact that somebody is a murderer need not be proof against his [verbal] style. But his style may prove that he is a murderer," Kraus writes in his *Fackel* (October 1907). His anger made him expose the mechanics of a language of a social, indeed, criminal respectability; his compassion, literally fierce, mediated between despair and shame. In the unremittingly precise recording of its persecutor's "acoustic mask" the victim preserves his own painful individuality.

Canetti, who chose the title *Die Fackel im Ohr* (1980, The Torch in My Ear) for the second volume of his autobiography dealing with the ten years, 1921-1931, that he spent in Vienna, was particularly impressed by Kraus's adamant stance against war. He had started going to Kraus's lectures in 1924 and very quickly became an addict to these consummate performances of the "master of horror" using his weapon of "literalness" with deadly precision, putting contemporary language on a trial such as it could not possibly survive. Many years later when writing about his complex (but not ambivalent) relations to Kraus,[13] Canetti said that the horror of the atomic bomb was already contained in Kraus's satirical pandemonium of voices, of acoustic masks, with which he constructed a model of what very soon afterward presented itself to the incredulous gullible world as the Third Reich. From Kraus, Canetti learned the feeling of unrelieved social responsibility, bordering on obsession, and he learned to listen. From now on the voices of reality would pursue him; like Kraus he would never be set free again. The novel *Die Blendung* brings them to full expression, a virtuoso performance subjecting the reader to the relentless persecution by the monotonous, powerfully inarticulate acoustic masks of the housekeeper Therese and the janitor Pfaff, who destroy those around them with their material greed and raw urge for power. Indeed, the novel and the two early dramas are the most persuasive witnesses to the effectiveness of Kraus's methods of literalness (*Wörtlichkeit*). But more and more Canetti comes to see that the limitations of this most impressive of teachers lie precisely in his illuminating aggressive concentration on the sentence: the exposed subhuman imperfection of the quote, the inhuman perfection of the comment. Canetti explains the ultimately dangerous exclusiveness of Kraus's method by describing how his sentences form a "Chinese wall,"[14] a perfectly closed structure that has by its very perfection sapped the empire it was meant to defend: "For the ashlars he used for building were *judgments,* and all that had been alive in the area around there had entered into them."[15]

His mother, whose emotional and intellectual influence cannot be overestimated—the first volume of the autobiography, *Die gerettete Zunge: Geschichte einer Jugend* (*The Tongue Set Free: Remembrance of a European Childhood*), makes this abundantly clear—had directed him with judgments. He had admired their clarity and decisiveness and above all the fact that she always gave him a reason. So of course did Kraus. Given the profound influence and, for a time, response of absolute devotion, Canetti's recognition of the essential insufficiency of any judgment had far-reaching consequences.

Increasingly Kafka's influence asserted itself; along with Kraus he is the most important writer for Canetti. Canetti writes: "Many years after the influence had become effective with Kafka something new had come into this world, a more precise feeling for the fact that it is questionable, which is, however, not coupled with hatred but with reverence for life. The interaction between these two intellectual and emotional attitudes—reverence for something that has been recognized as questionable – is unique, and once one has come to know it, one is unwilling ever to do without it again."[16] That Canetti retained this feeling is documented by all the texts published since *Die Blendung: Masse und Macht* (1960, *Crowds and Power*), the study of sociopsychological, philosophical, anthropological phenomena concerning the relations between crowds and power in the magnetic field of death; the drama *Die Befristeten* (1964, The Deadlined), aphoristic notes, collected in the volume *Die Provinz des Menschen* (1973, *The Human Province*), toward an open moral "system" set against the acceptance of death and as notations of intellectual poetic spontaneity meant to alleviate the sustained work discipline of *Masse und Macht*, decades in the making. There are also the gentle exposures of impotence, of children, of the poor, and of animals in the prose texts responding to travel experiences in Morocco *Die Stimmen von Marrakesch* (1968, *The Voices of Marrakesh*).

The book-length essay on Kafka's correspondence with Felice Bauer *Der andere Prozeß* (1968, *The Other Trial*) demonstrates through Kafka's superbly sensitive awareness of his own as of the other's life-center – the symbiosis of power and impotence – the fragmentary nature of human relationships too vulnerable to survive judgments and inflicted sentences. There are essays dealing with social and psychological aspects of all-powerful regimes and their attempts at total repression or destruction: on Albert Speer's memoirs, on an eyewitness to the apocalyptic explosion of the atomic bomb. A recent collection *Der Ohrenzeuge* (1974, *Earwitness: Fifty Characters*) goes back to acoustic masks from the world of *Die Blendung* with an added dimension of surreal ordinariness. Finally, there are the first three volumes of his autobiography,[17] which reveal the destructive (because limiting) properties of judgments, documenting Canetti's patient and passionate fascination for all the diverse forms of human life around him: everybody should be remembered, nobody should be excluded.

Canetti did not take too seriously the oft-noted "prophetic" quality of *Die Blendung*. "The prophets, lamenting, prophesy the known," he noted in 1945.[18] *Die Blendung*, referring to the burning of a scholar's magnificent library – the sinologist Peter Kien himself is the incendiary, having gone mad with intellectual and social isolation – is as much in anticipation of the burning of books ordered by Goebbels and carried out by enthusiastic university students in 1933 as it is reminiscent of the great burning of books in ancient China in the year 213 B.C. It was possible to predict such events by recording the voices of Viennese reality in the mode of Kraus, mastering horror and literalness. "My uncanny power was in chaos," Canetti notes in 1945. "I was as certain of that as I was of the world. Today even chaos has exploded. No structure was so senseless that it could not disintegrate into something even more senseless, and wherever I sniff, everything is heavy with the smell of extinguished fires." [19]

Chaos had been too safe in its brilliantly perfected presentation in the novel and the early dramas. The later work is set against chaos, its imagery simplified and purified, abandoning his earlier fascination for mimesis, the ultimately isolating mock surrender to the real. The differences between various voices have become more subtle, the nuances of the play with idioms and intonations more delicate. Yet these are voices recorded in many different places and periods of history, and in many different modes including the mythical. It is this greater restraint and subtlety that enabled Canetti to find meaning in speaking about contemporary totalitarian execution of power. Kraus had been permanently silenced by the "onset of hell" that he recognized very early in Hitler's regime. A poem published in the only issue of *Die Fackel* published in 1933 (October) "Man frage nicht" ("Don't Ask Me") ends with the well-known line: "Das Wort entschlief, als jene Welt erwachte" ("the word went to sleep when that world awoke"). One of the few antifascist writers who did not react violently to Kraus's remark, "Zu Hitler fällt mir nichts ein" ("I can't think of anything to say about Hitler") was Brecht, who understood that Kraus had been wise not to ask too much of satirical language. Brecht in his best works shared Kraus's method of capturing the weaknesses and the vices of men "in den Schlingen ihrer Redensarten" ("in the snares of their speech"); and he admired Kraus precisely for those acts of aggression that Canetti came to see as futile: "Als das Zeitalter Hand an sich legte, war er [Kraus] diese Hand" ("When the epoch laid its hand on itself, he was this hand.") [20]

In an issue of *Die Fackel* in July 1934 Kraus had admitted: "The great theme of the onset of hell is too much for the passionate cowardice of him whose work had been done in vain: to talk of the devil." [21] Even the most severe, the most ingenious cross-examination of language had not disclosed what a totalitarian regime in a terrorized mass society was capable of. It is not within the satirist's imagination to find possible solutions or to foresee that the impossible would indeed happen. Kraus's achievement was to reveal the impossibility of "solutions," of social conventions that had been accepted as possible. Greatly indebted to him, Canetti went further. He stopped writing fiction, that is, imposing an interpretation before he had understood what had happened. In the preface to the first edition of *Aufzeichnungen 1942-1948* (Notes 1942-1948), which were not published until 1965, he states that in order to force himself not to turn away from "the naked world" for even one moment, he started to collect as much information as he possibly could about the different ways in which men had lived together and had explained their attempts at coexistence. His appetite for information was indeed ferocious, and he developed a very flexible concept of history – "I would give a great deal to get rid of my habit of seeing the world historically," he noted in 1950, two years after he had started writing *Masse und Macht*.[22] History like fiction was too much of a construct, an imposed interpretation suppressing other social possibilities. In his *Aufzeichnungen* he therefore recorded sketches of utopian social arrangements or conventions based on taking literally certain social problems that we have agreed to take for granted, above all the determination of human beings through rationed time and through the acceptance of death: cities in which men are born old and get younger, where they live as long as they are loved, where they have at least two ages simultaneously, for instance 19 and 57, where everybody disappears for periods of time so that nobody can be taken for granted alive or in death, where religion does not console but sustains an ever acute despair about the human condition, that is, consciousness of the passing of time and the imposition of destructive changes that are as inevitable as they are alien, as accidental as they are programmed.

The more Canetti experienced death as omnipresent during the war, the more he began to doubt its "natural law." Freud had developed his concept of a "Todestrieb," *thanatos,* under the impact of witnessing so much dying during the First World War, which he had opposed from the very beginning. Accordingly, Canetti feels he had to protest all the harder. "With one problem which is the most important to me, the problem of death, I have found only opponents among all thinkers. That may explain why my own opinion comes forward with the energy of belief and never declares itself without vehemence and eagerness," he states in the preface to *Die Provinz des Menschen.*[23] He is puzzled that he alone seems to question what appears to him so eminently questionable: "The incomprehensible accepted by everyone as if it contained a secret justification."[24] It cannot, it does not. To the analytic philosopher, relegating death to metaphysics, Canetti points out that death is the oldest fact, "older and more incisive than any language";[25] the human sciences, on the other hand, have abstracted the concrete social problem of death into a natural law as it poses such difficulties. And death is always seen as an absolute, by definition outside life, removed from considerations like fairness, function, proportion. But it is precisely these considerations that Canetti wants appreciated, and he startles the reader with his consistent common sense. What he says about the acceptance of death makes sense in that it refers to a shared experience. Yet, strangely, the making sense itself seems the most startling, the calm assertion of the obvious the most provoking. Life is too short to accommodate all there is to know about potential, constructive change, about motion and surprise that is essentially human: "Who will give me the news when I no longer am, who will tell me?" Canetti asks.[26] He refuses to be excluded from the human future, and it is not so much the futility of such refusal that makes it so poignant, but its justification. If there is so much to know, so many worlds to enter, why should anyone be excluded?: "Death would not be so unjust if it were not *fated in advance.* Each of us, even the most evil, can claim the excuse that whatever he does never comes close to the badness of this predetermined sentence. We must be evil (*böse*) because we know that we shall die. We would be even more evil (*böser*) if we knew from the beginning when," Canetti writes in 1952, the year he completed the drama *Die Befristeten* (1964, The Deadlined).[27] Those scheduled for death in this play are for this very reason more evil, more distorted than the most grotesque characters from the early dramas or *Die Blendung.* Their surface normalcy, their calm, dulled voices are functionally deceptive: we have to identify with them so that we can then decide that we shall be different.

It is the shifting of differences and similarities, the merging, the diverging of the familiar and the alien that informs Canetti's texts after *Die Blendung.* For many years he did not "write," at least not in any form that would contain and solidify such fluidity. With amazing patience—friends and acquaintances in London remarked on its quixotic substance[28]—he collected information that eventually went into *Masse und Macht,* remaining true to his concept of human time: if he did not actually *have* the time to let the riches of information and insight accumulate, he ought to take it. All he permitted himself to write then were the *Aufzeichnungen,* spontaneous notations of his perception of social reality, his subjunctive mode of existence sustained in the remarkably self-reliant, as it were, natural assertion of each sentence: "His image of happiness: to read and write quietly a whole life long, without ever showing anybody one word of it, without ever publishing one word of it. Everything he has noted for himself is to be left in pencil, not to be worked on, as if it were not there for anything particular; like the natural course of a life that does not serve any limiting purpose but is fully itself and traces itself the way one walks and breathes: spontaneously."[29]

This perspective helps to explain the curiously open quality of Canetti's language, which is accessible to the reader and accommodating to thoughts, images, phenomena, and other voices. The speaker admits to being wary of the incisiveness of critical thought, the separation, the shock almost: "One sees thoughts stretching their hands out of the water, one thinks they are crying for help. What an illusion! Down below they live in perfect agreement and intimacy. Try it and pull out a single thought!"[30] It is rather the connections, the bringing together of the disparate, that Canetti concentrates on in his post-war texts. At the same time he insists on clarity and rational access: thoughts living together in undisturbed intimacy are also clearly defined individual articulations; interacting thoughts must not become "matted." The concentration on small units in perception and expression practiced in the *Aufzeichnungen* proves very useful to the writing of *Masse und Macht*. The complexity of the self, reflected in experience, is preserved in these small units of articulation that are not so powerful as to force it into any manipulable pattern. It can then be preserved as something growing, not completed: "The important part of each thought is what it leaves unsaid, how much it loves what has not been said, and how close it comes to it without touching it."[31]

The tentative movements of thoughts, the open but carefully organized verbal complexes in which the abstract and the concrete merge, the exploration of images shared, accessible in idiomatic speech, defy the construction of a system but not a consistent search for order, a clearly articulated emphasis on values. "Rarely has anyone been so at home in the mind, with so little ambivalence," Sontag writes,[32] trying to illuminate Canetti's peculiar achievement. In the contemporary intellectual context of cultural despair it is important to stress Canetti's passionate fascination with the potential of the human mind. But in order to understand the mixed nature of his texts and their surface directness, the writer's roaming curiosity *and* undogmatic insistence on selecting that which is useful to know, it is also important to point out that this fascination is nurtured by the achievement of others before him. It is precisely because others were so at home in the mind, trusting the potential of intellect and imagination, that Canetti, writing as our contemporary, can do without ambivalence.

Canetti's concept of the crowd, its power and its mystery, is based on intense personal experience, as are all his social concepts. He witnessed his first great demonstration on the occasion of Rathenau's assassination in 1922. In his autobiography dealing with the twenties, he mentions the very strong physical attraction exercised by the crowd on the individual (his) body, like gravitation, but also different in the sense that the bodies pulled into the crowd are not lifeless and therefore unchanged but undergo a complete change of consciousness. It was this change Canetti found as decisive as mysterious a phenomenon: "It was a mystery which has never released me, pursuing me for the best part of my life, and though I finally did find some clues, much has remained mysterious," he writes from the distance of almost sixty years.[33] The decision to write a book about the phenomenon of crowd behavior crystallized in 1925 in reaction to reading Freud's "Massenpsychologie und Ich-Analyse," a text by which he was repelled at first reading and still is today, fifty-five years later, because its author was not so much interested in understanding the dynamics of the crowd as in keeping it at a distance. What Freud's analysis lacked was recognition of a phenomenon which to Canetti seemed no less elemental than libido or hunger. To stress the fundamental aspect of the crowd, its dynamics and energies, the young Canetti used the term "Massentrieb" (drive of the masses), which he regarded as important as the sexual drive.[34]

In July 1927 the Vienna Palace of Justice was burned, an experience that proved to be highly important to the witness Canetti. The violent motions of flames and bodies merge: the fire assumes the properties of the crowd, the crowd spreads like fire. Distinct against the leaping flames and the convulsive body of the crowd Canetti sees a man flinging up his arms, lamenting the burning of all the files: "'But they've shot down people,' I said angrily, 'and you're talking about files!' He looked at me as if I wasn't there and repeated plaintively: 'The files are burning! All the files!'"[35] This memory went into the book-burning scene in *Die Blendung:* The incendiary, Peter Kien, a highly respected sinologist, is driven to this act of self-destruction by his petty-bourgeois persecutors, because in his scholarly isolation he accepts the destruction of others; his books are closer to him than human beings. His brother Georges, a very successful psychiatrist, had come to save him from his tormentors and had succeeded in restoring Peter's library damaged by their greed. He also chased away the predatory housekeeper Therese and the janitor Pfaff. Finally he suggested to his brother, whose illness he does not really understand although he seems to be able to control it, the idea and the image of magnificent self-consuming destruction: the fire and the crowd. Peter had been complaining about his isolation, which takes the form of a very grave but not exclusively neurotic misogyny. Georges, seeing only individual rather than social illness, approaches the problem by trying to persuade Peter that love is an obstacle to efficient work. Consider the termites, he says; most of them have been freed from sexual drives because such drives would cause too many disturbances in a very crowded society. But then he projects what might happen if the individual termites, blind cells in an organism beyond their grasp, rebelled against such limitation. In describing the rebellion, spreading like fire, destroying the whole colony, he gets carried away, creating images of passionate energy for such self-destruction that prove much more persuasive than his admonition to his brother to be reasonable and accept certain necessary limitations. The termites are victims of a grandiose delusion comparable to Peter's setting fire to his own library. Georges professes to an ever stronger belief in science, the rationality of the termite colony in its normal state, but the incendiary power of his rhapsodic description of the erupting crowd—like fire—moves Peter to act.

Georges, the psychiatrist, lives among the mad, is loved by them, needs their love. Rather than healing them, he tries to understand them, that is, to lose himself in their madness, which he diagnoses as the crowd within them that does not find satiation.[36] On the basis of Georges's comments the Austrian Marxist, Ernst Fischer, who knew Canetti in Vienna, criticized his concept of the individual's victory over and against death by immersion and dissolution of the self in the mass, the crowd, a totality. However, Canetti is not Georges, and he is not Peter. He shares characteristics with both brothers, but he is distinctly critical of them. He is fascinated by crowds and increasingly searches for documentation in cultural and political history—for instance, in the geneses of religious movements where crowds have often played a highly important part. He does not, however, suggest the collective of the crowd as a refuge or remedy for the threatened individual in a mass society. He is interested in analysis, not in evaluation or justification.

Peter's self-immolation—he burns to death with his books—is the result of his and his brother's failure to act with social responsibility. Peter becomes guilty by completely withdrawing from the world of demented housekeepers and janitors desperately fighting for their share; Georges does so by manipulating the mentally ill. Both worlds are horrible *and* comical—Canetti mentioned Gogol's influence on *Die Blendung*[37]—and they document the immensely difficult coexistence of individuals in a mass society, caught in their differences, their inequality. The destructiveness of the petty bourgeois has its roots in his imperturbable isolation. His asocial acts show an aggressive potential which can be fully brought out in certain mass movements where, through crowd manipulation, his obsessive "me, me" can be whipped into collective orgasmic attacks on reasonable, civilized social conventions. Georges is unaware of this danger because he cannot imagine that he would ever be in a situation beyond his control. Peter becomes aware of it too late. It is only when his sensibility has been sharpened by illness that he understands how dangerous Pfaff really is. The acoustic masks of the housekeeper and of the janitor document above all their grotesque inarticulateness. Their specific distortions, their mental mutilations are taken seriously, but there is no attempt to explain them. They are closed off to each other, to the intellectuals Peter and Georges, and to the intellectual reader. They appear as typical examples of petty-bourgeois authoritarian repression, greed, and aggression, whose acts are predetermined. Yet the imaginative variations of their monomaniac, monotonous masks, which are recorded with such precision, give them exotic distinctness: they are as alien as they are familiar.

Isolation so extreme that the result is chaos: the early plays, *Die Hochzeit* (1932, The Wedding), and *Die Komödie der Eitelkeit* (1964, Comedy of Vanity), demonstrate chaos so effectively that they have had great difficulties with their audiences, still causing theatrical scandals in the 1960s. Canetti said that the dramatic element is central to all his texts: the recording of voices, making them heard.[38] He clearly sees a relation between the acoustic mask, the physiognomy of a speaker made up of his particular five hundred words, and the visual masks used in the early cult theater, as well as to the animal masks so important to "primitive" cultures. The concept dramatic means for Canetti the interplay of fixation and transformation. In *Die Hochzeit* the fixation is greed, people owning objects as well as one another; in *Die Komödie der Eitelkeit* it is the self carried to the extreme because of a curious kind of social prohibition: there are no mirrors allowed in this particular dystopian society. However, the mirror does mirror the self not only in relation to itself, but also in relation to the other. Deprived of the possibility of looking at oneself, to prepare oneself for being looked at by the other, to anticipate and to a degree to control such an instant of interaction, proves to be disastrous in that it solidifies isolation to the point of madness. The different acoustic masks in "concert" display variations and transformations of greed and self-mania, a cacophonous chorus, almost overwhelming in its chaotic diversity.

What did the eruptions of murderous aggression manipulated by demagogues haranguing a crowd with nationalistic racist rhetoric have in common with crowd behavior during socially justifiable demonstrations or strikes? It was not, as Canetti saw it, the relation between the crowd and a leader; there were other much more important mechanisms. In London Canetti set out to understand more about them. He learned about crowd behavior in seventeenth-century England from the historian Veronica Wedgwood (who was sufficiently fascinated by *Die Blendung* to take upon herself the immense labor of an excellent translation). He received stimulation and information from the social anthropologists Mary Douglas and Franz Baermann-Steiner; he was fascinated by Arthur Waley's erudition. "I will have to say, though, that especially during the English period it was experiences with books which became as important, sometimes more important than those with people," Canetti stated much later.[39] Above all, he mentions the importance of myths, "countless collections of myths." A critic interviewing him in his London study describes the room as "not filled with, but consisting of books." And there was not one question touched on in a long far-ranging conversation that Canetti did not have an answer for – and the reference to a book.[40]

The list of texts, of scholarly studies, sources, reports, and documents that Canetti read and used for *Masse und Macht* is very long and very varied. The book is striking in its openness to a large number of different voices based on an intellectual attitude of not taking anything for granted, of mistrusting categories: "One ought not be duped by other people's beliefs; and to the conclusions reached by extensive reading one ought to grant time and air to breathe," Canetti notes while working on *Masse und Macht*. He also remarked: "To be so alone as to overlook no one anymore, no one, nothing."[41] He wants to learn to understand myths as if he believed in them. It is of central importance to give the phenomenon one's undivided attention, to concentrate on the individual voice.

The result of such concentration is not, as one might expect, chaos but a specific kind of order based on a highly personal selective perspective, which could be called poetic. The fusion of anthropological, sociopsychological documents, observations, and insights with the poetic sense for the concreteness and literalness of the image, for the significant substance of the phenomenon puts *Masse und Macht* between literary genres and between different distinct social sciences. It also removes it from the influence and protection of ideological models. The long list of texts that were important to the making of Canetti's analysis does not include Marx or Freud. In an interview in 1972, when asked about his position toward Marx and Freud and about a possible collection of his own and Lévi-Strauss's approach to myths,[42] Canetti explains how he had tried to avoid a conceptual system. After having stuffed himself (*vollgestopft*) with the experience of phenomena, he had used a terminology that had developed during the course of the study, retaining as much as possible the concrete energy and vividness of the phenomenon. Canetti agrees fully with Lévi-Strauss's insistence on the cultural achievements of so-called primitive societies, but in his concentration on individual myths he differs sharply from Lévi-Strauss's comparatist categorization of myths, which he rejects as a compulsively collecting and speculating rather than as a meaningfully ordering activity. His own respect for the achievement of a particularly interesting myth made him develop a unique way of retelling it, thereby clarifying the conflict central to its conceptual grid and its imagery and justifying its exemplariness.

The concept of objectivity informing *Masse und Macht* does not deny the importance of the person who looks and listens – the author, the reader, the myth-makers, chroniclers, and observers of historical events. The first sentences in *Masse und Macht* deal with the primordial social fact of fear of physical contact.

There is no analysis of psychological mechanisms, rather the reader is told of, is shown concrete repellent energies creating spaces around bodies. The main characteristic of the crowd—for the observer Canetti—is the reversal of such fear, directing energies toward the dense unification of bodies. It is only in the dense mass of bodies, in the crowd, that physical fear of the other body is benumbed and the limits of the physical self seem lifted or at least expanded. The heavier the mass of bodies, the denser the shared body of the crowd, then the less substantial the weight, the less the burden of individuality. The perspective is that of a mobile narrator, as Canetti was, for example, in mixing with the crowd on that day in July 1927 when the Palace of Justice was burned. He formed part of the crowd, is fascinated, *and* he observes. He is partly immersed but retains some distance, recording the puzzling formations and motions of the crowd, its drive to grow and to attract more bodies and at the same time the futility of this drive visible in violent discharges, eruptions, and dispersions. He sees and explains the familiar phenomenon of crowd vandalism as a radical attack on all boundaries: "Windows and doors belong to the houses. They are the most vulnerable part of their exterior, and once they are smashed the house has lost its individuality: anyone may enter it and nothing and no one is protected anymore. In these houses live the supposed enemies of the crowd, those people who try to avoid it. What separated them has now been destroyed and nothing stands between them and the crowd. They can come out and join it, or they can be fetched."[43] The crowd's rush against limits, translated into physical borders, helps to approach the initially incomprehensible aggression enveloping the individual who is temporarily immersed in the crowd, his violent dash against a house that is of no (personal) importance to him, and his single-minded pursuit of people he has never seen or known before.

The first chapter offers particularly precise observations of concrete crowd behavior. The properties of the crowd, its rhythms of motion, its blockades, are related to the rhythm of one's own footsteps, the menace of the other's footfalls, also to the steady rhythmic motions of large herds of animals in flight, to ecstatic tribal war dances. There are also the invisible crowds described in accounts of visions occurring in myths and legends: in the vision of a Siberian shaman space is filled with the anxiety of naked human beings, clinging together in clusters, spirits swirling among them like snowflakes. Persian stories tell about crowds of demons moving against one another; the thirteenth-century historian Cäsarius von Heisterbach reports on the huge crowds of devils pressing hard on a sinful priest on his deathbed.

Canetti is interested in demonstrating that and showing how the myths dealing with crowds make meaningful statements about sociopsychological behavior. Systems of signs change historically, as do the relations between signifiers and the signified. As he includes the phylogenetic aspect in his concept of history, he is aware that the signified – the experience connecting crowds and power in the field of force determined by death – has changed very little, whereas the signifiers have changed dramatically as there exists a very complex, richly articulated social historical consciousness. Meaningful social activity has been documented through many centuries in the most various forms, and it is this variety and complexity, accessible, as Canetti believes, to the unprejudiced reader, that is the essentially human achievement: the ability to sustain and demonstrate transformation. Canetti disagrees with Lévi-Strauss's forceful archaeological exploration of myths and the reconstitution of their meaning: his is an ingenuity of the visible rather than the hidden, of observation rather than speculation. Where Lévi-Strauss deals with a confrontation of sense and nonsense, Canetti traces the changes, the developments of meaning, the metamorphosis of social conflict.

The social world as much as the physical world presents a challenge; it can be understood, and such understanding can be shared so that it can be questioned. Canetti's method is informed by that openness to the reader's questions and that desire to be as clear, as accessible as possible, that calm conviction that communication is possible and that language is a highly satisfying method, not so much in terms of scientific rigor and caution, but in terms of the curiosity directed toward the other, the fascination for the wonders of the (social) world. These wonders are not created by the self, though it does of course participate in them; but they are there to grasp, and it is the act of grasping that bestows significance and substance on the self. There is a curious mixture of assertiveness and modesty in Canetti's method of dealing with the past and of presenting documents of social behavior: assertiveness, because there is no question that they are worth our consideration, and modesty, because the worth is theirs and not the interpreter's.

The most important human metamorphoses refer to animals. In understanding man's ability to undergo transformation as centrally human, Canetti both establishes and erases a clear demarcation between animal and man: rather, he is fascinated by complexly organized transitions.[44] Consider his argument for the connection between metamorphosis and consciousness in the context of an analysis of a special sub-form of the crowd, the "Increase Pack" (Vermehrungsmeute).

Man's weakness lay in the smallness of his numbers. It is true that the animals dangerous to man often lived singly or in small groups as he did. Like them he was a beast of prey, though one that never wanted to be solitary. He may have lived in bands about the size of wolf-packs, but wolves were content with this and he was not. In the enormously long period of time during which he lived in small groups, he, as it were incorporated into himself *by transformations* all the animals he knew. It was through the development of transformation that he really became man; it was his specific gift and pleasure. In his early transformations into other animals he acted and danced many of the species which appeared in large numbers. The more perfect the representation of such creatures was, the intenser his awareness of their numbers. He felt what it was to be many, and each time was made conscious of his own isolation in small groups.[45]

Potential faculties are always developed in interaction with the other, in this case the animal, by metamorphosis. This basic social fact is as important in the earlier stages of human development as in the later much more complicated stages of mass societies and their difficulties in communicating, as Canetti deals with them in *Die Komödie der Eitelkeit*. Contemporary mass societies, classless, hierarchically structured, rapidly changing but in many areas of social organizations profoundly afraid of change, grant little space to the individual's and the group's need and potential for transformation because this threatens the precariously balanced multitude of rigid arrangements which makes up our highly complex social systems. In the chapter "Verwandlung" (Transformation), Canetti traces particularly distinct forms of transformation: metamorphosis — often connected with hysteria and mania — to escape the multiplication and consumption of self in the double figure of the totem, the experience of mass and transformation in delirium tremens, imitation and simulation, figure and mask, and finally the prohibitions on metamorphosis and the institution of slavery.

This chapter presents the argument that the advantage as well as the threat of metamorphosis were much more clearly present in the social consciousness of earlier periods — an example would be the reaction to mental illness. As is shown in the myths of Proteus, or of Peleus and Thetis, a sudden arrest of the process of transformation was understood as imprisonment, as becoming a prey. The totem is of special interest because it makes possible the selection of a specific metamorphosis, connected with the activated influence on the totem animal, the self, which can then be ordered to multiply.[46] Figure and mask accentuate processes of metamorphosis, but also its limits; for Canetti the figure shows the process *and* the result of metamorphosis, the mask only the final stage. In drama the mask can become a figure and then mediate between the audience and danger. If it remains unchallenged in its formal perfection – the fascination of the mask has its roots precisely here – then its limitations, rigidity, and determination set against temporal flux, the medium of exprience, will have a negative influence. Canetti's emphasis on the social importance of transformation is supported by his plea for social pluralism. His curiosity is directed neither to the finite nor to the infinite but to the ever-changing scene of social conventions and conflicts; the only measure he recognizes records relatively and proportionally.

Canetti's method of retracing complex social phenomena to their earlier simpler more obvious forms is even more striking and provocative in the case of the command: it is the command to flee emitted by the stronger animal threatening to kill the weaker one. In the second volume of his autobiography he remembers his mother giving orders to a maid and making a point of rewarding her with food for those tasks that were especially difficult for the highly pregnant woman. His mother was proud of the fact that she did more than she "had to" according to her contract with the maid and complained that she could do the work better herself. It had been generous of her to hire the maid at all in her condition. The maid of course was very well aware of this and showed her gratitude by trying especially hard to comply with all the orders of the mistress. This perfectly ordinary incident becomes in Canetti's clarifying presentation an archetypical constellation of repression. He does not explicitly judge his mother, although her method of dealing with people had been shown to be a source of disagreements between them. He demonstrates his own uneasiness in the vividly remembered, tense and awkward verbal and physical behavior of unequals toward each other. An order, whether giving or receiving it, leaves a sting in the mind and the body, a profound irritation to the social balance of the self.

This sting isolates the individual and destroys his autonomy; it can be resolved only in the experience of merging with the crowd where the command strikes everybody simultaneously. The phenomenon of the demagogic orator, exciting his listeners and thereby creating a crowd, has to be seen in this context. Hitler had understood this connection. The extraordinarily aggressive, regressively cruel slogans that nobody took seriously in *Mein Kampf* became effective as threatening commands as soon as they were shouted at large audiences, which could then become one huge body receiving them.

Like death the giving and receiving of commands is a social problem of central importance, and the peculiar effect of Canetti's method in *Masse und*

Macht, in his essays, in *Die Befristeten,* in his aphorisms, and in his autobio-graphical texts lies in the stunning concreteness sustained by his perspective, the urgent vivid obviousness of deeply flawed social conventions. Because impotence is so unbearable, so destructive to the individual, Canetti insists on paying attention to it. If he had his way, it would not be explained away so easily, nor would the really intolerable pain of annihilation by death. A strong pedagogical impulse has motivated his writing since the war, but what he has taught himself about social conflicts is well worth sharing and he knows how to share effectively: he does not lecture, he demonstrates.

Among the many sketches about social alternatives collected in the *Auf-zeichnungen* there are projections of *Umkehrungen* (reversals), of the giving/ receiving direction of commands: humble human beings before the thrones of animals; the poor are given the rich as a present; the gods on their knees, asking to be forgiven for having survived too many humans; the owner of a restaurant in the power of the hungry children of Marrakesh, whom he had always brushed off like flies. In *Masse und Macht* he quotes from an ancient Indian treatise on sacrifices: "For whatever food a man eats in this world, by that food he is eaten in the next world."[47] The original situation is reversed: the victim finds, kills, and eats his devourer. The sting cannot be removed.

Like Kafka, Canetti postpones the abstracting, simplifying, metaphorical ordering of a highly complex, diverse social reality. He confronts it literally, that is, somatically. It is bodies that he sees, hears, and feels; it is through his body that he does so. The "unrealistic" aspects of his statements on death, the singlemindedness of his search for evidence documenting the disastrous consequences of human inequality, his insistent denial that there are no "givens" in the realm of social intercourse have led some readers to overstress the "utopian" quality of his texts, his passion for the life of the mind. Canetti is not interested in projecting the impossible, in speculating about absolutes. It is not the best life he is after, nor a life without death. It is a better life for more people and to him this means a longer life, better chances, more time to develop the human potential through transformation. It is ultimately to accept more fully the responsibility for this potential.

Notes

1. Susan Sontag, "Mind As Passion," *The New York Review of Books,* Vol. XXVII, No. 14 (25 September 1980), 47-52. Sontag's essay is a collective review of the Canetti texts made available in English to date by

Seabury Press. Sontag does not seem to be aware of the large number of articles and books on Canetti published in Germany and Austria during the past decade. For detailed bibliographical information see Dagmar Barnouw, *Elias Canetti* (Stuttgart: Metzler, 1979) (Sammlung Metzler, Band 180), pp. 115-136. My references unless stated otherwise are to the German texts; the translations are my own.

2. Elias Canetti, *Die gerettete Zunge. Geschichte einer Jugend* (München: Hanser, [3] 1977), p. 50.

3. Ibid., p. 61.

4. See below, p. 120.

5. Elias Canetti, *Die Provinz des Menschen. Aufzeichnungen 1942-1972* (München: Hanser, 1973), p. 73.

6. See Canetti's essay, "Der Beruf des Dichters," in *Das Gewissen der Worte* (München: Hanser, [2] 1976), pp. 257-267.

7. See Elias Canetti, *Die Fackel im Ohr. Lebensgeschichte 1921-1931* (München: Hanser, 1980), p. 197 ff.

8. *Die Blendung* has been translated into many languages: into English: *Auto-da-Fé*, translated by C. V. Wedgwood (London: Jonathan Cape, 1946) and *The Tower of Babel*, translated by C. V. Wedgwood (New York: A. Knopf, 1947); into French: *La Tour de Babel*, translated by Paule Arhex (Paris: B. Arthaud, 1949).

9. Interview with Dagmar Barnouw in August 1978.

10. See Idris Parry, "Elias Canetti's Novel 'Die Blendung,'" in *Essays in German Literature* I, ed. F. Norman (University of London: Institute of Germanic Studies, 1965), pp. 145 ff.

11. The early dramas have not yet been translated into English.

12. Elias Canetti, "Karl Kraus, Schule des Widerstands," in *Das Gewissen der Worte* (München: Hanser, 1976), p. 41.

13. Ibid., p. 44.

14. *Die chinesische Mauer* is the title of volume III of selected texts from *Die Fackel* (Wien: August Langen, 1910).

15. Elias Canetti, "Karl Kraus, Schule des Widerstands," p. 47.

16. Elias Canetti, *Die Provinz des Menschen*, p. 306.

17. The third volume of Canetti's autobiography, *Das Augenspiel* (München: Hanser, 1985) has not yet been translated into English.

18. Elias Canetti, *Die Provinz des Menschen*, p. 80.

19. Ibid., p. 79.

20. Quoted in Werner Kraft, *Karl Kraus. Beiträge zum Verständnis seines*

Werkes (Salzburg: Müller Verlag, 1956), p. 13.

21. Karl Kraus, *Die Fackel XXXVI* (July 1934), No. 890-905, p. 33.
22. Elias Canetti, *Die Provinz des Menschen*, p. 159.
23. Ibid., p. 8.
24. Ibid., p. 291.
25. Ibid., p. 346.
26. Ibid., p. 305.
27. Ibid., p. 166.
28. See Iris Murdoch, "Mass, Might and Myth," *The Spectator*, 7 September 1962, pp. 337 f. Robert Neumann, *Ein leichtes Leben. Bericht über mich selbst und Zeitgenossen* (München: Desch, 1963).
29. Elias Canetti, *Provinz*, pp. 217 f.
30. Ibid., p. 10.
31. Ibid., p. 43.
32. Susan Sontag, "Mind as Passion," p. 52.
33. Elias Canetti, *Die Fackel im Ohr*, p. 94.
34. Ibid., p. 168 f.
35. Ibid., p. 275; see also pp. 276-282.
36. Elias Canetti, *Die Blendung*, p. 454.
37. See Manfred Durzak, *Gespräche über den Roman. Formbestimmungen und Analysen* (Frankfurt: Suhrkamp, 1976), p. 95.
38. Elias Canetti, *Die gerettete Zunge*, p. 101.
39. Letter to Dagmar Barnouw, 10 June 1978.
40. Joachim Schickel, "Aspekte der Masse, Elemente der Macht. Versuch über Elias Canetti," *Text und Kritik*, Heft 28 (Elias Canetti) (October 1970), 13.
41. Elias Canetti, *Die Provinz des Menschen. Aufzeichnungen 1942-1972*, p. 60. Also Ibid., p. 39.
42. Elias Canetti, *Die gespaltene Zukunft* (München: Hanser, 1972), pp. 104-131.
43. Elias Canetti, "Destructiveness," in *Crowds and Power*. (New York: The Viking Press, 1963), p. 20.
44. See Ernst Fischer, "Bemerkungen zu Elias Canetti *Masse und Macht*," in *Literatur und Kritik*, I/H. 7 (1966), 12-20.
45. Elias Canetti, "The Increase Pack," in *Crowds and Power*, p. 108.
46. By contrast Lévi-Strauss sees totemism as a pure function of the differentiation of man from animal.
47. Elias Canetti, "The Reversal," in *Crowds and Power*, p. 324.

Works by Elias Canetti (German Editions)

Hochzeit. Drama. Berlin: S. Fischer, 1932.
Die Blendung. Novel. Wien, Leipzig, Zürich: Reichner, 1935/1936.
Komödie der Eitelkeit. Drama. München: Weismann, 1950.
Fritz Wotruba. Wien: Rosenbaum, 1955.
Masse und Macht. Hamburg: Claassen, 1960.
Welt im Kopf. Graz und Wien: Stiasny, 1962.
Die Befristeten. München: Hanser, 1964.
Dramen. (Hochzeit, Komödie der Eitelkeit, Die Befristeten). München: Hanser, 1964.
Aufzeichnungen 1942-1948. Frankfurt: Suhrkamp, 1965.
Die Stimmen von Marrakesch. Aufzeichnungen nach einer Reise. München: Hanser, 1968.
Der andere Prozeß. Kafkas Briefe an Felice. München: Hanser, 1969.
Die gespaltene Zukunft. München: Hansen, 1972.
Macht und Überleben. Drei Essays. Berlin: Literarisches Colloquium, 1972.
Die Provinz des Menschen. Aufzeichnungen 1942-1972. München: Hanser, 1973.
Der Ohrenzeuge. Fünfzig Charaktere. München: Hanser, 1974.
Der Überlebende. Frankfurt: Suhrkamp, 1975.
Das Gewissen der Worte. Essays. München: Hanser, 1975.
Die gerettete Zunge. München: Hanser, 1977.
Die Fackel im Ohr. Lebensgeschichte 1921-1931. München: Hanser, 1980.
Das Augenspiel. München: Hanser, 1985.

Works by Elias Canetti (English Editions)

Auto-da-Fé. New York: Farrar Straus Giroux, 1984.
The Conscience of Words. New York: Farrar Straus Giroux, 1984.
Crowds and Power. New York: Farrar Straus Giroux, 1984. Also New York: The Viking Press, 1963.
Earwitness. Fifty Characters. New York: Continuum, 1979.
Fritz Wotruba. Wien: Brüder Rosenbaum, 1955.
The Human Province. New York: Continuum, 1978.
Kafka's Other Trial. Letters to Felice. New York: Schocken, 1978.
The Plays of Elias Canetti. New York: Farrar Straus Giroux, 1984.
The Tongue Set Free: Remembrance of a European Childhood. New York: Continuum, 1980.

The Torch in My Ear. New York: Farrar Straus Giroux, 1982.
The Voices of Marrakesh: A Record of a Visit. New York: Farrar Straus Giroux, 1984.

Secondary Works in English

Strachey, Julia. "Elias Canetti: *Auto-da-Fé,*" *Horizon* 85 (1946), 60–63.

Fiedler, Leslie A. "The Tower of Babel," *Partisan Review* 3 (1947), 316–320.

McFarlane, J. W. "The Tiresian Vision," *The Durham University Journal* XLIX, 3 (1957), 109–115.

Parry, Idris, F. "Elias Canetti's Novel 'Die Blendung,'" in F. Norman, ed., *Essays in German Literature* I (London: London University, 1965), pp. 145–166.

Stenberg, Peter. "Remembering Times Past: Canetti, Sperber, and a World That Is No More," *Seminar* 17 (1981), 296–311.

Thomson, Edward A. "Elias Canetti's 'Die Blendung' and the Changing Image of Madness," *German Life and Letters* 26 (1972), 38–47.

Barnouw, Dagmar. "Doubting Death: On Elias Canetti's Drama 'The Dead-lined,'" *Mosaic* VII/2 (1974), 1–23.

Sokel, Walter H. "The Ambiguity of Madness: Elias Canetti's Novel 'Die Blendung,'" *Views and Reviews of Modern German Literature.* Festschrift für Adolf D. Klarmann, ed., Karl S. Weimar (München: Delp, 1974), pp. 181–187.

Russell, Peter. "The Vision of Man in Elias Canetti's 'Die Blendung,'" *German Life and Letters* 28 (1974–1975), 24–35.

Wiley, Marion E. "Elias Canetti's Reflective Prose," *Modern Austrian Literature* Vol. 12, No. 2 (1979), 129–139.

Barnouw, Dagmar, "Mind and Myth in 'Masse und Macht,'" *Modern Austrian Literature* Vol. 16, Nos. 3/4 (1983), 65–79.

Demet, Michel-François. "The Theme of Blood in Elias Canetti's 'Die Blendung,'" *Modern Austrian Literature* Vol. 16, No. 3/4 (1983), 147–153.

Hinderberger-Burton, Tania. "The Quixotic in Canetti's 'Die Blendung,'" *Modern Austrian Literature* Vol. 16, Nos. 3/4 (1983), 165–176.

Karst, Roman, "Elias Canetti's 'Die Blendung': A Study in Insanity," *Modern Austrian Literature* Vol. 16, Nos. 3/4 (1983), 133–145.

Schmidt, Hugo. "Narrative Attitudes in Canetti's 'Die Blendung,'" *Modern Austrian Literature* Vol. 16, Nos. 3/4 (1983), 93–109.

Zorach, Cecile C. "The Outsider Abroad: Canetti in Marrakesh," *Modern Austrian Literature* Vol. 16, Nos. 3/4 (1983), 47–64.

Major Secondary Works in German

Alfons-M. Bischoff. *Elias Canetti, Stationen zum Werk.* Bern und Frankfurt: Lang, 1973.

Dieter Dissinger. "Bibliographie zu Elias Canetti." *Canetti lesen. Erfahrungen mit seinen Büchern.* Ed. Herbert Göpfert. München: Hanser, 1975, pp. 136–166.

David Roberts: *Kopf und Welt. Elias Canettis Roman 'Die Blendung.'* München: Hanser, 1975.

Dagmar Barnouw. *Elias Canetti.* Stuttgart: Metzler, 1979.

Jeannie Ebner

August Obermayer

Jeannie Ebner is one of those artists who for reasons of personal modesty do not seek publicity at all costs. She relies solely on the literary quality of her work[1] and has, therefore, to be content for her name to appear on literary pages only and not to make headlines as some of the more flamboyant of her colleagues do—not always for artistic reasons. If a colorful and unusual biography can be responsible for the much-needed publicity without which no artist seems to be able to succeed in today's world, then Jeannie Ebner has deliberately deprived herself of this avenue by holding back information about her life and by relying on the reception of her literary output by readers appreciative of literary merit and not seeking the titillation of the exotic or scandalous: "Up till now I have always been of the opinion that my private life is not the public's concern. That is why I have produced laconic curricula vitae only, sometimes even with incorrect data, because I couldn't be bothered searching in documents."[2] Apart from uniformly recurring sparse lexicon entries there is indeed no further information on Jeannie Ebner available. It seems therefore appropriate to devote more space to biographical data than would otherwise have been the case.[3]

Her father, Johann Ebner (28 March 1870 Wiener Neustadt—16 January 1926 Wiener Neustadt), the black sheep of the family, who was employed as laborer by his moderately wealthy uncle, a wine merchant, was conveniently shipped to Australia at the age of nineteen in order to spare his middle-class family political embarrassment. At that time he was already married to a Viennese woman two years his senior, who followed him to Australia but soon began suffering from a mental disorder. She was taken back to Vienna, where she had relatives, and was placed in an asylum. Johann Ebner managed to accumulate a modest fortune and, after having lived alone for over twenty years, he desired to enter into correspondence with a Viennese woman. Accordingly he placed an advertisement in a Viennese newspaper. In this way he made the acquaintance of Ida Ganaus (26 January 1880 Vienna—3 April 1958 Vienna), whom he went to meet one week before World War I started. He fell in love with her but by then had become an Australian citizen and had to leave Austria when war broke out. He asked her to follow him to Australia, which she agreed to do. Having been sent the passport of Ebner's sick wife, Ida Ganaus tried to reach Naples using a false travel document. In the course of events she was twice arrested on suspicion of espionage and consequently missed the last passenger ship to leave Naples for Australia, fortunately for her, as it turned out, because the ship was torpedoed and sunk by a U-boat. At her own risk she took passage on an armored ship and made her way safely to Sydney. Johann Ebner, of course, was still married and according to his Catholic faith could not be divorced. It is therefore more than doubtful whether Johann Ebner and Ida Ganaus were ever properly married. On 7 November 1917 a son, Johann, was born to the couple. He died at the age of fifteen on 15 May 1932 in Wiener Neustadt. A year later on 17 November 1918 their daughter Jeannie was born in Sydney.

About 1920 the family returned to Europe. In his native Wiener Neustadt Johann Ebner invested his money in three houses, shares in a coal mine, two forwarding houses, an engineering works, and also, as a status symbol, acquired a burial vault for twelve persons. Furthermore he formally adopted his children and arranged for Ida Ganaus officially to bear his name. He died in 1926. Through inflation and the collapse of the trading banks, one of the preliminaries of the Great Depression, the family eventually lost everything but their shares in one of the forwarding houses.

Jeannie, who grew up bilingual, received all her schooling in Wiener Neustadt. For four years she attended elementary school, for another four years high school, and for two years she underwent training at a commercial college. She then served a full apprenticeship in the family's forwarding business and became qualified to manage the firm. When she reached the age of twenty-one she bought out the other partners and took over the business. In 1941 she enrolled at the Academy of Fine Arts in Vienna and began training as a sculptor, leaving the daily running of the business to a manager.

Early in 1945, when her business was bombed and burned to the ground and the flat in Wiener Neustadt was severely damaged, she decided to leave for the safer Tyrol. With her last cart and the surviving old horses she and her mother made their way to the Kitzbühler Horn, where they lived for a year in a converted mountain hut and then moved to Golling, near Salzburg. There it was possible for Jeannie to give English lessons in exchange for food and to find work as a painter and designer of souvenirs, which saved her and her mother from starvation.

In the autumn of 1946 Jeannie Ebner returned to Vienna, where she found work as a typist in a motor-repair shop of the American Military Forces. She held this position for three years, and during this time in 1948 she formed an association with Ernst Allinger, whom she married on 21 November 1964.

When she lost her job with the American Forces in 1949, she was already seriously considering writing a novel and possibly becoming a full-time writer. Whether or not she would become a free-lance artist would depend on the success or failure of the first novel. In the meantime she supported herself by doing part-time office work and by lending a helping hand to Hans Weigel, who was then editing the annual anthology *Stimmen der Gegenwart*. In 1954 her first novel, *Sie warten auf Antwort* (They Are Waiting for an Answer), appeared and was an immediate success with the critics. For Jeannie Ebner this was the determining factor in her decision to devote her life to writing. Although she received a number of literary prizes and honors,[4] financial reward was not forthcoming. It was, for instance, only in 1968 that she could afford her own study, and in the same year she took over the editorship of the distinguished literary journal *Literatur und Kritik*. Again she worked very hard for a very modest financial return. In a reply to a questionnaire which Peter André Bloch and his seminar prepared and sent out to contemporary authors in order to establish the means and conditions of the production of contemporary literature, Jeannie Ebner states her reasons for not being able to oblige as fully as requested: she was holding two full-time and two part-time positions at the same time and was therefore quite unable to engage in further activities, least of all unpaid ones. As full-time occupations she lists "editor, proofreader, typist, and office girl for the journal *Literatur und Kritik*" and translator of books. The income from these two occupations was just sufficient to live on. The part-time occupations were being a housewife for three hours every day (including Sundays), income: nil, and being a creative writer, income: pocket money.[5] When after ten years of service with the journal Jeannie Ebner retired from her position as editor in 1978 to concentrate on her writing again, she had achieved quite a remarkable success. Thanks to her devotion and her unique talent not only in publishing young Austrian writers, but also in attracting an astonishing number of overseas scholars as contributors, *Literatur und Kritik* had developed into a representative and highly respected international journal. Looking through the list of contributors over these ten years, it almost reads like a *Who's Who* in Austrian literature. All this Ebner achieved literally single-handedly. Whoever has seen this one-woman operation, a spartan editorial office in a backyard of an old palace, equipped with a desk, a chair, a telephone, a typewriter, and Jeannie Ebner, found it hard to believe that this was the place where a journal of such repute was put together. Since 1978 Ebner has been working on several projects and has completed another novel, *Drei Flötentöne* (1981, Three Sounds of a Flute) and a novella, *Aktäon* (1983, Actaeon).

For the dust cover of her first novel *Sie warten auf Antwort* (1954, They Are Waiting for an Answer) Jeannie Ebner provided a short biographical note, dealing mainly with her artistic development: "When I was twelve I wrote my first poem. This gave me such tremendous pleasure that I never abandoned this activity and I hope I shall never abandon it. When I was sixteen I spent my days working in an office; in the evenings I read Karl Marx and Rilke. The former I didn't understand, the latter made me want to die of consumption." Although this statement has to be taken cum grano salis, the early experience with poetry had a lasting effect. Jeannie Ebner has written poetry ever since, and indeed her first publication in book form, *Gesang an das Heute* (1952, *Songs for Today*), is mainly a collection of poems. The early encounters with Marx and Rilke do not seem to have had the same effect. Their influence cannot be traced, not even in her early work, which she began publishing in 1948 in several journals, literary magazines, and anthologies.[6] But her first novel *Sie warten auf Antwort,* which established her almost overnight as a recognized writer, shows two other possible influences. The characteristic mythological style of Ebner's early work, here already fully developed, is — as was the case with many writers at that time — very much reminiscent of Kafka.[7] The creation of a totally integrated and self-contained fictional world, of a mini-cosmos in its own right, functioning in accordance with its own laws and regulations, which do not necessarily correspond to the actuality of the everyday world, has often been described as being the "Kafkaesque" experience par excellence. Kafka's innovative approach has become readily available for aesthetic manipulation and therefore falsification, for although the style could be copied, the experience behind it could not. But in Ebner's case there seems to be an additional influence, an element of rationality counterbalancing the danger of slipping into mere decadence. This quality could have its origin in Musil,[8] because in spite of all allegorical and mythical disguise there is a very intellectual and highly conscious narrator in control, who is not hopelessly caught up in the events of the novel but who narrates with full knowledge of the problems and in full awareness of the situation. There is also the acknowledgment of the category of "the possible" on the part of the narrator and, according to Musil, whatever is possible is of no less importance than what is real.

The first chapter of *Sie warten auf Antwort*, explicitly titled "Introduction," deals expressly with matters of narration: "A story always begins with the fact that from a state of total equilibrium suddenly energy is set free, gets into motion without any apparent external cause but from inner necessity. This is how the action starts. The plot of which the story consists cannot be stopped anymore. It starts with a deed."[9] Thus the position of the narrator is established. It is in spite of all emotional concern a position of distance, an intellectual analysis of creative activities, a description of these activities. Thus it is possible that consciously created characters seem able to escape the narrator's control and manipulative power, but at the same time the narrator is fully aware of that happening. There is a certain degree of freedom for the character and therefore for the narrator, but once this freedom has been exercised and a decision has been taken, the events take over: "The net has caught him, he cannot escape from the course of the story, cannot find his way back, cannot free himself. The story progresses and sweeps him away like a boat without steering on the high sea. All that is left for him to do is to have trust in a star and fight for his life."[10]

Ebner thus provides two categories for the comprehension of the narrative act. There is the conscious, purposeful and planned arrangement on the part of the narrator on the one hand, and the accidental, fateful, and metaphysical occurrence taking over the narration on the other hand. These two extreme positions, the manipulative intellect and the unpredictable intuition, are always evoked within Ebner's work. They are frontiers, poles of human endeavor which, according to Jeannie Ebner's conviction, have to be brought together somehow in order to enable men to catch a glimpse of the truth. This approximation to the truth, if it occurs at all, takes place in a mysterious in-between region (*das Zwischenreich*).[11] Although this is a space metaphor, it denotes a mental condition.

Whatever happens is never the only possible result born of necessity but "one possibility, nothing else."[12] This conscious inclusion of the category of "the possible" allows the narrator to keep her distance from the narration, a distance resulting from the constant appreciation of all possibilities.

In *Sie warten auf Antwort* Ebner concerns herself with the phenomenon of helplessness. Originally the title of the novel was "Die Hilflosen" (The Help-less Ones), and it was changed to the present title only at the very last moment during the printing process. In an essay about her novel Jeannie Ebner claims that she was creating "symbols of helplessness" (*Symbole der Hilflosigkeit*) and states:

> For a long time I have had the impression that everything people do or say is somewhat accidental. This is what masks their actual being. If one gains insight, one discovers that all human beings—even the wise ones who are also in possession of the insight of their own helpless igno-rance—display a great deal of helplessness if they are confronted with the fact of existence. Even malice and brutality are often manifestations of an elevated form of helplessness.[13]

The behavior of the characters can therefore be seen as a conscious or unconscious attempt to overcome this helplessness, the activity of the narrator, however, as a quite distinct and conscious attempt, for the same purpose. This can be achieved by several means. Ebner chooses to create models of archetypal behavioral patterns, using constellations and situations prefigured by myth, religion, and literature. She adapts these patterns to fit her own time and reinterprets them accordingly. The action takes place in the capital of a geographically indeterminable country dominated by a large river (*das Stromland*). This river, which has traveled a long distance, has its source in a paradise-like country, peaceful, fertile, and universally beneficial to all peoples and all ages: "The river has its source in a quiet country with a good climate, rich fertility, and lasting peace. This country is an inexhaustible reservoir of energy and vivacity from which the great benevolent hand constantly distributes and even wastes without ever draining it. It is the granary of all ages and peoples ..."[14] This country—in spite of all similarities to known creation myths—is a literary landscape and is not only the source of the river but also the source of the story, because from it two figures, the angelic and esoteric Angelika and the Mephistophelian Muni, arrive in the capital city.

Both figures seem to the inhabitants of the capital city to be messengers from a world so distant that knowledge of it can be accessible only through legends, myth, and religion. Even Angelika and Muni have only a very faint recollection of their homeland. Angelika is the victim of her quest for the unknown. It was within her responsibility to take the first step and break away from the peaceful harmony of her existence, but once this is done a chain of reactions and consequences takes over, which forces her into a state of semiconsciousness, helplessness, and total dependence. Her opposite, Muni, represents the evil principle, the anarchist and irresponsible revolutionary, setting fire to the city and totally destroying it just for the fun of it. As Angelika inspires the simple, submissive, and humble janitor to acts of charity so Muni inspires the intellectual and skeptic Dr. Fröhlich to organize the revolution.

Life in the capital city is governed primarily by three seemingly all-powerful institutions: the Building Authority (*das Bauamt*), which is the only civil authority and is responsible for all worldly matters, the Organization (*die Organisation*), monopolizing all matters of religion and metaphysics, and the Gang (*die Bande*), an illegal but very influential association of outlaws and criminals having connections with all important departments. Both the Building Authority and the Organization derive their authority from a mysterious Masterbuilder (*der Baumeister*), whom no one has ever seen and whose very existence is doubted by skeptics like Dr. Fröhlich. Both institutions have developed a large bureaucracy, a network of endless rules and regulations, a set of customs and behavior which have become rigid, restrictive, and self-perpetuating and cannot really be fully comprehended by anyone.

The task of the Building Authority is to build houses. Therefore with great expense, energy, and planning activity they keep on building houses, half of which remain empty, are neglected, and deteriorate very soon, only to give way to new buildings that in turn will suffer the same fate.

The Organization deliberates on matters of the soul. They have invented a system that promises to get messages to the esteemed Masterbuilder, but because there is never any sign that these messages have been actually received, the system is suspected by the skeptics of being fraudulent. The Organization also arbitrates in questions of metaphysics and philosophy, and it presides over ceremonies and festivities.

The Gang with its connections and friends everywhere serves as a body that protects its members and looks after their interests.

These definite groupings within society cause the individual who is not a member of any of these groups—as is the case for the majority of people—and who is therefore helplessly subjected to the demands and expectations of these powerful institutions, to select his position, according to his inclination, between the two extremes of total subjection and the revolutionary act.

The novel introduces a number of characters, who, according to their abilities, predispositions, and education, master this situation in different ways. Their common denominator however is that they are all victims and that they are all basically helpless. Even the very educated, active, and caring Dr. Fröhlich, who early on suspects that all is not well in the city and finally instigates a revolution, displays in the final analysis only symptoms of helplessness. From the initially justified organizing of self-help he falls into the trap of intellectualizing and justifying any outrage for the progress of the cause. In a great vision at the end of the novel Dr. Fröhlich has to learn that all his life he has been asking meaningless questions, questions to which there are no answers, but at the same time he gains the insight and reassurance that he had to ask them, that it was the purpose of his life to ask them. When he finally reaches the stage where he can accept everything at face value without always having to ask the reason for it, he has also reached the end of his life. He has achieved what there is to achieve: not to take life too seriously, which consequently means he is also no longer suited for life. He dies peacefully, admiring intensely a blue butterfly.

For the reader, however, who goes on living, it seems a somewhat depressing insight that the aim of life, the harmonious and peaceful existence without preconditions and impositions, can be obtained only at the price of life. The novel discusses two alternatives: Dr. Fröhlich, the scientist, regards the world as a laboratory in which to experiment with forces bigger than life and greater than natural evolution; however, the old priest, a member of the Organization, regards the world as a garden in which it suffices to care reverently and tenderly for everything one meets. But both alternatives are equally helpless and susceptible to the temptation of evil. Activity can lead to criminality; contemplation and inactivity may provide evil with the opportunity of taking over unopposed. The aim is therefore to find a mode of existence that effectively controls and restrains evil. In this respect revolution of a certain kind may be appropriate, provided it can be kept under control:

> There is a type of revolution which restricts itself to specific aims, which can be reached in a defined span of time, a type of revolution which attacks the Establishment because it seems to have been stifled by the past and which strives to bring about better conditions for the future. Once this aim has been reached the revolution becomes superfluous and ceases to exist. But this is indeed a revolution that draws its energy from the heat generated by the battle of life. It is a progressive, far-reaching motion, a state of suspension consisting of impulses and initiatives, causes and effects which prevents life from cooling down. But there is also a type of revolt that aims to destroy everything that can be revolted against, which means the destruction of life itself. This type of revolt appears in the guise of ideas, and its nihilistic trait is not immediately apparent: total order, total justice, or total power. But life is never total. Whatever aims for total adjustment is against life.[15]

The former is the alternative for which the novel opts and the message it contains: permanent change as an expression of life. This permanent, meaningful, and just change—life itself—is the solution offered to the helpless. Hope is expressed by repeatedly emphasizing the human being's ability to learn. The first chapter ends with the reassuring statement: "They all don't understand, but they will learn, they surely will learn."[16] This phrase runs through the novel like a leitmotif[17] and thus becomes one of the key sentences for the interpretation. The development of mankind is a permanent process of learning, the human being is basically equipped with the capacity to overcome difficult situations. The process of learning will be different from individual to individual just as the degree of helplessness will differ from individual to individual. But as the individual is capable of overcoming his helplessness, so too is mankind.

The solution of the permanent revolt, the permanent process of learning suggested here, is offered as but one possibility, which is acceptable only as long as the nature of "the possible" is understood and as long as it does not claim to be the only solution. Thus through the presentation of the phenomenon of helplessness a means of mastering it has been shown.

Although Ebner evokes catastrophes and disasters of apocalyptic proportions, there remains always a glimpse of hope, an opening into a possible future. Ebner's characters are not caught by the absolute finality so frightening in Kafka's world. Her allegories, symbols, and metaphors are not totally hermetic; she always keeps open a small window on reality. It is therefore not surprising to observe a development toward a more realistic mode of presentation. Ebner wrote a considerable number of short stories in the style of her first novel, but by 1958, when her second novel, *Die Wildnis früher Sommer* (The Jungle of Early Summers),[18] appeared, a definite development had taken place. The emphasis has changed from a symbolic and mythological mode of presentation, to a psychological exploration of the characters; a more realistic style has therefore emerged. This development is not surprising, for Jeannie Ebner has always aimed at projecting her messages into figures, at creating characters who by means of their behavior and actions communicate the narrator's comprehension of the world and consequently fulfill the author's intention. But this development might have been helped along by the shock-like effect that Broch's famous dictum about simple "story telling" had on many young writers of that time. This phrase first appeared in letters to Friedrich Torberg written in 1943.[19]

When Broch's letters were published in 1957 it very soon became a catchphrase and shook the literary scene, although, at least so it seems, it was widely misunderstood and quoted out of context. Broch was searching for a new myth that could come to terms with the horrors of his age. Jeannie Ebner was about to create such a myth but turned back halfway and felt compelled to change. In her case, however, it was a change of the presentational mode rather than a change of theme or even content, because the ethical component was never lacking in her writing. In *Die Wildnis früher Sommer* Ebner is again concerned with this curious in-between region (*das Zwischenreich*). But now it is determined as a psychological state, a form of existence between truth and reality, which manifests itself in her protagonist's inclination to think and express herself in metaphors: "Her inclination to think in such metaphors was pronounced, and these metaphors were nothing but a shred of fantasy dipped into the water of reality. If one were to wring it out, it would shed a few drops of the truth."[20] But for Pin, the protagonist, these metaphors do assume the sphere of reality. She lives in an in-between state and does not distinguish between dream, fantasy, and reality, for these distinctions have been invented by the "technicians of life" and are of little value to a sensitive person. Everything Pin can perceive is equally real to her: "For any normal person like you and me they would be symbols, but Pin always saw everything as being quite real."[21] It is not surprising that such a person who determinedly refuses to grow up—"I do not want ever to grow up"[22]—does not outlive the age of sixteen. On the threshold of adulthood she perishes before she can be forced into an acceptance of the "real," which she has always despised: "Everything real she was indifferent to and found annoying. She was obsessed by her longing for the dream. Dreams were placed like big empty rooms one behind the other. She led a life under water, invented games only she could understand, and experienced things everyone else would have shrugged their shoulders at without feeling how mysterious it all was."[23]

The survivors are different people; they live within the boundaries of reality only; they ruthlessly oppress and finally destroy the dreamers, albeit sometimes unconsciously: "It is always the strong ones who are right, they are the survivors, the technicians of life. And sometimes the dark elements, too. They make all the deals on this earth and also make sure that the world does not unexpectedly turn into paradise. The fragile ones are destroyed by our recklessness and by our egoism."[24]

The girl Pin is a dreamer, doomed to be destroyed, but somehow she seems able to get closer to the truth than anyone else: "But Pin was moon-struck and walked over the unbridgeable abyss between reality and truth. She walked engrossed in a third state not in the reality of this world, not yet in the truth but still in a dream."[25]

But an existence in the dream world, especially in daydreams, is not without its risks, because it is bound to lead sooner or later to a serious conflict with reality, and one day Pin simply did not return from such an excursion into the realm of the dream.

This changeover from the symbolic and mythological mode to a more psychologically motivated and realistic one was not fully completed with the appearance of the second novel. Jeannie Ebner revised the work thoroughly for its third edition in 1978 and pruned it to two-thirds of its original length. It has thus become shorter and more concise, but also much more delicate and suggestive.

In retrospect Jeannie Ebner is fully aware of what had happened. In a letter dated 26 June 1979 she wrote: "The 'Jungle' was an attempt to free myself from parable and myth and to attain reality. But because I cannot write without any 'parable for the whole world' I invented as a background this family which is meant to be a symbol for Europe. There are two major sources for it: the Jewish religion and Greek science."[26] There is indeed a passage entitled "Die Chronik der Familie Abouan" ("The Chronicle of the Family Abouan") interrupting the realistic style, turning back to Ebner's original mode of mythological presentation and the form of the parable. The "chronicle" incorporates the fate of the individual member of the family into the context of the whole family and judging by the biblical names (Adam, Abel, Chaldäa) into the context of mankind. The individual fate thus becomes just a link in a chain of interdependent events. As the fate of the individual is determined by the family so the fate of the family is dependent on the fortune of its individual members. Here family history is presented in the form of a creation myth.

This might suggest that Jeannie Ebner is a religious writer, but although she makes repeated use of biblical images she also makes frequent use of Greek mythology and never displays devotional attitudes. She does however endeavor "to speak about God in a worldly manner" and does not hesitate to portray inhuman and antisocial behavior such as manslaughter, murder, incest, slander, and hubris. She aims, as Rion in the short story, Der Vater (The Father) does, at describing the invisible being in characters visible to the human eye: "I have to describe him the way one describes something that does not exist, circumscribe him with all those things that do exist by placing him in opposition to them. . . . What an undertaking to describe the invisible being with figures that for the human eye bear the characteristic of visibility."[27] This aim of presenting the invisible and inexplicable in concrete and visible figures makes it all the more understandable that Ebner came to choose a psychologically oriented style.

Reality is acknowledged as the realm of the strong ones, "the technicians of life," the rulers and survivors. Furthermore there is the state of truth, which seems to be something desirable but seemingly impossible to attain, and there is this curious in-between state (das Zwischenreich), the dream. This state seems to be the most that human beings can hope for. The dreamers are highly sensitive and delicate beings but not really fit for survival. They have come a step nearer to the truth but are always destroyed in the end because they lack the capacity to cope with reality.

This seems to indicate that there is no proof of the existence of the truth or for that matter of the invisible being. It is a concept constantly speculated about, permanently striven for, but never realized. It would seem therefore that Ebner's work, in spite of all its biblical imagery and Christian connotations, is not religious in the narrow sense of the word but is a critical analysis of basic philosophical concepts of the western world.

When in 1964 Ebner's third novel *Figuren in Schwarz und Weiß* (Figures in Black and White) was published, she was mentally and emotionally ready to deal with her own past, her own time and age, and her own personally experienced reality. The fully completed changeover to a realistic mode of presentation is one indication of this readiness. The background of this novel is clearly identifiable; it is Vienna and its society between 1925 and 1955. The novel itself is a social novel in the realistic tradition of Theodor Fontane, Gottfried Keller, and Thomas Mann, but theme and content again are character-istic of Ebner and do not differ greatly from her previous novels. Jeannie Ebner writes about this work:

> The only truly realistic novel (of mine) dealing with actual lives and real people who have been changed only as far as was necessary for literary reasons, because they were all still alive, is *Figures in Black and White*. But the "master" has been put together from three persons, and he actu-ally represents the Lord too. Stieglitzer is an invented character, he is the mouthpiece of rational thinking. The chapters up to the death of the brother are somewhat autobiographical, but from here on the plot does not correspond to my biography; the inner development of Theres, however, does.[28]

Again Ebner concerns herself with the concepts of good and evil and is also very aware of the fact that throughout history there have been changing and sliding scales of values, that good and evil are part of life and are not always clearly and easily distinguishable. Human beings are also prone to error and misjudgment, will make irreversible mistakes, and will have to bear with them.

In an intellectual exercise such as a game of chess positions can easily be defended or given up without causing any harm: "If the master took white, the color of China, Li-Tsen went into battle for the black king Europe. But both were surely much too polite to win and after they had reached a draw, they changed the colors and their point of view. It was only a game. The op-posing truths of the black and the white figures were equally necessary, other-wise there would be neither a game nor a discussion."[29] In life this is not so easily done, and the matter is complicated by society's constantly changing and constantly adjusting its values to suit new conditions. The change is some-times slow and evolutionary, sometimes, however, rapid and revolutionary. One such rapid change was the rise of National Socialism in Germany and the annexation of Austria in 1938. Ebner analyzes this phenomenon from a personal and subjective point of view, from the perspective of the middle class and upper middle class, a group which through its inactivity was largely instrumental in the unopposed takeover. It was a highly sophisticated and at the same time also incredibly naive stratum of society: sophisticated as far as education, social rituals, and patronage of the arts were concerned, naive in that its members did not care for politics and were quite unable to comprehend what was actually happening under their very noses. It was indeed thought to be a social asset to conform and adapt oneself to given situations and a social grace not to become so undignified as to concern oneself with politics. Hitler was in no way taken seriously by these people. He was regarded as being uneducated, vulgar, and therefore not even worthy of consideration:

> "Hitler? A devil? But he is simply stupid." "Stupidity is successful thanks to our belief that it is not necessary to fight it in time," said Guido. "But as soon as it establishes itself, it becomes two-faced. And its second face is demonic." "Stupid and vulgar," the former voice insisted. "Here in Austria it could never be successful . . ."[30]

This is precisely the attitude that renders one defenseless when evil strikes and, as history has shown, made Austria easy prey. A new system had taken over unopposed, new values had been forced upon a contemplative and unprepared society; things were taking place that could only be gazed at in dumbfounded bewilderment. Some people readily came to terms with the new power, but most carried on living as before, largely ignorant of the real situation. Again this was deliberate ignorance, as portrayed in the case of the main protagonist, Theres Meinhardt, who was concerned mainly with her personal problems and individual idiosyncracies: "Last night I dreamed I was a butterfly. And now I do not know whether I am a human being who dreamed she was a butterfly or a butterfly who is dreaming she is a human being."[31]

But the new order, the new system, was affecting the lives of the individuals, no matter how hard they tried to ignore it. At least for the thinking human being it became apparent very soon that there were two alternatives, each equally undesirable. "We have the alternative to be stupid and good, or clever and evil."[32] The option Theres Meinhardt chooses, inner resignation and escape into the in-between region of the dream, is to a certain degree also an option for "stupidity," as at this stage of her development she does not recognize social responsibilities or, if so, only on an individual and private basis.

After the collapse of the Third Reich it was still quite impossible for the characters to comprehend what had happened and how it could have happened. Documentation of the horrors committed in the concentration camps shocked Theres into the insight that ignorance is equal to guilt. And from this moment on she strives for both the intellectual and the intuitive perception of the world: "I like the reality as much as I like the dream."[33] She goes even further because it seems that these two spheres of experience are not of equal weight; the intellect is given a supervisory function over the dream: "My patron saint is best described as doubting Thomas. Because of his doubt he was able to place his hand into the wound of the risen Lord."[34] Theres Meinhardt refuses to believe blindly; she wants to believe but is prepared to do so only if the belief is compatible with reason. She is also not convinced that groupings formed for a specific purpose are an ethically acceptable solution to the problem. She had not cared for the National Socialist Party nor for the Resistance in its organized form. She is also quite skeptical of the newly founded Association for the Salvation of Europe, especially because it seems that some people do not find it difficult to claim membership in all these groups and unhesitatingly change from one to the other as circumstances require.

Not even grouping according to sex, a theme Ebner introduces here in antici-pation of much later feminist activities, is portrayed as an acceptable solution. The two main proponents of this idea, Antonia and Elisabeth, disappear at the end of the novel, Antonia into a mental asylum and Elisabeth into general insignificance. Theres Meinhardt is intelligent enough to distrust her own sex where it is warranted. She comes to learn that equal rights demand equal re-sponsibilities and also comes to accept that reaching a free decision is an exercise in supreme loneliness which cannot be lessened by any form of grouping.

She reaches her decision to become a writer in spite of not believing in the influence of literature on politics and on the basis of hope that her writing may be helpful to some individuals: "What is absolutely certain to me is the meaning writing has for the writer. Then the work is handed over to the world. And what the world makes of it or is willing to make of it is outside my con-trol."[35] To find the necessary strength to carry out this conviction requires a person full of faith: "It takes a basically religious nature in order to be able to live and write without any specific belief."[36] Again it is specified here that Christianity is part of our civilization, part of our tradition, a concept very much part of the "western reality": "Jesus Christ for me is a figure whom I love even if I do not believe in him."[37]

After a period of seventeen years in which quite clearly a process of artistic development and personal maturity has taken place, Ebner presented her fourth full-scale novel, *Drei Flötentöne* (Three Sounds of a Flute) in 1981. Although her themes seem to be those with which the reader of Ebner's work has been familiar ever since the appearance of her first novel and even the characters— especially the three female characters—seem to have surfaced again from earlier works, her mode of presentation, and the directness with which the message is put across are quite distinct innovations.

There are three stories, each concentrating on the life of a woman, inter-woven in such a manner that the result may be called a novel. For the first time Ebner uses first-person narration in a large prose text. As all three women narrate their life in this mode, and because the chapters as well as the lives of the characters are in many ways interconnected, the impression that the three women are not actually three different entities but three facets of one person projected and developed into a single figure becomes more and more of a certainty. The writer Gertrud, an energetic and rational person, is the only one of the three who actually manages to come to terms with life. She finds herself a partner in marriage with whom she can happily exist, she is engaged in an occupation that fulfills her, and she succeeds in adopting an attitude to life that enables her to accept the approach of old age gracefully and in a state of equilibrium and relative happiness. The other two women, however, are not so successful. Jana, a dancer who, after initial successes does not manage to reach the heights and glamor of a successful career on the stage, ends as a frustrated alcoholic committing suicide. Similarly Tschuptschik, a young idealistic dreamer, who tries to defy reality, is driven to suicide when she finds herself pregnant and is unable to bear the thought of bringing a child into a world that seems to her a very ill-equipped place for human habitation: "Images, sounds. Life pregnant with wishes and desire. And in an instant everything was gone. Was it more than three hesitant sounds of a lonely exultation or a lonely death? Three sounds of eternity. Only one of the three has survived: an old woman who had become very reflective."[38]

That Gertrud survives suggests that Ebner is here making a plea for reason and is rejecting the realm of dream, the in-between region, where so often in her earlier work the human being's chance to approach truth would lie. In a letter Jeannie Ebner states: "When I reached the age of sixty I felt strongly that I was now old enough and experienced enough actually to tell my readers something and not just to narrate stories."[39]

What Ebner is actually saying is that the ultimate achievement—even artistic achievement—seems to consist of finding a mode of survival in relative happi-ness in spite of all the temptation, vanity, and confusion that seems to surround us. It is the result of a compromise reached by a mature person. Jana and Tschuptschik, temptation, vanity or self-imposed ideals, youth and middle age are transitory; what survives is reason and the wisdom of old age: "In old age it is possible to smile in many situations where at an earlier age one might have wept."[40]

In 1983 Jeannie Ebner published a novella entitled *Aktäon*. The most remarkable stylistic feature of this text is the way that Ebner has developed of successfully combining the mythological mode of presentation of her early work with the realistic and psychological mode culminating in her latest novel *Drei Flötentöne* (1981). She achieves this blend by consciously redefining for her own purpose the myth of the Greek hunter Actaeon who spied on the goddess Artemis while she was bathing, was turned into a stag by her, and torn apart by his own dogs. Musing over the fact that the goddess would have had much more cause for indignation if Actaeon had ignored her altogether, Ebner narrates the story of a woman who has happily reached an age of over sixty and believes that all storms of emotion are a thing of the past, only to discover to her amazement that she quite distinctly registers the erotic presence of a male. But because the male was unaware of this affection—"luckily my Actaeon was blind"[41]—the narrator is able to reflect about it in a semidetached manner. She can observe herself being in love, and the results of these observations and reflections are turned into literature. Again, *Aktäon* is a book stressing the possibilities of happiness that old age has to offer, and, if one is to believe the author, happiness in old age is easier to achieve as maturity and wisdom increase, and vanity and personal demands decrease. So again Ebner, who is now anxious to share her wisdom with her readers, gives them the assurance that happiness is not the prerogative of the young. The only remaining question of course is whether the age of sixty-five, which Jeannie Ebner reached in 1983, qualifies as "old age."

Jeannie Ebner found her major theme very early in her writing career. It is a theme not only central to Ebner's thinking, but also equally central to mankind: the dilemma to be faced when one is trying to justify an ethical existence in an ever-changing world. In her struggle with this subject Ebner has changed her mode of presentation from a mythological and allegorical abstraction to a realistic and psychologically motivated treatise on her immediate past. Her novels are therefore not only interesting documents of their time and works of art in their own right, but in the sequence of their appearance they also demonstrate very convincingly the process of developing a means of communication from the general to the more specific and personal level.

Notes

1. Cf. the bibliography of Jeannie Ebner's work compiled by Jorun Johns in *Modern Austrian Literature* Vol. 12, Nos. 3/4 (1979), 209-236.

2. Jeannie Ebner in a letter to A.O. dated 5 August 1980.

3. Jeannie Ebner has sent a short biography containing all the facts reported here to A.O. on 5 August 1980. The manuscript comprises two pages A4, single spacing.

4. Cf. bibliography, *Modern Austrian Literature* Vol. 12, Nos. 3/4 (1979), 209-210.

5. *Gegenwartsliteratur. Mittel und Bedingungen ihrer Produktion.* Edited by Peter André Bloch (Bern, München: Francke, 1975), p. 312.

6. It appears that Ebner's first publication was the short story "Maschinenstadt" in *Basilisk*, Jg. 2, Nr. 2 (1948).

7. A possible influence by Kafka has already been noted by several critics: Victor Suchy, *Literatur in Österreich von 1945-1970. Strömungen und Tendenzen* (Wien: Dokumentationsstelle für neuere österreichische Literatur, 1971), p. 22. Adalbert Schmidt, *Literaturgeschichte unserer Zeit* (Salzburg, Stuttgart: Verlag Das Berglandbuch, 1968), p. 501. Ronald Heger, *Der österreichische Roman des 20. Jahrhunderts* (Wien, Stuttgart: Wilhelm Braumüller, 1971), Vol. 1, p. 126. Hilde Spiel in *Die zeitgenössische Literatur Österreichs,* ed. Hilde Spiel, *Kindlers Literaturgeschichte der Gegenwart* (Zürich, München: Kindler Verlag, 1976), p. 185. In an interview with A.O. on 28 September 1979 Jeannie Ebner insisted that at that time she was only familiar with Kafka's short story "Der Landarzt" and was not aware of being influenced by it.

8. Cf. August Obermayer, "Beiträge zu einer Bewältigung der Hilflosigkeit. Zu Jeannie Ebners Roman *Sie warten auf Antwort,*" *Modern Austrian Literature* Vol. 14, Nos. 1/2 (1981), 62-79. In the same interview on 28 September 1979 Jeannie Ebner also explained that she had no knowledge of Musil's work when she was writing her first novel.

9. *Sie warten auf Antwort,* p. 5.

10. Ibid., p. 5f.

11. Cf. Jeannie Ebner, *Protokoll aus einem Zwischenreich* (Graz, Wien, Köln: Styria, 1975).

12. *Sie warten auf Antwort,* p. 7.

13. This quotation is taken from the manuscript version of the essay entitled "Der Prozeß und der Heilungsprozeß." In the published version with the title "Die Symbole der Hilflosigkeit. Zu meinem Roman *Sie warten auf*

Antwort," *Forum. Österreichische Monatsblätter für kulturelle Freiheit* 1 (1954), H. 10, p. 28, this passage has been severely curtailed: "For it seems to me that almost all people—even the wise ones whose insights include the insight into their own helplessness—are completely helpless in the face of their own existence."

14. *Sie warten auf Antwort,* p. 9.

15. Ibid., p. 300 f.

16. Ibid., p. 16.

17. Cf. *Sie warten auf Antwort,* pp. 16, 135, and 378.

18. The title was suggested by Thomas Bernhard after he had read the manuscript.

19. Letter to Friedrich Torberg dated 10 April 1943: "Why the swear-word 'simple story telling' (Geschichtel-Erzählen)?" Also letter dated 21 August 1943: "It is, of course, very difficult to keep on polemicizing against the inadmissible simple story-telling." Hermann Broch, *Briefe von 1929–1951. Gesammelte Werke* 8 (Zürich: Rhein Verlag, 1957), pp. 184 and 193.

20. All quotations refer to *Die Wildnis früher Sommer,* (Graz, Wien, Köln: Styria, 1978) (third revised edition), Ibid, p. 33.

21. Ibid., p. 64.

22. Ibid., p. 105.

23. Ibid., p. 95.

24. Ibid., p. 71.

25. Ibid., p. 165.

26. Letter to A.O., dated 26 June 1979.

27. Jeannie Ebner, "Der Vater," *Protokoll aus einem Zwischenreich* (Graz, Wien, Köln: Styria, 1975), p. 34.

28. Jeannie Ebner in a letter to A.O. dated 26 June 1979.

29. *Figuren in Schwarz und Weiß* (Gütersloh: Sigbert Mohn, 1964), p. 30.

30. Ibid., p. 65 f.

31. Ibid., p. 92.

32. Ibid., p. 135.

33. Ibid., p. 203.

34. Ibid., p. 211.

35. Ibid., p. 380.

36. Ibid., p. 381.

37. Ibid., p. 445.

38. *Drei Flötentöne* (Graz, Wien, Köln: Styria, 1981), p. 268.

39. Letter to A.O. dated 12 February 1984.

40. Ibid.
41. *Aktäon* (Graz, Wien, Köln: Styria, 1983), p. 94.

Primary Literature

Gesang an das Heute. Gedichte. Wien: Jungbrunnen, 1952.
Sie warten auf Antwort. Roman. Wien, München: Herold, 1954.
Die Wildnis früher Sommer. Roman. Köln, Berlin: Kiepenheuer & Witsch, 1958.
   (Third revised edition, Graz, Wien, Köln: Styria, 1978).
Der Königstiger. Erzählung. Gütersloh: Sigbert Mohn, 1959. (Reprinted 1979).
Die Götter reden nicht. Erzählungen. Gütersloh: Sigbert Mohn, 1961.
Figuren in Schwarz und Weiß. Roman. Gütersloh: Sigbert Mohn, 1964.
Gedichte. Gütersloh: Sigbert Mohn, 1965.
Prosadichtungen. Salzburg: Otto Müller Verlag, 1973.
Protokoll aus einem Zwischenreich. Erzählungen. Graz, Wien, Köln: Styria,
   1975.
Gedichte und Meditationen. Gedichte. Baden bei Wien: Verlag G. Grasl, 1978.
Sag' Ich. Gedichte. Köln: Verlag Edward Hermansen, 1978.
Erfrorene Rosen. Erzählungen. Graz, Wien, Köln: Styria, 1981.
Drei Flötentöne. Roman. Graz, Wien, Köln: Styria, 1981.
Aktäon. Novelle. Graz, Wien, Köln: Styria, 1983.

Secondary Literature

Theodor Sapper, "Jeannie Ebners dichterisches Werk," *Literatur und Kritik*
   130 (1978), 578-599.
Gottfried Stix, "Jeannie Ebners Dichtungen und das Äußerste," *Literatur und*
   Kritik 130 (1978), 600-605.
August Obermayer, "Beiträge zu einer Bewältigung der Hilflosigkeit: Zu Jeannie
   Ebners Roman *Sie warten auf Antwort,*" *Modern Austrian Literature*
   Vol. 14, Nos. 1/2 (1981), 62-79.

Erich Fried

Jerry Glenn

Although Erich Fried published his first book of poetry in 1944 and his first collection of mature verse in 1958, he attracted little attention until the mid-1960s.[1] Since then he has remained in the public eye, an extraordinarily prolific writer and no less controversial figure. A man of many talents he has published more than thirty books containing original works—poetry, short prose fiction, a libretto, and a novel—in addition to numerous translations, and has also had several radio plays produced. His fame—or notoriety—rests, however, primarily on his late poetry. Since assuming a firm stance against the Vietnam War in the mid-1960s he has been the acknowledged leader among Germany's many political poets, and his position as the master of the word play, a device evident in his poetry from the 1950s until the present, is equally secure. In several respects he is paradoxical or even contradictory. This is reflected in minor ways: his poetry is called "epic" and his prose "lyric"; an intensely political person in his later poetry as well as in his private life, his translations are almost exclusively of writers whose work has little or no relevance to contemporary political issues. The most significant paradox, however, and the one around which much of the controversy focused on Fried revolves, is the fact that he, a Jew who lost many friends and relatives in the Holocaust, has become one of the leading spokesmen of the Palestinian cause; he is a vehement anti-Zionist, although not, he rigorously insists, an anti-Semite.

Born in Vienna on 6 May 1921, Fried has lived in London since he sought refuge there in 1938. His reasons for deciding not to return to a German-speaking country are complex, but an extremely important factor was his dissatisfaction with political developments in Germany—an attitude often reflected in his poetry. He held numerous and varied jobs, including that of political commentator for the BBC from 1952 to 1968, but has long considered himself first and foremost a writer. Although best known for his poetry he has also produced a substantial amount of prose fiction, beginning with the novel *Ein Soldat und ein Mädchen* (1960, A Soldier and a Girl),[2] which occupied Fried for some fourteen years and is often cited in discussions of the intricacies of his thought. Set at the time of the war-criminal trials in Germany, it was inspired by, if not actually based on, the case of Irma Grese, a guard in a concentration camp who was sentenced to death. In the novel the condemned woman is granted a final request: to spend her last night with one of the soldiers assigned to guard her. The man she selects is a Jewish member of the Allied occupation forces, and the book probes this soldier's reflections on his situation and on the question of German guilt as reported (and commented upon) by a narrator. In spite of his background and the effect the Holocaust had had on his own life, Fried displays a remarkably open attitude, refusing to accept any form of the concept of collective German guilt that was quite prevalent at the time the novel was written. Far from exonerating the Nazis he sees and examines the complexity of the issues involved (a complexity reflected in the structure of the book) without offering pat answers.

Recognition as an accomplished translator, primarily of English literature, preceded by a number of years the establishing of Fried's reputation as a poet in his own right. The publication of a German version of Dylan Thomas's *Under Milk Wood* in 1954 was followed by highly acclaimed translations of several other writers including T. S. Eliot, John Arden, and Sylvia Plath. An invitation to do a modern version of Shakespeare's *Midsummer Night's Dream* in the early 1960s led to other Shakespeare translations and eventually to a project of truly major proportions; Fried has now rendered more than twenty of Shakespeare's plays into German. Although no extensive scholarly study of the translations has been undertaken, commentators are virtually unanimous in their praise. Christian Enzensberger, for example, has called Fried's versions "the most conscientious and precise" of the numerous translations available in German.[3]

Fried's first two collections of verse, *Deutschland* (1944, Germany) and *Österreich* (1945, Austria), gave little indication that their author would someday come to be a highly respected poet. The form is quite traditional. Each poem has a regular meter; some, especially those of a reflective nature, are written in iambic pentameter, and many are modeled on the folk song. All are rhymed. Word plays, later to become Fried's stylistic hallmark, are present in limited numbers, for example: "Hart mach mich, doch nicht verhärt mir das Herz" (Make me hard, but don't harden my heart, *Deutschland*, p. 26).[4] The word play is not without sophistication—there is a progression from the word "hart" to a related word having a different sound ("verhärt") to a third word, entirely different in meaning but in turn similar in sound to the preceding one ("Herz"), and a bilingual pun on English "heart" and German "hart" is also present. But such instances are not common, and otherwise there is little of a formal nature in these early poems that can be found in Fried's mature work.

On the other hand many of the symbols, motifs, and themes of his later poetry are seen in the juvenilia. As the titles suggest these works are highly political. Furthermore the young Fried consistently reveals an awareness of the complexity of the moral and political issues raised by the war and the Holocaust. He insists on the guilt of those who "passively watched the misfortune" (*Deutschland*, p. 15) as well as of those who actively participated, but as in *Ein Soldat und ein Mädchen* there is no blanket condemnation of Germany and the Germans. In the introduction to *Deutschland* he clearly states: "I am an Austrian. . . . I have encountered Germans as enemies when they occupied my native land, and as friends in exile" (p. 4), a position also reflected in the poetry. An unexpected sympathy is frequently expressed for the German soldiers; much more blame is allotted their elders, who formed them and sent them to war. His attitude toward his native Austria is no less complex. He longs for, yet fears return; he loves the country but is aware of its active participation in the course of recent history. As he says in "An Österreich" (To Austria, *Österreich*, p. 13), "To cloak your guilt in silence would be no sign of love."

Here, scarcely less than in his later poetry, Fried's position is one ruled by "doubt" (*Zweifel*). This is most clearly expressed in "Der Richter" (The Judge, *Deutschland*, p. 26): "On that day when no longer I must doubt/all my beliefs, intentions, and decisions, . . . on that day I deserve to meet my death." The poem is a *Rollengedicht*, one spoken by a persona, and refers at least on the primary level to the position of, and the attitude desirable in, a judge; but it is no less applicable to Fried's own philosophy of life. This too remains a characteristic of his later works: an intense involvement, often to the point of identification, with persons who find themselves in difficult situations. Unlike most recent German poets of the political left he neither advocates nor practices a separation of the personal and political spheres. Similarly two subjects that continue to be common in his poetry for the next thirty years are already significant here: children and nature. In *Deutschland* sympathy is expressed not only for children tortured and killed by the Nazis, but also — surprisingly perhaps and more frequently — for the children in Germany, who are portrayed as innocent victims of their parents' sins. Later in the collection the emphasis shifts from children as individuals to the young in the sense of "posterity" (the German word "Erbe" often appears). Fried's love of nature is expressed in the first poem of *Österreich*, which concludes with the words: "You my mountain, my stream, my tree" (p. 5). Nature, especially animal and plant life, will later come to be extremely important in his poetry; the tree, as will be shown, often appears in association with human beings in poems expressing a reverence for life.

Although issued by a major German publisher, Fried's next collection,

Gedichte (1958, Poems), attracted little attention. Those critics who did comment tended to praise Fried's ability to manipulate language, sometimes citing a serious element, but speaking about the content only in general terms. This is in retrospect readily understandable; there is little focus, little "content," in the collection. There are very few references to Germany, past or present (one poem contains the dedication "to the dead of Hamburg," p. 75, and another a brief reference to "a chamber full of gas," p. 47), or to other current or historical events; indeed, it is difficult to discuss these poems other than to point to the ingenious use of language. The form, too, offered little upon which a commentary could be based. Most of the poems are written in free verse, like much other poetry by younger writers being published in Germany at the time; rhyme appears sparingly and then typically for a special effect. The following poem, while in some respects extreme in its use of word plays, is not atypical:

Logos

Das Wort ist mein Schwert	The word is my ax
und das Wort beschwert mich	and the word taxes me
Das Wort ist mein Schild	The word is my buffer
und das Wort schilt mich	and the word buffets me
Das Wort ist fest	The word is sportive
und das Wort ist lose	and the word is loth
Das Wort ist mein Fest	The word is my sport
und das Wort ist mein Los (p. 31)	and the word is my lot[5]

This poem is what it seems to be: a playful yet serious statement by the poet on his relation to his poetry. It and others like it led Fried to be classified as a writer for whom language takes precedence over reality, over the world and its problems.

From today's perspective, however, it is possible to see in these poems evidence of the concerns for which Fried is now known. References to children and nature are found, as in the following lines from "Mexikanisches Regenopfer" (Mexican Sacrifice for Rain, p. 11), a poem expressing sympathy for poverty-stricken people: "Ins rissige Feld fällt der Regen/auf die zerrissenen Kinder" (In the parched field rain falls/on the mangled children). Yet even here word-plays seem to be as important as the subject: "Feld" (field) and "fällt" (falls) have the same, or virtually the same, sound: "rissig" (parched, cracked) and "zerrissen" (torn apart, mangled) have a similar sound, a pun further complicated by a common meaning of the latter, "torn/shabby," in reference to clothing. Similarly, in another poem, "Wer weiß etwas von einem" (Who Knows One, p. 89), "doubt" (*Zweifel*) appears in a context in which it is difficult to determine which is paramount, the concept or the pun: "Eins ist die Einsamkeit/Zwei ist der Zweifel . . . die Verzweiflung des Zweiflers." These lines, untranslatable without either changing the meaning radically or losing the puns, have the following literal meaning: "One is solitude/two is doubt . . . the despair of the doubter," and are based on the fact that "Einsamkeit" (solitude) and "Zweifel" have as their first four letters the German words for "one" and "two," respectively, and that the word for "despair" is formed by adding a prefix to the word for "doubt." The entire poem is rich in puns, yet it is also very serious in nature. It is based on, and could perhaps be called a parody of, a Jewish song ("One is our God alone/Two are the tables of the Covenant"), an allusion that would be missed by the vast majority of non-Jewish German readers in spite of the presence of the Hebrew title, "Echod mi jodea," as a subtitle of the poem.

The poetry of the early 1960s is in some respects transitional. *Reich der Steine* (1963, Kingdom of Stones) is a collection of cyclical poems or, more accurately, long poems divided into shorter segments, written over a period of time and having little in common except their length. Later Fried was to make frequent use of the long poem in the interest of clarity and completeness, and he has commented on the cyclical nature of his collections, on the importance of the context for the understanding of individual poems.[6] *Warngedichte* (1964, Warning Poems) and *Überlegungen* (1964, Reflections), on the other hand, reveal an increasing willingness on Fried's part to include references to politics and current events in his poetry. The poems of the former have much in common with those of *Gedichte*. But, as the title suggests, the poet attempts to make more apparent the relation of the poems to the problems of the world, to let the reader know that the puns and other devices for manipulating language are not present for their own sake but rather to move the reader to ponder the paradoxical nature of reality. As Fried says in a text printed on the dust jacket, "These verses are not warnings in the sense of an inflexible view of the world or of a political party." They reflect rather "the dull feeling upon awakening or upon not being able to fall asleep, . . . or the sense of embitterment upon suddenly grasping the relationships between different newspaper reports."

Überlegungen, an unpaginated book containing twenty-two numbered but untitled poems forming a unified sequence, is clearly and directly political. Here Fried espouses a kind of nondoctrinaire and non-Stalinist Marxism, and does so in a language that is often prosaic and dry. The third poem begins:

"We learned/to interrupt/our striving for freedom/in order first to build/its foundations/and later freedom." The building metaphor is sustained through much of the volume and points both to the necessity to sacrifice some freedom now in the interest of establishing a state based on the proper social principles (contrary to prevalent western thought) and, of equal importance, the ultimate goal, freedom and prosperity within this context (contrary, at least in practice, to many socialist governments of eastern Europe). In spite of the didactic tone, however, the message is not always clear; Fried's earlier tendency toward obscurity has not yet been overcome here in his first sustained attempt to write specifically political verse.

The poems of *und Vietnam und* (1966, and Vietnam and) are an entirely different matter; they are not only highly political, but also clear and unambiguous, leaving little room for misunderstanding. Although critics have pointed out, and Fried has confirmed, that the presence of the word "and" in the title is meant to underline the author's conception of the Vietnam War as one violent period among many in the history of the world, the poems themselves emphasize the event, not the broader context. Throughout the collection we find expressions of opposition to the war that range from vehement to venomous. Fried's personal dedication to the principle of life and his opposition to violence coalesce with his political belief in Marxism in these poetic statements. That is not to say, however, that they are all alike. Several styles emerge as well as several perspectives or objects of attack. "17.-22. Mai 1966" (May 17-22, 1966), one of Fried's most famous, will illustrate one type: "From Da Nang/for five days/came the daily report:/sporadic fire//On the sixth day came the report:/In the fighting of the last five days/in Da Nang/so far about a thousand victims" (p. 23). The primary target is probably the author's conception of American disregard for human life—a thousand deaths are dismissed as the result of "sporadic fire"—although the inaccuracy of the press in reporting the war, something addressed more prominently elsewhere in the book, is also an issue.

Other poems rely on word plays, but now there is never any doubt that the content behind the puns is of paramount importance:

Logik	Logic
Wenn es	If we
gestattet ist	concur
daß man	that the
die Kinder	children

bestattet	be interred
dann	then
ist es	we
auch	also
erlaubt	have leave
daß man	to strip
die Bäume	from the trees
entlaubt (p. 25)	the leaves

Before discussing this poem, which is more complex than the one cited immediately above, a word on the translation is in order. The translation given here, which generally captures the *meaning* of the original, sounds a little like Ogden Nash, whereas Fried's poem most assuredly does not. Fried's effect rests upon the tendency of the German language to form common words with very different meanings simply by varying the prefix of a basic root. In this case the words are "gestatten" (allow/permit) and "bestatten" (bury/inter), and "erlauben" (allow/permit) and "entlauben" (defoliate). Hence the dry, matter-of-fact, "logical" tone of the poem is impossible to capture in an English version that attempts to retain the puns. If the language of the translation is that of Ogden Nash, the logic of Fried's poem, reflecting his view of the logic of the war, is that of Lewis Carroll: since "bestatten" and "entlauben" sound like words for "permit," the actions they describe are permissible. Upon further reflection an even greater problem becomes apparent: the priorities are backward. The more serious crime, burying (murdering) children, is used as a justification for the lesser, defoliating trees.

Whereas many Germans (and more than a few Americans) would even in 1966 have been in total agreement with the sentiments expressed or implied in the poems quoted above, in other poems Fried becomes more controversial and often more subjective. "Messung eines Staatsoberhauptes" (Measuring a Chief of State), for example, contains the following lines clearly, if perhaps not unambiguously, referring to Lyndon Johnson: "Already very remarkable/ by far not/as great/as Hitler/but on the other hand/for example/already greater/than Nero" (p. 49). And in "Preislied für einen Freiheitskrieger" (Song of Praise for a Freedom Fighter) we read: "Whoever is like you/can also . . . throw children/into gas chambers/which kill with less pain than napalm" (p. 60). Using Hitler or the Holocaust as a point of reference or comparison for other wars or atrocities is sure to arouse the ire of many Jews and some gentiles, and this reaction was recorded soon after the publication of *und Vietnam und,* for example, by Herbert Andreas: "Hitler and his followers may well be encouraged by this amazing declaration of exoneration, coming, as it does, from such an unexpected source [i.e., a Jew who had fled Nazi-controlled Europe]."[7] This issue, which will be discussed below, was to assume considerable importance in the years to come.

Before the end of the Vietnam War Fried published six more volumes of new poetry, and the war continued to play a central role in these works. "Gespräch über Bäume" (Conversation about Trees) from *Anfechtungen* (1967, Contestations), quoted here in excerpts, illustrates Fried's preoccupation as well as elements of his poetic technique:

> Since the gardener pruned the branches
> my apples have been larger
> But the leaves of the pear tree
> are diseased. They are involute
>   in Vietnam the trees are defoliated

> My children are all healthy
> But my younger son concerns me
> he hasn't adjusted
> to his new school
>   In Vietnam the children are dead

> . . .

> What a bore!
> Whatever you talk about
> he starts in on Vietnam!
> You can't object to a fellow's having a little peace and quiet
>   A lot of people in Vietnam have their peace and quiet
>   You have no objections (p. 60).

The title refers to Bert Brecht's poem "An die Nachgeborenen" (To Posterity), which contains the lines: "What kind of an age is it, in which/A conversation about trees is almost a crime,/Because it necessitates a silence about so many misdeeds,"[8] Fried shares Brecht's concern: in an age dominated by political atrocities it is "almost a crime" to devote one's thoughts to the trivial — or the "beautiful" — and thereby ignore the state of the world. Fried, however, explicitly introduces an important element: the motives of those who would carry on trivial discussions about trees. The person speaking with the poet in the framework of the poem directly verbalizes the attitude left buried deep below the surface, if present at all, in Brecht: the desire to ignore the terrible, if distant, political reality.[9]

The styles of "Gespräch über Bäume" and "Logik" are quite different. The former is more verbose and more direct in its statement, and it relies on the reader's anticipated approval of the poem's final ironic line, whereas the latter is laconic and based on the effect of the puns. In each, however, Fried bases his appeal on the war's destruction of children and trees. Without trivializing the difference in importance between the two, Fried here, as often, utilizes them in the same poem as symbols of his conception of this war's especially great incompatibility with the principle of life. Children represent the future of the human race, and trees mankind's affinity with nature, both of which, no less than the actual trees and children in Vietnam, are represented as being in peril.

Other political themes also appear in Fried's poetry of the late 1960s and early 1970s (most prominently American involvement in Latin America), and the tone of the poems becomes even more venomous. One, for example, "Ablehnung einer Tragödie" (Rejection of a Tragedy), suggests that Johnson was responsible for the assassination of John F. Kennedy (*Zeitfragen,* 1968, Questions of the Times, pp. 86-87). The use of scatological language increases rather dramatically — a readily understandable reflection of Fried's conception of the state of the world — as do instances of other shock effects. Even the most shocking, however, are not without a constructive purpose. At first reading "Marienlegende" (Legend of Mary) seems to have no raison d'être other than blasphemy for its own sake: the scene is recreated in which Jesus says "He that is without sin among you, let him first cast a stone" (John 8:7), whereupon Mary does so (*Die Freiheit den Mund aufzumachen,* The Freedom to Open Your Mouth, p. 46). The object of Fried's satire, however, is not Jesus or his teachings but the Catholic Church's doctrine of the Immaculate Conception and in general its tendency to emphasize esoteric theology at the expense of human charity.[10] Fried's views on this matter are expressed quite clearly in an interview with Dick van Stekelenburg, in which he says: "Socialism has adopted basic elements of Christian ethics" and goes on to remark: "Ecclesiastical dogmatism is far removed from the 'truth' of early Christianity."[11] Seen within this context Fried's poem assumes an added dimension. Mary was "without sin," and in casting the first stone she was only following her son's "command" to do so. The doctrine then is not merely ridiculed, but is also represented as being incompatible with the primary thrust of Christ's teachings. The absurdity of the specific situation is indicative of Fried's general view that the doctrine often subverts the basics. Here, however, as often in the poetry of this period, the constructive intention is obscured by the polemical stance.

Not all the poetry of this period corresponds to the categories discussed above. A new object of attack, socialism or Marxism as it is currently practiced, makes its appearance, and in these poems the tone is typically rather subdued:

After the Changes Are Made

For Ernst Fischer

Imagine socialism
freed of everything
that disturbs you

Ask yourself
who would then
find it disturbing

That person alone
is and really remains
your enemy

(*Die Beine der größeren Lügen,*
1969, The Legs of the Bigger Lies, p. 43)

The sins of the Soviet Union and the failings of the form of Marxism practiced in it and in its satellites had long been assailed and ridiculed by poets living in the German Democratic Republic (e.g., Wolf Biermann and Rainer Kunze; both it should be noted, are dedicated socialists). Fried, on the other hand, had with few exceptions been conspicuously silent in his poetry, if not in speeches and essays, throughout the 1960s. Now, as the post-Stalin era enters its third decade, the poet's impatience begins to show. The tone, however, is muted, at least in comparison with the stridency of his attacks against the west, and the criticism in the poem under discussion also includes capitalists (who, of course, would find socialism "disturbing," even "after the changes are made"). But the appearance of this kind of poem lends credibility to Fried's claim that he attacks injustice and oppression wherever they may be found, without expressing allegiance to any political party.

On the whole Fried continues to focus his attention on the west. Another poem from *Die Freiheit den Mund aufzumachen* further defines his position as the Vietnam War approaches its end and foreshadows the directions his political verse will take:

Elucidation of Obscure Points

American military courts
have cleared
the officers in charge at My Lai
of the accusation of committing atrocities

Chief Justice Lord Widgery of London
has found that English paratroopers in Ireland
only did their duty
on Bloody Sunday

Investigations by the West Berlin authorities
into the death of the prisoner Georg von Rauch clearly reveal
that the police had cause to open fire
Baader-Meinhof, you know

If after 1945 the explanation
of the events at the Jewish settlement in Auschwitz
had been left to the SS we would have been spared
photographs and films, statistics and reports

Isolated excesses
would of course have been found here and there
but on the whole only the performance of duty
and never a bloodbath (p. 12).

In this poem three instances of violence followed by a cover-up are cited from recent history: Vietnam, now approaching its end; Northern Ireland, not to become a primary concern of Fried's but rather to represent numerous situations considered similar by the poet, as in Latin America or in Iran under the Shah, and, soon to become one of his primary targets, the Federal Republic of Germany, where Fried sees an alarming increase in "terrorism" directed by the state against the so-called terrorists of the militant left. Also of significance is the use of the Holocaust as a point of comparison. Although those opposed to this idea would probably not find the present context especially offensive, they definitely did take offense at Fried's use of it in another context that surfaces in one of the poet's first post-Vietnam collections, *Höre, Israel!* (1974, Hear, O Israel), in which Zionism and Israel bear the brunt of his wrath.

   This collection, which contains several poems that are reprinted from earlier books as well as numerous new ones, opens with a poem, "Benennungen" (Naming, pp. 7-8), in which Fried attempts to state his position as directly and clearly as possible: although there is a relationship between Jews and Zionists, the two are not to be equated; the Zionists are guilty of the mistreatment of the Palestinians; there is no justification for either anti-Semitism or Zionism ("Zionism" referring to those who support the aims of the State of Israel). This poem is followed by a five-page discussion written in clear and dispassionate prose, in which Fried reiterates his intention to attack in his poetry oppression in every form, wherever it is manifested: in Nazi Europe, Vietnam, or now in Israel. He expressly justifies his comparison of Nazi to Israeli atrocities on the grounds that he wants to help prevent the comparison from becoming "more and more valid and compelling" (p. 11). It is interesting to note in this commentary the presence of Fried's concern for posterity; he wants "the Jews now living in Israel, their children and their children's children" to be able to hope for a peaceful future.

   The collection itself can only be described as eclectic. Poems in most of the styles and reflecting most of the moods discussed above are present, as are a number of "found poems," texts taken verbatim from other sources (many from Theodor Herzl) and rearranged into verse. One common denominator is the clear intention to avoid all misunderstanding. Whereas in his other works Fried generally assumes that the reader is familiar with the historical and contemporary allusions, here he takes great pains to provide explanations and documentation. The poem "Wer weiß etwas von einem," for example, is reprinted, and a note on the frame of reference is added. This desire to avoid ambiguity results in the presence of a large number of directly didactic poems that read much like sermons, such as the long title poem, where Israel is told that the powers that brought Hitler to power "want the same thing from you/ that they wanted from Hitler" (p. 53), and that "you are no longer victims of the others/you yourself want to victimize others" (p. 55).

   There is, of course, another side to the complicated political question, and this kind of attitude won Fried many more personal enemies than converts to his cause. Just as those Vietnam poems in which the wanton destruction of life was exposed were more effective than the ones attacking Lyndon Johnson, whose position was recognized as a difficult and complex one even by many opponents of the war, so too the best poems of *Höre, Israel* address the suffering of innocent people who have fallen victim to the harsh realities of the violence prevalent in the Middle East. Perhaps the most noteworthy of these—and there are not many—is "Kreuztragung 1972" (1972, Carrying the

Cross). After setting the scene—a Palestinian woman is carrying a tree—the
poet comments:

> She is carrying her tree
> which the Israelis
> uprooted
> when she herself was uprooted
>
> out of her destroyed village
> going somewhere or other
> where she hopes to be able to plant it
> before it dies
>
> The plaster eyes of Jabotinsky
> and Golda Meir
> stare at the dusty path
> and do not see her (p. 102).

The poem, which is accompanied not only by explanatory notes but also by
three photographs of the scene showing the woman and the busts of the political
figures mentioned in the final stanza, is indeed a poignant expression of both
the suffering of the innocent victims of the situation and the politicians' indifference. Although the political attitudes can be explained by those sympathetic to the Israeli position, the emotional appeal of this woman's pathetic
situation is difficult to counter. The suffering of innocent children is similarly
portrayed in some poems, most notably in "Deir Yassin" (pp. 63-64), in which
pictures of Palestinian children (some of them reproduced in the book) are
compared with pictures of children in the Warsaw ghetto. Again, although those
opposed to Fried's interpretation of the situation in the Middle East can find
good arguments to oppose his views and his methods, the case for a similarity
between the situations of these children and Jewish children under the Nazis
is compellingly made on an emotional level. It is perhaps worth noting that
just as the suffering of the South Vietnamese at the hands of the Viet Cong
was never mentioned, so too are the sufferings of innocent Israelis at the hands
of the PLO passed over in silence.

Besides the Vietnam War and the Middle East the third subject deemed
important enough by Fried to warrant a book devoted exclusively to it is the
political situation in the Federal Republic of Germany, which receives scathing
treatment in *So kam ich unter die Deutschen* (1977, Thus I Came among the

Germans). Although some of these poems are reminiscent of the folksong or nursery rhyme, most are direct and conversational like the majority of those in *Höre, Israel!;* some—more than in *Höre, Israel!* but fewer than in most of Fried's collections—are based on word plays. Literary allusions (including the title, taken from the German poet Friedrich Hölderlin) also play a significant role here as in Fried's later poetry in general.

After a brief introduction, in which Fried expresses his disappointment in the way West Germany has developed, the poet proceeds to assail various aspects of that nation's society, most in some way related to the use of force — "terrorism," a word he would not limit to leftists who resort to violence in their opposition to the government—to combat political opponents and harness dissent. A number of poems deal with the case of Ulrike Meinhof, one of the leaders of the "Baader-Meinhof" group, whose death in prison under questionable circumstances was ruled a suicide, and several other individuals are specifically named and their cases described. Although some of these persons and events are explained in notes, most are not. Perhaps Fried assumed his German audience would be familiar with them or he was less concerned about being fully understood than was the case in *Höre, Israel.* In any event, readers not intimately familiar with events in the Federal Republic are likely to miss many specific allusions, even if the basic point—the prevalence of oppression—is only too clear.

Many Germans, including some in positions of prominence, took offense at these poems. One in particular, "Auf den Tod des Generalbundesanwalts Siegfried Buback" (On the Death of Attorney General Siegfried Buback, pp. 103–106), was singled out for censure. It was discussed in the German parliament and was used as justification for removing Fried's works from schoolbooks.[12] To be sure, Fried does not attempt to justify the assassination, but he explicitly places greater blame on Buback than on the assassins, referring to "his death/by which I am repulsed almost as much/as I am by his life." This was one of the primary reasons for the furor.

The end of the Vietnam War gave Fried no cause for optimism, and his poetry of the mid-1970s reveals many causes for pessimism in addition to Israel and Germany. Although concern about injustices perpetrated by western nations remains paramount, a return to a more general sense of disquietude, similar to but more intense than that seen in the pre-Vietnam verse, is noticeable. In *Gegengift* (1974, Antidote), for example, the increasing number of references to "doubt" is significant. Fried's basic position, in essence unchanged through the years, is restated in the poem "Angst und Zweifel" (Fear and Doubt):

Do not be in doubt
about the person
who tells you
he is afraid

But be afraid
of the person
who tells you
he is not in doubt (p. 20)

His doubts about Marxism also become more pronounced, as in the longish
poem "Drei Aussagen über die Verteidigung einer Lebensaufgabe" (Three
Statements on the Defense of a Life's Goal, pp. 34-35): "Doubts are expressed/
about whether he is a good Marxist/but perhaps it would be good if there were/
more doubting Marxists . . . Those who/most severely//condemn him/are the
very ones//who are guilty of/making him what he has become." As was noted
above, Fried did not select acts of Soviet aggression and oppression (e.g., the
invasion of Czechoslovakia or Afghanistan) as events worthy of sustained attack
in his verse, perhaps for the reasons expressed in the poems of *Überlegungen,*
i.e., sympathy with the necessity of curtailing freedom during the establishment
of a socialist form of government. But here and elsewhere in the late poetry
Fried does voice his concern on a theoretical level about the failure of Marxism
to make strides toward the just political system that he and others had envisioned.

A very different kind of "doubt" is at the core of the long poem "Zweifel
an der Sprache" (Doubts about Language), also from *Gegengift* (pp. 69-79).
In this poem, virtually untranslatable on account of the numerous — and highly
effective — puns, Fried is at his critical, insightful, and semioptimistic best.
His contribution to a discussion on the topic named in the title, an extremely
important issue in recent German literary criticism, it more persuasively than
most essays on the subject lays bare the silliness as well as the perniciousness
of the position that language is suspect: "Doubts about language/lead to a
language of doubt/Those who speak it/arrive at speechlessness." Fried acknowledges that language is imperfect, but the best way to prevent a car from
going in the wrong direction is to keep it in neutral; given the inevitable choice
between going nowhere and taking the risk of a wrong turn — between keeping
silent and risking a false or inappropriate statement — he will opt for the latter
any time. There is language, and there is language: "*Who* has doubts/about a
cry for help/about a scream/about words like 'you' and 'I Miss You?'" Political

slogans can be absurd ("Germany awaken," the Nazi slogan) or all too clear, if sometimes complex ("Judah perish"); some political statements, on the other hand, need no commentary: "Military putsch in Chile." "Therefore have doubts about those who say:/'Language can do anything'... Therefore have doubts about those/who in painstakingly cultivated language/painstakingly disparage/ cultivated language." Language is open to misuse as well as misinterpretation; it is a product of human beings, and it is what those who use it make of it. Beware of those who misuse it and, no less so, of those who view it as an end rather than a means.

Subtle but significant changes can be detected in Fried's most recent poetry. While political verse and word plays are still encountered, they are less frequent and less aggressive. As Manfred Riedel has aptly commented, there is now "more sadness than wrath."[13] References to children and nature become much less frequent. Poems about poets and poetry increase; exile, sometimes alluded to previously, but not a major theme since *Österreich,* more often comes to the fore. One recent collection even has the title *Liebesgedichte* (1979, Love Poems), and it is not meant ironically, just as the phrase "I miss you" cited above is to be taken at face value as an expression of a basic and important human emotion. In spite of the occasional appearance of politics and word plays these are on the whole insightful, introspective, and often melancholy poetical statements of an aging man with a growing awareness of death as he searches for meaningful relationships.

It would be difficult to find a poem that could be called "typical," but the following, from *Lebensschatten* (1981, Shadows of Life),, can perhaps serve to illustrate the tenor of Fried's most recent poetry:

Left Right Left Right

> If a leftist thinks
> that a leftist
> merely because he is on the left
> is better than a rightist
> then he is so self-righteous
> that he has moved to the right
> If a rightist thinks
> merely because he is on the right
> that he is better than a leftist
> then he is so self-righteous
> that he is a right-wing extremist

And because I
am against rightists and
right-wing extremists
I am against
leftists
who think
that they are better
than rightists
And because I am against them
I sometimes think
I have a right to think
that I *am* better than they are (p. 19)

The intensity of Fried's devotion to the leftist cause has not decreased, but he is more aware or more ready to state his awareness of the weaknesses of many of his fellow leftists, especially their lack of concern for humanity, which stands in direct contradiction to his conception of what it means or should mean to be a leftist. Finally, his introspection, here manifested in the form of self-irony (a quality not often found in contemporary German leftist poets) is also revealed.

Fried's importance as a political poet is an unquestioned fact, as is his mastery of the poetic word play; furthermore, his books sell: *Liebesgedichte* reached the remarkable total of 25,000 copies in print a year after publication. His stature as a poet, however, is still an open question. He has won literary prizes —e.g., the International Publishers Prize (1977) and the Prize of the City of Vienna (1980)—but not as many as other poets whose names are far less familiar. All but his most ardent admirers concur that he publishes too much, i.e., by no means all of his poetry displays the polish and control that might be desirable. And there is also considerable disagreement on the quality of even his best poems. In a review of *Lebensschatten* Manfred Riedel, after quoting one piece, comments, "A great poem, a beautiful poem."[14] Jürgen P. Wallmann, on the other hand, says in a review of the same volume after quoting some poems, "Of what use are these kinds of trivial occasional verse (*Poesiealbumsprüche*), however well-intentioned they might be? And they are even among the best in this book," and he later adds, "A text like this may belong to any number of genres, but it is certainly not a poem."[15] The critics' view of Fried, like Fried's view of the world, is complex and not without paradoxical elements.

Notes

1. Most of the substantial studies of Fried, exclusive of interpretations of individual poems, are listed in the bibliography below: I am indebted to many of them to a greater or lesser degree.

2. Complete bibliographical information on Fried's works is given in the list of publications below.

3. Quoted in Hanjo Kesting, "Erich Fried," *Kritisches Lexikon zur deutschsprachigen Gegenwartsliteratur,* ed. H. L. Arnold (München: Text + Kritik, 1980), p. 6; a list of Fried's translations can be found in Volker Kaukoreit, "Auswahlbibliographie zu Erich Fried," *Freibeuter,* No. 7 (1981), 29–30. For a discussion of Fried as translator see Rex Last, "Erich Fried: Poetry and Politics," *Modern Austrian Writing: Literature and Society after 1945,* ed. Alan Best and Hans Wolfschütz (London: O. Wolff; Totowa, N.J.: Barnes & Noble, 1980), pp. 190–192; and Manfred Mixner, "Zweimal Shakespeare: Die Übersetzungen von Erich Fried und die Bearbeitungen von Karl Kraus," *Literatur und Kritik,* Nos. 136/137 (1979), 413–420.

4. Because of space limitations, quotations will generally be given only in English translation; when some aspect of the original is especially significant, as in this quotation, the original will also be given. All translations are my own.

5. Here, as occasionally below, I have attempted to reproduce Fried's puns; literally the four pairs are: sword/burdens me; shield/scolds me; firm/loose; festival/fate.

6. Erich Fried, "Rede in der Hand," *Doppelinterpretationen,* ed. Hilde Domin (Frankfurt am Main: Athenäum, 1966), p. 248.

7. *Neue Deutsche Hefte,* No. 112 (1966), 151.

8. Brecht, *Gedichte,* 6 (Frankfurt am Main: Suhrkamp, 1961), p. 143.

9. Fried's attitude toward the relationship between nature or nature poetry and politics is typically complex; he is no less concerned about engagement being viewed as an end than about *l'art pour l'art.* See Wilhelm Große, "Erich Fried: Neue Naturdichtung," Peter Bekes, et al., *Deutsche Gegenwartslyrik* (München: Fink, 1982), pp. 86–99; and Hiltrud Gnüg, "Gespräch über Bäume: Zur Brecht-Rezeption in der modernen Lyrik," *Basis,* 7 (1977), 102–104.

10. Rolf Hochhuth attacks this attitude much more directly in *The Deputy,* where Pius XII is portrayed as more interested in the cult of the Blessed Virgin than in the fate of the Jews.

11. *Deutsche Bücher,* Vol. 5, No. 1 (1975), 12.
12. For a discussion of the case see Christian Schultz-Gerstein, "Aus Liebe zum Gegenteil," *Der Spiegel,* April 9, 1979, pp. 225-228.
13. "Lebensschatten – Lebensformen: Über die späten Gedichte von Erich Fried," *Neue Zürcher Zeitung,* 26-27 June 1982, p. 70.
14. Ibid.
15. *Literatur und Kritik,* Nos. 169/170 (1982), 99.

Books by Erich Fried

They Fight in the Dark: The Story of Austria's Youth. London: Young Austria in Great Britain [1944].

Deutschland: Gedichte. London: Austrian P.E.N., 1944.

Österreich: Gedichte. London and Zürich: Atrium, 1945.

Gedichte. Hamburg: Claassen, 1958.

Ein Soldat und ein Mädchen. Hamburg: Claassen, 1960.

Reich der Steine: Zyklische Gedichte. Hamburg: Claassen, 1963.

Warngedichte. München: Hanser, 1964.

Überlegungen: Gedichtzyklus. München: Hanser, 1964.

Kinder und Narren: Prosa. München: Hanser, 1965.

und Vietnam und: Einundvierzig Gedichte. Berlin: Wagenbach, 1966.

Arden muß sterben: Eine Oper vom Tod des reichen Arden von Faversham. London: Schott; New York: Associated Music Publishers, 1967.

Anfechtungen: Fünfzig Gedichte. Berlin: Wagenbach, 1967.

Zeitfragen: Gedichte. München: Hanser, 1968.

Befreiung von der Flucht: Gedichte und Gegengedichte. Hamburg: Claassen, 1968.

Die Beine der größeren Lügen: Gedichte. Berlin: Wagenbach, 1969.

Unter Nebenfeinden: Fünfzig Gedichte. Berlin: Wagenbach, 1970.

Die Freiheit den Mund aufzumachen: Achtundvierzig Gedichte. Berlin: Wagenbach, 1972.

Gegengift: 49 Gedichte und ein Zyklus. Berlin: Wagenbach, 1974.

Höre, Israel! Gedichte und Fußnoten. Hamburg: Assoziation, 1974.

Fast alles Mögliche: Wahre Geschichten und gültige Lügen. Berlin: Wagenbach, 1975.

So kam ich unter die Deutschen: Gedichte. Hamburg: Assoziation, 1977.

Die bunten Getüme: Siebzig Gedichte. Berlin: Wagenbach, 1977.

100 Gedichte ohne Vaterland. Berlin: Wagenbach, 1978.

Liebesgedichte. Berlin: Wagenbach, 1979.
Lebensschatten. Berlin: Wagenbach, 1981.
Zur Zeit und zur Unzeit: Gedichte. Köln: Bund-Verlag, 1981.
Das Nahe suchen: Gedichte. Berlin: Wagenbach, 1982
Das Unmaß aller Dinge: 35 Erzählungen. Berlin: Wagenbach, 1982.
Das Mißverständnis. Ill. Rainer Hofmann. Frankfurt am Main: Alibaba, 1982.
Es ist was es ist: Gedichte. Berlin: Wagenbach, 1983.
Angst und Trost: Erzählungen und Gedichte über Juden und Nazis. Frankfurt
    am Main: Alibaba, 1983.
*Ich grenz' noch an ein Wort und an ein andres Land: Über Ingeborg Bachmann –
    Erinnerung, einige Anmerkungen zu ihrem Gedicht "Böhmen liegt am
    Meer" und ein Nachruf.* Berlin: Friedenauer Presse, 1983.
Beunruhigungen: Gedichte. Berlin: Wagenbach, 1984.
Kalender für den Frieden 1985. Köln: Bund-Verlag, 1984.
*Und nicht taub und stumpf werden: Unrecht, Widerstand und Protest: Reden,
    Polemiken, Gedichte.* Dorsten: Multi-Media, 1984.
In die Sinne einradiert. Ill. Catherine Fried-Boswell. Köln: Bund-Verlag, 1985.

Erich Fried in English Translation

Arden Must Die: An Opera on the Death of the Wealthy Arden of Faversham.
    Tr. Geoffrey Skelton. London: Schott; New York: Associated Music
    Publishers, 1967.
Last Honours. Tr. Georg Rapp. London: Turret, 1968.
On Pain of Seeing. Tr. Georg Rapp. London: Rapp & Whiting; Chicago: Swal-
    low, 1969.
Four German Poets: Günter Eich, Hilde Domin, Erich Fried, Günter Kunert.
    Tr. Agnes Stein. New York: Red Dust, 1979.
100 Poems without a Country. Tr. Stuart Hood. London: Calder, 1978; New
    York: Red Dust, 1980.

Selected Bibliography

Gross, Ruth V. *PLAN and the Austrian Rebirth: Portrait of a Journal.* Columbia,
    SC: Camden House, 1982, pp. 108-112.
Hartung, Harald. "Lyrik als Warnung und Erkenntnis: Zur Zeitlyrik Erich
    Frieds." 1966: rpt.: *Geschichte der deutschen Literatur aus Methoden.*

Ed. Heinz Ludwig Arnold. Frankfurt am Main: Athenäum, 1973, III, pp. 71-77.

Hinderer, Walter. "Sprache und Methode: Bemerkungen zur politischen Lyrik der sechziger Jahre: Enzensberger, Grass, Fried." *Revolte und Experiment.* Ed. Wolfgang Paulsen. Heidelberg: Stiehm, 1972, pp. 98-143.

Holzner, Johann. "Gegennachrichten: Zu den Gedichten von Erich Fried (1966-1974)." *Formen der Lyrik in der österreichischen Gegenwartsliteratur.* Ed. Wendelin Schmidt-Dengler. Wien: Österreichischer Bundesverlag, 1981, pp. 41-55.

Kaukoreit, Volker. "Auswahlbibliographie zu Erich Fried." *Freibeuter,* No. 7 (1981), 27-32.

Kaukoreit, Volker. "Der Weg eines bunten Getüms: Eine vorläufige Biographie des Dichters Erich Fried." Ibid., pp. 20-23.

Kaukoreit, Volker. "Erich Fried im Londoner Exil." *Die Horen,* No. 134 (1985), 59-72.

Kesting, Hanjo. "Erich Fried." *Kritisches Lexikon zur deutschsprachigen Gegenwartsliteratur.* Ed. Heinz Ludwig Arnold. München: Edition Text + Kritik, 1980.

Kesting, Hanjo. "Gedichte ohne Vaterland: Der Lyriker Erich Fried." Hanjo Kesting, *Dichter ohne Vaterland: Gespräche und Aufsätze zur Literatur.* Bonn: Dietz Nachf., 1982, pp. 39-51.

Kane, Martin. "From Solipsism to Engagement: The Development of Erich Fried as a Political Poet." *Forum for Modern Language Studies,* 21 (1985), 151-169.

Last, Rex. "Erich Fried: Poetry and Politics." *Modern Austrian Writing: Litarature and Society after 1945.* Ed. Alan Best and Hans Wolfschütz. London: Oswald Wolff; Totowa: Barnes & Noble, 1980, pp. 181-196.

Wallmann, Jürgen P. "Erich Fried." *Argumente: Informationen und Meinungen zur deutschen Literatur der Gegenwart.* Mühlacker: Stieglitz, 1968, pp. 161-169.

Wertheimer, Jürgen. "Erich Fried." *Die deutsche Lyrik 1945-1975.* Ed. Klaus Weissenberger. Düsseldorf: Bagel, 1981, pp. 344-352.

Zeller, Michael. "Im Zeichen des ewigen Juden: Zur Konkretion des politischen Engagements in der Lyrik Erich Frieds." *Gedichte haben Zeit: Aufriß einer zeitgenössischen Poetik.* Stuttgart: Klett, 1982, pp. 153-196.

Barbara Frischmuth

Donald G. Daviau

Barbara Frischmuth (born 1941) is an excellent example of the transition of Austrian literature in the past decade from the preoccupation with language that dominated the 1960s to a more traditional mode of literature featuring social concern. As a member of the Forum Stadtpark, the organization of writers in Graz, and through her training as a translator, she confronted the language skepticism that was so prevalent when she began to write, as she stated in an early radio interview entitled "Zweifel an der Sprache."[1]

Concern about language, particularly language used to inculcate ideas, is reflected in Frischmuth's first narrative tale *Die Klosterschule* (1968, The Convent School), an autobiographical depiction of life in a girls' Catholic boarding school. This work brought her considerable attention, although some of the publicity was in the form of notoriety rather than appreciation of the work as a literary achievement, for the book created controversy because of its attack on the traditional form of Catholic education.[2] In *Die Klosterschule,* which reflects the influence of Handke in subject matter and style, an attempt is made to demonstrate how the young impressionable schoolgirls are brainwashed by the constant repetition of dogmas that present an orthodox Catholic philosophy of life. Frischmuth examines the preconceptions and presuppositions that are contained in the phraseology, which is intended as a subtle form of thought control. She presents the formulations and propositions in a straightforward precise manner and without further commentary allows the reader to react to the delimiting and demeaning view of women that they contain.

Frischmuth has an excellent ear for language, and the impact of the book is strengthened also by the fact that she is writing from experience. She is not attacking linguistic abuse but rather protests a misuse of language by those who utilize it for purposes of indoctrination. The girls are presented with a view of woman's mission in life intended to prepare them for their future roles as wives and mothers in a manner prescribed by the church. Frischmuth is fighting specifically against the idea of training women for a purpose in life that in her view does not correspond to the new enlightened social concept of women in the twentieth century. This work clearly shows the dedication of Frischmuth to the feminist ideals of women's liberation, a theme that continues to become more pronounced in subsequent works. In *Die Klosterschule* Frischmuth demonstrates that it is harder for women to achieve independence, to be themselves, if they ever manage it at all, after having been exposed constantly throughout their educational years to old-fashioned ideas about women's subordinate role in life. That the weight of the church is behind this attempt to use language to restrict women in the options they feel are open to them makes this pedagogical system all the more insidious.

From this first work with its concentrated tendentious emphasis on an examination of language Frischmuth has evolved into a writer of great imagination, inventiveness, emotional sensibility, and social concern. The narrow preoccupation with language has broadened into a more traditional literary approach, stressing personal dilemmas and social problems either of individuals growing toward maturity or of couples trying to find the inner resources to build a life together. She treats the problems of women without being a strident feminist. Indeed the balanced, moderate approach of her writings to complex issues is one of her strongest positive features. The course of her artistic development, which in effect mirrors the trend of Austrian prose during the 1970s, will be examined in the following discussion.

The evolution evident in the progression of Frischmuth's writings not only involves a shift of perspective from language to character, but also includes a return to an emphasis on nature, a feature that was largely ignored by writers during the phase of linguistic experimentation in the late 1950s and 1960s. She has noted recently the renewed feeling for nature evident in contemporary literature: "I would even go so far as to consider this feeling for landscape in contrast to urban phenomena and vice versa a characteristic of contemporary prose in Austria."[3] Frischmuth herself exemplifies this change, and nature has become a prominent feature in her recent novels. Her attraction to nature is seen also on a personal level, for, although she lives in Vienna, she feels an inner need to spend time in the country, by which she usually means Alt Aussee, where she was born the daughter of an innkeeper. She considers the possibility of alternating between city and country a desirable strengthening factor and regards as foolish any attempt to view the city and the provinces as adversaries.

In the decade and a half since *Die Klosterschule* Frischmuth has produced a variety of works in different styles. She has a degree from the Interpreter's Institute in Graz in Turkish and Hungarian, which she also studied in Erzurum and Debrecen as well as at the University of Vienna from 1964 to 1967. She has made translations from both languages into German. In addition she has recreated children's language in the two collections of fairy tales for adults as well as children, *Geschichten für Stanek* (1969, Stories for Stanek), and *Amoralische Kinderklapper* (1969, Amoral Children's Noisemaker), and in the children's books *Der Pluderich* (1969, The Pluderich), *Philomena Mücken-*

schnabel (1970, Philomena Mosquito Beak), *Polsterer* (1970, Polsterer), *Die Prinzessin in der Zwirnspule* (1972, The Princess in the Yarn Spool), *Ida – und ob!* (1972, Ida – And how!), and *Grizzly Dickbauch und Frau Nuffl* (1975, Grizzly Potbelly and Mrs. Nuffl). These works show her rich imagination in plot invention, her humor, and her playful facility in creating a children's vocabulary not accessible to their parents. In form the stories contain the same blend of the real and the fairy-tale world that characterizes her subsequent major novels.

In 1971 Frischmuth produced the volume *Tage und Jahre. Sätze zur Situation* (Days and Years. Sentences on the Situation), a collection of vignettes in which she attempts to describe as precisely as possible a series of basically disconnected actions, phenomena, and events. The various segments or entries parallel the technique of pointillistic painting. Since Frischmuth does not provide any transitions between the individual descriptions, she forces the participation of the reader, who must provide the sense of continuity and interconnectedness and thus help create a unified literary work out of the given facts. The feelings of the protagonist are not described but must be deduced from her actions. The entries, which are written in simple, unadorned language, are not aphorisms, anecdotes, or commentaries, but simply factual observations, documentations, and memories ranging from a few lines to a few pages in length. For example, in the first half of the book subtitled "Tage" (Days) the first entry reads: "I press out stars. The tin breaks. I have cut myself. My finger bleeds into the dough."[4] There are descriptions concerning the weather, the mail, pets, workers, television, in short, episodes describing routine everyday life in the country for an intellectual woman.

The statements in the second half of the book, "Jahre" (Years), are longer, corresponding to the longer time unit. Here Frischmuth deals with her childhood in a hotel by the lake in Alt Aussee. The recall of the past permits interspersing some flights of fancy with the reality of the present. The reader is presented with a series of independent, nonsequential mosaic tiles consisting of experiences and thoughts and must create his own context for them. In this sense the work is like a series of finger exercises for the more complex writings to follow. It may be possible to see in *Tage und Jahre* the continued influence of Handke, who in 1967 expressed his distaste for plot.[5]

In the next two years Frischmuth produced two volumes of stories, *Rückkehr zum vorläufigen Ausgangspunkt* (1973, Return to the Provisional Starting Point), and *Haschen nach Wind* (1974, Grasping for the Wind), as well as the novel *Das Verschwinden des Schattens in der Sonne* (1973, The Disappearance of the Shadow in the Sun), a fictionalized account based on the summer she spent in Istanbul. In all three works Frischmuth explores the theme of women in contemporary society from different perspectives. The style remains objectively realistic, and the narratives feature the blend of experienced and observed details found in *Tage und Jahre.*

The nineteen stories comprising *Rückkehr zum vorläufigen Ausgangspunkt* are heterogeneous and again make no attempt to achieve a unified whole. They are all autobiographical, and primarily recall the world of her childhood. Together they display Frischmuth's range of interests at the time from children's stories to tales of horse racing reminiscent of *Ida – und ob!* (Frischmuth's former husband was a racehorse trainer) to impressions of Istanbul. As in *Tage und Jahre* the reader can deduce the larger scene from the aggregation of individual experiences presented in pointillistic manner.

The major change in *Haschen nach Wind* is that these four tales are no longer experimental like the previous works. There is a noticeable shift from the topic of language to a concern for people, specifically for women and their problems in trying to balance marriage, family, and career. The theme is not emancipation as such but the problem of interpersonal relationships, of surviving as an individual within a relationship with another person. There are no answers provided, only questions raised. The mood, however, is pessimistic, and none of the tales ends happily. As Paul Kruntorad notes appropriately: "The tales in *Haschen nach Wind* show in somewhat uneven division Barbara Frischmuth's sureness in the genre of so-called women's literature. She fills it out with new sobriety and precision, even if not with particularly new emotions."[6] Or as Reinhard Urbach has commented: "They are stories with dead ends: things cannot continue this way any longer, think the women, who no longer know which way to turn. But things do continue this way.... These stories are for reliving, for recalling, for self-recognition. They do not help us out of the problems, they help us into them" [7]

The first tale "Bleibenlassen" (Let Things Be) concerning the breakdown of a marriage is told exclusively from the woman's point of view, as are the other stories. The men in all of Frischmuth's works are only foils, and the reader is shown little of their thoughts, feelings, and desires except indirectly. In this psychological tale Frischmuth presents the thought processes of the protagonist, a graphic artist, who tries to hold an unsatisfying marriage together while at the same time pursuing her career. She wants to be married, but at the same time she wishes to pursue her career and retain her individual freedom. Her difficulty with creativity reflects her troubled spirit and her worry about her marriage. Finally she is confronted with her husband's infidelity and, feeling threatened, she is thrown into a state of shock and confusion. Her husband considers her behavior madness (she suddenly begins beating him irrationally out of sheer frustration), and it is not clear what the resolution will be except that she is determined to fight as hard as she can to stay in her home. Whether she is really insane, and whether the ominous approaching footsteps are those of her husband or people coming to take her to an institution are unanswered questions which conclude the story on a note of threatening ambiguity.

In "Baum des vergessenen Hundes" (Tree of the Forgotten Dog), a bitter tale of a marriage in the process of dissolution, the protagonist Sybil also flees out into nature to recover from the spiritual strain of a joyless marriage that is wearing her down emotionally. She feels trapped and threatened by the thought of being subservient to another person and plans to return to work in an antique shop where she had been happy and can regain her sense of individuality:

> You mean you intend to leave me? He had stood up and was coming toward her. Leave, leave, she mocked him, what does it mean to leave? I am simply going, I am going my way. I can no longer stand it, I do not want to go on anymore, I want to be alone![8]

The tale ends on a brutal note: he buries his head in her lap in lost confusion, she fantasizes about stabbing his exposed neck, "so that it would be over once and for all, and she would no longer have to torment him."[9]

The problem does not lie in the outer circumstances, which are not presented as difficult or problematical, but in the psychological attitude of the women protagonists, who, for reasons that are not specified and which they themselves seem not to know, cannot adjust to a life style that accommodates another person. They feel spiritually inhibited and restricted in their potentialities. They live in apprehension and dread of demands upon them even before they are made. What is missing here, as in all these stories, is the essential ingredient of love. These women protagonists seem to be immature in the sense that they retreat into themselves or into fantasy, unable to cope with reality or to communicate with their partners.

This state of dreamy isolation can be seen in the title story "Haschen nach Wind," which portrays a young schoolgirl who tries to live her romantic fantasies by becoming involved in an affair with one of her teachers. She yearns for love and fantasizes that the teacher will eventually marry her. However, the reality of the relationship brings no fulfillment of her dreams and indeed little pleasure of any kind. The tale ends tragically: when her pregnancy causes him to reject her, she retreats to the woods to commit suicide. Her lonely death is bitter, and the knowledge that the teacher will face disciplinary action gives her no solace.

The final story "Unzeit" (Bad Time) describes the life of Euridice, a divorced woman with twins. She had married Felix in college, had dropped out when she became pregnant while he finished his studies, and then they separated: She does not know what direction to follow in the future, for she finds nothing satisfying. She engages in temporary relationships with various men but does not want to enter into any permanent arrangement again. Her life is lonely, uncertain, and incomplete while she searches for direction and meaning. Above all she fights to maintain her independence while bringing her life into equilibrium and is not close to anyone, even her children. Her ex-husband's visit at Christmas time causes her to let down her guard only to be hurt by him again: "and then she knew that she would never be able to see him again in this friendly way, that she now must be on guard against him just as against all others. Whatever their names might be."[10]

Although there is more stress on emotions or inner states of mind in these pessimistic tales, the author still maintains an objective distance from these characters. These realistic works, which present various relationships like specimens for examination, are designed to appeal more to the mind than to the heart. While there are some typical features, it is not possible to generalize on the basis of these "world histories," for these three women as well as the fourteen-year-old girl are all immature dreamers unable to cope with other people and lacking the strength to find the life they want. Their problems are created within them rather than caused by external forces. Whether and how they finally face reality and whether they will eventually find happiness is left undecided, but the future is open. The title *Haschen nach Wind* symbolizes the futility of their aspirations thus far but does not preclude the possibility of improvement except for the tragic teenager.

A major turning point in Frischmuth's literary development is the ambitious novel *Das Verschwinden des Schattens in der Sonne* (1973), which represents a great advance over the previous works technically and in thematic complexity. The opportunity to retell Turkish historical legends enabled her to combine her gift for fantasy with her talent for accurate description. The anonymous protagonist and narrator vividly captures the exotic sights and sounds of Istanbul as seen by one who is open-minded, favorably predisposed, and determined to like what she sees. The plot concerns the attempt of a Viennese university student to carry out a summer research project in Istanbul, tracing the history of the medieval Dervish order of the Bektashi. She lives with Aytem, a young Turkish teacher, and Turgut, a university student actively involved in a radical political group. The protagonist is thus placed between the old and the new and must learn that her research into the country's past is not an accurate guide to its present or future.[11]

Despite her openness, receptiveness, and eagerness to be accepted into this society the anonymous narrator finds it impossible to be regarded as anything more than a tourist passing through. Neither her love for Turgut nor that for her mentor Dr. Aksu is strong enough to overcome the barriers that separate them. She discovers that one cannot be accepted into a new society, particularly into a politicized situation, without commitment and true inner engagement. As long as she has a passport and a return ticket home in her pocket she remains a stranger and outsider, no matter how much she desires to be accepted:

> ... You know us, you live with us, you are interested in everything that concerns us, that means everything that has affected us, you speak our language, you are informed about our history, and still you do not really look around you, you do not perceive a great deal that is happening around you. ... You walk around as if in a dream. I want to warn you that you should not believe that you will understand everything better if you go further and further back in time. It is not only our tradition that has made everything the way it is.[12]

Eventually she is defeated in her research project as well as in social and personal terms. When her friend Turgut is shot by police during a political demonstration after having told her that he was leaving for the provinces to avoid involvement with the law, she perceives that she has always been an outsider to him and to all her other Turkish friends. The magic spell of Istanbul is broken, and she returns home gratefully, wiser in the ways of people and nations. As she notes in a moment of sober reflection: "I would wake up one day and all this would no longer affect me, at least directly."[13] She has learned that life is not the way she imagines it to be in her dreams, but unlike the fourteen-year-old in "Haschen nach Wind" who pays for this lesson with her life, or the other women there who have not yet awakened to reality and consequently exist on the edge of despair, the protagonist here has matured through her experiences and is ready to seek and explore new possibilities of life in the future. This novel is as optimistic as *Haschen nach Wind* is pessimistic, although the theme of striving for an impossible goal is similar. The difference is that here the protagonist learns from her failure, and in this sense the work is a *Bildungsroman*. Her return home is not a defeat but a victory for herself. The summer in Istanbul has been a process of growth and transformation to a new self, more confident, more knowledgeable about the world, more sensitive to people, and more dedicated to a sense of social commitment. The title *Das Verschwinden des Schattens in der Sonne* emblemizes this awakening from a dreamy state of fascination to the sobering clarifying light of reality, but the heroine makes the transition without suffering, for the exotic atmosphere of Istanbul has caused the entire experience to seem to be more a dream than reality. The valuable lessons learned remain but not the pain.

Das Verschwinden des Schattens in der Sonne, although more complex than any of Frischmuth's previous works, contains the same blend of fairy-tale world and reality that characterizes her other works. However, it has brought Frischmuth to a new broader level of concern, for she has advanced from the limited perspective of a single individual or of a couple to the more complex confrontation of an individual with society. Her protagonist has sought entry into an alien community through knowledge of its past, which she felt could be the key to the present, but to her misfortune she finds that her grasp on both is illusory. Despite her knowledge of many details of history, she still cannot synthesize the material because of its complexity: "I grew dizzy from the interpretive possibilities which the story offered."[14]

The protagonist's quest in Istanbul has in a sense been a *Haschen nach Wind,* which is symbolized in the novel in several ways. It is reflected in her vain attempts to find a certain Süheyla (why she is so difficult to locate is never explained), who seems to serve only the purpose of adding another element of mystery, vagueness, and uncertainty to the novel. Another symbol of transitoriness and the loss of continuity from the past to the present is the fact that the quaint old house in which she lives will soon be torn down to make room for a modern building. Finally the title of the novel itself reflects the impossibility of the protagonist's quest to bring the mystical legends of the past into the light of present reality. The two cannot be reconciled, and the myths dissipate before her eyes like the shadows before the sun.

Now that the protagonist sees things clearly for the first time, she can return home without regret and face the future with new understanding, inner resolve, and self-confidence. Through the cathartic effect of Turgut's murder she has undergone a total internal transformation of values and personality, and these in turn awaken many new possibilities for the future. The ending is tragic in terms of Turgut but open-ended and totally positive in terms of the protagonist. As a writer the protagonist is ready to turn her attention realistically to social problems of which she has become aware. In this sense she agrees with the view expressed by Franz Fühmann in discussing this novel that "Literature always has to do with those unsolved problems which constantly have to be overcome anew because they recur again and again, and one must take a position on them."[15] One can see this shift of emphasis in Frischmuth's next novel *Die Mystifikationen der Sophie Silber* (1976, The Mystifications of Sophie Silber), where she grapples with major contemporary social questions that require resolution.

The ambiguous ending of *Das Verschwinden des Schattens in der Sonne,* which stresses life's possibilities or alternatives, leads directly to *Die Mystifikationen der Sophie Silber*, the first volume of a trilogy dealing with the problem of women's liberation. While not an educational novel in the same sense as its predecessor, it still fits loosely into this category. All of the qualities that have been discussed so far—objective realistic descriptions, imaginative plot invention, the blend of the fairy-tale world and reality, and a protagonist who is a sensitive, receptive observer—are combined here in a novel that features in addition great warmth, charm, and humor. The new feature here is the engagement of the author with major social issues of the day. Certainly this novel surpasses all of her previous works in terms of inventiveness, for here Frischmuth has created her own fictional world and populated it with fairies, elves, water, mountain, wind and other spirits, all anthropomorphized representations of nature, who can assume human form at will and live as comfortably in the real world as in their own.

Frischmuth's fondness for the fairy-tale form or for what she calls "adult fantasy" has already been noted, and her fascination with myths and legends also fits into this category.[16] In fact, there seems to be a carryover to *Die Mystifikationen der Sophie Silber* from the novel *Das Verschwinden des Schattens in der Sonne* where the narrator tries to fathom the disappearance of the fourteenth-century order of the Dervish of the Bektashi, which had been absorbed into society so completely that it was still recognizable only to initiates if at all. The spirits in *Die Mystifikationen der Sophie Silber* adopt this solution of disbanding their formal order and integrating into society at large in their efforts to preserve the natural world from destruction. The major sources for the novel, however, according to the author herself, are old Celtic legends and George MacDonald's novel *At the Back of the North Wind.*[17] This novel also fits easily into the tradition of German and Austrian fairy-tale literature from Ludwig Tieck and E.T.A. Hoffmann to Ferdinand Raimund (particularly *Der Alpenkönig und der Menschenfeind,* The King of the Alps and the Misanthrope), and Hugo von Hofmannsthal.[18]

The events in the book demonstrate the truism that nothing in the world has permanence. Everything is transitory and subject to change, including the role played by the spirit world, which is not immune to earthly developments.

In this fairy tale of reality ("Wirklichkeits-Märchen"), which blends artistically the world of spirits and the world of the mortals, Frischmuth shows how the two worlds are mutually dependent, a fact that human beings seem to have forgotten. Although the spirits have followed a certain pattern of existence for an indefinite time, the callous exploitation of natural resources by the mortals has reached such proportions that the representatives of the spirit world are being threatened everywhere. For that reason they have gathered from all parts of the world for a major meeting at Aussee to discuss their future.

Sophie Silber, who is related in an unspecified manner to the spirit world, has been mysteriously invited to the meeting at the request of Amaryllis Stern-wieser, the leading fairy and Sophie's guardian angel. Through Sophie the spirits hope to become informed about current developments in the world. Sophie, who has led a colorful and full life as an actress in a wandering troupe of players, never learns that she is in the company of spirits but she benefits greatly from the experience. She is at a turning point in her life, for she has just been engaged at a major theater in Vienna and is ready to begin a new career at the prime of her life. The main purpose of Amaryllis' invitation is to help Sophie remember her past life and gain confidence about herself so that she can face the future with awareness, assurance, and a spirit of independence.

Through Sophie Silber's presence the novel is brought into the category of emancipation literature, at least on this one level. It is noteworthy that Sophie has descended from the von Weitersleben family, in which the children never know who their fathers are. This family custom already establishes the independence of the women from men. Sophie continues the tradition and does not know who fathered the son she has neglected for eighteen years. Her decision to rejoin with him now is a sign that she is ready to integrate the past and present in her life. She is now truly independent and can start her new life without the further protection of Amaryllis Sternwieser, who had planned this step to prepare Sophie for the day when her guardian angel would no longer exist; Amaryllis, who is really a more central character of the book than Sophie, is preparing to undergo a drastic transformation to cope with the changing world.

Apart from Sophie's personal story the novel is a parable of contemporary social and environmental problems. The spirits voice their opposition to war, pollution, exploitation of resources, and a host of other ills of modern society. Since they cannot halt the devastation of their realm, they decide to assume new roles as mortals and to continue their existence in a manner that will enable them to influence events. Amaryllis states the alternatives facing the spirits and details the reasons for her decision to become mortal:

We can assume the form of wives and children and divide the power anew, divide it in such a way that the mortals no longer represent a danger to the world. We can try above all to teach them friendliness, sympathy, the pleasure in all beings and things, and the unity and the multiplicity, the spirit of one for all, and the forms of continued life. . . . We can satisfy their curiosity to such a degree that their fantasy will awaken again, and they will be able to imagine a better way to act than the manner to which they have succumbed.[19]

The solution of Amaryllis to attempt to alter the course of the world by infiltrating it in the form of women and children is an ingenious way of stressing their newly gained importance in society. Thus this seemingly tranquil fairy tale with its idyllic pastoral setting, quaint characters, whimsical customs, and stylized language contains a feminist program and in a sense presents an ingenious version of events leading to the women's movement. However, neither Sophie Silber nor Amaryllis in her mortal form of Amy Stern will become a political activist, a radical, or a revolutionary. They will simply live normal, well integrated, happy, and successful lives as independent career women and thus serve as encouraging models for other women to follow. When the numbers of such women are sufficiently large, they will be able to influence events. Thus the two parts of the novel, the real and the fantasy world, are united by the theme of women's emancipation and by the ideal that women must play a greater and more important role in the world.

On the basis of the feminist theme and the environmental and pacifist issues the novel is completely contemporary. Yet the basically cheerful and optimistic tone seems to reflect an earlier less troubled age than the present, at least as it is usually presented in the literature of today. Frischmuth has returned delicacy of feeling, gentleness, and gracefulness to prominence, and has made literature enjoyable again through the pleasant atmosphere and attractive humorous characters even while presenting a serious social "message." Instead of the "Anti-Heimat" (anti-homeland) stance found in Bernhard, Jonke, Innerhofer, and others Frischmuth lavishes her descriptive powers on creating a charming setting of idyllic beauty and peaceful harmony in the manner of Stifter. Nature is serene and sublime, marred only by the effects of pollution. Yet despite her fondness for nature Frischmuth is never a sentimental idealist but always practical. Hence the decision of the spirits to transform as the world is doing rather than to retreat into hiding in Avalon, as they could do, or to try to keep things as they are. She knows that the world cannot return to an earlier stage of development, and she does not indulge in utopian unrealizable solutions to difficult and complex problems. Instead she makes only the modest and sensible suggestion that the future must be planned differently if the world is not to suffer irreparable damage. At the same time she advocates a more influential role for women in the decision-making process.

Die Mystifikationen der Sophie Silber is an ambitious attempt to grapple with fundamental social issues without becoming polemical. Although the novel projects a natural, idyllic, pastoral world of spirits, it is pragmatic in outlook, for it recognizes that even the spirit world cannot cling to past ideals. It is necessary to remain a part of the world and to change with it in order to try to direct it into a more desirable course in the future. To avoid social themes or to adopt a pessimistic view toward life like Bernhard, or to concentrate on shocking bourgeois audiences like Wolfgang Bauer is in each case a course of action that Frischmuth rejects in favor of more positive optimistic alternatives. She recognizes the problems of contemporary life but does not despair because she does not know any immediate solutions. Life offers multiple possibilities to effect change and, according to Frischmuth, women can become an important force in helping to bring about improvement in the world.

The life of Amaryllis after her transformation into human form becomes the subject of Frischmuth's next novel *Amy oder die Metamorphose* (1978, Amy or the Metamorphosis). The humanization of Amaryllis is depicted as she proceeds through social commitment, love, and childbirth. The novel ends with Amy determined to have her child as a single parent and prepared to cope with life on her own resources.

Despite the greater realism of *Amy oder die Metamorphose* the magical aura of the fairy-tale world of *Sophie Silber* still prevails, because Amy is not yet completely human and fully released from the other world. The birth of her child breaks all connections to the spirit world,[20] and the third part of the trilogy *Kai und die Liebe zu den Modellen* (1980, Kai and the Love of Models) dealing with Amy as an unwed mother combining a career as a writer with parenthood, is written in a completely realistic manner without any further references to spirits.

The metamorphosis of the title does not refer solely to the physical change of Amaryllis Sternwieser into Amy Stern's body but rather to Amy's personal development. At the beginning she is tentative and irresolute, exploring various alternatives and possibilities for her future, until finally her pregnancy brings her the maturity and strength to choose a course of action that will best serve her child and her career.

The exposition with its mixture of fairy-tale world and reality is followed by a series of short vignettes as Amy tries to learn about life by listening to

various women discussing their relationships with men. As an observer she
is exposed to some of the alternatives she faces in life. She hears from women
who are dominated by their husbands and from others who have pursued careers
instead of, or combined with, marriage. At the same time Amy meets other
women in the laundromat who tell stories of life with oversexed, impotent, or
boring men. None of these tales is particularly inspiring or edifying, and they
are useful to Amy only as examples not to follow. Amy is a good listener, and
her urge to learn is plausible, since she has not had a "human" background
on which to draw. Eventually she determines to give up the study of medicine
to become a writer, a twist which brings the novel into an autobiographical
vein. As it progresses the novel becomes increasingly realistic and focuses on
the problems faced by a career woman in a male-oriented society. Amy has an
affair with Klemens, the son of Sophie Silber who now lives with his mother
in Vienna, but their relationship seems to be one of mutual convenience rather
than of true love on either side. Unfortunately, Klemens does not rise above
being a cardboard figure, and Frischmuth has yet to portray a fully developed
male character. Like all of the men in Frischmuth's works Klemens plays only
a secondary role. For her part Amy, like her predecessors in the earlier works,
refuses to relinquish any of her independence and freedom. Although she and
Kelmens say they love each other, each values a career more. As Amy notes:
"Sometimes there is even the feeling that they are opponents more than partners. Opponents in a game. . . ."[21] When Amy finds herself pregnant, Klemens
perfunctorily and with great reluctance offers to marry her, but it is clear that
he does not want the responsibility. He would prefer that she have an abortion.
However, with a defiant decision that is more emotional than logical Amy
dismisses him and determines to keep her child. Thus, after all of the explora-
tions of alternatives in life *Zufall* makes the final decision for Amy. No matter
how many life stories one hears or knows, human problems cannot be general-
ized, and the circumstances of each situation still determine the personal course
of action.

Because of its episodic nature this novel is not as tightly integrated and
structured as *Sophie Silber*. Like the protagonist in *Das Verschwinden des
Schattens* Amy seems here to be more an observer than a participant in the
events, at least until circumstances force her to act at the end. Like its predecessors it is an educational novel: Amy is given the opportunity to compare
alternatives until she finds an acceptable course for her life. The novel ends
on the optimistic note that old traditions are giving way to new perspectives
and that the role of women is becoming more prominent. Amy's decision to
have her child is one facet of the new feminist spirit. Another contribution

will be her writings, through which she hopes to influence society. There is no solution in sight but only a goal to pursue. As a writer Amaryllis/Amy will carry out her promised aims.

Having set the previous two novels in the past and present, respectively, Frischmuth concludes her ambitious trilogy with a projection of the future in *Kai und die Liebe zu den Modellen* (1979). In this autobiographical novel, which is narrated in the first person in contrast to the previous volumes, Frischmuth projects her tentative hopes for a changed society more favorable to marriage and children. A theme of women's emancipation continues to predominate, and a number of possible models for women (and men) to follow are presented, although none is advocated as the ideal course that will solve the problems of all women attempting to combine a career with marriage and family. At the end of the novel Amy has yet to resolve this conflict in her own life, and there is a genuine possibility that she never will, for many of her difficulties are psychological in nature and, as for the earlier characters, lie more within her than in outer circumstances. However, she is constantly maturing and changing, and at the end she at least knows the direction that she and society should follow.

Amy approaches the feminist program conservatively and realistically. She recognizes that society is in a process of transition that will take time to complete. She is no militant revolutionary but stresses a program of moderation and education that will produce change by evolution. Although directed toward a different problem of society, Frischmuth's stance automatically calls to mind Hofmannsthal's idea of a Conservative Revolution. All of Amy's discussions with friends concerning possible models for women to follow fail to provide any new insights or ideas on the subject, and no concrete conclusions are offered. In this sense Amy resembles Maya, who models in wax because she is reluctant to put anything into permanent form and likes to keep all possibilities open. The main conclusion offered by this novel and by the entire trilogy is only to point the direction for society to follow: greater participation of women in society, increased importance of children, and more attention to the education of boys, so that they will be more uderstanding of women when they become men. Schools should also play a role by teaching boys new priorities, deemphasizing the stress on a career.

Emphasis on children represents the other major level of the novel, for they are the real hope for a changed and improved future society: "If there were a new morality, its basis would have to be a genuine interest in children."[32] Amy cannot understand why people consider children the property of two parents and why all adults do not feel related to all children. She attempts to serve as a model by the way she raises Kai, whom she treats as an equal and as a companion. She allows him complete freedom to develop in the hope that he will be the new kind of male needed in the future. Some of the best scenes are those of children at play, where Frischmuth has an opportunity to display her talent for capturing the language, the games, and the vitality of young people. She knows how children with their naiveté and ingenuousness can break down barriers between adults. Along with the ideas of child rearing the novel also touches upon such related issues as child abuse and problems facing the children of guest workers.

Kai und die Liebe zu den Modellen is completely realistic in characters, setting, language, and tone. The blend of fantasy with the real world has given way here to an objective minute description of everyday life. The trilogy has proceeded from the macrocosm of the world at large to the microcosm of Amy's personal conflicts. It is a tribute to Frischmuth's artistry that she can sustain interest even when treating familiar prosaic events. Her objectivity also enables her to portray potentially sentimental situations with sensitivity without lapsing into pathos.

Frischmuth's next two tales, *Entzug – ein Menetekel der zärtlichsten Art* (1979, Withdrawal – A Most Tender Warning) and *Die Reise ans Ende der Welt* (1979, The Trip to the End of the World), provide additional testimony to Frischmuth's virtuosity and also document eloquently how far she and Austrian literature have come in the past decade from the objectivity and avoidance of emotionalism of the 1960s to the complete restoration of lyrical subjectivity. In *Kai und die Liebe zu den Modellen* Frischmuth portrayed the anguish of Amy as, filled with desire, she yearned for her ex-lover Klemens to come to her. However, such emotional scenes were carefully controlled and restrained. Here in these two tales of unrequited love, handsomely illustrated by Heinz Treiber, Frischmuth in a major departure from her usual objective manner gives free reign to descriptions of erotic and spiritual longing in an effusive lyrical style employing richly sensuous imagery and sexual symbolism.

The title story describes the thoughts of a mature intellectually liberated woman addressed to an absent lover. One could easily imagine Amy writing such a letter to Klemens if she had ever spoken honestly or openly to him about her feelings. The longing for closeness and love is described by a series of metaphors and similes depicting various transformations. Among other things the protagonist fantasizes about changing into a rose which her lover will pick and press between the covers of a book. When the day comes to be together again she wants an indication from him that his feelings have been as strong as hers: "Then will come the time when all my words are used up and even the

most poetic sentence will not be able to cover the void. Without your nearness
I can no longer last the winter. . . . So far must love drive one. Not in order to
say, come, I am here if you need me! But: I need you!"[22]

The second tale, *Die Reise ans Ende der Welt,* is written in the same sensuous
imagistic style. A young elementary school teacher, who cannot find her ideal
lover in reality, creates him in fantasy. In this sense she is distantly related to
the teen-age heroine of *Haschen nach Wind.* Here the girl hears the voice of her
imaginary lover, Osman, the son of the ship builder, and follows it into the
ocean. As she searches for him in the depths of the water we learn of her past
life, of her mother's unhappiness that her daughter cannot find a husband, of
the various men in her life, and of her insecurity as a teacher. Her travels in
pursuit of Osman lead her to Alexandria, which she has always wanted to visit,
and to the desert. Suddenly she feels Osman's presence near her, although she
cannot see him, and her happiness is fulfilled. At this point her lifeless body
rises out of the water, ". . . and frightened to death a few people taking a harmless canoe ride."[23] With this grotesquely humorous ending Frischmuth breaks
the spell of the tragedy and of the passionate mood she has created.

Firschmuth's next two short novels *Bindungen* (1980, Relationships), and
Die Ferienfamilie (1981, Family on Vacation), are both interim works that
continue and amplify the themes of her trilogy: the struggles of the emancipated career woman, the possibilities and limitations of personal development,
the difficulty of relationships between people with different approaches to
life, and the proper way to raise children. In *Bindungen* Frischmuth presents
an emancipated young career woman named Fanny, who is studying for a career
in archaeology. The novel examines Fanny's attempt to regain the equilibrium
of her life after the breakup of an affair. In the wholesome regenerative atmosphere of nature and amidst the harmonious homelife of her sister Malwina's
family Fanny surmounts her suffering and at the end is ready to return to
the university.

The novel is prefaced by two quotations. The first, from E.T.A. Hoffmann,
deals with the language of children, a specialty of Frischmuth displayed here
through the conversations of Fanny with Zeno, her sister's bright but undis-
ciplined child. The second quotation, by Lou Andreas-Salomé, deals with love-
hate relationships and alerts the reader to the ambivalent relationship of the
two sisters, who are opposites in their outlook on life and in basic personality.
Fanny is an outsider who has difficulties in relationships with others most
probably because she inherited the domineering characteristics of her mother.
Malwina is totally oriented toward the surface of things and is determined to
have a happy harmonious family life while at the same time pursuing her career

as a painter, at which she is modestly successful. Malwina seems to have everything that Fanny at least subconsciously desires: a happy marriage, a family, inner harmony, relative freedom, and professional success. Fanny on the other hand prefers to dig through the surface to get to the bottom of things even though her former professor had once told her that in life as in archaeology one can destroy everything if one digs too deeply and too vigorously.

The major problem in *Bindungen* and also in Frischmuth's other works is the discrepancy between outer freedom and inner dependency. Fanny needs other people and wants their love but on her own terms. Until she learns that it is necessary not only to bind but also to be bound, as Hofmannsthal said so eloquently in *Death and the Fool,* she will always be disappointed in every relationship and feel like an outsider. At the conclusion of this realistic novel there is no indication that Fanny has undergone any inner transformation or growth that will make life easier in the future. However, the novel does not end with any sense of resignation but on the positive note of life's possibilities and promise. While there are no false illusions there is at least hope, for she is a whole person again.

In the highly autobiographical novel *Die Ferienfamilie* (1981) Frischmuth continues her examination of relationships that are disrupted or that do not function as they should. It might be termed an adult children's book, whose aim is to sensitize adults to the world of children, particularly children from broken marriages, to their special language and to their needs and feelings. At the same time it makes children aware of the problems that adults face. It is narrated in a completely realistic style with detailed descriptions of everyday life.

An intellectual woman with the symbolic name Nora, who earns her living as a writer, moves with her son and two other young children from broken marriages to a small house in the country for the summer. Through Nora's private discussions with each of the children their feelings toward absent parents and their life style emerge. The didactic conversations between Nora and the children concern marriage, life, and raising children. Frischmuth stresses the idea that all adults should love all children and not leave that responsibility solely to the chance mother and father. At the same time Nora defends parents against the children's accusations of being ignored, noting how difficult it is in confronting life's complexities to find the time that one should take for children. She also shows the hardships faced by a single parent in trying to organize a household and also to find the hours that are needed for work, in her case as a writer.

Die Ferienfamilie presents a good examination of children and adults who are "unbound" and are seeking connections with others. Since there is no plot there is also no resolution. The novel is brought to a conclusion when one of the children has an accident on his bicycle, and his father, who is honeymooning with his third wife, indicates that he will return immediately to see his son. While Nora and the three children emerge more closely knit as a group than they were at the beginning and hope to repeat this summer vacation again the following year, the personal situation of each individual has not altered. However, the novel ends on a positive note with laughter indicated as the proper attitude toward life: "And then all three had to laugh aloud, for how else, I beg you, should they have reacted to all of the complexities in this complex world."[24]

In her most recent works, the drama *Daphne und Io* (1982), which had been performed but not published, and the novel *Die Frau im Mond* (1982, The Woman in the Moon), Frischmuth attempts to raise her familiar material — the relationships of men and women — to literary significance by introducing a dual level to the narrative: allusions to mythology in the drama and to the tradition of Columbina and Pierrot in the novel. By this device she lends greater significance to the characters. Unfortunately, while she was credited for her ambitious efforts, critics failed to consider either work a success. However, such works show that she knows the direction to follow to produce the major work she is capable of writing.

The thirteen selections in her newest collection of prose titles *Traumgrenze* (1983, On the Boundary of Dreams), prose tales show again the blend of the spirit world with the real world, as she has so successfully done in a number of works, particularly in the novel trilogy. Here, as there, the two worlds are not separate but intermixed. These tales again provide eloquent testimony of her vivid sense of fantasy, which for her, as for many great writers, is as vital as reality. They also show Frischmuth's increasing turn to reflectiveness, for thoughtful comments and observations are interspersed throughout the stories. Like the other works of the last few years these tales may be considered experiments showing her continuing development both as a thinker and as a stylist.

Frischmuth is a genuinely gifted author, whose writings show a constant progression over the span of her career to date. As she has shifted away from a narrow focus on language to concern for social problems she has developed steadily in sureness of technique, style, maturity of theme, and particularly in her unique ability to combine her own fictional worlds, whether they be that of spirits and elves or of children at play, with the real world. She has consistently expanded the range of her forms and themes, and she shows every indication of continuing to progress toward more demanding accomplishments in the future. The hope is that at some point she will find it possible to combine all of her rich talents to produce the major work which she is so eminently capable of writing and on which her lasting reputation will be based.

Notes

1. Barbara Frischmuth, "Zweifel an der Sprache," ORF, quoted in Paul Kruntorad, "Prosa in Österreich seit 1945," in Hilde Spiel, *Die zeitgenössische Literatur Österreichs* (Zürich und München: Kindler Verlag, 1976), pp. 246-269.

2. Cf. Dietmar Grieser, "Eine leidige Angelegenheit: Barbara Frischmuth und 'Die Klosterschule': eine Feedback-Studie," in *Schauplätze österreichischer Dichtung* (München: Albert Langen Verlag, 1974), pp. 169-179.

3. Barbara Frischmuth, "Österreich, versuchsweise betrachtet," in *Glückliches Österreich. Literarische Besichtigung eines Vaterlands,* edited by Jochen Jung (Salzburg und Wien: Residenz Verlag, 1978), p. 70.

4. Barbara Frischmuth, *Tage und Jahre* (Salzburg und Wien: Residenz Verlag, 1971), p. 7.

5. Peter Handke, *Ich bin ein Bewohner des Elfenbeinturms* (Frankfurt am Main: Suhrkamp, 1972), p. 24.

6. Paul Kruntorad, "Prosa in Österreich seit 1945," in Hilde Spiel, *Die zeitgenössische Literatur Österreichs,* p. 270.

7. Reinhard Urbach, "*Haschen nach Wind.* Vier neue Erzählungen von Barbara Frischmuth," *Neue Züricher Zeitung,* 14 December 1974.

8. Barbara Frischmuth, "Baum des vergessenen Hundes," in *Haschen nach Wind* (Salzburg: Residenz Verlag, 1974), p. 72.

9. Ibid., p. 73.

10. Barbara Frischmuth, "Unzeit," in *Haschen nach Wind,* p. 143.

11. Waltraut Schwarz considers this tension between rebellion and return the theme of all of Frischmuth's major works, Cf. "Barbara Frischmuth — Rebellion und Rückkehr," in Herbert Zeman, ed., *Studien zur österreichischen Erzählliteratur der Gegenwart* (Amsterdam: Rodopi, 1982), p. 230.

12. Barbara Frischmuth, *Das Verschwinden des Schattens in der Sonne* (Frankfurt am Main: Suhrkamp, 1973), pp. 141-142.

13. Ibid., p. 218.

14. Ibid., p. 222.

15. "Gespräch über Barbara Frischmuth," (Franz Fühmann, Dietrich Simon

and Joachim Schreck), in *Sinn und Form,* 28. Jahr 2. Heft (1976), 436.

16. In the series "Mein Kinderbuch" in *Die Zeit* Frischmuth discussed her attraction to fairy tales and listed among her favorite early reading such works as *Thousand and One Nights,* the two Alice books of Lewis Carroll as well as *Die Jagd nach dem Snark, Water Babies* by Charles Kingsley, and the works of George MacDonald. Cf. Barbara Frischmuth, "Als die Wünsche noch an den Bäumen hingen" (When Wishes Still Hung from Trees), *Die Zeit,* 4 June 1979.

17. Barbara Frischmuth, "Als die Wünsche noch an den Bäumen hingen," *Die Zeit,* 4 June 1979.

18. Although Frischmuth in a personal conversation denied any influence of Hofmannsthal, there are many points of similarity between them: the inclination for the fairy-tale form, the stress on transformation, the idea of growth through adversity and renewed love, and the concept of selective forgetting to enable one's new self to approach the future without being crippled by thoughts of the past. Interest in the Orient is shared by Hofmannsthal, and concern for the problems of women, of the family, and of marriage is a dominant feature of his writings. His view of women, however, is far removed from Frischmuth's concept.

19. Barbara Frischmuth, *Die Mystifikationen der Sophie Silber* (Salzburg: Residenz Verlag, 1976), pp. 315–316.

20. There are similarities in this motif with Hofmannsthal's *Die Frau ohne Schatten.*

21. Barbara Frischmuth, *Kai und die Liebe zu den Modellen* (Salzburg: Residenz Verlag, 1979), p. 67.

22. Barbara Frischmuth, *Entzug – ein Menetekel der zärtlichsten Art* (Pfaffenweiler: Pfaffenweiler Presse, 1979), p. 20.

23. Barbara Frischmuth, "Die Reise ans Ende der Welt," Ibid., p. 41.

24. Barbara Frischmuth, *Die Ferienfamilie* (Salzburg: Residenz Verlag, 1981), p. 132.

Selected Bibliography

Die Klosterschule. Frankfurt am Main: Suhrkamp, 1968.
Amoralische Kinderklapper. Frankfurt am Main: Suhrkamp, 1969.
Geschichten für Stanek. Berlin: Literarisches Colloquium, 1969.
Der Pluderich. Kinderbuch. Frankfurt am Main: Insel, 1969.
Philomena Mückenschnabel. Frankfurt am Main: Insel, 1970.

Polsterer. Kinderbuch. Frankfurt am Main: Insel, 1970.

Tage und Jahre. Sätze zur Situation. Salzburg: Residenz, 1971.

Ida – und ob. Jugendbuch. München, Wien: Jugend un Volk, 1972.

Die Prinzessin in der Zwirnspule und andere Puppenspiele für Kinder. München: Hellermann, 1972.

Rückkehr zum vorläufigen Ausgangspunkt. Erzählungen. Salzburg: Residenz, 1973.

Das Verschwinden des Schattens in der Sonne. Frankfurt am Main: Suhrkamp, 1973.

Haschen nach Wind. Erzählungen. Salzburg: Residenz, 1974.

Die Mystifikationen der Sophie Silber. Roman. Salzburg: Residenz, 1976.

Amy oder die Metamorphose. Roman. Salzburg: Residenz, 1978.

Kai und die Liebe zu den Modellen. Roman. Salzburg: Residenz, 1979.

Entzug – ein Menetekel der zärtlichsten Art. Zwei Erzählungen mit Illustrationen von Heinz Treiber. Pfaffenweiler: Pfaffenweiler Presse, 1979.

Bindungen. Erzählung. Salzburg: Residenz, 1980.

Die Ferienfamilie. Roman. Salzburg: Residenz, 1981.

Das Leben des Pierrot. Erzählungen. Salzburg: Residenz, 1982.

Die Frau im Mond. Roman. Salzburg: Residenz, 1982.

Traumgrenze. Erzählungen. Salzburg: Residenz, 1983.

Kopftänzer. Roman. Salzburg: Residenz, 1984.

English Translations

None available at present.

Secondary Literature

Dietmar Grieser, "Eine leidige Angelegenheit: Barbara Frischmuth und 'Die Klosterschule': eine Feedback-Studie." In *Schauplätze österreichischer Dichtung.* München: Albert Langen, 1974, pp. 169-179.

Franz Fühmann, *Sinn und Form,* Jg.28, Heft 2 (März/April 1976), pp. 423-426.

Muhammad Abu-Hatab Khaled, "Versuch einer kritischen Analyse zum Bild der islamischen Mystik in Barbara Frischmuths Roman 'Das Verschwinden des Schattens in der Sonne,'" in *Veröffentlichungen* der Deutschabteilung der Al-Azhar Universität, Kairo, Januar 1978. pp. 37-56.

Muhammad Abu-Hatab Khaled, "Das Orientbild in Barbara Frischmuths Roman 'Das Verschwinden des Schattens in der Sonne,'" in *Österreichische Literatur in Ägypten*. Veröffentlichung der Deutschabteilung der Al-Azhar Universität, Kairo, 1978, pp. 9–35.

Hans Gstrein, "'Das Verschwinden des Schattens in der Sonne'–Religionssoziologische Einsichten und Anliegen im politischen Werk von Barbara Frischmuth." Ibid., pp. 39–45.

Christa Gürtler, *Schreiben Frauen Anders? Untersuchungen zu Ingeborg Bachmann und Barbara Frischmuth*. Stuttgarter Arbeiten zur Germanistik, 134. Stuttgart: Akademischer, 1983.

Jürgen Serke, "Barbara Frischmuth: Die Macht neu verteilen, so daß sie keine Gefahr mehr für die Welt bedeutet!" in Jürgen Serke, *Frauen schreiben*. Ein Stern-Buch. Hamburg: Gruner & Jahr, 1979, pp. 150–163, 320–321, 330, 331.

Donald G. Daviau, "Neuere Entwicklungen in der modernen österreichischen Prosa: Die Werke von Barbara Frischmuth," in *Modern Austrian Literature*. Sonderheft. Vol. 13, no. 1 (1980), 177–216.

Ulrike Kindl, "Barbara Frischmuth," in *Neue Literatur der Frauen*. Hrsg. von Heinz Pukuns. München: Beck, 1980. pp. 144–148.

Jorun B. Johns, "Barbara Frischmuth: Eine Bibliographie der Werke und der Sekundärliteratur bis Herbst 1980," in *Modern Austrian Literature*, Vol. 14, no. 1 (1981), pp. 101–128.

Jorun B. Johns and Ulrich Janetzski, "Barbara Frischmuth," in *Kritisches Lexikon zur deutschsprachigen Gegenwartsliteratur*. Hrsg. von Heinz Ludwig Arnold, Band I. München: Edition Text & Kritik, 1978. S. A-G.

Peter Handke

Francis Michael Sharp

Peter Handke was still an adolescent schoolboy when in the mid-1950s the two dominant figures of twentieth-century German drama and prose, Bertolt Brecht and Thomas Mann, died. He was born in a mountainous region of southern Austria in 1942, nine years after Hitler had seized power in Germany and four years after his triumphal march into Austria itself. By both the date and the place of his birth, Handke escaped the full burden of guilt and need for expiation that National Socialism exerted on the direct successors to Brecht and Mann among the older postwar German writers such as Heinrich Böll, Günter Grass, Martin Walser, Peter Weiss, and Rolf Hochhuth, to name only a few. And it has only been in Handke's more recent works that the tainted episode of the Nazi past, a heavily dominant theme in postwar German-language literature, has surfaced as a theme in his works.

By declaring the theater to be useless as an institution to promote social or political change Handke pointedly distanced himself early in his career from the activist legacy of Brechtian dramaturgy. Yet it was not Handke's first works for the stage or his repudiation of political theater that initially brought him into the limelight of the German cultural scene. In April 1966 he traveled to Princeton to attend the annual meeting of *Gruppe 47,* a loose association of German writers who had met for readings and critical discussions since 1947. It was here on the last day of meetings that Handke, under the watchful eye of the press, unleashed his attack on the "impotence of description" in the works of his older, more established colleagues. Whether calculated or not, Handke's impertinence toward the establishment won for him immediate notoriety as a publicity seeker who had no ground for support in his own sparse literary production. Even twenty years and numerous plays, stories, and poems later, Handke's works are still accorded a mixed critical reception that often reflects the original controversy surrounding him.

Shortly after his outburst in Princeton Handke published a clarification of his complaints against what was known as the New Realism.[1] Description in literature itself, he insisted, was not the target of his attack, but rather the type of description he saw being practiced that identified objects in language with those in the phenomenal world. That literary reality has a linguistic base was to Handke an elementary truth that his colleagues appeared to overlook. For them to treat language as an inert medium by which phenomena of the world might be reproduced without distortion was a naive and potentially dangerous presumption. Although such linguistic considerations were of course not new with Handke, they were far from the mainstream of a literary establishment that was still deeply involved in coming to terms with recent political history and that prized the social and political commitment of a writer above everything else. Handke's heresy lay not only in his brashness and youth, but also in his focus on what seemed merely formal concerns to writers consumed by moral and ethical questions. In the intellectual atmosphere of the sixties, however, the heretic was an embodiment of cultural heroism, and the spectacle of an assault on authority attracted a great deal of sympathetic attention to the young aspiring writer.

These aspirations would have to wait until the seventies to be fully realized, but they had been at the center of his fantasies, Handke has said, since he was twelve. Except for the years from 1944 to 1948 he had spent most of his life to his twelfth birthday in Griffen, his hometown in southern Austria. During this interim Handke and his mother lived in Berlin with the parents of his father, a soldier in the German army. In 1948 they returned to Austria where the boy began the years of his formal education that were to stretch, essentially uninterrupted, until 1965. At this point in his life the Suhrkamp publishing house accepted his first novel, and Handke immediately gave up the study of law, which he had embarked on four years previously. He had originally chosen law mainly because a teacher had advised him that it was the one course of study that would leave him plenty of free time for his own writing.

In *Wunschloses Unglück* (1972, *A Sorrow Beyond Dreams*), the story of his mother's life and suicide, Handke gives her credit for his own early acquaintance with literature. Later, as a student in a Catholic preparatory school for the priesthood, Handke was drawn particularly to William Faulkner and George Bernanos, both authors forbidden by the school authorities and thus that much more alluring to the rebellious side of his nature. The literary worlds of these writers took on heightened significance and reality for the boy depressed by the rigid authoritarianism of the school. During his years at the university in Graz Handke continued his literary education alongside his law studies primarily through his association with the artists in the "Forum Stadtpark" and his participation in the Graz Group of young avant-garde writers. His first publication, a short prose piece entitled "Die Überschwemmung" ("The Flood"), was published in 1964 in the journal *manuskripte,* where parts of *Die Hornissen* (1966, The Hornets), his first novel, also appeared. A collection of short prose works from these early years, *Begrüßung des Aufsichtsrats* (Salutation of the Board of Directors) was published in 1967 by a publishing house in Salzburg. In addition to *manuskripte* the local radio station became an outlet for Handke's creative production, broadcasting several of his short stories as well as his commentary on literature, the Beatles, and soccer. It was also in the mid-sixties that the fledgling writer began his "speech plays" and a second novel, *Der Hausierer* (1967, The Peddler), which he read from at Princeton.

Neither of Handke's first novels caught the attention of the literary world to the same degree as his public outburst. Fragmentary and discontinuous, the narrated events of *Die Hornissen* revolve around a blind man named Gregor whose reflections on his life blend with the memories of a book he had once read about a similarly afflicted character. The narrator's autobiographical reminiscences and fiction merge into an undifferentiated stream of occurrences populated by several vaguely drawn members of his family. Handke's novelistic debut met none of the traditional generic expectations and, as was smugly noted by those commentators who were aware of Handke's remarks at Princeton, it was full of descriptive detail.

An ironic observer of the Princeton meeting characterized the mood that greeted Handke's reading from his second novel, *Der Hausierer,* as one of a "lively rigor mortis."[2] In an interview some years later Handke himself expressed aesthetic reservations about this novel as well as two of his early speech plays.[3] From hindsight these works seemed to the author overly formalized, too limited in their adherence to the model upon which they were based. In *Der Hausierer* the model is the murder mystery or detective story, and Handke devotes the first part of each of the twelve chapters to an abstract sketch of its rules and developmental stages. By laying bare the skeletal structure that individual variations of the genre have in common he intended to make the reader aware of its mechanics. The first section of each chapter is set off in italics from a narrative text that might be found at the corresponding stage in a conventional murder mystery. Handke's interest, however, was to expose, not to imitate convention, and instead of a suspenseful tale his narrative resembles a mosaic of sentences lifted from various stories.

With the performances of his speech plays in 1966 and 1967 Handke's reputation as a serious antagonist of the literary status quo began to acquire legitimacy. Following its première in June 1966 in Frankfurt's avant-garde Theater am Turm, *Publikumsbeschimpfung* (*Offending the Audience*) moved to Berlin where it ran for five years. *Weissagung* (*Prophecy*) and *Selbstbezichtigung* (*Self-Accusation*) were first performed on German stages in October 1966, *Hilferufe* (*Calling for Help*) the following year in Stockholm. By the end of 1967 the young upstart from the Austrian provinces had received the prestigious Gerhart Hauptmann prize awarded by Berlin's *Freie Volksbühne*.

While there are scarcely any elements of the theater that Handke leaves untouched in his speech plays, the most fundamental change is in the use of language. Unlike traditional theater, language in the speech plays creates neither plot, image, nor illusions. The actors' function, with variations in each work, is limited to speaking. Instead of creating a separate world on the stage by dramatically declaiming the author's text, the speakers underscore the unity of their world with that of the audience. The elevated language of classical drama is as out of place in the speech plays as it might be on the street corner. Handke demonstrates here what he had asserted at Princeton: the building blocks of literature are words, not objects. He calls to mind the fundamental difference between the signifier and the signified, between the linguistic skeleton of language and its suprastructure of meaning. The radicality of his demonstrations corresponded to the degree to which his fellow writers and their audiences seemed to have neglected, confused, and suppressed this difference.

For the four speakers in *Publikumsbeschimpfung* the playwright provided no precise division of labor, merely designating that each should be heard for about the same amount of time. The list of rules that precedes the text points to various acoustic and visual models as expressive and rhythmic guides. Everyday sounds and sights as well as the litanies of the Catholic church are listed alongside the music of the Rolling Stones, the Beatles' movies, and the hit parade on Radio Luxembourg. The allusions to the symbols of popular culture gave Handke's works a special note of relevance in the minds of young theatergoers in the sixties.

The audience, the real topic of Handke's first speech play, should get no clue about what awaits it before the curtain parts. Handke's instructions direct that the usual formalities of theater ritual and etiquette be observed in every detail. Neither the improperly dressed spectator nor the latecomer should be allowed to take a seat. The usual pre-performance noise from behind the curtains is in evidence as is the gradual dimming of the lights and the buzzer that usually signals the opening act. Only after the curtains have opened does the special nature of the performance begin to become evident. As the four speakers step toward the front of a bare stage, the lights are again turned up until stage and audience are equally illuminated. The expectation in the spectators' mind of a theatrical reality about to unfold on stage has been quashed even before the speakers can disillusion them directly.

Nothing seen or heard in this linguistic performance—the litany of disavowals begins—will stand for something else. In this "argument with the theater" (14) the imaginary wall between stage and auditorium falls as the spotlight shifts from the play to the playgoer. The argument focuses on that element of playgoing society which perpetuates theatrical tradition by its habituated patterns of action and thinking. Handke's speakers verbalize these patterns, bring them to the consciousness of the public whose behavior, they maintain, has become ritualistic, its reactions predictable and easily manipulated. During the last few minutes of the performance the speakers turn from analysis of their theme to insult and bombard the audience with a rich array of invective that ranges from the humorous and silly to the outrageous and obscene. As any other writer who writes for more than his own satisfaction, however, Handke too needs and courts a public. The insults in *Publikumsbeschimpfung* are not meant to alienate the audience but to "switch" it "on" (29), to interrupt its complacency and break the spell of traditional theater. This accomplished, Handke's first speech play can really become what he insists it is, a prologue both to the future habits of his audience and to his own work for the stage.

Although there are no roles in *Selbstbezichtigung* and only one personal pronoun, an "I" which Handke labels an impersonal, grammatical entity, the stage directions prescribe two speakers, one male and one female. They stand on an evenly lit, bare stage and here speak *for* the spectator rather than at him. The list of propositions that describe the birth, the physical and perceptual development of the "I" has been abstracted from the particular, yet refers to an everyman: "I came into the world. . . . I grew older. . . . I moved. . . . I spoke. . . . I saw. . . . I learned" (37). The most significant step of its development is from the natural to the moral world when capacities for actions come into conflict with prohibitions, when "I can" begins to clash with "I should." "I learned rules," the everyman determines, "rules for behavior and thought, . . . rules for inside and outside . . . rules for things and people . . . general and specific rules" (39). Beyond this capacity to learn rules, the "I" proves itself particularly adept at the more satisfying human function of breaking them. Delight rather than remorse stands behind its confessions. In accusing itself of its multitude of errors, failings, misdeeds, and offenses, it revels in its humanity and marvels at the web of restrictions and interdictions that it can ignore or violate.

Weissagung, Handke has noted, "is no play on meaning, but a play on language," a comment that rings equally true for *Hilferufe* as well.[4] In the latter speech play the speakers declaim a series of increasingly brief sentences, phrases and words in what Handke declares to be a search for the word "help." Until the word has been found at the end, when paradoxically "help" is no longer needed, an emphatic "no" follows each segment of the spoken text. As a prologue to the other equally short text Handke quotes from a poem by Ossip Mandelstam:

> Where to begin?
> Everything is out of joint and totters.
> The air quivers with comparisons.
> No word is better than the other,
> the earth booms with metaphors. . . .[5]

Spoken by a chorus of four speakers, both individually and in varying configurations, Handke's text is a series of tautological statements that parody a language overburdened with meaningless comparisons and empty metaphors. Comparing one object with another, he wrote in an essay in 1968, reflects an impotence to distinguish details of the first object, an inability to perceive its uniqueness.[6] In *Weissagung* the normally distinct elements of a comparison or metaphor are identical. Handke's statements are meaningless absurdities, a rhetorical device employed to strengthen the critical bite in this play on language.

"Literature is romantic," Handke declared in the title of a provocative essay written in 1966, a piece aimed primarily at Sartre's littérature engagée.[7] Such an avowal was by no means a quietistic surrender to prevailing social and political circumstances, but was bound to irritate the political left schooled in Brecht, Peter Weiss, and the documentary theater of the sixties. For Handke protest and activist sentiment had their place in forms of discourse other than the literary. Yet *Kaspar* (1968), Handke's first full-length play, reflects a struggle between power and powerlessness, a struggle between an imposing force and a passively innocent figure that might well be termed abstractly political. While Handke may have banned overtly political argument from literary discourse, the theme of his play is the insidious politics of language. These politics conform to the fundamental contours of an authoritarian system with language itself in the role of the master and Kaspar as its servant. The play depicts Kaspar's training for this role, an apprenticeship directed by three disembodied voices or prompters related to the speakers in the earlier speech plays.

By christening his protagonist Kaspar, the first character named in his plays, Handke makes an historical allusion, but not, he insists, for historical purposes. In 1828 in Nuremberg a mysterious figure in his mid-teens, Kaspar Hauser, stepped out of an apparent lifelong isolation into human society for the first time. He brought with him an almost total ignorance of language, the prime characteristic shared by Handke's Kaspar. Struggling onto the stage out of the folds of the curtain, the theatrical figure undergoes a symbolic second birth like that of his predecessor. He utters his one linguistic property, a single sentence, over and over: "I want to be a person like somebody else was once" (65). Kaspar's sentence is at this point, however, simply a series of words grammatically ordered but without stable meaning. As the prompters point out in following and commenting on his movements, he uses his sentence to mean anything and everything as a kind of all-purpose tool to adjust to his environment. Their function is to destroy and replace this uniquely variable sentence with conventional language, to take from Kaspar a sentence he controls and to deliver him over to a language that controls him.

Through a process of "speech torture" (59), suggested by Handke as an alternate title for the play, the prompters exorcise Kaspar's sentence by slowly grinding it down to its constituent sounds until Kaspar finally becomes silent. Then reversing the process, they bombard him with a cacophony of "speech material" (75) that gradually initiates him into speech. Handke suggests the structuring, normative power of this lesson in language by a change in the sequence of events on stage. Initially, the prompters' sentences are adjusted to Kaspar's movements, but gradually the order is reversed until his movements are visibly coordinated with the rhythm of the prompters' sentences. As language extends its mastery over him, several other identical Kaspars appear on stage, a propagation that underscores his loss of uniqueness. For the prompters and eventually for Kaspar, language is a means for establishing order among the objects of the world: "Ever since I can speak I can put everything in order" (78). In ordering, in impressing its order on the chaos of the phenomenal world, language bridges the natural alienation between subjective and objective realities, making the strange familiar and changing the expression of "astonishment" on the face of the original Kaspar to one of "contentment" on the faces of the clones. Handke focuses in *Kaspar* on this capacity of man to appropriate phenomena by naming them, to overcome the astonishment of speechlessness. The goal of Gregor Keuschnig, the protagonist of his later narrative, *Stunde der wahren Empfindung* (1975, *A Moment of True Feeling*), is to find his way back to this astonishment, to penetrate the layer of familiarity and contentment that language superimposes on the world.

Audiences and critics in Germany, Austria, Switzerland, and elsewhere greeted *Kaspar* with such enthusiasm that it became the young writer's most often produced and most thoroughly analyzed theatrical piece. Having conquered the stage with plays obsessed by language and saturated with speech, Handke turned next to a theater without words and wrote the descriptive text for a play of gestures, situations and apparently trivial events entitled *Das Mündel will Vormund sein* (1969, *My Foot My Tutor*). Two male actors in a bucolic setting, masks covering half their faces and dressed in work clothes, act out in silence a series of individual and interactive episodes. As the curtain opens, one of these figures, the ward, sits eating an apple in front of a painted stage setting of a farmhouse. Handke's text provides a moment-by-moment account of the details of the setting, its changes and the activities on the stage from the perspective of the audience. The "action" begins when the warden or guardian enters, sees the youth eating a second apple and stares at him until he lays the half-eaten apple aside. This very unexceptional event sets the tone for a relationship of dominance and subservience accentuated by allusions to violence. These allusions take a particularly grisly turn, at least in the spectator's imagination, when in the last scene, the ward, under the cover of a dark stage, may or may not be taking a horrible revenge on his oppressor.

While one reviewer called *Das Mündel will Vormund sein* "a repetition of *Kaspar* with other means," another stressed its theatrical quality, relating it to Samuel Beckett and to American "happenings," and labeling it "pure theater."[8] The silence on stage at its première must have contrasted starkly with the pandemonium caused by the production of *Selbstbezichtigung* earlier the same evening, a performance that featured nude speakers and had to be halted long before the final curtain.

The spoken word becomes instrumental once again in Handke's *Quodlibet* (1970), a clever play on and with language that, like *Das Mündel will Vormund sein*, the author considered a preliminary exercise for his longer play, *Der Ritt über den Bodensee* (1971, *The Ride Across Lake Constance*). In *Quodlibet*, Latin for "What you will," the cast of fourteen provides its own text. Handke merely directs that only snatches of the various conversations on stage be intelligible to the audience and that these be acoustically planned to elicit predictable patterns of response. For what the author called "a piece about the aesthetics of perception," the members of the audience make new sense out of the fragments they hear, a sense that has nothing to do with the speakers' intent, but relies instead on habits of thought and expectations that confirm "listener clichés."[9]

As Handke demonstrates in *Der Ritt über den Bodensee*, the stimulus for such stereotyped responses need not be spoken but may be a simple bodily motion or gesture. In one of the more lucid moments of a dialogue that is often disjointed and out of focus the discussion centers on this very point:

Porten: Someone keeps looking over his shoulder while he's walking. Does he have a guilty conscience?

Bergner: No, he simply looks over his shoulder from time to time.

Porten: Someone is sitting there with lowered head. Is he sad?

Bergner   (assumes a modeling pose for her reply): No, he simply sits there with lowered head (107).

Such stereotyped responses, Handke implies, characterize the half-conscious, unthinking relationship of most of us with our surroundings. Perceptions of external as well as internal facts and events become so glazed over with hackneyed routine that we act out most of our lives in the dreamlike, somnambulistic state of the characters on stage.

The title of the play refers to a nineteenth-century German ballad about a man who rides horseback across the frozen Lake Constance on a winter's night. On reaching the other side he learns from his amazed friends that the ice he had traversed is no more than an inch thick. Hearing this, he drops off his horse, dead from fright. Like the rider in the ballad, the characters in Handke's play move and act in a state of unawareness, held above a potentially threatening reality by a thin layer of language. Their somnambulistic facility with language contrasts with the initial state of Kaspar whose speechlessness made him vulnerable to the chaos of the phenomenal world, but also left him acutely aware of this disarray to the point of constant astonishment.

With a display of simple human emotion new to Handke's plays, Hermann Quitt, the main character of *Die Unvernünftigen sterben aus* (1973, *They Are Dying Out*), opens what is to be Handke's last dramatic work of the seventies. "I feel sad today" (165), the powerful capitalist entrepreneur confides to his servant Hans who reminds him that a man of his position and wealth can ill afford such moods. But Quitt perseveres throughout the play in search of a core of individualism that can find contact with the world directly through an exterior hardened by his ruthless market strategies. In Handke's closest approximation to the theater of illusion Quitt meets in the play with several of his colleagues to revamp these strategies. Although they reach an agreement on price fixing that will benefit them all, Quitt proceeds to undermine their accord and bring his associates to financial ruin. He sets this "tragedy of business life" in motion as a sign that his identity has not entirely been lost in his role as businessman: "I'm going to ruin their prices and them with it. I'm going to employ my old-fashioned sense of self as a means of production. . . . It will be a tragedy. A tragedy of business life, and I will be the survivor" (211). Yet Quitt himself recognizes that the "genuine signs of life" behind his actions are nothing but the "raw sewage" (211) of the self, anachronistic remnants of a nineteenth-century individualism. As the "sole survivor" (252) of his species he too is fated for extinction, and the play ends with his suicide.

Handke has said in an interview that Shakespearean tragedy provided him the prototype for his play, a prototype he then found played out in the financial pages of daily newspapers. Indicative of his development away from detachment and from writing according to models, however, he stressed to the interviewer the complementary subjective side of his play: "It wouldn't interest me to transform something I've merely observed into literature. Somehow my own stories and entanglements also have to be there. . . . I try every time to bring in my entire unconscious and all my dreams."[10] As the subjective component of the creative impulse grew more insistent in the seventies, Handke turned increasingly to the narrative as an outlet.

Apart from his preoccupation with the stage during these years, however, Handke wrote critical essays, radio plays, and edited as well as contributed to an anthology of "new horror stories."[11] His first financially successful publication was a collection of poems, *Die Innenwelt der Außenwelt der Innenwelt* (1969, *The Innerworld of the Outerworld of the Innerworld*), language constructs resembling concrete poetry in their graphic appeal and linguistic awareness. Some consist simply of language appropriated from another context: number 24, for example, reproduces the Japanese hit parade of popular songs from 25 May 1968. Like other young artists interested in reshaping the media of their expression, Handke was drawn to film and film making, above all as an alternative to traditional theater. Interviewed about his first efforts for the screen, *Chronik der laufenden Ereignisse* (1971, Chronicle of Current Events), a script he wrote and directed as a television film, Handke focused on the potential for existential change inherent in the medium: "You see a possibility in the best film of how you yourself could live." Later in the interview he continues: "It happens so seldom that you see something which has to do with art . . . and you say I simply have to change my life."[12] Since *Chronik der laufenden Ereignisse* Handke has written a second filmscript, *Falsche Bewegung* (1974, False Movement), directed the filming of his narrative *Die linkshändige Frau* (1976, *The Left-Handed Woman*), and translated Walker Percy's *The Moviegoer* (1980, *Der Kinogeher*).

Handke himself has been an avid moviegoer since his student days in Graz. His infatuation with film finds fictional representation in the thematic structure of two longer narrative works published in the early seventies. The first of these, *Die Angst des Tormanns beim Elfmeter* (1970, *The Goalie's Anxiety at the Penalty Kick*), revolves around the murder of a box office cashier by the work's protagonist. On the best-seller list in Germany and the first of Handke's narratives translated into English, it again exploits the pattern of the popular murder mystery, not to re-dissect the genre but to explore the experiential anomalies of a character who has fallen out of the network of signs and meanings with which others make common sense of their environment.

Josef Bloch, a former soccer goalie, arrives one morning at the construction site where he works, and because only the foreman takes notice of his arrival,

he concludes that he has been fired. Following this capricious act of interpretation, Bloch wanders aimlessly through Vienna, his puzzled reactions to
commonplace events marking his withdrawal from the system of experiential
grammar that gives these phenomena stable significance. His alienation conditions his first reaction to the cashier. He is struck by the natural way in which
she accepts his money when he enters the theater and is fascinated by her unthinking participation in their trivial exchange. Several days later he follows
her home, spends the night with her and, after painful attempts at conversation
the next morning, he strangles her. Handke offers no explicit motivation for
either the attraction to the cashier or for her murder. The initial allure for the
alienated Bloch, however, is plainly his fascination with the automatic nature
of her response to "the wordless gesture with which he'd put his money on the
box-office turntable" (4). Conversely, his fascination turns to irritation, disgust,
and finally murderous rage at the growing familiarity that the girl wants to
impose on him after they have slept together. She volunteers her name, appro-
priates as her own the things he tells her, and finally seems to know what he
will say before he has spoken. Viewed from Bloch's perspective, the slaying is
an act of self-defense, an act of ontological assertion against a threatening
familiarity.

Bloch flees the scene of the crime by bus to a remote border town where
he makes renewed contact with a former girlfriend. Here he passes time drinking,
reading newspapers, repeatedly trying to phone friends and his ex-wife, walking
and constantly misinterpreting the details of his surroundings. These details,
whether they are snatches of overheard conversations, noises, gestures, or
objects lying on the ground, begin to take on the function of a private language
that contains messages for Bloch alone. Referring to a conversation between
the postmistress and a mailman, he concludes: "And it wasn't only the conversation that was insinuating; everything around him was also meant to suggest
something to him. 'As though they winked and made signs at me,' thought
Bloch. For what was it supposed to mean that the lid of the inkwell lay right
next to the well on the blotter and that the blotter on the desk had obviously
been replaced just today, so only a few impressions were legible on it?" (95).
Handke has clearly moved beyond his position in *Kaspar* of exposing and demonstrating the power that language alone exerts on experience and behavior.
For Josef Bloch, objects across his entire field of perception become endowed
with significance, "talk" to him and issue regulations as insistent as those of
purely linguistic codes.

The narrative ends on a soccer field with Bloch lucidly explaining to a stranger the fine points of a penalty kick from the perspective of the goalie. The

murder remains unsolved and the criminal at large, loose ends to the fictional model that indicate its subordinance in Handke's plan. Bloch describes the goalie's task of anticipating the direction of an undefended penalty kick as nearly impossible even though the goalie on the field receives the attempted shot directly into his arms by standing absolutely motionless. The acute awareness of the insuperable odds that the goalie faces in view of the deceptive kicker separates Bloch, the ex-goalie, from the goalie still playing the game. Bloch stands on the sidelines of the larger game as well, an astute observer of the semiotic process functioning around him, but no longer a player.

Handke drew heavily from autobiographical materials in two major works published in 1972, *Der kurze Brief zum langen Abschied* (*Short Letter, Long Farewell*) and *Wunschloses Unglück* (*A Sorrow Beyond Dreams*). The separation from his wife whom he had married in 1967 and his travels in the United States supplied the narrative backbone for the first work, a story whose strong plot line and allusions to literary tradition underscore its distance from the experiments in the sixties. And the reviewers took notice, reminding Handke of earlier aspersions cast at narratives with a story to tell and questioning his oversight of the more controversial aspects of America, its ghettos, and its war in Southeast Asia.[13]

On the map of the United States inside the book's back cover, the reader can trace the narrator's journey from the east coast to St. Louis, from there to Tucson, and finally to Oregon and California. A thirty-year-old Austrian writer who has given up work on a play to write "stories" (150), the narrator is pursued from coast to coast by his estranged wife. She sends him a threatening birthday card with "last" scribbled between the words "Happy Birthday" and later fires a revolver at him, although the attempt on his life is ambiguously described in dreamlike, imprecise language. Handke locates the central autobiographical influence in the "fundamental psychic constellations of the book," maintaining that "the surface story is fictitious" in spite of the numerous details taken from his life.[14] He had actually been in only a few of the cities along the path of the fictional journey and totally invented the final episode with John Ford.

Part of the way across the country the narrator travels by car with Claire, a young American professor of German who represents the link with German literary tradition on the exotically foreign American landscape. She functions more as a sounding board for the narrator anxious to escape the self worn down by psychological battles with his estranged wife than as a new love interest. He reads passages to her from *Der grüne Heinrich* (*Green Henry*), a nineteenth-century novel of development that focuses on the growth of a central figure toward an accommodation with society. Clearly from the past the novel still gives the narrator pleasure in its representation of a time that believed in personal change. At points nauseated by his own sense of identification, he desperately longs to escape into the fictional worlds of literature (*The Great Gatsby*) and film (Ford's *Young Mr. Lincoln*). This kind of identification with fictional characters evolves at times into a fantasy of re-forming the elements of the self and its circumstances rather than magically negating them. Handke has pointed to the conclusion of *Der kurze Brief zum langen Abschied* as just such a reformulation of autobiographical elements, a "fairy-tale ending" to a bitter marital episode.[15] Following the ambivalent depiction of the attempt on the life of his fictional alter ego, Handke transports the couple, their aggressiveness spent in the act of catharsis, to the last scene with the venerated John Ford. The presence of the aging director, his own films testimony to the deep-seated need of the human spirit for fiction, validates for Handke his own transformation of a painful experience into a fantasy that finally sends the couple in separate directions, at peace with themselves and one another.

Early in 1972, seven weeks after his mother had taken her life with an overdose of sleeping pills, Handke began to respond to a need to write about her that he had first felt at her funeral. *Wunschloses Unglück* is both the "life story" of his mother, an Austrian of peasant stock and Slovenian lineage, as well as the reflections of a writer-son on the particular difficulties of his topic. The differing perspectives of the opening two paragraphs express his dilemma. The first paragraph cites a reporter's account of the suicide, a one-sentence notice of the essential facts stripped of everything personal, even the name of the deceased. Handke's reclamation of his mother from anonymity begins with the first words of the second paragraph in the recognition of the nameless figure as "my mother" (3). As a writer, however, Handke is aware that his subject must remain on middle ground between the general and the particular and that he must maintain the balance between the exemplary and the unique qualities of her life.

Maria Handke, fifty-one years old at her death, spent most of her life on the small farm in southern Austria which her father owned. Frugality was a way of life, a pattern internalized at an early age and carried into adulthood as self-denial. The German title, literally translated as "contented unhappiness," reflects the results of this denial, the loss of the capacity to even desire happiness. Handke reveals the deep imprint of this pattern on his mother's character, but shows as well her innate resistance to it. Maria Handke was by nature unable to fully content herself with a joyless life lacking hope and expectations, a life to which women especially fell heir. As a young girl she left home in defiance of her father in order to learn something even though, Handke remarks, learning to cook was the only course open to her. The natural exuberance of her adolescent years was heightened by the gaudy pageantry of National Socialism, its political malignancy hidden underneath its festive surface. She fell in love for the first and last time with an army sergeant, a married man whose child she bore and whose memory she clung to through the long years of loveless marriage to Handke's stepfather. Late in life she found in great literature a release mechanism that allowed her access into the core of her individuality deeper than she had ever known before. In a setting in which "the word 'I' seemed stranger to the speaker himself than a chunk out of the moon" (33), she learned to talk about herself and to reveal something about this self to her son. A feeling of pride wells up inside him as he travels to her funeral, an emotion born of the knowledge that her suicide was the most radical statement of discontent that she could have made about her unhappy life.

Calling his own writing an "exploitation of consciousness," Handke has listed his mother's death, the birth of his daughter, and the separation from his wife as the events that have affected him most profoundly.[16] During the early seventies he traveled between Düsseldorf, Paris, Austria, and Cologne, settling for a while into a suburb outside Frankfurt in late 1971. Over the next three years he received three literary prizes and, in addition to the publications already mentioned, published two volumes of his collected plays, one of critical essays mostly from the sixties, and a diverse group of "Poems, Essays, Texts, and Photos" of more recent vintage.[17] By the mid-seventies, Handke had not only established an impressive literary reputation, but also had found the intrinsic bond between his life and work that he would continue to exploit in the years to come.

Die Stunde der wahren Empfindung (1975, *A Moment of True Feeling*), the story of two frightening, yet strangely exhilarating days in the life of Gregor Keuschnig, press attaché to the Austrian embassy in Paris, stands at the very edge of nakedly subjective expression, according to its author.[18] Gregor, whose name and sudden existential transformation recall the protagonist in Kafka's *Die Verwandlung* (*Metamorphosis*), wakes up one morning from a dream in which he committed a murder and is convinced that he is no longer the same person he was the night before. No longer anchored securely in the network of systems, codes, and roles that previously defined his place in the world to himself and others, he has lost the basis of his identity. During the next forty-eight hours as his alienation gradually becomes evident to those who knew him, and as the external breaks are made with his wife and daughter, his mistress, his profession, and his personal past, Gregor experiences a sense of release from the all-too familiar that alternates with a sense of terror at his unstructured freedom. Looking in at his daughter on the morning following the dream, "he felt as though he were taking leave of something; not only of the child, but of the kind of life that had been right for him up until then. Now no kind of life was right for him" (7). Gregor's life ceases to cohere as it did before the dream, its previous form inexplicably lost with no prospect of a replacement. His experience becomes random and fragmented like that of Josef Bloch, but what was a cognitive dilemma for the ex-goalie is an existential problem for Gregor Keuschnig.

His initial impulse is to try to hide the problem from the co-participants in his daily rituals. For most of the first day Gregor manages to uphold the pretense of carrying on his former life although his encounters with other people, the seemingly trivial events along his way as well as the momentary failure to remember his own name and to recognize his own face in the mirror cause him extreme anxiety. In the evening an Austrian writer visiting in Gregor's home exposes his masquerade. His probing eye sharpened by an obsession with detail, the writer had observed Gregor's feigned behavior earlier in the day and confronts him with the truth. Humiliated, Gregor totally loses control of himself, disrobes, smears food on his face, and physically assaults his interrogator. As the final destructive blow to his own lies, he jeeringly blurts out the admission of an infidelity to his wife.

After unsuccessfully trying to live in a kind of subjunctive mode of un-reality as if nothing had happened, the implications of the dream become unavoidable: "That dream must have been the first sign of life since God knows when. . . . it wanted to turn me around. To wake me up and make me forget my somnambulistic certainties. It has always been easy for me to forget dreams. It will be difficult to drop my certainties, because they will cross my path day after day – though in reality others have merely dreamed them for me" (25). The inversion of life and dream, a theme with a long tradition in literary history, has had special appeal to Austrian writers. The dream of Handke's protagonist transforms his life from the stale, static repetition "of internationally certified forms of experience" (52) into a dynamic, open-ended process of becoming. To live without the certainties prior to his dream becomes the challenge of Gregor's orphaned existence as well as the opportunity to discover the world anew.

Momentarily in the grip of a mystical trance at one point during his wanderings through Paris, his inner eye opens to the power of the subject to create experiential coherence. On the basis of this incident he becomes conscious of the capacity to rewrite the script of his own life. In the last paragraph as

Gregor walks toward a rendezvous with a woman he has never met and whose phone number he found scribbled on the sidewalk, the narrator ceases to call him by name, referring instead to the male figure crossing the square simply as "a man" (133). The man once oppressed by the role of Gregor Keuschnig has achieved total alienation from this role into a new anonymity and appears to have begun work on a new life's script.

For most of the time between 1973 and 1978 Handke made his home in a suburb of Paris, the setting of the screen version of *Die linkshändige Frau* (1976, *The Left-Handed Woman*). When he rewrote the original filmscript as a narrative, however, he relocated the story to a housing development outside a large German city resembling his residence near Frankfurt. The book, a best seller for weeks, begins on a winter afternoon inside one of the bungalows of the complex. Here the main character Marianne, simply called "the woman" by the narrator, waits for evening to come when she will drive to the airport to pick up her husband who is returning from an extended business trip in Finland. He arrives, they drive home, put their son to bed, and walk to a nearby hotel where they eat dinner and spend the night. On their way home the next morning, Marianne unexpectedly tells her husband Bruno that she has had an "illumination" (13) about their relationship. He will leave her, she says, and she insists that it happen that very day. As if Bruno had half expected this turn of events, he calmly agrees and returns to the hotel until later when he moves in with Franziska, a mutual friend. His initial compliance with his wife's bizarre request, however, only serves to deepen the perplexity of the reader who is almost entirely excluded from the psychological and emotional processes taking place within the characters. The reader is no longer permitted the access to an inner life that he had had to Josef Bloch, Handke's mother, and Gregor Keuschnig but must content himself with clues to Marianne's inner life indirectly betrayed in her eyes, gestures and a few of her remarks.[19]

To support herself and her son, Marianne resumes a career in translation. Her new life as a wage-earning, single parent shows few signs of either fulfilling the dire consequences that a sobered and wounded Bruno foresees or of meeting the feminist expectations of Franziska. Following an encounter with Bruno who harshly suggests electroshock as the cure for her ailment, then solicitously warns her about isolating herself, Marianne's complaints about her life emerge in a short soliloquy addressed to the mirror: "I don't care what you people think. The more you have to say about me, the freer I will be of you . . . From now on, if any one tells me what I'm like, even if it's to flatter or encourage me, I'll take it as an insult" (23). Franziska's repeated invitation to attend a meeting of feminists brings out a similarly individualistic response. She goes to the meeting place but remains outside the room, observing the mute gesticulations of the others through the window. The only political action she could imagine, she tells Franziska later, "would be to run amok" (55).

Handke introduces several other figures into the narrative cast: Marianne's publisher, her father, an actor who professes to love her, and a salesgirl, but Marianne and her insistence on autonomy remain the center of the story. At the end the characters gather for a spontaneous party at her home, talk, interact, and finally leave. Marianne remains to one side for most of the evening, not aloof but detached and mostly silent. After everyone is gone, she turns to her mirror once again: "You haven't given yourself away. And no one will ever humiliate you again" (87). Through the limits that Handke puts on the reader's insight into Marianne's thoughts and emotions, he formally accentuates the value that she herself attaches to her privacy and independence. Proud of the ability to have maintained her self-possession she represents a fictional counterpart to Handke's portrayal of his mother's biography, an existence stagnating in its roles and definitions.

While at work on *Die linkshändige Frau* Handke simultaneously kept an almost daily journal of his random impressions, thoughts, and reflections, a record of mental activity that touches on a broad spectrum of topics from the trivial to the sublime. The entries in *Das Gewicht der Welt* (1977, *The Weight of the World*) cover the time span from November 1975 to March 1977, a period mainly spent in Paris together with his daughter. In a prefatory note to the German edition he writes that he had originally planned to form the raw material of his notes into a narrative or dramatic work, but it was the miscellaneous bits of experience that finally captured his imagination. He abandoned the design in which these bits had no place and concentrated instead on the spontaneous linguistic reactions to stimuli of both inner and outer sensibilities. Handke's journal became in essence a running commentary on consciousness, a means to reflect its varying responses to the "weight of the world." In no other work does he describe more succinctly and demonstrate more clearly what he calls his life's occupation: "When as a child I first experienced *myself* as a ghostly event in the symbol-free everyday world, I knew that my self would keep me busy for the rest of my life (that I would never finish thinking myself through)" (240).

Most entries are no longer than a few lines and only occasionally are several grouped around the same theme. Among the recurring stimuli are fantasies, dreams, emotions, physical sensations and the automatic patterns of everyday speech, gestures and behavior that Handke observes in himself and others. By far the clearest human image is that of his daughter, identified only as "A."

Reflections of public events are noticeable by their absence, while the outlines of a few private events such as the death of a friend, sessions with a psychoanalyst, and a hospital stay are more readily distinguishable. Literature and film are two of the more pressing and regular stimuli. The fascination with Novalis, Friedrich Schlegel, Friedrich Hebbel, Hermann Hesse, Heimito von Doderer, and above all with Goethe is not so much with their literary art, however, as with the reactions of the diarist himself to this art.

In the two additional journals published since *Das Gewicht der Welt*, the accent has shifted from Handke's "passion for perception" (104) to an obsession with his mission as a writer. If the earlier journal is filled with illustrations of a hypertrophied capacity to respond to the minutiae bombarding his physical senses, emotions, and intellect, *Die Geschichte des Bleistifts* (1982, The Story of the Pencil) and *Phantasien der Wiederholung* (1983, Fantasies of Repetition) give evidence at times of a condition bordering on megalomania. At such points Handke's immodesty seems to soar beyond the bounds of judicious self-appraisal, particularly in the euphoric afterglow of a completed work of fiction. And during the years covered in the two journals, 1976–1980 and 1981–1982 respectively, he finished a tetralogy of three narratives and one dramatic work as well as his most recent novel. He has found his colleagues, he declares, among the "classical authors" of world literature, Aeschylus, Homer, Vergil, and Goethe.[20] When the focus turns to literature and writing, as it often does, the vocabulary and the tone come from the temple rather than the workshop of art. Yet while Handke seeks the semisacral community of tradition, he remains an implacable foe of every group, an inveterate believer in his own individualistic artistic vision.

Recognized for this vision by his contemporaries with the Kafka prize in 1979, Handke reacted with the unconventionality now almost expected of him and passed the award on to two younger writers. In the autumn of that same year he returned to Europe after an extended stay in the United States and settled in Salzburg. The emotional and intellectual consequences of this homecoming find literary expression in what Handke considers a tetralogy of works published between 1979 and 1981. *Langsame Heimkehr* (1979, *The Long Way Around*), the first of the series, bears the title (literally "Slow Homecoming") that symbolizes the significance of the group as a whole.[21]

Valentin Sorger, the main character in *Langsame Heimkehr,* is a geologist working in a sparsely inhabited region in the far north of the North American continent. Although he is a scientist, his drawings and measurements of the pristine landscape—where nameless paths pass by huts without numbers, and roads meander aimlessly until they end in thickets—have a quasi-religious character. Sorger is ultimately motivated by private, subjective concerns rather than scientific goals. A casualty of the modern maladies of alienation and fragmentation, he is in desperate search of personal coherence and wholeness. He finds temporary remedy for the discontinuities of his existence in his activities as the architect of order amidst the chaos of nature. By projecting form onto the formless world of the north, by creating bounded spaces where no others exist, he acquires the momentary capacity to give form and definition to his perception of self as well. Yet this limited remedy to Sorger's existential uncertainties bears with it the hazards of solipsism. Shortly before he leaves the far north for the return to California, an intermediate stage in his homeward journey to Europe, he has a presentiment of the isolation he faces if he continues to pursue his narrowly egocentric activities. A voice from the darkness issues a cryptic warning to him about the dangers of going blind from gazing "too long into the snow" (81). Over an extended period, the voice implies, staring into the chaos of the snowy north country, which is unsystematized and uninterpreted by cultural codes, can overwhelm even the most creative producer of subjective forms and turn his vision entirely inward, blinding him to the world outside the self.

During the stopover in California Sorger emerges from his egocentricity, takes up contacts with friends and rediscovers the reliance of the self on the other. At the home of his neighbors the "divine other" enables him to utter the elementary "It's me" with conviction (135). From this point on Sorger's preoccupation with the construction of a cohesive identity gradually dissipates. Although he has been unable to mend its disjunctions he comes to terms with them, accepting them as part of the "irreparable defect" (198) that pervades the whole of existence. Sorger's reconciliation with his imperfect life extends to an acceptance of a nemesis with which Handke quarreled in *Das Gewicht der Welt*, the recent historical past. As a counterbalance to the blight that National Socialism left on this past, Sorger attaches himself to the forward flow of time and the opportunity to help determine its direction. By the end of the narrative on the flight from New York to Europe the narrator addresses Sorger directly: "You no longer knew who you were. Where was your dream of greatness? You were No One" (200). The narrator's final diagnosis describes an existential state diametrically opposed to the one in which Sorger found himself at the beginning of *Langsame Heimkehr*, a state of self-forgetfulness that foreshadows the next work in the tetralogy.

The first-person narrator of *Die Lehre der Sainte-Victoire* (1980, *The Lesson of Mont Sainte-Victoire*) is a writer who has just returned to Europe and, as he points out, a close fictional relative of the geologist Sorger who has undergone a kind of literary metempsychosis on the flight across the Atlantic. More an essay on art, the aesthetics of perception and artistic creation than a narrative, this second volume of the tetralogy focuses on the narrator's contemplation of Cézanne's paintings during the last decade of the artist's life, particularly those of the mountains of Sainte-Victoire in southern France. For the writer Cézanne becomes a mentor, an instructor in aesthetics whose works embody a relationship to nature that he strives to emulate in the terms of his own artistic medium. The paintings function as "suggestions" (81) to him, drawing him first to the physical presence of the mountains and subsequently calling forth an artistic response to the landscape parallel to that of Cézanne.

While the geologist Sorger found the site of his activities in a virginal setting scarcely seen by human beings, the writer-narrator of *Die Lehre der Sainte-Victoire* discovers the spur to his next work in a landscape already filtered through the most refined of human capacities, the power of artistic creation. More than a simple shift in geography from North America to Europe, the change of locale signals Handke's recognition of the role of artistic tradition in engendering his own writing, the recognition that his task as a modern writer intent on originality is to cultivate the bonds to his rich cultural heritage, not to attempt to circumvent them. Handke gives abundant testimony in his journals to a new awareness of his indebtedness to this heritage.

From his study of Cézanne's paintings Handke's narrator learns to suppress the egocentric perspective on nature that had initially been Sorger's despair as well as a temporary salvation. He acquires the ability from the French painter to "stand in the colors" (16), to experience himself as part of the object world, not as its organizing center. Patterning himself on Cézanne's example, he rejects evil and human despair as the principles of his artistic vision, turning instead to the "réalisation" (21) of nature in its purest state of immediacy and lack of adornment. Unlike Sorger, the writer rejects the invention of form and its projection onto nature. His goal in his artistic relation to the object world is to eradicate traces of the self, to escape individuation into the typological role of "the writer" (72). Only when the artist can attain perfect self-effacement in his work, only when "the conventional self (becomes) entirely No One" (72) can natural forms be "realized" in a work of art uncontaminated by subjective distortions. The final achievement of Handke's narrator lies neither in the analytical precision with which he dissects the significance of Cézanne's art nor in the attempt at the end of the work to turn his theoretical musings into literary practice. It lies rather in the strikingly lucid metaphorical language with which he illuminates the artistic process, metaphors that penetrate its very interiority.

In the same year that *Die Lehre der Sainte-Victoire* appeared, Handke also published a collection of poems, essays, and prose texts, *Das Ende des Flanierens* (The End to Dawdling), written between 1966 and 1980. The volume consists mainly of reviews of contemporary writers and their works, two short pieces on Kafka as well as commentary in prose and poetry on a variety of topics all written for special occasions and originally published in magazines and journals. *Kindergeschichte* (1981 *Child's Story*), the third part of Handke's tetralogy, appeared the following year.

Declaring a maxim of Goethe's on naturalness and innocence as his guiding principle in the new work, Handke turns sharply away from the essayistic discourse on art and aesthetics to an artlessness and naiveté encompassing content and form.[22] His most directly autobiographical work since *Wunschloses Unglück,* even though persons and places remain unnamed, *Kindergeschichte* depicts the period during the early years of his daughter's life. Soon after her birth, Handke's marital problems culminated with his wife's departure to resume her career. Alone and in inescapably close quarters with the child, "the adult" as Handke calls his narrator, must adjust his inner and outer life to the rhythms of a toddler. Cut off from his daily fantasies, his work habits interrupted by the child's constant claim on his attention, he lashes out at her at a central point in the story, hits her, and is immediately overwhelmed by guilt and the need for penance.

After this episode, the adjustments become easier as the joys of the father keep the frustrations of the writer in check. Postponing work on a larger literary project for the nearly six years they spend alone together, he devotes most of his time and energy to the normal paternal functions of loving and protecting his offspring. In the series of changes of residence and schools, of daily tragedies and triumphs her sorrows and happiness become his own, and Handke seems to have been unwilling to make "literary" compromises with this story from his life.

At one point in *Wunschloses Unglück,* Handke writes of his disgust with the honesty and openness of autobiographical writing and expresses a wish to write a work in which he could "lie and pretend, a piece for the theater, for example" (94). *Die Unvernünftigen sterben aus* appeared just one year later. This was his last play to date until the "dramatic poem" *Über die Dörfer* (1981, Beyond the Villages) was published as the final segment of the tetralogy. Wim Wenders directed its first performance at the Salzburg Festival in August 1982, a location giving Handke the overt link to tradition he has increasingly sought.

The dramatic situation in *Über die Dörfer* is rooted in a dispute between three siblings about the family home. Legally it belongs to the oldest brother Gregor, an artist living in a distant city, but at the moment the drama begins the younger brother Hans, a construction laborer, lives there together with his wife and family. Hans, however, has recently written Gregor for permission to allow their sister Sophie, a department store clerk, to transform the family home into a business. Appalled by the plan, Gregor has made the journey home to voice his disapproval and to preserve their heritage from commercialization. In two long expository speeches in the first scene he fills in the background of the dramatic situation and describes his relationship with his brother and sister. On stage listening and offering him counsel on a philosophical plane about his attitudes and course of action is Nova, a godlike female figure whose lofty sentiments recall Nietzsche's Zarathustra.

The long speeches of the second scene belong mostly to Hans, whom Gregor has sought out on the job at a construction site. For extended passages the family dispute recedes into the background as the younger brother, supported by three companions, defends and celebrates the dignity of the common laborer in an elevated language common to all the play's characters. Counteracting Gregor's implicit claim to prerogatives of age and wisdom they turn the occasion of his visit into a festive demonstration for workers' rights, rights that have little to do with Marxist orthodoxy. Hans asserts the essential mystery of workers' lives and their revolt against the clichés and patterns through which others view them:

> When will the man of letters restore my rights?
> When will I be able to desire
> instead of wanting to gain victory? (49)

Sophie, the aspiring entrepreneur, brings the dramatic focus back to the dispute in the brief third scene, persuasively arguing her case for independence and, like Hans, effectively undermining Gregor's position of initial advantage. All three are in the right, Handke remarks in a prefatory note to the actors. But in the denouement of the final scene, acted out—or more precisely, declaimed—in front of the village cemetery, the bitterness aroused by the conflict remains unalleviated, justice incompletely served in each case. Sophie finally plagues her brother with insults until he gives in, but her harsh denunciation of his life devoted to art deepens his alienation to home and family beyond remedy. "Return home to a foreign land," the old woman of the fourth scene tells him: "Only there are you *here*" (74). Gregor's bitterness turns into a blanket condemnation of his family in the past and present as well as the future.

Hans, the "eternal sacrifice" (15) in his brother's eyes, willing to give up the roof over his family's head for his sister's ambitions, reveals himself in the last scene as a nihilistic demagogue calling down destruction on a world devoid of hope.

Handke's *deus ex machina* is Nova, the self-proclaimed messenger of the "spirit of the new age" (96), the "new woman" whose function according to classical dramatic tradition should be to return harmony to the feuding family members. The play, however, has a modern open ending. In a long and eloquent final speech Nova addresses the assembled group from atop the cemetery wall, yet the effect of her words on the dramatic personae remains unstated and uncertain. Just before the curtain falls, Nova places a crown on the head of Hans's son, an act omitted from the Salzburg première apparently because of its overstated symbolism. The symbolic efficacy of her gesture, however, remains as unclear as the efficacy of her message. For Handke the literary realization of a Nova-like figure has a value in itself even in times when the belief in what she represents seems remote, her symbolism drained of its power. Such fictional representation has been able to perpetuate a tradition of classical ideals about self-overcoming and human renewal through even the bleakest of historical moments: "Chaplin too appeared as Nova at the end of *The Great Dictator* [1940], as a human being of a new age. And since time immemorial there have been many to appear as Nova. Of what use has it been? That again and again someone else could appear as Nova."[23]

An American reviewer recently wrote that Handke's "language seems to offer the reader everything before it recedes, without closure. Some will soar into its openings, entranced; others, finding no support, will fall away."[24] Although referring to the translated narratives of the tetralogy, the appraisal is particularly appropriate for the language in Handke's journals as well as his latest narrative work, *Der Chinese des Schmerzes* (1983, The Chinese of Suffering). And the extremes of German readership have reacted as the reviewer predicted, some finding the language too tentative, others captivated by the suggestiveness of its poetic passages.

It is such passages that not only frame the narrative core of *Der Chinese des Schmerzes* at its beginning and end but are interwoven as well into the fabric of the entire work. The subject of this epic poetry is the landscape in and around Salzburg, the sights and sounds of the mountains, valleys, and rivers blended together with the multifarious aspects of human activity as registered on the acutely responsive sensorium of Handke's protagonist, Andreas Loser. Loser finds himself like Gregor, however, a foreigner on his native soil, once mistaken by a passing child for an Indian. A lover bestows upon him the title of endearment "my Chinese of suffering" (218). Through the first-person voice of this poet of the mundane, Handke retards the rush of time in order to record the full enchantment of his senses, creating a mood of serenity and calm that links him to the great nineteenth-century delineator of literary land-scapes, the Austrian Adalbert Stifter. Referred to as "the Observer" in the titles of the subsections, Loser relates his name to a verb in colloquial parlance mean-ing "to listen" (32). Despite the natural acuity of his senses, however, he con-templates an even more profound penetration of phenomenal reality, a kind of seeing alluded to in the Greek verb *leukein* in which perceptual capacity merges with the power of imagination.

Before the narrative begins, an incident on a city street has intensified Loser's natural passiveness as an observer and sent him into a state of stagnant isolation. Reacting to the jostling of another pedestrian, he counters with such force that the man falls to the ground. The stranger is unhurt, but Loser's shock in recognizing the violence lurking so near the surface of his personality persuades him to take temporary leave from his teaching post. He has for some time already been living in an unsettled separation from wife and family.

A teacher of classical languages by profession, Loser devotes his leisure hours to amateur archaeology. Over the years he has developed a specialized expertise in locating the thresholds of structures in ruins, a key to the diagram-matic recreation of entire houses, temples, and settlements. A central narrative leitmotif, the threshold turns up in a variety of concrete and symbolic forms, in nature as well as in human affairs. Following the incident on the street, Loser describes his condition as one of suspense or irresolution, an experience of being at a crossover with no decisive impulse to move in any direction (19, 23). He seems to have come to a point of existential stasis, no longer able to pass through one stage of his life to the next. This stasis is broken only by another, even more violent incident. On the way to a small gathering of friends for an evening of tarok Loser discovers that the mountain rocks have been defaced with the swastika, the emblem of his archenemy. As if moved by a pent-up inner imperative, he pursues and kills the culprit, finally hurling the body down the steep slope of the mountain into the thicket below. The violence that had so shocked him before gains a kind of fictional, if not moral ground, and through his deed Loser deals a symbolic deathblow to a troublesome psychic antagonist that has plagued other Handke protagonists as well.

His action also marks a recovery of forward momentum, a break from the curious state of suspense in which he had previously felt immobilized. With the traditional symbolism of the Easter season apparent in the background, Loser overcomes his condition of stasis and is restored to life. After a spontaneous erotic encounter with a stranger at the airport hotel, a flight to the birthplace of his beloved Vergil and then further south to Sardinia where his children were conceived, he returns to Salzburg and the classroom. Emotionally, he moves closer to his son as the "witness" of his story, not as the source of absolution, but as the other in whose eyes he regains a sense of his reality. During the entire epilogue to the narrative, Loser surveys the beauty of the landscape from the middle of a bridge. As an area of transition from one bank to another, the bridge serves Handke as one last metaphorical embodiment of his central leitmotif, the threshold.

Although the literary rebel of the sixties has made his peace with his fore-bears in tradition, it is far from a peace of submission or slavish emulation. From all indications he will continue along the path of constant renewal and innovation that he began in his youth and will remain among the most absorb-ing of those in the literary vanguard, an artistic elite whose métier is to expose the commonplace and hackneyed. Handke's recent work is difficult precisely because it disappoints expectations and forces the reader to make leaps of association more common in poetry than in prose or drama. Its most funda-mental aim is to restore by aesthetic means a sense of wonderment at the world, to gain back through art what has been lost in man's encounter with the world. For Handke perception and imagination, reality and fiction, life and art are interlocking elements of a whole that is immeasurably greater than either of its parts.

Notes

1. "Zur Tagung der Gruppe 47 in den USA," *Ich bin ein Bewohner des Elfenbeinturms* (Frankfurt: Suhrkamp, 1972), pp. 29-34. (If available, English translations of Handke's works have been used and are referred to in the text itself. I have used my own translations for titles and quo-tations not already translated as well as for material from other Ger-man sources. The date in parentheses is that of the original German publication.)

2. As quoted in Nicholas Hern, *Peter Handke* (New York: Frederick Ungar, 1972), p. 7.

3. "'Nicht Literatur machen, sondern als Schriftsteller leben': Gespräch mit Peter Handke," *Als Schriftsteller leben: Gespräche mit Peter Handke, Franz Xaver Kroetz, Gerhard Zwerenz, Walter Jens, Peter Rühmkorf, Günter Grass,* Heinz Ludwig Arnold, ed. (Reinbek bei Hamburg: Rowohlt, 1979), pp. 10-11.

4. Quoted and translated in June Schlueter, *The Plays and Novels of Peter Handke* (Pittsburgh: University of Pittsburgh Press, 1981), p. 28.

5. Quoted in Schlueter, p. 28.

6. *"Theater und Film:* Das Elend des Vergleichens," *Ich bin ein Bewohner des Elfenbeinturms,* pp. 65-66.

7. "Die Literatur ist romantisch," Ibid., pp. 35-50.

8. Hellmuth Karasek, "Von Äpfeln, Fussnägeln und Katzen" and Peter Iden, "Das pure Theater des Peter Handke," *Über Peter Handke,* Michael Scharang, ed. (Frankfurt: Suhrkamp, 1972), pp. 149, 146.

9. In Rainer Litten, "Theater der Verstörung: Ein Gespräch mit Peter Handke," Ibid., p. 158.

10. "'Für mich ist Literatur auch eine Lebenshaltung': Gespräch mit Peter Handke," *Gespräche über den Roman,* Manfred Durzak, ed. (Frankfurt: Suhrkamp, 1976), p. 320.

11. *Der gewöhnliche Schrecken: Neue Horrorgeschichten* (Salzburg: Residenz, 1969).

12. In Heiko R. Blum, "Gespräch mit Peter Handke," *Über Peter Handke,* p. 81.

13. In Michael Schneider, "Das Innenleben des 'Grünen Handke'" and Reinhard Baumgart, "Vorwärts, zurück in die Zukunft," ibid., pp. 95, 91-92.

14. "Die Ausbeutung des Bewußtseins: Gespräch mit Peter Handke," *Schreiben und Leben: Gespräche mit Jürgen Becker, Peter Handke, Walter Kempowski, Wolfgang Koeppen, Günter Wallraff, Dieter Wellershoff,* Christian Linder, ed. (Köln: Kiepenheuer und Witsch, 1974), p. 43.

15. In Hellmuth Karasek, "Ohne zu verallgemeinern: Ein Gespräch mit Peter Handke," *Über Peter Handke,* p. 88.

16. Linder, pp. 33-34.

17. The essays from the sixties are collected in *Ich bin ein Bewohner des Elfenbeinturms.* The title of the more recent volume is *Als das Wünschen noch geholfen hat* (Frankfurt: Suhrkamp, 1974).

18. Arnold, p. 20.

19. See Peter Pütz, *Peter Handke* (Frankfurt: Suhrkamp, 1982), pp. 91-92.

20. *Die Geschichte des Bleistifts* (Salzburg and Wien: Residenz, 1982), p. 232.

21. Although the three narratives of the tetralogy have recently been translated and published (see bibliography), they were unavailable to me and I have quoted from the original German using my own translation.

22. *Die Geschichte des Bleistifts,* p. 185.

23. Ibid., p. 246.

24. Russell Schoch, "Using Language to Transform," *San Francisco Chronicle,*

11 August 1985, p. 4.

Works in German

Die Hornissen. Frankfurt: Suhrkamp, 1966.
Publikumsbeschimpfung und andere Sprechstücke. Frankfurt: Suhrkamp, 1966.
Der Hausierer. Frankfurt: Suhrkamp, 1967.
Begrüßung des Aufsichtsrats. Salzburg: Residenz, 1967.
Hilferufe. Frankfurt: Suhrkamp, 1967.
Kaspar. Frankfurt: Suhrkamp, 1968.
Hörspiel. Köln: Kiepenheuer & Witsch, 1968.
Hörspiel Nr. 2. Köln: Kiepenheuer & Witsch, 1969.
Prosa, Gedichte, Theaterstücke, Hörspiele, Aufsätze. Frankfurt: Suhrkamp, 1969.
Die Innenwelt der Außenwelt der Innenwelt. Frankfurt: Suhrkamp, 1969.
Deutsche Gedichte. Frankfurt: Euphorion Verlag, 1969.
"Das Umfallen der Kegel von einer bäuerlichen Kegelbahn." *Der gewöhnliche Schrecken: Horrorgeschichten.* Salzburg: Residenz, 1969.
Quodlibet. Frankfurt: Suhrkamp, 1970.
Die Angst des Tormanns beim Elfmeter. Frankfurt: Suhrkamp, 1970.
Wind und Meer: Vier Hörspiele. Frankfurt: Suhrkamp, 1970.
Der Ritt über den Bodensee. Frankfurt: Suhrkamp, 1970.
Chronik der laufenden Ereignisse. Frankfurt: Suhrkamp, 1971.
Stücke I. Frankfurt: Suhrkamp, 1972.
Der kurze Brief zum langen Abschied. Frankfurt: Suhrkamp, 1972.
Wunschloses Unglück. Salzburg: Residenz, 1972.
Ich bin ein Bewohner des Elfenbeinturms. Frankfurt: Suhrkamp, 1972.
Stücke 2. Frankfurt: Suhrkamp, 1973.
Die Unvernünftigen sterben aus. Frankfurt: Suhrkamp, 1973.
Als das Wünschen noch geholfen hat. Frankfurt: Suhrkamp, 1974.
Falsche Bewegung. Frankfurt: Suhrkamp, 1975.
Die Stunde der wahren Empfindung. Frankfurt: Suhrkamp, 1978.
Der Rand der Wörter. Stuttgart: Reclam, 1975.
Die linkshändige Frau. Frankfurt: Suhrkamp, 1976.
Das Gewicht der Welt: Ein Journal (November 1975–März 1977). Salzburg: Residenz, 1979.
Langsame Heimkehr. Frankfurt: Suhrkamp, 1979.
Die Lehre der Sainte-Victoire. Frankfurt: Suhrkamp, 1980.

Das Ende des Flanierens: Gedichte, Aufsätze, Reden, Rezensionen. Frankfurt:
    Suhrkamp, 1980.
Kindergeschichte. Frankfurt: Suhrkamp, 1981.
Über die Dörfer. Dramatisches Gedicht. Frankfurt: Suhrkamp, 1981.
Die Geschichte des Bleistifts. Salzburg: Residenz, 1982.
Phantasien der Wiederholung. Frankfurt: Suhrkamp, 1983.
Der Chinese des Schmerzes. Frankfurt: Suhrkamp, 1983.

Works Translated into English

Kaspar and Other Plays. Trans. Michael Roloff. New York: Farrar, Straus &
    Giroux, 1969. (Includes *Offending the Audience, Self-Accusation,
    Kaspar.*)
Offending the Audience and Self-Accusation. Trans. Michael Roloff. London:
    Methuen, 1971.
Kaspar. Trans. Michael Roloff. London: Methuen, 1972.
The Goalie's Anxiety at the Penalty Kick. Trans. Michael Roloff. New York:
    Farrar, Straus & Giroux, 1972.
The Ride Across Lake Constance. Trans. Michael Roloff. London: Methuen,
    1973.
Short Letter, Long Farewell. Trans. Ralph Manheim. New York: Farrar, Straus
    & Giroux, 1974.
The Innerworld of the Outerworld of the Innerworld. Trans. Michael Roloff.
    New York: Farrar, Straus & Giroux, 1974.
A Sorrow Beyond Dreams. Trans. Ralph Manheim. New York: Farrar, Straus,
    & Giroux, 1975.
The Ride Across Lake Constance and Other Plays. Trans. Michael Roloff. New
    York: Farrar, Straus & Giroux, 1976. (Includes *Prophecy, Calling for
    Help, My Foot My Tutor, Quodlibet, The Ride Across Lake Constance,
    They Are Dying Out.*)
Nonsense and Happiness. Trans. Michael Roloff. New York: Farrar, Straus
    & Giroux, 1976.
A Moment of True Feeling. Trans. Ralph Manheim. New York: Farrar, Straus
    & Giroux, 1977.
Three by Peter Handke. Trans. Michael Roloff and Ralph Manheim. New York:
    Farrar, Straus & Giroux, 1977. (Includes *The Goalie's Anxiety at the
    Penalty Kick; Short Letter, Long Farewell; A Sorrow Beyond Dreams.*)
The Left-Handed Woman. Trans. Ralph Manheim. New York: Farrar, Straus

& Giroux, 1978.

Two Novels by Peter Handke. Trans. Ralph Manheim. New York: Farrar, Straus & Giroux, 1979. (Includes *A Moment of True Feeling* and *The Left-Handed Woman.*)

The Weight of the World. Trans. Ralph Manheim. New York: Farrar, Straus & Giroux, 1984.

Slow Homecoming. Trans. Ralph Manheim. New York: Farrar, Straus & Giroux, 1985. (Includes *The Long Way Around, The Lesson of Mont Sainte-Victoire, Child Story.*)

Secondary Sources in English

Critchfield, Richard. "Parody, Satire, and Transparencies in Peter Handke's *Die Stunde der wahren Empfindung,*" *Modern Austrian Literature,* Vol. 14, nos. 1/2 (1981), 45-61.

Gilman, Richard. "Peter Handke," in *The Making of Modern Drama: A Study of Büchner, Ibsen, Strindberg, Chekhov, Pirandello, Brecht, Beckett, Handke.* New York: Farrar, Straus & Giroux, 1974, pp. 267-288.

Hayman, Ronald. *Theatre and Anti-Theatre: New Movements Since Beckett.* New York: Oxford University Press, 1979, pp. 95-123.

Hays, Michael. "Peter Handke and the End of the 'Modern,'" *Modern Drama,* Vol. 23, no. 4 (January 1981), 346-366.

Hern, Nicholas. *Peter Handke.* New York: Frederick Ungar Publishing Co., 1972.

Innes, Christopher. *Modern German Drama: A Study in Form.* Cambridge: Cambridge University Press, 1979, pp. 235-255.

Klinkowitz, Jerome and James Knowlton. *Peter Handke and the Post-modern Transformation: The Goalie's Journey Home.* Columbia: University of Missouri Press, 1983.

Miles, David H. "Reality and the Two Realisms: Mimesis in Auerbach, Lukacs and Handke." *Monatshefte,* Vol. 71, no. 4 (Winter 1979).

Rorrison, Hugh. "The 'Grazer Gruppe,' Peter Handke and Wolfgang Bauer." *Modern Austrian Writing: Literature and Society after 1945,* ed. Alan Best and Hans Wolfschütz. London: Oswald Wolff, 1980, pp. 252-266.

Schlueter, June. *The Plays and Novels of Peter Handke.* Pittsburgh: University of Pittsburgh Press, 1981.

Sharp, Francis Michael. "Literature as Self-Reflection: Thomas Bernhard and Peter Handke," *World Literature Today,* 55 (Autumn 1981), 603-607.

White, J. J. "Signs of Disturbance: The Semiological Import of Some Recent Fiction by Michael Tournier and Peter Handke," *Journal of European Studies,* 4 (1974), 233-254.

Major Studies in German

Durzak, Manfred. *Peter Handke und die deutsche Gegenwartsliteratur: Narziß auf Abwegen.* Stuttgart: W. Kohlhammer, 1982.

Gabriel, Norbert. *Peter Handke und Österreich.* Bonn: Bouvier, 1983.

Nägele, Rainer and Renate Voris. *Peter Handke.* München: C. H. Beck, 1978.

Pütz, Peter. *Peter Handke.* Frankfurt: Suhrkamp, 1982.

Pütz, Peter. "Peter Handke." *Kritisches Lexikon zur deutschsprachigen Gegenwartsliteratur.* Ed. Heinz Ludwig Arnold. München: edition text + kritik, 1978.

Scharang, Michael, ed. *Über Peter Handke.* Frankfurt: Suhrkamp, 1972.

Text und Kritik, 24 (October 1969), 24/24a (July 1971), 24/24a (September 1976).

Franz Innerhofer

Gerald A. Fetz

Of the impressive number of talented Austrian writers who have stormed the German literary scene since the late 1960s Franz Innerhofer is one of the most highly regarded. He was assured a significant place in contemporary German literature by the publication of a widely acclaimed trilogy of autobiographical novels in the mid-1970s: *Schöne Tage* (1973, *Beautiful Days*), *Schattseite* (1975, Shadow Side), and *Die großen Wörter* (1977, The Big Words).

A biographical sketch of Franz Innerhofer reads very much like a summary of the content of these three novels. Born in 1944 in the rural mountain village of Krimml in the Salzburg region as the illegitimate son of a young farm girl, Innerhofer spent his first two years in foster care, the next four with his mother, and then at the age of six was uprooted again and sent to his father's large farm several villages away. By his own account Innerhofer endured the next eleven years under extremely repressive and traumatic circumstances. Even as a very young boy he was forced to work long hard hours at every conceivable farm task and had to submit to the brutal discipline of his patriarchal father. As the "bastard son" he was neither fish nor fowl and belonged in reality neither to the family nor to the farmhands; consequently he spent the next eleven years as an outsider, isolated in most ways from both master and servants. Neither school nor the church provided any relief from the labor and drudgery or any opportunity for genuine human contact; on the contrary both merely added new tasks and new forms of repression. Against all odds he achieved a certain amount of independence by mastering the newly acquired farm machinery and finally freed himself from his father's tyranny in 1961. He started an apprenticeship in a machine shop in the nearby village and in spite of multiple difficulties succeeded in completing it. But even more importantly it was here that he discovered and became enchanted by the world of words.

Innerhofer fled from the country and took a job in Salzburg as a welder in a large factory. He enrolled in evening classes, eventually managed to finish school, and finally received a scholarship to the University of Salzburg. After six semesters, however, Innerhofer's fascination with and hope in the academic world dissolved into disenchantment. He left the university and began to write. In a personal crisis he claims he read Peter Handke's novel about the suicide of his mother, *Wunschloses Unglück,* and was inspired to try to write about himself and his difficult past.[1] Innerhofer had apparently contemplated suicide himself on many occasions, just as his protagonist Holl does throughout the trilogy and, according to Ulrich Greiner, actually began his first novel as a "justification for suicide."[2] In the course of writing *Schöne Tage* he managed to overcome the crisis and establish himself as a significant young writer. *Schöne Tage* enjoyed a very enthusiastic reception by critics and public alike and gained Innerhofer the prestigious Bremen Literature Prize in 1974.[3] This first novel has been translated into English under the title *Beautiful Days* and was also made into a television film for Austria and West Germany in 1980.[4]

Innerhofer's trilogy stands as an extraordinary statement about one individual's anachronistically oppressed childhood and youth, his attempts to cope with and ultimately free himself from emotional and physical slavery, and his hopes and then profound disappointments in trying to adapt to a very foreign environment: the "world of words." While displaying unique qualities, these novels are also works that are both deeply rooted in literary traditions and reflect affinities with the works of other contemporary, particularly Austrian, writers. Even though the number of critical discussions of Innerhofer is not yet great, his novels have been mentioned in connection with several important prose traditions in German literature, including the "Heimatroman" (regional novel), the closely related "Bauernroman" (farm novel), novels of youth, and even the "Bildungsroman" (educational novel).[5] In two very thoughtful articles, for example, Jürgen Koppensteiner has analyzed Innerhofer's novels, particularly *Schöne Tage,* in the context of "Anti-Heimatliteratur."[6] Klaus Heydemann compares and contrasts *Schöne Tage* with Ebner-Eschenbach's *Das Gemeindekind* (The Foundling) and Waggerl's *Das Jahr des Herrn* (The Year of the Lord), pointing out how Innerhofer's novel is indebted to the "Heimatliteratur" (regional literature) tradition, but also the ways in which it rejects and negates many of the tradition's central features.[7] The most thorough analysis of the entire trilogy to this point, however, is Ulrich Greiner's discussion in *Der Tod des Nachsommers,* (The Death of Indian Summer), which, in spite of several journalistic oversimplifications, succeeds admirably in placing Innerhofer in the context of contemporary Austrian literature.[8]

In the reviews and critical assessments of his novels Innerhofer has frequently been mentioned in connection with earlier writers to whose works his trilogy displays parallels or affinities. The intensity of his writing, particularly in the first two novels, has called forth comparisons with Georg Büchner's *Lenz;*[9] the rural despair in the same two novels has reminded some critics of Jeremias Gotthelf;[10] and the emotional isolation and suffering of the young Holl have led still others to observe similarities with *David Copperfield* and *Anton Reiser.*[11] But more fruitful, perhaps, are the comparisons between Innerhofer and his contemporaries, especially those who have written "Anti-Heimatliteratur." Few contemporary Austrian authors portray their country or its famous countryside in images corresponding to the pastoral visions found in the traditional "Heimatliteratur" or in the promotional materials of the Austrian tourist industry. The rural reality depicted in recent literature has little in common with those stereotypical pictures of awe-inspiring landscapes, rosy-cheeked farmers and maidens, and contented cows. A claim by one critic that Innerhofer provides a "necessary corrective to the field-, forest-, and meadow 'Alpine-ness' of Heinrich Waggerl . . ."[12] could be applied equally well to numerous fellow Austrians.[13] For Innerhofer and many others the *Wunschbild* (dream) of rural existence has clearly become a *Schreckbild* (nightmare).[14] The extent to which Innerhofer reverses the clichés, however, by confronting us with such vivid and concrete examples of abuse, brutality, alienation, and despair, together with the straightforward, unadorned manner in which he does so, particularly in the first two novels, are characteristics of his writing which begin to distinguish him from the other contemporary Austrian writers.

The final novel in the trilogy, *Die großen Wörter,* does not fit into the category of "Anti-Heimatliteratur." Its setting is no longer farm or village but the city, and the overall style of the novel changes accordingly. And although it is a direct extension of the first two novels, *Die großen Wörter* establishes a completely new tone and a new set of themes and problems.

One critic has remarked that the three novels should be read and understood as a single unit.[15] It is true that each novel concerns itself with a specific stage in the development (*Bildung*) of the autobiographical protagonist, and if one expects to gain a clear understanding of the genesis of many of the problems confronting Holl in the third novel, then familiarity with the first two is essential. Yet that fact should not overshadow their significant differences nor undermine their integrity as individual novels, as will be shown by analyzing Innerhofer's novels first as single works and then as a trilogy unit.

Schöne Tage. Innerhofer's directness and economy of language are evident from the first page: wasting neither time nor words, the opening lines lead the reader to the heart of the matter. Holl is described as a frightened two-year-old child, alone and isolated in a strange setting, having just been taken abruptly from the environment that was familiar and secure. The perspective here, sustained throughout the novel, is clearly that of Holl, filtered somewhat through the narrator. It is feelings rather than thoughts that are expressed in the prose, and these feelings are rarely reflected upon. Accordingly, the language is simple and concrete, and the descriptions are essentially visual images, of objects, movements, and actions.

The contours of Holl's reality come quickly into focus, and these change very little through the novel: "Coming from a small world into a world of buffetings and beatings, mostly exiled into some corner . . . From dawn to dusk the child was told what he was not allowed to do and what he had to do; anything else he heard was incomprehensible, consisting of alien words, directed to alien people" (*BD*, 1-2; *ST*, 7).[16] We see throughout how Holl suffers and struggles against the circumstances of his life, how he attempts to cope with the continuous flood of hardships and humiliations that descend upon him, and how finally at the age of seventeen, he almost miraculously frees himself from the oppressive world of his youth with the hope of finding a better life.

Holl is sent at the age of six to his father's farm. Once again he is torn from an environment that was at least familiar. Again he is disoriented, confused, and afraid. Quickly he discovers that communication on his father's farm, "Hof 48," takes place almost exclusively in the form of commands, and he responds by resisting: "Holl put up a struggle. Father beat him, beat him again, and again, until Holl's resistance collapsed . . ." (*BD*, 7; *ST*, 28). Yet Holl never completely gives up, he merely seeks new forms of defense, new means of resistance, and the sides are drawn in one of the most incredible father-son conflicts in literature.

The world of "Hof 48," with which Holl must cope is a primitive, pre-industrial world where hard labor is demanded from morning to night. His father is a feudal lord who rules his medieval fiefdom by means of fear and force. Holl refers to himself and the other farm workers as "Leibeigene" (indentured serfs) and frequently calls the place a "Bauern-KZ" (peasants' concentration camp).

Holl's world is also basically without language. Only the father, stepmother, priest, and teachers possess and use language, for language is power, the vehicle for commanding, punishing, forbidding, and humiliating: "No one spoke, the only modes of expression were hoarse whispers or bellows; there were no explanations, only orders and slaps in the face" (*BD*, 11; *ST*, 20). Holl's lack of language, of words capable of ordering his thoughts and feelings, of communicating with others, only causes his confusion, anger, and sense of worthlessness to grow. This lack of language (*Sprachlosigkeit*) is a plight that Holl shares with the other farm laborers, who "were aware of their misery, but they had no words, no language to express it in . . ." (*BD*, 16; *ST*, 26). Since language is a weapon, the "serfs" are not allowed to possess it. Withholding language from them is a very effective means of maintaining power over them. And without language their rather feeble attempts to relate to each other are limited to meanness, violence, and primitive sexuality. With regard to the latter we read: ". . . the laborers tried to usurp their nights, at least, and thus they perpetuated themselves from one darkness into the next" (*BD,* 16; *ST,* 27). Holl, of course, since he is only a child does not enjoy even this fleeting relief from labor and abuse. For Holl, a bed-wetter, nights are just another kind of terror and an additional source of humiliation: "To lie there in his own urine was so horrible; no matter how he strained to avoid it, it kept happening to him. Each time it destroyed him" (*BD,* 28; *ST,* 43).

Any mistake Holl makes and any sign of resistance on his part leads to physical or psychological punishment or both. Whippings and beatings are so frequent that the surroundings become a landscape of slaps in the face (*Ohrfeigenlandschaft*). His anger and hatred toward his father grow increasingly stronger as does his feeling that he is a ridiculous person himself. Because Holl is an illegitimate child, he is neither fully integrated into nor fully excluded from his father's family. To defend himself against this ambiguous position, he rejects this half-family and its values, aligning himself at least emotionally with the other "serfs," even though he is also not really one of them. He feels a kind of unarticulated solidarity with these fellow "victims," and they become a substitute but inadequate family. Yet this is hardly satisfactory compensation and ultimately does little to ameliorate Holl's isolation.

During his first years at "Hof 48" he attempts to build up sources of hope and relief in his mind, but these inevitably lead to painful disappointments. For instance, in spite of experiences that should have taught him otherwise, he allows the hope to remain alive that his mother, once she knows exactly what he has to endure, will rescue him. After being falsely accused of vandalizing a wayside crucifix near the village, very appropriately named "Haudorf,"[17] (Beating Village) and suffering a particularly severe beating by his father, Holl runs away to his mother's farm. He is immediately returned, however, and is forced to dismiss his mother as a source of hope. Holl had also allowed himself to hope that his entry into school would bring a reduction in his numbing workload and lead to positive changes in his life. Yet school freed him from nothing and proved to be just another extension of the brutality and authoritarian environment he knew at home. And the Church, although he places no great hope in it, proves to reinforce and support the repressive hierarchy of the father and the society around him: ". . . God now seemed to correspond better to his previous image of the devil. God was the Terrible One . . . Life was hard enough as it was, punishment enough: why then be judged and punished by God all over again?" (*BD,* 77; *ST,* 114).

Paradoxically and ironically the work and hard labor that lead to so much suffering for Holl also become his refuge: "Only by immersing himself in work up to his eyebrows was he able to secure himself against the constant excesses, at least in the daytime. The work served him as a shield, front and back" (*BD,* 66; *ST,* 98-99). Holl throws himself into the most agonizing work and thereby extends the limits of his endurance not only for work, but also for all forms of abuse. Not surprisingly he begins to define himself in terms of work; but his suffering continues year after year, and thoughts of murdering his father alternate with thoughts of suicide.

In spite of the dulling effect of his surroundings Holl becomes a keen, if inarticulate, observer of those surroundings and of those who exist therein. He is overwhelmed by the innumerable impressions that penetrate his thoughts, basically because he is still without adequate means of ordering those impressions. But he begins to recognize the importance of achieving linguistic independence and resolves to practice, even if it means talking to himself: "He did talk to himself a lot, told himself time and again: I have to talk" (*BD,* 136; *ST,* 150).

It is perfectly understandable why Holl's observations of the world around him are essentially frightening and negative, and reflect oppression, decay, and despair. The following passage is not atypical: "They were indeed standing in snow up to their ankles, stretching across a ditch and, in a wide curve, down to the ravine. There were probably hundreds of cow skeletons down there, rotten, half-rotten, and bare, and among them, most likely, human skeletons as well, of deserters who had lost their footing in pitch-dark night, of suicides and murder victims" (*BD,* 105; *ST,* 153-154).

Something positive for Holl finally occurs at "Hof 48." His stepmother has burned herself and a temporary cook arrives to fill in for her. Helga, the cook, is observant and bold. She generalizes from her extensive experience about such farms as "Hof 48," and we see, as does Holl, that this situation is hardly an exception. "She has wasted half her life on farms, and wherever she had been she has encountered the same ridiculous scene ... For quite some time now she had felt she was not working in kitchens but in mortuaries" (*BD,* 116; *ST,* 169). She chastises Holl's father and stepmother for the way they treat Holl and the others. Remarkably for Holl they not only tolerate her insolent behavior, but also actually retreat. He watches her intently, impressed particularly by the way she speaks, the way she uses words and language to fight tyranny rather than extend it. Although her stay is brief Helga's impact on Holl is great. She inspires him, gives him a glimpse of actual liberation, a hint that the "feudal lord" is not invincible. Most importantly, perhaps, she articulates and gives language to thoughts and feelings that Holl has known only too well but for which he can find no means of expression.

Holl's world does not change overnight. By the time he is thirteen he is able to withstand the beatings and floggings administered by his father so well that even his father has to recognize that this method of punishment and humiliation is no longer effective. When the tractors and other machines arrive on the farm in the late 1950s, the first sign at "Hof 48" that the industrial revolution had even taken place, Holl quickly masters them and, as the only one who does so, begins to achieve some independence. The archaic feudal structure of "Hof 48" starts to collapse.

The year is 1959 and farm laborers are harder to find and keep. They no longer accept the same degree of abuse as they had even a few years earlier. With the encouragement of the new milkhand, Holl asserts himself more boldly toward his father until finally the father has to back down from a confrontation. The physical struggle between father and son is over; but Holl will require additional time to free himself emotionally. Determined to leave the farm in spite of his terrible anxiety, Holl seizes the first opportunity, an apprenticeship in Haudorf.

In 1961 at seventeen years of age Holl begins a new phase in his life: "A new world towered tall in front of Holl. In the mornings he was glad to enter the workshop with the master. Large doors and large windows, white walls and machines, all of which aroused his instant interest. The master did not shout but quietly explained the various routines to him, and while they were working he also talked to him about people and books and ways of dealing with people" (*BD*, 168; *ST*, 239). In the master's mother, Helene, Holl finds a teacher who is both warm and determined to help educate him. He is more than willing: "Holl was sitting at table with the others and admitted that he really did not know anything, nothing about the world, nothing of the world, but he said he wanted to make a start now" (*BD*, 169; *ST*, 241).

Schöne Tage gives us an unusually powerful story of a terribly mistreated child in an incredibly archaic rural world. The reality confronting us is as far removed from the idyllic settings and romanticized characters of the traditional "Heimatroman" as is imaginable. And after following Holl through the unmitigated misery of his first seventeen years the light and hope that appear at the end, although not completely without preparation, still come as a surprise: intuitively we feel that the ending is simply too good to be true, "beinahe märchenhaft"[18] (almost fairy-tale like), as one reviewer puts it. In fact, as we will soon learn in *Schattseite*, it is too good to be true.

Holl's story is told with such intensity and density of narrative that it allows us as little relief as Holl's world of work allowed him. The chronological and episodic narrative, all in the third person, is simultaneously captivating and objective, engaging and coolly distant. Innerhofer obviously identifies with the autobiographical character, but there is a remarkable absence of pathos and sentimentality. He is able to maintain control over the anger and other emotions that the reader is forced to feel throughout. His considerable literary achievement is evident in part in his having created an oxymoronic engaging protocol, an emotion-wrenching report.

In an early review of the novel Karin Struck called it "linguistically powerful,"[19] and it is in the language itself that we find one of the most extraordinary aspects of the book. Paradoxically the language documents and reflects a world essentially without language. The language of the novel does not describe Holl's inarticulatenesss and his struggle to overcome it as much as it draws us into that struggle itself. In a language realistic but only rarely naturalistic, Innerhofer gives profound expression to the silent and inarticulate feelings and thoughts of his protagonist. He has claimed in an interview that "whereas in other places people talk constantly about trivialities, here they remain silent about the things that are most horrible."[20] Into this silence Innerhofer breathes linguistic life.

The basic questions raised in the book are not existential questions in the philosophical sense. They are questions of existence in the physical sense. The lives portrayed here are archaic and tortured, but life in general is not absurd. One perhaps useful comparison in establishing some of the unique qualities of this work is that between Innerhofer and Thomas Bernhard. Günter Blöcker has observed that "Innerhofer stops where Thomas Bernhard begins."[21] Although the brutal rural setting here is very similar to the settings one finds in such Bernhard works as *Frost, Watten, Verstörung,* or *Ungenach,* the two authors approach their material from opposite directions. "Innerhofer," as Greiner has pointed out, "comes from below, strenuously achieving distance. Reality still has him."[22] Bernhard approaches the material from above: intellectually, abstractly, even ironically. His language is convoluted, involved, abstractly theoretical, cerebral, neurotic; Innerhofer's language is simple, direct, concrete, and physical. The milieus of both are characterized by mass ignorance, brutality, despair, and human isolation; the characters in both are often suicidal, and nature is perceived as an enemy. But whereas for Bernhard such themes are often metaphors for existential illnesses, they are never such for Innerhofer, for the causes of the maladies are discernible.

Schöne Tage is a devastating novel. It is both compelling autobiography and engaging fiction, ". . . a book which appears to have overcome the difference between art and reality, which beyond being a document of one individual's liberation can perhaps provide impetus for a collective liberation."[23] It is a novel worthy of the praise granted it by reviewers, critics, and readers. The outrage and anger with which it was met in certain rural circles in Austria can be viewed only as an indication of its power and effectiveness.[24]

Schattseite. This second novel concerns itself with Holl's three years of apprenticeship. As an indication of Holl's developing sense of identity, Innerhofer finally grants him a first name and significantly it is his own: Franz. An important shift in narrative perspective also occurs: *Schattseite* is narrated in the first person, eliminating the distinction between narrator and protagonist and reducing the distance between author and protagonist as well.

The structure of the novel remains basically episodic and chronological, although because this novel covers only a three-year time span the chronological aspect is less significant. The focus on certain episodes with lengthy time lapses in between still prevails. The shift in narration, from a character who is caught in a "pre-language" situation, described by a third person, to one who is in the midst of achieving both a linguistic and personal identity and who now tells his own story, makes this second novel more subjective, more personal, and more reflective. The "Außenwelt" (external world), to borrow from Handke,[25] retains its importance, for this novel too treats a specific, recognizable external reality, but the protagonist's "Innenwelt" (inner world) also assumes major significance. The protagonist begins to reflect—on himself, on the others with whom he comes into contact, on his environment, and with increasing frequency on the nature of power and authority. Holl's thoughts and reflections, however, lead more often to questions than conclusions, and they are neither complex nor abstract but grounded firmly in his reality.

In a very profound sense *Schattseite* is a "Bildungsroman," a novel in which the hero moves from ignorance toward knowledge, aided in that progress, which is more dialectical than linear, by a kind and effective teacher. It is a novel in which the protagonist struggles with and finally achieves a relatively positive self-identity. It is also a "Bildungsroman" in the literal sense, a novel about education, for Holl gradually discovers and becomes absorbed by books and learning.

This novel too begins with an abrupt, frightening, and confusing change in milieu for Holl. Over the first several pages of *Schattseite* Innerhofer retraces and elaborates on the steps already described at the end of *Schöne Tage*, steps leading Holl away from the horrors of "Hof 48" and to the promising and friendly environment of his apprenticeship. Yet this time around the appealing world of the master's shop and home has turned rather sour. In the retelling Holl does not feel optimistic and relieved but awkward, confused, and deceived:

feelings he knows only too well from earlier. The past, his past in particular, weighs heavily upon him when he is forced to realize that he was able to flee the location of that past but not its substance, that he had liberated himself physically but not emotionally: "... it struck me that I was still a prisoner; I had liberated my body but not my past. I dragged it around behind me like a washrag, was afraid of it and wanted to flee·from it" (S, 9).[26] Fleeing his oppressor does not prove to be the cure-all Holl had naively expected it to be.

Even though the farm, "Hof 48," represents for him a "childhood of horrors lived through one upon the other ..." (S, 19), it had been a self-contained world in which it was relatively easy even for Holl to gain an overview and in which the power structure, however brutal, was at least overt and clear. His disorientation now is like that experienced by a long-term prisoner suddenly released. It is significant that Holl reflects: "Imprisonment itself, I thought, is probably tolerable, but then to be set free. Free for life!" (S, 49). Having known virtually no relief from constant work and having learned to define himself in terms of work, Holl cannot deal with unstructured time and moves clumsily from one brief and trivial activity to another. Although the village is very small, it is a new and complex world for Holl.

Holl has arrived at the master's house two days early and is treated over the ensuing weekend with warmth, openness, and friendliness. But on Monday morning everything seemed so different: "Everyone suddenly so serious. A very different feeling came over me ... Bruckmann looked at me coldly. The others too, his wife, Georg, and Helene, directed their looks at me. So, Bruckmann said, now your life will start to get serious. Pig! Swindler! I cursed to myself ... The bread and butter turned into a gooey paste in my mouth ... I felt myself flung back to a time when my days began in desperation ..." (S, 20). Holl thinks briefly about fleeing even further, perhaps to another country, but he manages to bring himself under control and goes to work: "I have nothing to lose, somehow it must work. Wait it out, the worst you can do is die." (S, 35).

Alienated from his external reality and from those who inhabit it, Holl also feels alienated from himself. Very conscious of his physical and social clumsiness, Holl constantly changes positions and moves about aimlessly: he is simply not at home in his own skin. Holl becomes immediately frustrated by his inability to master the new tasks set before him and is certain that he will never live up to Bruckmann's expectations: "It won't work. I can't weld. I can't make my hands do what they're supposed to do ..." (S, 33), and his hands, overly large, misshapen, and swollen, become the symbol of his social awkwardness and self-alienation. His estrangement, extending to virtually everything, leads to almost total despair: "A withered blade of grass, a rock, a broken fence post, anything, I wanted to be anything, just not me . . . I pretended as much as possible to be carefree and I continuously gave myself orders: smile you jerk, sit down you jerk, eat you jerk, don't make such a dumb face" (S, 43). Holl's clumsy and infrequent attempts to enter into intimate relationships with girls end in equal frustration: "We stood still a hundred times and searched for a tender feeling, but we couldn't find one because our bodies seemed so foreign to us" (S, 203). His lack of a strong sense of self also leads him to avoid strangers: "I walked as if I were busy with something, as if these people were of no interest to me, so that no one would speak to me, because I was afraid of being asked 'Who are you? where do you belong? what do you do?' and with 'oh' I would be crushed again" (S, 48).

Holl's feelings of awkwardness, loneliness, and anger are exacerbated by his sense of a conspiracy (Prozeß) against him in and around the village. Rumors of bed-wetting, vandalism, laziness, incompetence, and stupidity follow and haunt him. Occasionally he feels himself dragged back into earlier terror, even questioning in his own mind whether the rumors and assertions might not be true: ". . . on top of everything else, it struck me that the people who had passed judgment on me up to now might have been right" (S, 34).

Gradually, however, Holl throws himself into his work, masters it, and begins to view his situation in less catastrophic terms. As part of his apprenticeship Holl is sent for three months to a vocational school in an even more remote village. The school is run in an authoritarian manner, and the methods of instruction are designed to instill fear and make the apprentice submissive. Holl reacts allergically to the repression; during his second term at the school he becomes involved in an insurrection that comes very close to leading to his dismissal. It is only through Bruckmann's intervention that Holl is allowed to remain in school and thereby complete his apprenticeship. These episodes are significant for the novel in that they represent Innerhofer's first social-critical statements about his society and its institutions in a general way. This social-critical aspect will increase in importance in his work from this point on.

As Holl becomes more secure he begins to achieve some distance from himself that allows him to expand his observations and reflections to include others. Realizing that he is not the only person who has suffered at the hands of this rural environment, he feels a growing sense of solidarity with his fellow "victims." He contemplates the rapid changes visited on both village and rural countryside by sudden economic development, primarily as a result of the expanding tourist trade: ". . . the memory of the village, but the village now only exists as a hindrance to development . . . It is a village which is torn apart. The tourist office has become sacred. The tourists are now our gods" (S, 171).

As the traditional village and rural structures break down, many people are uprooted and leave the area. Others quickly advance economically, forming a new "petit bourgeois" class, but very few of these are prepared for such radical changes and adjust, if at all, in form but not in substance. The pedantry, artificial sophistication, triviality, and meanness of the "petite bourgeoisie" is merely added to the brutality and dullness that characterized these individuals when they were still farmers or small merchants.

Through Holl's descriptions we get a particularly vivid and depressing glimpse at the boring and desperate lives of young people in this rapidly changing village world. Alienated from themselves, each other, their daily routines, and even the nature that surrounds them and attracts the tourists, they pass their time drinking, fighting, committing stupid crimes, or indulging in unfeeling sexuality. Many die, usually violent deaths, often in car accidents or by suicide. Holl remarks at one point: ". . . it could be that an entire generation will drown itself in alcohol and gradually kill itself night after night in its cars . . ." (*S,* 183). The desperate indifference with which many of these young people view their lives is summed up in such passages: "A young laborer said – tavern, workplace, bed – I don't have much more. What's the real difference whether tomorrow I'm still alive or under the ground?" (*S,* 168). Their horizons are extremely narrow, their hope even more so. Their only real choice is to flee, but where to? Karin Struck has made a keen observation in her review of *Schöne Tage,* which relates directly to this question and anticipates many of the difficulties Holl will encounter when he too flees from the land to the city: "The country has to be left behind, but where have the people gone, where do they go? They flee 'from' the country and then dream of fleeing 'back to' the country."[27]

Gradually Holl begins to escape such a fate of dullness, boredom, and meaninglessness. In one of the most remarkable descriptions in contemporary literature of the liberating power of books we watch as Bruckmann's mother, Helene, pushes and shames Holl into confronting books and ideas: "I was exhausted and wanted a little rest after work, wash myself, eat, and remain sitting behind the table in my work clothes. But Helene needled . . . I came up with more and more arguments which were intended to excuse my ignorance, but secretly I began to recognize that I could only justify my past with them, not my present . . ." (*S,* 82–83). Finally Holl asks Helene to loan him a book she thinks he can read. His response upon finishing it is important for his further development:

It was a story about Carinthian farmers, about romance . . . The hero was

the proud son of a powerful farmer. After two days I gave Helene back
the book, which I had read from cover to cover, and said that I hadn't
liked it at all, I would like to read another book, that I know more about
farmers myself. Afterwards I was very angry about the book and at
Helene: how can she offer me a book full of such lies, a book in which
not one single example of farmers' meanness appears, no Holl, no conspiracy, no cursing servants? (*S*, 86).

Slowly Holl develops a critical, although not yet sophisticated, reading sense.
He rejects such traditional "Bauernromane" and is driven toward books that
open up new worlds far beyond his experience. His experience with the second
book is much different:

I held the book with my big hands and read eagerly words phrases sentences paragraphs pages and absorbed them, hyphens periods colons
quotations marks just got in the way. I discovered completely different
people there. Nothing reminded me of my world. Tender, soft hands . . .
People have time. I came alive. Lying in bed, I came alive, turned the
pages . . . The desire to experience that which I never had, hope, things
and situations which I had never experienced, pushed me on. . . .(*S*,
86, 88)

Fortunately for Holl he was not left totally to his own devices as he read
his way into new worlds. He was not allowed to use literature merely as an
escape. Helene forces him to discuss the works with her and gradually they
become engaged in a continuing conversation not only about books, but also
about films, newspaper articles, and social problems. The emotional and intellectual progress that Holl makes throughout the novel is not without its
setbacks and contradictions, but it is profound nonetheless. As one reviewer
claims: "The object Holl gradually becomes a subject who sees, reads, thinks,
and experiences: FRANZ Holl who tenaciously and under the most difficult
conditions achieves his first name, his identity."[28]

Over holidays Holl occasionally visits his mother on her small farm, even
though most of these visits result in conflict between them. In this setting
Holl is confronted with and forced to relive portions of his past. The tension
is heightened by his recognition of the significant differences in his situations
past and present and between his mother and Helene: "I had to think about
Helene. The one is a stranger who wants to help me in every way. The other
is my mother who wants to drive me back into a miserable situation, who

only knows how to dominate and be dominated . . ." (*S,* 127). The visits become focal points for Holl's renewed attacks on the Church, about which his mother is particularly defensive, and on the schools. Innerhofer's social criticism, directed at these antiquated and inhumane institutions, comes clearly into the foreground.

Yet in spite of Holl's critical stance toward his past there are moments when it is still the only world that seems to make real sense to him. At one point early in the novel, after much vacillation about whether he should do so or not, Holl visits his father in the hospital: "After everything I had experienced in Bruckmann's household, in the vocational school, in the settlement Z., the world of Lein [his father] seemed to make the most sense. Hayseed welder! Fool! Farmer! Whatever there had been between him and me, I told myself, it is not as bad as being made ridiculous by ridiculous people. Farm work is hard, but it is not ridiculous" (*S,* 79). We are reminded of Karin Struck's comment cited above and point out that although such sentiments are expressed only rarely in *Schattseite,* they become more significant and problematical in *Die großen Wörter.*

In contrast to such feelings here, very shortly after this hospital visit we hear Holl assert: "The farm house in which I took my meals and slept on work days seemed more and more like a fairy tale to me" (*S,* 81). It is these positive sentiments about his current situation that increase and prevail in the novel; Holl gradually achieves a healthy self-image as a worker, substantiated by Bruckmann's comment that ". . . you can depend on Franz . . ." (*S,* 148). He also gains, through Helene's encouragement, confidence in his own speech and thought.

At the end of the book Holl has passed his final exams and met all other requirements for a successful apprenticeship. With that behind him he looks for and finds a job in a local factory; but before actually starting work he abruptly decides to flee to Salzburg and find a job there. The last few pages of the novel show Holl overwhelmed by the city. He is alone and disoriented once again: "I was confused. The strangers confused me. I acted like a foreign worker . . ." (*S,* 247). Nonetheless, he manages to secure a job in a large factory and throws himself into the struggle of coming to terms with yet another world.

Schattseite is in most respects a more contemporary novel than is *Schöne Tage.* Its events, problems, and characters do not seem as exotic or historically as far removed. *Schattseite* is also a more directly social, even political novel than the first in that Holl develops a critical stance toward institutions and social circumstances as well as the means to express that stance. He also becomes aware of many of the stifling authoritarian structures and attitudes in society at large, whereas earlier he had only been cognizant of them in the microcosmic world of his father and "Hof 48."

The reviewers and critics of *Schattseite* have been almost as unanimous in their praise as they have been for *Schöne Tage*. Where criticism has been expressed it has usually focused on the contention that Innerhofer's work becomes weaker the more it moves away from the concrete and toward the abstract, the more it moves away from the realistic description of the external world and toward the realm of ideas.[29] Yet Innerhofer still has a clear overview of his protagonist and the world in which he lives and he maintains clear control over the novel's content. And as a *Bildungsroman*, as a testimony to the liberating power of books, learning, and good teaching, *Schattseite* is an extraordinary novel.

Die großen Wörter. In the final novel of the trilogy the self-enclosed rural world of the first two novels gives way to the more complicated world of a modern city; the question arises whether Innerhofer can maintain overview and control of the content. The prose style changes radically, reflecting Holl's moving increasingly and rapidly into the "world of words." As the emphasis on physical experience and concrete events diminishes, lengthy discussion of ideas, extended self-analysis and substantial dialogue, reported now indirectly by the third-person narrator, start to dominate the prose. Clearly the "Innenwelt," the realm of ideas and subjective responses to the external reality has replaced the "Außenwelt," the realm of concrete experience and objective descriptions of reality, as the central focus.

The novel commences with Holl's return to civilian life following a tour of duty with the army. A period of time has thus elapsed between the end of *Schattseite* and the beginning of *Die großen Wörter*, a lapse enabling Holl to gain some distance from and reflect back on his earliest experiences in Salzburg and the thoughts and feelings that had accompanied them. The pattern in Holl's life whereby he allows his hopes and expectations to rise unrealistically only to have them firmly dashed, reemerges here in these reflections: "Yes, that miserable time came back to him again, the time when he saw his hopes and himself turned upside down within a few days. His hasty flight to the city and the sudden panic he experienced because the world which he had sought did not exist . . ." (*DgW*, 10). [30]

Among his several naive expectations Holl had anticipated that he would discover a genuine feeling of solidarity among his fellow workers in Feinstein's factory and in them a group to which he could finally belong. What he found, however, was far from a sense of solidarity: opportunism, crass materialism, indifference toward one another, lack of ideals, and a general "petit bourgeois" mentality. Holl had also enrolled in evening school, expecting to find access to his esteemed "world of words" and an environment in which he could continue to grow intellectually with the aid of enlightened teachers, teachers even better than Helene had been. Instead, he was confronted with pedantic, insensitive teachers and an exhausting workload.

Illusions shattered and hopes dashed, Holl nevertheless clings to his remaining hopes and occupies himself with the task of progressing toward them. When fellow workers and pedantic evening school teachers disappoint him, he focuses his hope on the university, which symbolizes for him the highest station in the "world of words." He is determined to gain entry to that world whatever the cost and strain: "Out of fear of not being able to say 'yes' to anything in the world, he held tightly to the conviction that at least the university was free of the ridiculous . . ." (*DgW*, 85). Holl is in awe of the university, fascinated with students and professors alike, and is amazed when one of the students who lives in the same dormitory actually becomes a friend. It is obvious to the reader, conscious of the pattern of high expectations that lead to terrible disappointments, that Holl's naive perception of the university and those affiliated with it only invites further disillusionment. This is particularly evident when we realize that Holl expects to find ultimate answers and to experience the university as the place where everything finally makes sense.

Holl's life remains full of dualistic tensions. Still working at Feinstein's factory while taking evening classes, Holl has one foot in each world and is thus a resident in neither world completely. As a "Milieuwechsler," one who exchanges one world or environment for another, he appears forever caught in the middle, attracted to and repulsed by both milieus sometimes simultaneously, sometimes alternately. And as a newcomer to the more complex world of the city, Holl has considerable difficulty distinguishing between appearance and reality. For all of these reasons, Holl is basically homeless. Homelessness with its profound and often disastrous results concerns Innerhofer throughout the novel.

A very specific tension that asserts itself increasingly in Holl's life is that between past and present. The attraction of the past becomes at times a romantic yearning for a world that, in spite of its unforgotten hardships, made sense for Holl. It was a world of physical labor, the usefulness of which was immediately evident, a world in which the social and economic structures were not obscure, a world in which one could determine who and what the enemies were. Occasionally it seems that the bitter irony of the first novel's title, *Schöne Tage*, is about to be retracted. Holl's memory is not so bad that he forgets the abuse, brutality, and inhumanity of that world completely. Nonetheless he yearns for certain features of that world and compares them favorably to some of the negative and troubling aspects of his urban world. Those dangers for Holl (and Innerhofer) that Karin Struck observed in her review of *Schöne Tage* have obviously become very real: "In all of his sentences full of disgust for farm work and his father there glimmers somewhere also the yearnings of a man who has been thrown into industrial and office work, there also glimmers somewhere the danger that Holl's past will actually, in retrospect, turn into 'beautiful days.' With the 'serfs' there were at least hints of community. And what kind of community is there for a student of German literature?"[31]

The many tensions in Holl's life, between past and present, between different milieus, between physical labor and intellectual pursuits, between romantic illusions, whether these are projected into the past or the future, and the disappointments of reality are the focus around which the entire novel revolves. All of the episodes in Holl's life that are described, his reflections on himself and the world, the dialogues with friends and acquaintances, and finally his attempts to reach political conclusions display these basic tensions.

Holl overcomes his great anxieties and actual failures to complete the first year of evening school. Disillusioned with the teachers, he learns to perceive school as a means to an end. Despite the disappointments to his idealism he remains sufficiently convinced that education is the route to liberation; he quits his factory job to take a lesser position as janitor/caretaker in his dormitory in order to devote more time and energy to his studies. This is a difficult decision to make, for Holl is an excellent worker and has advanced rapidly in the factory; by contrast his success in school has been moderate at best. He is also troubled by the nagging feeling that intellectual work is not real work, not totally legitimate. Having defined himself for so long in terms of physical work, he has to combat a guilty conscience about removing himself from the world of physical labor to pursue the interests of his mind.

The contrasts between the worlds of work and school reach a climax, as does Holl's dilemma in reflecting upon them, when he reluctantly takes several school friends to a high Alpine hut on his father's farm for a winter excursion. The trip becomes grotesque for him when he is confronted by his friends' anxiety about the rustic surroundings, their utter incompetence in performing minor chores, and their complaints about the need to do them: "Even the thought that some still perish silently at their work and the others, who live from them, become defensive when work is even mentioned, drove Holl crazy ..." (*DgW*, 120). Holl's disdain for these friends and his impression that their world is pampered and artificial increase markedly with this experience. As a result, "... farmers and the working populace now stood for Holl far above the 'world of words'" (*DgW*, 112).

Even though such experiences severely test Holl's image of the university and what it represents, he fails to surrender his hopes altogether. Nonetheless he begins to avoid his classmates and frequents a mechanics' bar. That his dangerous romanticizing of the rural world has been extended to this unlikely realm becomes obvious when Holl sings the praise of the bar and its visitors: "The people he met in the mechanics' bar were real" (*DgW*, 87). Holl quickly falls into the cliché of the academic world versus the "real" world. Mechanics, prostitutes, pimps, ex-convicts, neo-Nazis—these are the "real" people whom Holl finds in the bar: "They either talked about politics thoroughly or not at all . . ." (*DgW*, 89). "In order to talk about literature, he had to go to the mechanics. bar. There sat people who came alive at the mention of literature" (*DgW*, 128). One must be skeptical of such assertions, but it is understandable that Holl is attracted to the bar and can find refuge there among other outsiders, others who have known hard work and poverty, who have not been integrated into bourgeois society, who also have large and disfigured hands. The mechanics' bar represents for Holl a step backward into his past, a place where he can temporarily feel secure, where he can escape anxieties about his place in the "world of words," but it is not a solution, for Holl does not really belong to this group either.

At other times, rather than stepping back into his past, Holl attempts to overcome it altogether. Faced with the first extended vacation of his life, Holl decides to travel: "When he had seen London, Prague, Florence, Paris, and Rome, he hoped he would have eradicated completely his own past with the help of these big-city impressions . . ." (*DgW*, 101). Needless to say his naive hopes are not fulfilled in this way either.

Holl finally succeeds in finishing school, receives his "Matura" (diploma), and is awarded a fellowship to study at the University of Salzburg. But even now on the threshold of his longstanding goal of being a university student Holl's dissatisfaction with himself and his life continues: "The irony was that Holl described his progress, as far as school was concerned, as a mistake and folly. He did not accept the achievement and tenacity of evening students which was admired by many. As soon as it was mentioned, he pointed to the mountain farmers and said that they had every bit as much right to be admired for their achievement and tenacity. Holl always had reason to be dissatisfied with himself . . ." (*DgW*, 116). Surprisingly, however, he pushes all of his criticisms of this "world without work" aside and announces that he wants to become a writer.

Political reflections played but a minor role in the first two novels of the trilogy, but in *Die großen Wörter* they assume major significance, for much of the dialogue between Holl and others is concerned with political questions. His thoughts about politics are very subjective, growing as they do from his disappointments and realization that a wide gap exists between his ideals and reality. We have already noted his disappointment upon discovering that solidarity was no more than an empty phrase among his fellow workers, which he blames in large part on the unions. Although he is attracted to certain aspects of Communism, Holl also firmly rejects pressures to join the "tiny" Communist Party in Austria because he fears he would have to support party positions with which he disagrees. Since he is forever vacillating between polarities, between two worlds, it is no surprise that Holl cannot accept ideologies.

But Holl is a political person: he becomes indignant when he discovers or contemplates injustices, when he reflects, for instance, on history and the exploitation of the workers who constructed the marvelous buildings of Salzburg. He is also fascinated —but in a romantic way—by revolutions that such workers attempted, and not only in Austria. His analyses of political structures and power remain inconsistent, eclectic, and largely superficial. He lashes out at the United States, West Germany, and capitalism in general. He attacks the Nazis and neo-Nazis, the Communists, and politicians in general. Within this disaffection, however, one recognizes certain tendencies: his intellectual sympathies lie clearly with the causes of the left, his emotional make-up, though, renders him vulnerable to attitudes of the right.

Holl is aware of these dangerous emotional tendencies and condemns them intellectually. While reflecting on his military service he sees: ". . . that it had been no accident that he had volunteered as a tank driver, that he had felt very powerful in the midst of the monstrous motor noise and that he would have driven into a group of demonstrators on command. And at some point it had simply snapped in him. At some point he simply believed that the beatings he had suffered had been right, that they had made a strong person out of him" (*DgW*, 93). Holl's consciousness of this side of his character enables him to control it, but he cannot eradicate it completely.

Holl's political thinking remains vague and confused to the very end. Clichés from the social and political criticism of the student movement of the 1960s dominate, but the deeper analyses characterizing at least part of that movement are missing. The final scene of the novel involves a discussion between Holl and one of his acquaintances, appropriately named Stürzl,[32] who tries to convince him of the merits of his own queer and mystical brand of Communism, which he refers to as the "Summerauer Manifest" (Summerau Manifesto). Holl becomes extremely irritated by the half-crazed Stürzl and his chaotic and contradictory manifesto. One suspects, however, that a good part of Holl's irritation is due to his realization that his own political thinking is as confused as Stürzl's.

Throughout the years in Salzburg Holl's relationships with women, as infrequent as they have been, have also been marked by problems and ambivalence. Near the end of his schooling, he halfheartedly enters into a relationship with one of his classmates, Fräulein Gärtner, whom he claims to dislike because she reminds him of his stepmother. Yet the flesh is weak. After passing his final exams, however, Holl decides to break off with all of his former classmates including Miss Gärtner. But she locates him, announces that she is pregnant and wants to marry him. He refuses, telling her that if she really is pregnant, she undoubtedly planned it that way in order to trap him. Holl remains firm in this decision and does not succumb to additional pressure from her and others, but it is evident that this episode represents a crisis for him of lasting consequences: he is aware of the similarity between his decision and the decision his father must have made when he decided not to marry his mother. Is he repeating his father's sins?

To escape from this situation Holl flees to Italy. In spite of a scholarship waiting for him his long-sought-after center of the world of words, it is obvious that Holl no longer anticipates that the university will be a panacea. On the contrary his general state of mind is evident when, on his return trip from Italy, he laments: "I'm alive, he thought . . . How awful" (*DgW*, 141).

The novel, and thus the trilogy as well, ends with Holl's final hope in his long and arduous climb to the pinnacle of the "world of words" solidly dashed. The narrator observes, for example, that "during the first two semesters his enthusiasm diminished gradually, and a more powerful world, the archaic world of farm laborers and farmers, began to command his attention . . ." (*DgW*, 142). Many factors have contributed to Holl's ultimate disappointment, but the crucial factor, one must suspect, is that the world he had sought did not exist. We are left with the inescapable conclusion that Holl's worst fear has come true: at some point not to be able to say "yes" to anything in the world.

Thus the central problems and tensions in the novel and in Holl's life remain unresolved, as they perhaps must, for they are the problems and tensions of the twentieth century for which there appear to be no ultimate solutions. They reflect the modern predicament from which existentialist, absurdist, and other modernist art perspectives have arisen. The open end of *Die großen Wörter*, its lack of conclusions, its avoidance of (simple) answers, and the disappointment, even alienation of the protagonist make it a novel much in the modernist tradition.

The critical reception of this third novel has not been as unanimously enthusiastic as that afforded the first two. The main criticisms have stressed a perceived lack of control and objectivity, a much less convincing prose style as Innerhofer leaves the realm of concrete descriptions and enters the world of abstractions, a lack of understanding on Innerhofer's part of the complexities of urban as opposed to rural life, and an abundance of clichés. In the opinion of some critics Innerhofer has simply been unable to render into literary form the more complicated world of words and the city.[33]

Other reviewers have viewed the novel much more favorably. Franz Schwabender, for instance, places *Die großen Wörter* above the highly praised *Schöne Tage* and *Schattseite:* "Linguistically, 'Die großen Wörter' seems to me to be even denser, more genuine than the previous two books. It reflects with its watchful, circumspect reality the position of a man who, through his upbringing, through his formation in the worlds of the farm, labor and the intellect has become a not so easily integrated member of society."[34] Alexander Auer adds that he finds the language ". . . even more concise, more expressive and fluid . . ." and sees the novel's more open form and the fact that the story line does not flow neatly from beginning to end as positive qualities.[35]

The reviews are mixed, but I think that some of the criticisms are inaccurate and stem from false expectations and rather one-sided literary standards. Each of the three novels has its unique qualities and to a certain extent must be judged on its own terms. The first two novels can stand more securely as independent novels than can *Die großen Wörter. Schöne Tage*, for instance, requires no prior knowledge about the protagonist or his world: the reader could understand all details of this first novel whether the remainder of the trilogy had been written or not. *Die großen Wörter*, however, is in most ways a conclusion, and as such it depends much more on its place within the trilogy.

Die großen Wörter is also a much more difficult and puzzling novel than the first two, largely because the subject matter is much more inconclusive. If unity of form and content is a reflection of good literature, as is frequently asserted in the positive reviews of *Schöne Tage*, then *Die großen Wörter* should qualify as good literature at least on that account. The perspective of the novel is that of Franz Holl, and his perception of himself and the world is full of contradictions and tensions. It seems only fitting that this perception be reflected in a prose style that underscores the contradictoriness, fragmentation, and disillusionment in his life. The disjointed style reflects his confusion and the struggles within him between his illusions and reality, between his yearnings for answers and his recognition that there are none; in sum, it reflects his "modern condition." It is true that clichés abound in this novel, but Holl like many others is trapped in these clichés when he searches for solutions to unanswerable problems. To assume that Innerhofer is uncritical of Holl or of the clichés into which he lapses, or that author and protagonist are one and the same at all times, as some critics do, results from a rather careless reading of the novel. Holl is an autobiographical character, to be sure, and the distance between Innerhofer and Holl is not always great; but there are also numerous indications of Innerhofer's criticism of much of Holl's thinking as well as his insights into the dangerous aspects of Holl's character. It is also clear from the narrator's comments about Holl that Innerhofer has an appreciation and understanding of the complexities of urban society and the world of words—an understanding that Holl does not share. When Innerhofer points out the folly of Holl's high and naive expectations or underscores the fascist tendencies that Holl displays, he is certainly not to be equated with Holl, or at least he is a Holl who is far beyond the Holl of the novel.

With the first two novels in the trilogy the reader had come to expect some kind of resolution. *Schöne Tage,* as noted, concluded with an almost fairy-tale liberation. *Schattseite,* although the ending leaves no doubt about future difficulties that Holl must face, also ends conclusively. The reader cannot help but feel a great deal of satisfaction from the resolutions of these first two novels: put simply, good and evil are clearly defined, and good emerges victorious. *Die großen Wörter,* however, is a completely different kind of novel. Not only are Holl's expectations and hopes of finding genuine liberation in the "world of words" brutally squelched, but also our hopes and expectations as readers as well. Because Innerhofer so successfully makes the reader identify and sympathize with Holl in the first two novels, the reader has taken on and is faced with the same disappointments and confusion as Holl. Good and evil have become blurred in this third novel, and the enemy vanishes or changes form when one tries to grasp him. The question even arises here for the first time as to whether Holl might be responsible for some of his problems and suffering himself. Because many of his apparent strengths now appear as weaknesses it has become much more difficult to identify with him. His world (and ours) has changed from being brutal but comprehensible to being brutal and perplexing. The hope and vision of a happy end to his struggles, a fairy-tale ending in the "world of words," disappear into thin air.

When asked why he was unable to give *Die großen Wörter* the positive ending he had once intended, Innerhofer responded: "That had to do with Marxism. I have written about individual or isolated people in whom no group is interested. In part those are people who fail. A positive ending in light of that would have seemed to me to be a mean trick on them. I am concerned about the individual who tries to make something of himself. Marxism is concerned with general conditions, not with individuals. These have to adjust whether they like it or not."[36]

In spite of the clear distinctions and differences in the three novels, taken together they form a unified and coherent whole, which reveals a continuity and progression from beginning to end. The conclusion to Holl's arduous journey is disappointing and disturbing, but it makes complete sense in the context of what preceded it. That is not the same as asserting that no other conclusion would have been possible: Innerhofer's original intention of giving the novel a positive ending and his own growth, which led him beyond a dilemma similar to what Holl experiences at the end of the novel, indicate otherwise. But the internal logic of the trilogy proves unmistakable when one reads the novels closely and in sequennce.

Let us briefly look at these three novels not as single literary works but as a trilogy. Holl is the central focus throughout. His life, his surroundings, his realities are viewed primarily from his own perspective, even though one must be careful not to view narrator (or author) and protagonist as identical in the two novels where a third-person narrator exists. Where the prose style changes it reflects changes in Holl, his world, and his perception of that world. Even the abrupt stylistic shift between *Schattseite* and *Die großen Wörter* parallels the radical changes in Holl's life, brought about by his move from country to city.

A thematic continuity also manifests itself when one considers the trilogy in its entirety. It was certainly not one of Innerhofer's primary intentions to write an allegory, nor is there any explicit indication in the texts themselves that he was conscious of the possibility for seeing Holl's (his own) development in allegorical terms; but the trilogy can be read on one level clearly as an allegory of western man's journey from his well-defined, if often difficult, position in rural, preindustrial society to his complicated and perplexing existence in the modern, technological, and urban world, a journey that has led him from physical, but comprehensible hardship to a confusing alienation of the spirit. This alienation of the spirit has become of course one of the major themes of artistic expression in the postindustrial, twentieth-century world. It is precisely that world—the world of Kafka, Beckett, and Bernhard—that Holl has finally "attained." And there is no more possibility, in spite of his ambivalent yearnings in that direction, of a return to the simplicity of the negative "Eden" from which he fled than there is for modern man to return to his preindustrial condition or any of the specific "Edens" that are the object of his retrospective yearnings.

The secondary literature on the trilogy as a whole is not yet abundant. But those assessments that have appeared are singularly positive. Franz Schwabender, for instance, has claimed the following: "With the conclusion of the autobiographical trilogy of this Salzburg writer, one of the most remarkable undertakings in recent German literature has reached fulfillment . . . Franz Innerhofer has completed this trilogy with great tenacity and profound reflection. Like Thomas Bernhard he has thereby underscored the uniqueness of his literary talent."[37] Alexander Auer has termed the trilogy "a superbly readable text, completely self-contained and personally shaped, which shrinks back from no problem and which shows neither affectation nor falsehood. Contemporary Austrian literature had been missing a 'Bildungsroman' of quality. Franz Innerhofer has succeeded in writing it."[38]

In fact, just as *Schöne Tage* and *Schattseite* have been cited as outstanding examples of the "Anti-Heimatroman," it could be argued that the trilogy, which concludes by raising serious questions about the positive attitudes toward traditional education that prevail in the "Bildungsroman," can be understood as a kind of "Anti-Bildungsroman." Given the fact that *Die großen Wörter* negates the positive "Bildungsroman" characteristics of *Schattseite*, it threatens to stand the nineteenth-century tradition of the "Bildungsroman" on its head as well.

Franz Innerhofer is a radical, honest, and important writer. Let us hope that his current silence is only temporary and that he will break through it once again with a literary work that lives up to the quality and promise of this exceptional trilogy.

Notes

1. Cf. Helmut Olles, "Franz Innerhofer—'Schöne Tage,'" *Die Welt der Bücher*, 3 (1975).

2. Ulrich Greiner, *Der Tod des Nachsommers* (München: Hanser, 1979), p. 107.

3. See, for example Reinhard Baumgart, "Auf dem Lande: Menschenfinsternis 'Schöne Tage,' der erste Roman von Franz Innerhofer," *Süddeutsche Zeitung*, 12/13. Oktober 1974; W. Martin Lüdke, "Herrschaft und Knechtschaft. Franz Innerhofers erster Roman 'Schöne Tage,'" *Frankfurter Rundschau*, 30. November 1974.

4. Franz Innerhofer, *Beautiful Days*, trans. Anselm Hollo (New York: Urizen Books, 1976). The translation frequently fails to capture the linguistic

power of the original, but because it is the only translation available in
English I have nonetheless quoted from it throughout.

5. Cf. Werner Thuswaldner, "Die Tage werden noch nicht schöner–der
    Roman 'Schattseite' von Franz Innerhofer...," *Salzburger Nachrichten,*
    25. September 1975; Helmut Schödel, "Abkehr vom Aufstieg. Inner-
    hofers Roman von den großen Wörtern," *Süddeutsche Zeitung,* 12. Ok-
    tober 1977; Alexander Auer, "Nach Haudorf und Anderswo Hin," *Austri-
    aca* 7 (1978), 37-44.

6. Jürgen Koppensteiner, "Anti-Heimatliteratur. Ein Unterrichtsversuch
    mit Franz Innerhofers Roman 'Schöne Tage,'" *Unterrichtspraxis,* 14/1
    (1981), 9-19, and "Das Leben auf dem Lande. Zu den Anti-Heimat-
    romanen österreichischer Gegenwartsautoren," *Akten des VI. Intern.
    Germ. Kongr.,* Basel 1980 (Bern, Frankfurt am Main, New York: Verlag
    Peter Lang), pp. 545-550.

7. Klaus Heydemann, "Jugend auf dem Lande. Zur Tradition des Heimat-
    romans in Österreich," *Sprachkunst* 9 (1978), 141-157.

8. Greiner, op. cit.

9. Jürgen Lodemann, "Menschenfinsternis-Franz Innerhofer: 'Schöne Tage,'"
    Die Zeit, 15. November 1974.

10. Cf. Johann Keckeis, "Ein Bauernspiegel 1974: Franz Innerhofers 'Schöne
    Tage,'" *Zürichsee Zeitung,* 18. April 1975.

11. Cf. Lodemann or Auer, both op. cit.

12. Hans Esderts, "Die Stimme der Sprachlosen. Zum Roman Franz Inner-
    hofers 'Schöne Tage'...," *Bremer Nachrichten,* 25. Januar 1975.

13. Such authors as Peter Handke, Gerhard Fritsch, G. F. Jonke, Hans Lebert,
    Elfriede Jelinek, Peter Rosei, Michael Scharang, Gernot Wolfgruber, and
    Thomas Bernhard have all written works that come quickly to mind in
    this context.

14. The terms originated with F. Sengle, "Wunschbild Land und Schreckbild
    Stadt," *Studium generale,* 16 (1963), 619-663, but are used frequently
    in the secondary literature on "Anti-Heimatliteratur."

15. Auer, p. 37.

16. Page numbers cited first are from the Hollo translation, those cited second
    are from the *suhrkamp taschenbuch* German edition.

17. One possible translation of "Haudorf" is "Beating-ville."

18. Erwin Hartl, "Eine merkwürdige Entdeckung: Franz Innerhofers 'Schöne
    Tage,'" *Die Presse,* 14/15. September 1974.

19. Karin Struck, "Für die Arbeit gezeugt," *Der Spiegel,* 50 (1974), 136.

20. Greiner, *Der Tod des Nachsommers,* p. 105.

21. Günter Blöcker, "Zwei Kindheiten," *Merkur*, 2 (1975), 189.
22. Greiner, p. 108.
23. M. K., "Befreiung von der Sprachlosigkeit . . ." *Neue Züricher Zeitung*, 5 May 1975.
24. Greiner, p. 105.
25. Reference is to Handke's *Die Innenwelt der Außenwelt der Innenwelt*.
26. Because no published translations of either *Schattseite* or *Die großen Wörter* exist in English, the translations in the text are my own. The page numbers in parentheses are from the *suhrkamp taschenbuch* edition of *Schattseite*.
27. Struck, "Für die Arbeit gezeugt," p. 136.
28. W. Martin Lüdke, op. cit.
29. Cf. Inge Meidinger-Geise, "Fortsetzung vom Prozeß," *Die Tat*, 21. November 1975; Hans Haider, "Ein Landarbeiter wird Schmied," *Die Presse*, 29. Oktober 1975; Jürgen Lodemann, "Stromboli in Salzburg," *Die Zeit*, 10. Oktober 1975.
30. My translations from this third novel are taken from the Residenz Verlag original edition, 1977.
31. Struck, "Für die Arbeit gezeugt," p. 136.
32. One meaning of *stürzen* is "to overthrow."
33. Cf. Lothar Sträter, "Holls Leiden an sich selbst," *Rheinische Post*, 22. Oktober 1977; Norbert Schachtsiek-Freitag, "Erfahrungen in der Redewelt. 'Die großen Wörter' . . " *Badische Zeitung*, 7. Januar 1978.
34. Franz Schwabender, "Unbehaust in der Welt. Franz Innerhofer hat seine autobiographische Trilogie abgeschlossen," *Oberösterreichische Nachrichten*, 4. Januar 1978.
35. Auer, op. cit.
36. Innerhofer, Interview with Gisela Ullrich, *Frankfurter Rundschau*, 29. März 1978.
37. Schwabender, op. cit.

Primary Works

Schöne Tage. Novel. Salzburg: Residenz Verlag, 1973 (Paperback edition, Frankfurt am Main: Suhrkamp, 1977 = st 349).

Beautiful Days. Novel. Translation of *Schöne Tage* by Anselm Hollo. New York: Urizen Books, 1976.

Schattseite. Novel. Salzburg: Residenz Verlag, 1975 (Paperback edition, Frankfurt am Main: Suhrkamp, 1979 = st 542).

Die großen Wörter. Novel. Salzburg: Residenz Verlag, 1977. (Paperback edition, Frankfurt am Main: Suhrkamp, 1979 = st 563).

Secondary Works
(excluding newspaper and magazine reviews)

Auer, Alexander. "Nach Haudorf und Anderswo Hin." *Austriaca,* 7 (1978), 37–44.

Caputo-Mayr, Maria Luise. "Überlieferung aus neuer Sicht: Zur jüngsten österreichischen Prosaliteratur." *Perspectives and Personalities. Studies in Modern German Literature Honoring Claude Hill,* ed. Ralph Ley et al., Heidelberg: Carl Winter, 1978, pp. 89–100.

Frank, Peter. "Heimatromane von unten—einige Gedanken zum Werk Franz Innerhofers." *Modern Austrian Literature,* Vol. 13, no. 1 (1980), 167–175.

Greiner, Ulrich. "Franz Innerhofer." In U. G. *Der Tod des Nachsommers,* München: Hanser, 1979, pp. 101–121.

Heydemann, Klaus. "Jugend auf dem Lande. Zur Tradition des Heimatromans in Österreich." *Sprachkunst* 9 (1978), 141–157.

Koppensteiner, Jürgen. "Anti-Heimatliteratur. Ein Unterrichtsversuch mit Franz Innerhofers Roman 'Schöne Tage.'" *Unterrichtspraxis,* Vol. 14, no. 1 (1981), 9–19.

Koppensteiner, Jürgen. "Das Leben auf dem Lande. Zu den Anti-Heimatromanen Österreichischer Gegenwartsautoren." *Akten des VI. Intern. Germanisten Kongresses, Basel 1980.* Bern, Frankfurt, New York: Peter Lang, 1980, pp. 545–550.

Schink, Helmut. "Vergewaltigung der Kindheit—Franz Innerhofers 'Schöne Tage.'" In H. S. *Jugend als Krankheit?* Linz: Oberösterreichischer Landesverlag, 1980, pp. 147–174.

Ernst Jandl and Concrete Poetry

Fritz H. König

Jandl's poems invite "jandln," a verb that has all but entered the German language and means, loosely and in a very general sense, the same as taking a poetic *homo ludens* approach to language. A good example is Klaus Jeziorkowski's four-liner:

> Marjandjosef
> mag ich das jandl mögen
> das marjandl
> im ernst.[1]

It is a play on Jandl's name with religious, pejorative, sexual, and amicable overtones that obviously defies translation into English. Another critic, Jörg Drews, wrote an article entitled "Ernst, ach Ernst, was du mich alles lernst!"[2] again an untranslatable name pun. Jandl seems to have this influence on his readers and critics: namely, to become creative and also try some witty language manipulation. I can think of very few poets past or present who have this capacity to incite their readers and listeners to try their hand at poetry manufacturing themselves, a fact that seems to indicate at least that Jandl's poetry is very much alive, potent enough to fertilize the mind of the reader, and, most importantly, to beget children. To create "living" poems is indeed Jandl's goal. He says: "The goal of my work, today and earlier, is functioning, living, effective, direct poems, guided, from whatever material they evolve and in whatever form they may appear, by all that is contained in myself of direction and inclination, joy and rage. What I want are poems that leave no one untouched."[3]

Throughout this study we will have to listen to Jandl's own words about his own poetry. He finds it necessary to make critical and theoretical comments, partly because the critical apparatus on the type of poetry he writes is still largely absent. There is also the matter of lending the audience a guiding hand, of preventing it from looking for things that are not there (and in so doing overlooking those that are).

Jandl has often been labeled a "concrete" or "experimental" poet. To this labeling Robert Acker enters the following caveat:

If we consider "concrete" to mean a reduction of the linguistic medium to the bare essentials or to imply a literature that only investigates the (im)potency of its own medium, then the label can only partially be applied to these authors [Jandl and Mayröcker], and only to some of their works. . . . If we consider "concrete" to mean a moderate restructuring of language in order to illuminate new perspectives about this language, about exterior reality and about one's self, then the term may be appropriate. Thus the word *experimental,* when applied to these authors must be used with care. They do indeed employ unusual or strange stylistic devices, but they do not haphazardly or wildly indulge in linguistic juggling. Their "experimentation" lies in perfecting and improving their own . . . styles.[4]

Jandl himself refuses to specify to which poetic school he belongs. He is ready to accept the terms "concrete" and "experimental" only when they can help him to consider the works of others or to reconsider some of his own. He is proud to have coined the word *Sprechgedicht* (speaking poem), which applies to a series of his own poems, but he is otherwise happy to leave the arduous task of categorization and denomination to others.[5] However, in his brief "Self-Portrait 1966" he says that Reinhard Döhl in Stuttgart accepted his *experimental poems* and helped him to a breakthrough, thus implicitly acknowledging the applicability of this term to at least part of his poetic production. In the same essay he also acknowledges stimuli from such friends as Mayröcker, Artmann, Rühm and poetic models from Stramm, Arp, Schwitters, and Gertrude Stein.[6]

In another essay, "Austrian Contributions to a Modern World-Poetry,"[7] he speaks of a need in the 1950s to create a new type of poetry, based on language manipulation, that received the attributes "concrete" or "experimental." Founded by a Swiss writer, Eugen Gomringer, the new poetry soon grew into an international movement. Disillusioned with the literary postwar atmosphere in Austria, a number of writers, the so-called "Wiener Gruppe" (Viennese Group), started to work and experiment with complete disregard for poetic conventions and artistic limitations. H. C. Artmann, Gerhard Rühm, Konrad Bayer, Oswald Wiener, and Friedrich Achleitner all belonged to the Viennese Group. Jandl places himself outside yet in a "tangential" position to this group, acknowledging a relationship and some cross-fertilizsation. He then proceeds to describe this type of new "World-Poetry":

This modern World-Poetry is poetry which . . . does not make us think of something else. It is not illusionistic or didactic . . . does not contain anything that one can "know." It is "concrete" because it realizes possibilities inside language and makes objects out of language. . . . It is not measurable in an extralingually imagined world. . . . It is poetry which produces closed systems of relations. . . . It does not suggest. It clarifies. It clarifies surfaces. . . . It is a poetry of our consciousness, the unoccupied intelligence as premise for the reception of this poetry, and as a result of the contact with it . . .[8]

Jandl, implicitly, is part of this "World-Poetry," if not its foremost exponent— at least as far as the literature of the German-speaking countries is concerned.

Besides Jandl there have been other writer-theoreticians, chiefly Gerhard Rühm, Peter Waiermair, and Heinz Gappmayr. However, on the whole the Austrian experimentalists with the exception of Jandl and Rühm show little interest in formulating theory. Rühm is especially interested in the "constructivists" who work *with*, unlike the surrealists who worked *in* the language. In his formulation the written fixation of language already has an informative function, and therefore form is not a means of expressing content but rather already *is* content. The concrete text does not describe, it shows (*zeigt*).[9]

In his essay "The First Steps" Jandl professes that it is precisely this urge to "show" that motivates him: "It has always been fun for me to make something that one can show . . . what really interests me is not so much what something is made of, but rather that it is something that is made in order to be shown, and that people look at it and that some like it and some get angry, a thing just for this and nothing else."[10]

Rühm's aesthetic considerations, though yielding some valuable insights— e.g., Rühm is the first to discern between "reading" and "hearing" texts ("Lese-" und "Hörtexte")—never quite jell into a system of theory. A more successful theoretician is Eugen Gomringer who offers the following definition of concrete poetry:

It is clear from what theoretical explanations the concept "concrete poetry" could evolve. Generally speaking: the concrete poet pays close attention to the material that he either wants to express (*zur darstellung bringen*) or in which he expresses (*darstellt*). He even prefers to offer little content (the content that is barely there still), only to be able to master content in its concrete linguistic form; to master it under all the influences of modern schools of thought. He is interested in language at the starting point, in the very complex and simple creative act of speaking/thinking, and analogous to that, in the visual beginning of language.[11]

Gomringer uses this definition in order to draw a clear division between the new movement and the preceding Dadaists and Expressionists, granting at the same time that these literary trends were not without influence on concrete poetry. But he does not look only to the past, he also looks to the future: "... One will see, furthermore, that concrete poetry will again lead to the real existence of the word and the letter ... beyond the details, one will see that concrete poetry begins to realize the idea of a universal common poetry. Perhaps it is time then to profoundly revise concepts, knowledge, beliefs, and disbeliefs concerning the poetic (*das dichterische*)."[12]

Of course Gomringer is right when he mentions a relationship with the Dadaists and Surrealists. After all, concrete poetry was not born into a vacuum. Milestones on the road toward a so-called "absolute language art" (*absolute Wortkunst*) are the thoughts of some French poets, above all Mallarmé, as expressed, for instance, in Marinetti's "Futurist Manifesto," or Joyce's manipulation of prose style. The Swiss Dadaist idea of the "total work of art" (*Gesamtkunstwerk*) played a role as did Picasso's and Kandinsky's experiments in painting.

Picasso's and Kandinsky's paintings as well as those of many of their contemporaries are generally referred to as "abstract art." To avoid a confusion of terminology it is helpful to consult Viktor Suchy's clarification in his excellent survey, "Concrete and Experimental Poetry in Austria":[13] "Important for the theoretical formulation of experimental and concrete poetry of our time is the difference in the perception of abstract and concrete poetry. The concepts "abstract" and "concrete" have almost gone through the same change as, for instance, the terms "idealistic" and "realistic" did from scholasticism to modern times. They went through a 180-degree turn, i.e., a complete exchange."[14]

Speaking earlier about Jandl's capability to incite his audience and critics to language manipulations themselves, I used the expression "poetry manufacturing." Recognizing the influence of modern linguistics on concrete poetry C. J. Wagenknecht stated in 1968: "Poems become possible whose content is their own manufacturing (*ihr eigenes Machen*)."[15] They are the "poetic exploration" of linguistic facts. Therefore Wagenknecht calls these poems "linguistic poetry" and equates them to abstract painting. This then is the final consequence of a trend that started with Gottfried Benn's famous sentence: "A poem is rarely born, a poem is made."[16]

In the meantime the development from the early poems of August Stramm, concentrating on the function of the single word without completely cutting the relation to the object (Jandl acknowledges being influenced by Stramm), to the Viennese Group and the Forum Stadtpark in Graz—both centers for

poetic language experimentation—is not linear. The development is interrupted
by the fascist era, which abhorred this type of poetry, calling it "degenerate
art" (*entartete Kunst*). In this context it might be pointed out that Marxism
generally favors concrete poetry, although, as Suchy remarks, orthodox Marxism
has misunderstood the avant-garde as bourgeois decadence.[17]

Summing up at this point, it can be stated then that Jandl is indebted to the
Expressionists, to the Dadaist sound poem, to the language experiments of
Stramm, Schwitters, and Gertrude Stein and, last but not least, to the Viennese
Group as well as to his friend and associate Friederike Mayröcker. But Jandl's
poetic endeavors are not epigonic; on the contrary, Jandl is an individualist,
developing his own theory of art. Throughout his career he oscillates between
more "traditional" poetry and new experiments. R. Acker's admonition has to
be remembered: it is not quite appropriate to simply categorize Jandl as a
"concrete" or "experimentalist" poet, even though he has made major contributions to this type of poetry.

A. Haslinger sees in Jandl's biography "a permanent tension between his
teaching profession and his 'poetic existence.'"[18] This tension, according to
Haslinger, is also evident in Jandl's frequent travels abroad. Yet who better to
talk about his biography than Jandl himself? In his "Self-Portrait" of 1966 he
says:

> I was born in Vienna in 1925. Consequently I spent the greater part of the
> NS-era [National-Socialist era] and the war as a pupil in secondary school,
> which was a haven. I had the luck to be with peers who felt the same way.
> The majority of us in this school, in my class were against Hitler/war/
> victory. I only joined the military in '43 after the university entry exam
> and became an American POW in '45, which was a liberation. 10 months
> in England, although behind barbed wire, gave me an idea of that country
> and enough of its language to decide my profession. March '46 back in
> Vienna I studied German and English without detours among the mass
> of the repatriated. In '49 after my exam for a teaching certificate, which
> was followed in '50 by the doctorate, I began to teach. This work in
> Vienna was twice interrupted for a year: In 52/53 I was in England as a
> German teacher, during 64/65 I took leave, translated Robert Creeley's
> novel *The Island,* and went to England to try out my own lyrical experi-
> ments. That I was going to write was a fact for me already in high school,
> likewise the teaching profession. Both seemed to go well together, even
> in the university. Work on the poem, to which I felt challenged by my
> poem-writing mother who died when I was 14, was reserved for the

time after my studies, without any thought of a "poetic existence."
Even today this idea seems to me romantic nonsense, but the coexistence
of both activities did not go smoothly, and between the two many things
disintegrated that otherwise belong to life.[19]

Jandl's poems started to appear in magazines and periodicals in 1952. His
first collection of poetry in book form came out in 1956 under the title *Andere
Augen* (Other Eyes). This book consisted of poetry written with more or less
conventional poetic devices. A turn to the grotesque, to experimentation, came
afterward, when contacts had been established with the Viennese Group and
after he had met Friederike Mayröcker. Jandl's biography would not be complete without mentioning that since 1951 he has been a member of the Austrian
Socialist party and since 1970 a member of the Academy of Arts in West Berlin
as well as of the Forum Stadtpark in Graz. In 1973 he co-founded the *Grazer
Autorenversammlung* (Graz Author's Society).

Jandl has traveled extensively. During 1970/1971 he spent some time in
West Berlin as a guest of the DAAD in the West Berlin artists' program; in 1971
he was Visiting German Writer at the University of Texas in Austin, and in 1972,
together with Friederike Mayröcker, he made a lecture tour through the United
States for the Austrian Ministry of Education and Art. The literary awards
Jandl has received in recognition of his work include the Austrian prize of
the War-Blind for prominent radio plays (together with Friederike Mayröcker)
in 1968; the Georg-Trakl-Prize for Poetry (1974); the City of Vienna Prize
for Literature (1976); the Austrian State Prize for Literature (1978); and the
Mülheim (West Germany) Dramatist Prize (1980).

Judging by his invitations and the numerous prizes he has received, Jandl
is recognized as one of the major contemporary poets of the German-speaking
countries. But fame and recognition came more slowly in Austria than abroad.
On the occasion of his receiving the Georg-Trakl-Prize in 1974 A. Haslinger,
who gave the awarding speech, felt it necessary to point out somewhat apolo-
getically: "There are Austrian authors who still need an introduction at home
while they have been famous for a long time abroad."[20] And in his "Self-
Portrait" Jandl himself points out that with his first experimental works the
possibilities for publication in Austria ended. In 1963 he had to travel to Germany where Reinhard Döhl in Stuttgart accepted the experimental poems
for publication and helped him to "overcome the isolation."[21]

Critics have repeatedly claimed that the poetry in Jandl's first collection,
Andere Augen (1956, Other Eyes) is "conventional." In the absence of definition, however, "conventional poetry" is a questionable concept at best. In

this context it is a term used merely to mark the difference from Jandl's later experimental poetry, in which the syntax is often dissolved and the words are dissected into individual letters and sounds.

But it should be pointed out that already in this first collection, reminiscent of the American poet William Carlos Williams's poetry, the poems are reduced to their bare essentials. The emphasis is on seeing these essentials. The audience does not necessarily need "other eyes" to see but rather needs to divert its eyes from the unimportant ornate ballast to the core of the matter, and then to transmit its innate qualities directly to the brain without detours. One example:

while we waited

while we waited,
a woman stepped into the garden, woman,
said one of us then, the woman
looked over to us, woman,
each of us thought then, the woman
smiled over to us, each of us —
but the woman
turned and left the garden.[22]

This poem expresses in very compressed form the essence of "woman," the perennial coquettishness and the primeval desire on both sides. It also expresses the usual course of events: the game remains just that, a game. The result is only a vibrant sense of stimulation. The building blocks of the poem are the calculated repetition of the words "woman" and "us" and the quick procession of action verbs. In the sixth line, the climax of the poem, the syntax crumbles. Thus even if this poem is termed "conventional," it is not difficult to perceive this type of poetry as a starting point for further language experimentation.

For the next seven years Jandl does just that: experiment with language. Frustrated about not being able to publish his experimental poetry in Austria, he goes to Germany where he finally achieves a publication breakthrough. His *lange gedichte* (Long Poems)[23] appear in 1964, and in the same year also *klare gerührt* (title untranslatable).[24] *mai hart lieb zapfen eibe hold* (title untranslatable),[25] a playful phonetic transcript of the famous Wordsworth poem, "My Heart Leaps up When I Behold" by means of a meaningless string of real German words follows in 1965, as well as *Hosi-Anna!*[26] These publications culminate in 1966 with the first book-length collection of experimental poetry:

Laut und Luise (Sound and Louise).[27] The title commemorates his mother, Luise, who also wrote poetry, and alludes as well to the contrastive adjective pair *laut/leise* (loud/quiet).

With this book, twice republished in 1971 and 1976, Jandl firmly established himself as an experimental concrete poet. This work, divided into thirteen thematically organized parts, is extremely versatile. The poems range from visual to acoustic experimentation (many are a combination of both). In daily usage the word "experimentation" has some negative aspects in so far as it has the flavor of the yet "unfinished" product. Jandl's experimental poems are not to be taken in that sense; they are indeed finished poems, although the "experiment," or to stay with the image, the laboratory experience, is very much in evidence. Looking at Jandl's experimental poems, we may feel that the very word "poem" could also present a problem, because what we actually see or hear is so different from what we are accustomed to. Jandl's poems do not fit within the usual field of association conveyed by the word "poem." Heissenbüttel in his postscript to *Laut und Luise* accordingly feels the need to belabor the concept "poem." He successfully expands the term to include concrete poetry by taking the concept out of its historical context: "A poem consists of sentences whose content and form are historically conditioned. But it is neither identical with historically conditioned phrases, nor with its historically conditioned special grammatical forms."[28]

Thus, according to Heissenbüttel, Jandl does not write poems by reflecting mood, sentiment, or atmosphere in condensed "poetic" form, nor does he turn his contact to sun, moon, lake, forest, roses, a girl's eyes into "conjuring formulas of magic." How does Jandl *make* poetry in his laboratory? By exploring language. He does not take language as a means to intuitively express imaginings; rather he takes language as an end in itself, not unlike a sculptor the looks of whose products, the texture, color, and size very much depend on the materials used. What interests Jandl are the dynamics and the possibilities of language, its visual and acoustic appearance, the various speech registers, its idiomatic use, slang, even dialect. In order to use "language" in his poems, he dissects it into its smallest parts, i.e., individual words, sounds, or letters. He frequently exploits the discrepancy between letter and sound as well as juxtaposes "meaning," e.g., different meanings of the same word. Grammatical logic is of no consequence, the reigning principle is the surprise. The surprising twist is the motor of the poems. Since surprise is also a basic element of humor, many of Jandl's poems are indeed humorous. His complete irreverence toward language as well as his tendency to ask idiomatic parts of speech for their meaning, to turn the familiar around until it becomes new and unfamiliar, further contribute to the hilarity in the poems.

V. Suchy goes one step further; not only does he stress the humor in these poems, but (with Heselhaus), points to their grotesque features: "The cabaret-like, the grotesque is clearly visible in Jandl's poetry and thereby connects with the best traditions of social-critical minor art (*Kleinkunst*) of the period between the two world wars."[29]

In an essay, "Doubts about Language" ("Zweifel an der Sprache"), Jandl doubts that "doubts about language" are possible: "Language has no alternative, and therefore there can be no 'doubts about language.' This is not proven wrong by the possibility of thinking of a destruction of language as a consequence of the destruction of mankind; that this destruction, the work of man, is thinkable, does not generate doubt about language, but doubts about man."[30] It seems that his point of departure in writing concrete poetry is not a purely critical stance vis-à-vis the validity of language, i.e., its usefulness as a means of communication, but rather a basic enjoyment of language, a playful approach. This clearly separates him as a poet from other experimentalists like Heissenbüttel and Gomringer.

Laut und Luise is a collection of poems written over a decade, so that the experimentation is multifaceted. There are pure sound poems of the kind Schwitters wrote (e.g., "talk"), there are grotesque Morgensternian inventions ("das blumenhorn"), prose poetry that recalls Arp's experiments, excursions into dialect ("doode") à la Artmann, baroque-like figure poems. The book is a veritable treasure chest of experimental possibilities, moving in five or more directions at once, exploring a multitude of poetic manufacturing processes.

One of the first poems in the collection is entitled "chanson." The poem consists of four words "l'amour / die tür / the chair / der bauch." This is also the first stanza. The next three stanzas repeat the same words, only that the nouns now change position. In the following three stanzas the articles are interchanged (le tür / d'amour etc.) and in the last part of the poem the sounds of articles and nouns are transposed (am'lour / tie dür etc.). The arrangement of four-line stanzas is broken three times by refrain-like three-liners 'l'amour / die tür / the chair). This poem, obviously, has to be read aloud. On being read aloud, it shows rhythm, musicality. Furthermore, in the *chanson* the words are unimportant; they always deal with love or other aspects of daily life, and these words are usually repeated in the same song or others, ad nauseam. Jandl somehow duplicates all this in the poem with the simplest means possible. At the same time he pokes fun at the *chanson:* the progression l'amour / die tür / the chair / der bauch rather crassly (as many *chansons* tend to) suggests the act of lovemaking and in a crescendo of sounds the words dissolve into nonsense;

what remains is the proverbial "catchy tune."

Music is the theme also of the poem "pi":

> pi / ano / anino / anissimo
> pi / pi / o / nano / nanino / nanissimo
> o / pi   (*Laut und Luise*, p. 9)

The word "piano," simultaneously noun and adjective, is combined with the diminutive form "pianino" and the superlative "pianissimo." In addition, some of the syllables involved are separated and lead a life of their own. This poem conveys a humorous dichotomy between the musicality, the solemnity of the act of piano playing and the obvious scatological (pi / ano / anissimo), sexual (onano / onanissimo) and narcotic (opi[um]) references. This type of poem is accessible only to the linguistically adept. To appreciate the next poem "calypso": "Ich was not yet / in brasilien / nach brasilien / wulld ich laik du go" etc., also requires a certain degree of bilingualism. English teacher Jandl likes to extend his linguistic experimentation to that language (another example in *Laut und Luise* is the poem "stilton cheese").

Much of Jandl's experimentation is based on mishaps in the spoken language, transposition of letters "eile mit feile," or distorted pronunciation, "spül düch / meun künd." (Ludwig Thoma uses this device in his books in order to affect "Prussian" pronunciation.) One of the most interesting poems in this context is the poem "16 jahr": "thechdthen jahr / thüdothdbahnhof / wath tholl / wath tholl / der machen," etc. This poem also builds on linguistic deviation. The /th/ sound as a substitution for /s/ is difficult to produce for Germans. Besides suggesting a severe speech impediment, the sound is also commonly associated with the speech of homosexuals. Although this poem has comic overtones then, in the line "wath tholl / der machen," helplessly repeated twice, the social stigma involved is articulated; a social comment is being made, the poet's personal engagement comes to the surface. The same section of the book that contains the poems just mentioned has the heading "volkes stimme" (people's voice). Naturally it also contains dialect experiments. The intriguing part of the dialect is the sound again signifying deviation from standard language. The dialect poems are sound arias for which the letters and words on the page are only imperfect renderings; they are like notes on a sheet of music that have to be translated into sound in order to come to life. "doode schbrooooochn" is such a poem. Again letters are exchanged. "Sanskrit" appears as "graaanzgrid" and "Kirchenslawisch" as "slirchenkaaawisch." The mispronounced words with the sound system of the dialect suggest a) the state of education of the dialect speaker and b) the distance of these "dead" languages from the live dialect, making them even more dead, if this is possible. Inherent here might also be the question why anyone would want to learn these dead languages.

The third section, "war and such," culminates in the famous "ode auf N," in which one word "Napoleon" is dissected into syllables and sounds, arranged in a skinny, continuous procession over three entire pages. Riha calls it a "breathing-, coughing-, rasping-aria."[31] The sounds of war reverberate in the onomatopoeic poem "schtzngrmm." This poem consists of the word "Schützengraben" (trenches), which, deprived of its vowels, is allowed to hiss and explode over the page like so many cannons and grenades.

To make his poems more accessible and with a didactic purpose in mind, Jandl has commented on a number of his own poems, has told how the poems came about, how they were made. "schtzngrmm" ·is a case in point. He calls this poem a "speaking poem" (Sprechgedicht). As such he describes it as a combination of "word"- and "sound"-poem.[32] The vowels are missing "because war does not sing." The last line of the poem reads t-tt. The sound is derived from "schtzngrmm" and suggests as a climax the word "tot" (dead). Murdoch and Read observe: "Jandl explodes the phonological dimension, using sounds from the base word, but not in random or aleatory manner. He sets up a soundpicture of a battlefield in which may be heard the staccato t-t-t of the firing guns, the sch- of missiles, the whole a deliberate chaos of phonological associations."[33]

War too, more precisely the time before the war, is the topic of the poem "wien: heldenplatz" (Vienna: Heroes' Square). The effect of this poem is based on the tension created by using standard syntax together with a vocabulary that consists of innovative nominal combinations, such as "maschenhaft," "männchenmeer," "maskelknie," "hoffensdick," "gottelbock," "stimmstummel," etc. These combinations alluding very much to the vocabulary of hunters, evoke the scenery of the stalkers (the Nazis) and the stalked (the Austrians). They also contain sexual connotations alluding to the wooers and the wooed. Jandl explains the origin of the poem: "Material for [this poem] was an event from the spring of 1938 . . . I stood at the age of 14 on the Ringstraße in Vienna, squeezed in a crowd that had come to a public meeting. A woman directly in front of me protested vociferously against an unintentional, and in the crowd unavoidable, movement of my knee, by which she felt molested. This scene made an impression on me and resulted 24 years later in the lines: 'drunter auch frauen die ans maskelknie / zu heften heftig sich versuchten, hoffensdick' and 'und den weibern ward so pfingstig ums heil / zumahn: wenn ein knieender sie hirschelte.'"[34]

Hitler himself seems to have given the public address in the scene above, although cleverly his name is avoided, but the noun "stirnscheitelunterschwang" is clear enough. The SA is present "hünig" and "balzerig." And the entire scene is war-prone ("aufs bluten feilzer stimme"), death-prone, like the hunt. Invented verbs like "brüllzten" (from "brüllen") and "kechelte" (from "hecheln"), by association also invoke the hunt, but here are expression for the general hysteria, the seduction of the people.

The fifth section, "author's voice," is a visual arrangement of sound effects. The sixth "small geography" commences with the poem:

niagaaaaaaaaaaaaaaaaaa

ra felle

niagaaaaaaaaaaaaaaaaaa

ra fella
(*Laut und Luise*, p. 58)

Again, we have a dual effect: the sound of the falls and the visual projection of the geographical facts, the duplicity of the falls.

The next poem "amsterdam" is of interest owing to its methodological relationship to "wien: heldenplatz." Jandl's comment: "Similarly related to expressionism, like 'wien: heldenpla'tz,' is 'amsterdam;' as far as the method is concerned, it is an inversion of the former. There the word was changed, the syntax maintained; here, except for the compound 'profilschmalz,' each word is taken from daily speech, but between the words exists a relation of syntactical dissolution. This results in tension, without which a poem cannot exist. . . . The reader can, as he likes, make semantic connections or not."[35] This kind of poem ("die haus stiehlst zum mütze. / an wäre kalten die fagott" etc.), is, despite Jandl's comment, much more inaccessible than the ones in which visual and sound effects dominate.

Section seven bears the title "cures" ("kuren"), an expression which in German could also mean "to take the waters"; the title probably has both meanings here. On the one hand, Sebastian Kneipp, the founder of this type of health program, is present; the "stilton cheese" refers to another type of cure.

Of interest to anyone who has ever studied English phonetics at the university level are the "three visual lip-poems" "dedicated to the mustache of daniel jones, the great english phonetician." The three poems consist of a vertical arrangement of vowels and consonants, which are not meant to be sounded out, hence "visual." Before the poems Jandl inserts the following remarks: "The visual lip-poem is the opposite of the visual paper-poem. The reciter is the paper of the visual lip-poem. The visual lip-poem is spoken without sound. It is written into the air with the lips. The inexperienced reader speaks the visual lip-poem in front of the mirror. . . . He who learns visual lip-poems by heart will never grow completely blind . . " (*Laut und Luise*, p. 8).

Probably the best poem of section nine, "seasons," is "a snow-picture" ("ein schneebild"). Three horizontally interspersed columns provide a flood of associations. These associations, one leading to the other, are not arranged mathematically, symmetrically, but rather in a way that suggests the dynamics of one specific moment. This section concludes (logically?) with the poem "dezem" (short for December). The poem has an iconographic character: the calligraphic imprint of a crow's foot in the snow (the latter fact is surmised from the "snowiness" of the preceding poems and the indicated time of year). The key word is "kalligrafiert," which suggests "telegrafiert" (by reason of homonymity). The imprint of the crow's foot thus announces the season telegram-style. The poem is visual in so far as the first three lines, the actual imprint, are closer together and also horizontally arranged in the shape of a bird's foot.

Jandl employs yet another method in the poem "in the country" ("auf dem land"): "fininininininininDER / brüllüllüllüllüLLEN / schẃeineineineineineineineinE / gŕunununununununununZEN . . ."[36] from section eleven ("bestiarium"). Jandl explains that he derived this "reduplication method"[37] from the so-called reduplicating verbs in classical Greek. And he adds: "To write a poem of this kind, no other program is needed than that a writer take position on the other side of language. It's where language exists as raw material that one busies oneself with language, and the themes come by themselves."

It has been stated earlier that Jandl's poems are very often humorous. In section twelve, "epigrams," concerned about the lack of humor ("and not in poetry only"),[39] he asks outright and emphatically with drawn-out vowels and consonants "wo bleibb da / hummoooa? " One example of how Jandl provides "hummoooa":

lichtung

manche meinen / lechts und rinks / kann man nicht / velwechsern. /
werch ein illtum!   (*Laut und Luise*, p. 135)

The mechanism of this poem is based on the Chinese-Japanese phonemic problem when speaking western languages; it is a simple demonstration of lambdacism-rhotacism. The starting point is a set phrase from everyday speech. The humor lies in the fact a) that Jandl manipulates a much belabored phrase which, like most proverbs and truisms, has a tendency to grate on one's nerves and b) that he creates comic tension between the grammatically, syntactically, and semantically correct statement and the phonological trick. The joke is not at any individual's expense. A didactic undertone is present. This didactic undertone grows into full-fledged social criticism in the two-liner "BESSEMER-BIRNEN / als mehr kanonen" (also from "epigrams"). "Bessemerbirnen" are devices to produce steel. This coupled with the proverbial butter/cannon choice and the original meaning of "Birne" (pear) makes up three semantic layers in the poem, combined in a very ingenious manner. Language is being alienated. The humor is contained precisely in this alienation process, which also makes the social comment doubly emphatic.

The last section of poetry in *Laut und Luise*, entitled "klare gerührt," is one long visual poem of very little narrative content. Its effect, based on increasing and decreasing print size and geometrical shapes, is visual-aesthetic. It seems that only a rudiment of semantic areas distinguishes this type of poem from the purely visual arts. (This poem had already been published two years earlier.)[40]

It was necessary to look at *Laut und Luise* in some detail, first, because this book is Jandl's first large collection of concrete poetry; second, because it comprises approximately the first ten years of Jandl's production; and, last but not least, because the book demonstrates a multitude of methods of concretization, of successful poetic language experiments. Not unlike Snorri Sturluson's *Edda*, *Laut und Luise* could be considered a textbook, a book that demonstrates poetic methods, ways to language experimentation. The texts become doubly useful when combined with Jandl's own explanations and comments.

The next major publication after *Laut und Luise* is *sprechblasen* (1968).[41] The title means "speech bubbles," reminiscent of the manner in which speech is commonly rendered in cartoons. As the title indicates, the poems contained in this volume are "speaking poems." They assume significance only when read aloud; the human voice is an essential element of the poem.

In 1970 a new collection of poetry appeared: *der künstliche baum* (the artificial tree). About this work A. Okopenko says: "In 'the artificial tree' the entire spectrum of Jandl's possibilities unfolds again: visual poems, puns, collages, permutations, sound shifts, speaking texts, foreign language gags, and notes for acoustic experiments. The thematic areas too . . . remain: the characteristics of life, animals and things, noise and disgust, eros, family problems, literary and leftist troubles, word-content-analysis, religion."[42] Okopenko further remarks that it would be pointless to compare this new book with Jandl's earlier works, because no "vertical development" is evident, only an "ant-like scurrying in different directions" [of experimentation].

The title of this volume alludes to both "art" and "artifice." More importantly, though, the "artificial" tree can do things that other trees are not capable of doing, such as bearing fruit simultaneously above and below, expressing movement and mirror-effects. The branches let the light through, a light that might let the individual fruit appear in a different, unaccustomed light; moreover, the fruit may be lined up on a branch together with many others, it may fall or be part of the chaos below on the ground, split open, and show its contents. This description, however, does justice neither to the title poem nor to the entire book, because it is metaphoric, and metaphors are diametrically opposed to Jandl's *modus operandi*. Metaphors presuppose conventions in the usage of language, etymologies, the sense of historical growth. Jandl on the other hand lets words pass through *un*conventional contexts and watches their behavior; he plays with double meanings, evoking new and startling associations; he stretches and compresses words, plays with their sound and visual appearance. Put differently, the tree is "artificial" because it is constructed, made of unusual material. It is *not* a copy of nature, the words do not depict a tree, describe its seasonal mood, nor do they suggest elements of the symbolic, such as the cycle of life, etc. They simply *are* the tree.

Der künstliche baum was followed by a book-length collection of poetry *dingfest*[43] (1973, title untranslatable). This volume contains poems written between 1952 and 1968. As opposed to those in *Laut und Luise, sprechblasen,* and *der künstliche baum,* these are not "concrete" in many ways, especially as far as form is concerned; they are more closely related to Jandl's very first book, *Andere Augen.* This duality in Jandl's work has to be stressed; for his production of concrete poetry and poetry with more conventional forms during the same period of time is another reason for the difficulty in classifying this writer.

Because the poems presented in *dingfest* were composed during a period extending over almost two decades this is not a homogeneous work. Poetic techniques and methods vary widely. The unity of the poems arises from the fact that objects (*Dinge*) and/or situations become solid (*fest*), that is, they take shape and become tangible. The latter word could serve as a very loose translation of the title *dingfest*. How is tangibility provided? Through language that invents new word combinations, occasionally ignores syntax, dives down into slang and dialect, enumerates and repeats, exploits double and triple meanings, but does not dissolve words into mere sounds or visual effects.

The poem from which the collection takes its title was written in 1958:

auf einem stuhl	on a chair
liegt ein hut.	lies a hat.
beide	both
wissen voneinander	know nothing
nichts.	of each other.
beide	both
sind	are
so dingfest.	so tangible.

(*dingfest*, p. 113)

Objects know nothing of each other. By inference they know nothing of us, and we know little of them. Yet they are tangible. The German word "fest" expresses more than tangibility; it also expresses the idea of immobility, of unchangeability. In other words, the objects have their own unchangeable world, their own laws and dynamics. Our relation to them does not change their perennial quality, their shape, or *raison d'être*. Looking beyond the poem quoted above, it should be noted that the attributes of the spatial dimensions (objects) also seem to apply to the chronological dimension. Time, periods of time, and situations, though tangible and alive, are just as massive, unmovable, and unchangeable to us as objects, e.g., the unavoidability of war, its archetypal character is expressed in the ballad "die sieben schwaben" ("the seven swabians" — the title alludes to the fairy tale by the same name). Sometimes time and objects are even allowed to intermingle, to permeate each other. In the seventh stanza of the poem "als das flugzeug ankam" ("when the plane arrived") we find: "I stood at the edge of the landing strip / and negotiated with minutes / which swayed in helicopters . . ."

Although it seems to me to be problematic to offer an interpretative statement for a collection of poetry that demonstrates so much variety in form and themes, H. Mayer in his postscript interprets the poems in *dingfest* as follows: "The immobility that can be discovered again and again is not, as in Benn, the enthusiastic dogma of a poet who with Nietzsche is convinced of the eternal return to the same. Jandl is bitter and frightened about the fact that things won't change. By that he means both society's immobility and the troubling sameness with which the human being progresses from birth to death."[44]

One comment on the formal aspects: as mentioned above, fairy tales are present ("the seven swabians"); Biblical style is imitated ". . . und es wird sich erheben / einer aus der schar . . ." (from: "wartezimmer"); we are reminded of Brecht's ballads ("the seven swabians," "visitor from abroad," "goldfish"); word-creations à la Becher are frequent in the early sixties: ". . . die sternstirn an des königsgauklers schädel, / hält steinern hamlet stein im stein der hand" (from: "hamlet"); Jandl often seems to yield joyfully to the force of the rhyme, resulting in amusing Morgensternian couplets: "das kind den goldfisch stellt / aufs wasser das nicht hält" (from "der goldfisch"). The list could be continued, but these few examples serve to illustrate the technique.

The ever-present humor and irony is one element tying this collection of poetry to Jandl's earlier books. As Mayer points out, however, the irony often has a tendency to become bitter. The smile with which we start to read a poem often freezes after a few lines, for instance in the very last poem (obviously it is no coincidence that this is the last poem):

sie gruben nach dem sarg	they dug for the coffin
der eine leiche barg	which contained a corpse
die einmal einer war	who once was someone
der unvergleichlich war	who was incomparable

So far one smiles because of the banality of the rhyme in the first two lines and the rather lighthearted progression in the logic. With the repetition of "war," though, we become unsure of the comic intent at the end of the stanza:

sie hätten gern gefragt	they would have liked to ask
den mann wer der einst war	the man who he once was
dazu war es zu spät	for this it was too late
wie rasch die zeit vergeht	how fast time passes

(*dingfest,* p. 185)

The tone remains light, but the content dissipates any hilarity. Not even the formula, the cliché, of the last line, "how quickly time passes," can bring relief; quite on the contrary the cliché assumes meaning and sheds its habitual void in the context of this poem. Although we start reading the poem with a smile, the poem turns the tables on us, grins back at us through the vacant eyes and mouth of the skull.

The year 1974 saw three Jandl publications in book form: *serienfuß* (no translation possible), *wischen möchten* (to want to wipe), and *für alle* (for everyone).[45] The first two collections are again devoted to experimental poetry.

The last contains material of a very varied nature. The variety provides a basis for a claim Jandl makes on the cover: "my table (i.e., writing desk) is set for everyone." Few poets can make such a claim, but in Jandl's case it sounds credible.

für alle is divided into six parts. The first part reprints twenty-nine poems from Jandl's very first book *Andere Augen* (poems written from 1952 to 1954). The second part consists of one long poem describing the Hitler era: "deutsches gedicht" (german poem) from the year 1957 and explanatory remarks written in 1972. Words are conjured up, repeated, letters are exchanged: *werkriegt-weltkrieg*, one concept changes almost unnoticeably into a new one: English expressions are introduced. The latter technique allows a look at the contemporary Austro-German situation and its reflection of the Nazi era from the outside (abroad) and from the inside. The two points of view are frequently permitted to intersect. The result, as far as the seventies were concerned, is a strange amalgam of forgetting, guilt, pride, and unchangeable tradition. The look into the future at the end of the poem gives no reason for hope. Each future millennium (the chronological spacing is certainly not a coincidence) is static and very similar to the poem "früherinnerung an." The imagination, straining to look into the future, gets stuck in the repetition of the words "im jahre / jahre / jahre . . . ," making the poem open-ended, stimulating the audience to take over the thought process, the individual to substitute his own imagination.

The third and longest section presents a large number of "scattered poems" (thus the subtitle) composed between 1956 and 1974, some of which are here in their second versions: There are no sound poems. The poetic devices used are mostly repetitive schemes (both entire lines and individual syllables), the occasional loss of syntax, and onomatopoeia. Thematic homogeneity is lacking.

Section Four is entitled "exercise in prose" ("übung in prosa"). The prose texts are all very short, most of them less than one page long. It would be very difficult to find a generic name for these pieces other than "short prose texts." Some of the texts simply describe a situation from daily life, such as two women getting on a bus ("autobus"). Gestures and words are dictated by conventions, more individualistic behavior shows in the facial expression. In another story Jandl relates his visit to the POW camp in England where he spent several months after the war. He describes only trivial details of the visit. But it is precisely these details which give a very powerful impression of the tedious, boring life in a POW camp ("rückkehr an einen ort"). "betten" describes camp life directly. There are six paragraphs, each consisting of one long sentence, each paragraph with a heading: stones, mattresses, hollows, straw 1, straw 2, folding beds. This arrangement makes the text appear to be the outline for a novel. If "betten" is the outline for a novel, the text "essen und schlafen" must be the outline of a play. It contains a similar paragraph arrangement which, however, soon turns into dialogue. The last six texts of this section are actually prose poems, most of them based on sound effects not unlike the speaking poems we met earlier. The best is probably "ein gewitter" (a thunderstorm), which onomatopoeically, by repeating the words "blitz," "donnern," "regen," causes a thunderstorm to march by.

Of all these prose texts the best is the shortest one, "das gleiche" (the same): "on receiving the news about the death of his mother I saw my father cry for the first time. My mother held him like a child and stroked his head. when the same happened to me a few years later I tried in vain to follow my father's example. Then, of course, I did not have a mother to hold me" (*für alle*, p. 154). Jandl describes with utter economy of language his reaction to the death of his mother. The *pointe* of this short text lies in the use of the word "mother," which changes meaning depending on the context.

Section Five "ins theater" (to the theater) starts out with a poem by the same name. The first "play" is entitled "parasitäres stück" (parasitical play). The title is derived from the recommendation that this "play" is to be added to a preceding "classical speaking play" (*klassisches sprechstück*). The "parasitical play" consists simply of some stage directions, the most important of which is that the last ten minutes of the text from the preceding play have to be repeated with the tongue hanging out of the actor's mouth. The centerpiece of this section is the "play" "szenen aus dem wirklichen leben" (scenes from real life). The characters have mathematical designations: m1, m2 etc. After two "beginnings," the headings of the "scenes" ("the confederation," "the oath") suggest Schiller's *Wilhelm Tell*. The "performance" is interrupted by a chorus, a commercial, general chaos ("tohuwabohu"). Just as there were two beginnings, there are two conclusions. The text is a collage of sound poems published much earlier, for instance in *Laut und Luise*.

Jandl has periodically tried his hand at the dramatic. His goal is usually satire. Just as in his concrete poetry, where we have seen language being used as the subject matter, in the radio plays, too, action is language and vice versa. One of his longer plays is the rather recent "die humanisten" (*the humanists*).[46] A detailed and perceptive discussion of this play by Ingrid Haag and Eduard Wiecha appeared in *Modern Austrian Literature*.[47] Starting with the well-known play "fünf mann menschen" (five men people), Jandl wrote many of his radio plays together with Friederike Mayröcker. Also with Friederike Mayröcker and Heinz von Cramer he made a TV movie "Traube" (Grape) in 1971.

The last section of *für alle* consists of prose remarks of a biographical and theoretical nature: "statements and peppermints." I have already quoted extensively from this section while discussing some of the poems earlier. As K. Riha points out,[48] lately Jandl has worked more with criticism and theory. Also contained in *für alle* are longer essays and interviews, most notably "gespräch" with Peter Weibel (1976),[49] notes to "the humanists,"[50] remarks on the poem "ottos mops,"[51] and various book reviews he has written over the years. Although in the mid-seventies Jandl wrote many radio plays and essays of a theoretical nature, poetry production did not stop. The cycle of fourteen poems called *tagenglas* appeared in 1976.[52] The language is reminiscent of "Gastarbeiterdeutsch" (the speech of German foreign workers); the verbs are not inflected, the syntax can usually have several meanings, punctuation is completely lacking. Again, the poems are clearly experimental. The last poem of the cycle is entitled "wie eltern zu land" (like parents to country):

dies mich hauen hinunter	this me beat down
dies mich heben hinauf	this me lift up
daß ich nicht wissen schweben	that I not know hover
nicht trauen ersticken und ersaufen	not dare to suffocate and to drown
ich noch in kaltem land	I still in cold country
manchmal spüren meines mutters hand	sometimes feeling my mother's hand
schweigen mein verstand	quiet my intellect
an ihr sein lang kein rühren	in her be long no touching
schweigen mein verstand	quiet my intellect
durchsausen meine ohren	my ears sound through me
neu nicht werden ich werden geboren	new not become I am born
bevor ich erden ich gehen wie eltern	before I earth I go like parents
zu land	to country

The English translation is only a very rough approximation; the rhyme, of course, is totally lost, and many of the verbs (e.g., "durchsausen") are more limited in English at their various semantic levels. The origin of pain in the first line ("dies") remains uncertain, which makes the desperation even more pronounced. To end this pain two modes of dying are suggested. But the sufferer is unable to make this choice ("nicht trauen").

The suffering takes place in the cold country of childhood (rendered obvious through the title as well as the reference to the mother who can give consolation only infrequently and for a short time). P. H. Neumann[53] refers to the change of correct and faulty noun inflection in the fifth line: "The grammatical correctness confirms the chill of the 'cold country.' The 'mistake' (false genitive) confirms the change to another level of time and consciousness. This genitive exudes a special emotional effect that can be explained. A feminine noun is inflected with a masculine ending, which would be appropriate for the word *father*. However, it is applied to the *mother;* in the last line the 'parents' are mentioned."[54] Twice, in lines seven and nine, the intellect is excluded. Only through this exclusion can the choice to die be made. The mention of the parents refers to a different state of being; death is equated with birth. The atmosphere of the poem is Kafkaesque. The entire cycle is steeped in deep pessimism.

Jandl also uses the same technique of little or no inflection in the volume *die bearbeitung der mütze* (treatment of the cap), which appeared in 1978.[55] The book contains poems written between 1970 and 1977. These are literally poems of life and death; the irony and humor are lost. What remains are occasional glimpses of sarcasm. The poems are in the form of a diary, arranged chronologically. Jandl's existential frustration seems to be ever increasing. One poem, symptomatically, says: "ich was suchen / ich nicht wissen was suchen . . ." (I something seek / I not know what to seek). The reduced language might indicate Jandl's reduced self-image, doubts about himself as a person and a poet. R. Acker also sees: ". . . his feeling of helplessness and impotence in the face of approaching old age and death, his fear of not being able to find material and inspiration for future poems, his 'deteriorating' friendship with Mayröcker, his frequent depressions which are bridged with the help of whiskey, pills, and cigarettes, and the imminent collapse of his own self-image . . ."[56]

But Jandl's poetic well has not dried up. The year 1980 saw the publication and performance of *Aus der Fremde. Sprechoper in 7 Szenen,*[57] for which he received international recognition. Chronicling his friendship with Friederike Mayröcker, the play revolves again around Jandl's creative crisis and the stagnation of his friendship with Mayröcker. The end of the play brings no solution to the problems: the "he" hides under the bedcovers. The state of limbo prevails.

The year 1980 also saw the publication of Jandl's most recent collection of poetry: *der gelbe hund* (the yellow dog).[58] Much of the format, many of the poetic devices deployed in *die bearbeitung der mütze* are also used in this volume. It contains poems from the years 1978 and 1979, again in chronological order. The autobiographical character is evident. The themes have not changed much either; the existential problems, the crisis in his authorship are still there: in one poem he awaits Mayröcker's blessings and criticism (". . . daß ihm geben du dein säge"), in another his creative efforts are frustrated: "there I sit down / in order to make a poem . . . there it received life / there it has failed." In a third he considers "an entire language, an entire life" not enough to make poems. But this volume of 231 pages, written in just two years, provides little credibility for these somber thoughts. He had to do more than ". . . sit in front of the typewriter / and let my fingers / rattle along a little" (from the poem "ohne fremde hilfe"). Death is present in many of the poems either literally, as in "der schnitter" (the harvester with the scythe), or in the abysmal poem "der horizont" (the horizon), which moves down and no new sky appears. And again his thoughts stray to his work, in "die spuren" (the tracks) he is not worried about his productivity but about the durability of his work, whether or not "a breath of air" could annihilate it.

Although many of the poems here also make use of the *Gastarbeiter* – or childlike uninflected, unpunctuated language with ambiguous syntax – there is a return to reinstating inflection, correct syntax, and punctuation. The new language, however, remains extremely simple, still childlike. K. Jezior-kowski in his book review in *Die Zeit*,[59] uses for this type of language the term "Bauklötzchen" (a child's building blocks), which seems to be very appropriate. In *der gelbe hund* Jandl gives a brief theoretical comment, explaining that from the simple language one should not construe that he is trying to write "poems from (about?) childhood," but rather that the author carefully directs the language.

Today, in 1985, Jandl is sixty years old. He can look back on a poetic work of monumental proportion and variety. He is one of the few "experimental" or "concrete" poets (and considering his entire work this nomenclature does make more sense than any other) who enjoys popularity, not only with literary *connoisseurs*, but also with a wide spectrum of the population, especially with school children. Furthermore, his fame is not restricted to Austria but encompasses all German-speaking countries and even some others. His social comments, subtle as they may be, are always to the point. His cultural and existential pessimism is shared by many Europeans.

His lasting contribution is dual: he alerts us to the power and dynamics of language, but also to its limitations and thus to the more general problems of communication. His experimental, innovative approaches stimulate the readers to be creative themselves.

Notes

1. Klaus Jeziorkowski, "Das Wiener Wunderhorn," a review of Jandl's recent poetry collection *der gelbe hund, Die Zeit,* 17 April 1981, p. 26.
2. Jörg Drews, "Ernst, ach Ernst, was du mich alles lernst!", *Die Zeit,* 8 August 1975.
3. Ernst Jandl, "selbstporträt 1966," *für alle* (Darmstadt und Neuwied: Luchterhand, 1975), p. 219. All translations of Jandl's poetry and prose into English in this study are my own. Jandl radically uses lower case letters, even at the beginning of sentences and in names. Since lower case letters in English do not change the appearance of written language nearly as much as in German, I chose not to adopt lower case letters in the translations.
4. Robert Acker, "Ernst Jandl and Friederike Mayröcker: A Study of Modulation and Crisis," *World Literature Today,* Vol. 55, no. 4 (Autumn 1981), 597.
5. Ernst Jandl, "orientierung," *für alle,* p. 214.
6. Ibid., p. 219.
7. Ibid., p. 220.
8. Ibid., p. 222.
9. Gerhard Rühm, ed., *Die Wiener Gruppe* (Achleitner, Artmann, Bayer, Rühm, Wiener; texts, collaborations, actions), (Hamburg/Reinbek: n.p., 1967), p. 9.
10. Jandl, *für alle,* p. 215.
11. Eugen Gomringer, *konkrete poesie deutschsprachiger autoren* (Stuttgart: Reclam 9350/51, 1972), p. 153ff. My translation.
12. Ibid., p. 155.
13. Viktor Suchy, "Konkrete und experimentelle Poesie in Österreich," *Helikon,* Sondernummer, 1979, pp. 239–246.
14. Ibid., p. 231. My translation.
15. Ibid., p. 236.
16. Gottfried Benn, "Probleme der Lyrik," *Gesammelte Werke,* ed. D. Wellershoff (Wiesbaden: n.p., n.d.), p. 1059. My translation.
17. Suchy, p. 235.
18. Adolf Haslinger, "Ernst Jandl-Georg Trakl-Preis-Träger 1974," *Literatur und Kritik,* no. 94 (1975), 145.
19. Jandl, *für alle,* p. 218.
20. Haslinger, p. 145.
21. Jandl, *für alle,* p. 219.

22. Ernst Jandl, "während wir warteten," *für alle* (Darmstadt und Neuwied: Luchterhand, 1975), p. 12.

23. Ernst Jandl, *lange gedichte* (Stuttgart: rot-text 16, 1964).

24. Ernst Jandl, *klare gerührt* (Frauenfeld: Eugen Gomringer Presse, 1964).

25. Ernst Jandl, *mai hart lieb zapfen eibe hold* (London: Writers Poets II, 1965).

26. Ernst Jandl, *Hosi-Anna!* (Bad Homburg v.d.H.: Gulliver Press, 1965).

27. Ernst Jandl, *Laut und Luise* (Olten: n.p., 1966); new editions: (Neuwied: Luchterhand, 1971), (Stuttgart: Reclam, 1976). All quotes from the last edition.

28. Jandl, *Laut und Luise*, p. 157.

29. Suchy, p. 244.

30. Jandl, *für alle*, p. 258.

31. Karl Riha, "Ernst Jandl," *Kritisches Lexikon zur deutschsprachigen Gegenwartsliteratur* (München: Text und Kritik, 1978), p. 5. My translation.

32. Jandl, *für alle*, p. 242.

33. Brian Murdoch and Malcolm Read, "An Approach to the Poetry of Ernst Jandl," *New German Studies,* no. 5 (1977), 137.

34. Jandl, *für alle*, p. 224.

35. Ibid., p. 227.

36. Jandl, *Laut und Luise*, p. 109.

37. Jandl, *für alle*, p. 240.

38. Ibid.

39. Jandl, *für alle*, p. 230.

40. Jandl, *klare gerührt.*

41. Ernst Jandl, *sprechblasen* (Neuwied: Luchterhand, 1968); new edition: (Stuttgart: Reclam, 1979).

42. Andreas Okopenko, "Baum seitlich der Kunstbaumgruppe," *Wort und Wahrheit,* no. 3 (1971), 286. My translation.

43. Ernst Jandl, *dingfest* (Darmstadt: Luchterhand, 1973).

44. Ibid., p. 188. My translation.

45. Ernst Jandl, *serienfuß* (Darmstadt: Luchterhand, 1974); Ernst Jandl, *wischen möchten* (Berlin: Literarisches Colloquium Berlin, 1974).

46. Ernst Jandl, *Die Humanisten,* Westdeutscher Rundfunk, 1977 (Köln: Kiepenheuer und Witsch, Theaterverlag, 1977); also in *Modern Austrian Literature,* Vol. 15, no. 1 (March 1982), 97–114.

47. Ingrid Haag and Eduard Wiecha, "Konversation auf Abwegen – zu Jandls Bühnensatire *Die Humanisten,*" *Modern Austrian Literature,* Vol. 15, no. 1 (March 1982), 115–126.

48. Riha, p. 6.
49. Peter Weibel, "gespräch," *Neue texte* 9, Linz, 1976.
50. Ernst Jandl, "Anmerkungen zum Stück 'Die Humanisten' und Meine bisherige Arbeit an Stücken," *Programmheft der Vereinigten Bühnen Graz* to Ernst Jandl *Die Humanisten* und Reinhard Gruber/Ernst Wünsch, *Oscar,* season 1976/1977.
51. Ernst Jandl, "Ein bestes Gedicht," *Kinder, Dichter, Interpreten: Zehn Minuten Lyrik,* ed. Rudolf Riedler (München: R. Oldenbourg, 1979), p. 58 ff.
52. Ernst Jandl, "tagenglas," *Merkur,* no. 11 (1976), 1045 ff.
53. Peter Horst Neumann, "'Tagenglas'—Versuch über Ernst Jandl," Ibid., p. 1053 ff.
54. Ibid., p. 1063.
55. Ernst Jandl, *die bearbeitung der mütze* (Darmstadt: Luchterhand, 1978).
56. Acker, p. 598.
57. Ernst Jandl, *Aus der Fremde. Sprechoper in 7 Szenen* (Neuwied: Luchterhand, 1980).
58. Ernst Jandl, *der gelbe hund* (Neuwied: Luchterhand, 1980).
59. Klaus Jeziorkowski, *Die Zeit,* p. 260.

Works by Jandl

Andere Augen. Wien: Bergland-Verlag, 1956 (Neue Dichtung aus Österreich, Vol. 21).

wir, die autoren. Vorrede zu: publikationen. Nr. 2. Ed. H. C. Artmann. Wien: n.p., 1957.

"ich begann mit experimenten," *zwischen-räume.* Ed. Reinhard Döhl. Wiesbaden: Limes Verlag, 1963. p. 119 f.

lange gedichte. Stuttgart: rot-text 16, 1964.

klare gerührt. Fraunfeld: Eugen Gomringer Press, 1964 (konkrete poesie 8).

mai hart lieb zapfen eibe hold. London: Writers Poets II, 1965.

Hosi-Anna! with illustrations by Thomas Bayrle and Bernhard Jäger. Bad Homburg v.d.H.: Gulliver-Presse, 1965.

Laut und Luise. Olten: Walter Verlag, 1966 (Walter-Druck 12). New editions: Neuwied: Luchterhand Verlag, 1971 (Sammlung Luchterhand 38); Stuttgart: Philipp Reclam jun., 1976.

No music please. London: n.p., 1976 (Turret Booklet 9).

Sprechblasen. Neuwied: Luchterhand Verlag, 1968. New edition: Stuttgart: Reclam, 1979. With a postscript by the author: "Autobiografische An-sätze," (Reclams Universalbibliothek 9940).

Musikalischer Genuß aus Worten und Geräuschen. Die Ansprachen von Ernst Jandl und Friederike Mayröcker bei der Entgegennahme des Hörspielpreises der Kriegsblinden, epd/Kirche und Rundfunk, 23. 4. 1969. Under the title *Fünf Mann Menschen. Die Reden von Ernst Jandl und Friederike Mayröcker, Frankfurter Allgemeine Zeitung.* April 23, 1969.

"Konkrete Poesie in Großbritannien," *Neue texte 2.* Linz. May 1969.

der künstliche baum. Neuwied: Luchterhand Verlag, 1970 (Sammlung Luchterhand 9).

Beitrag zum Thema "the death of concrete," *Stereo Headphones.* Ed. Nicholas Zurbrugg. Kersey, Suffolk, England. 1970. No. 2/3.

flöda und der schwan. Stierstadt/Taunus: Eremiten-Presse, 1971.

Fünf Mann Menschen, together with Friederike Mayröcker. Neuwied: Luchterhand Verlag, 1971.

"Ich mit Umwelt," *Motive. Warum ich schreibe. Selbstdarstellung deutscher Autoren.* Ed. Richard Salis. Tübingen: Horst Erdmann Verlag, 1971, p. 159 ff.

"Poetologische Reflexionen eines Schriftstellers. Erstfassung des Vortrags, Voraussetzungen, Beispiele und Ziele einer poetischen Arbeitsweise," *Germanistik – Beiträge zur Lehrerfortbildung.* Vol. 4. Wien: Österreichischer Bundesverlag, 1971, p. 213 ff.

dingfest. Darmstadt: Luchterhand Verlag, 1973 (Sammlung Luchterhand 121).

übung mit buben. Berlin: Berliner Handpresse, 1973.

die männer. ein film. Düsseldorf: Eremiten-Presse, 1973.

"Zur Problematik des freien Schriftstellers," *Neue Rundschau.* 1974. Vol. 1, p. 54 ff.

serienfuß. Darmstadt: Luchterhand Verlag, 1974 (Sammlung Luchterhand 157).

wischen möchten. Berlin: Literarisches Colloquium Berlin, 1974 (LCB Edition 34).

für alle. Darmstadt: Luchterhand Verlag, 1974.

"Ein neuer poetischer Raum. Zur Prosa von Friederike Mayröcker," *Views and Reviews of Modern German Literature. Festschrift für Adolf D. Klarman.* Ed. Karl S. Weimar. München 1974, p. 285 ff.

"Die poetische Syntax in den Gedichten von Friederike Mayröcker," *Manuskripte 45.* 1974.. Vol. 45, p. 49 ff.

Gott schütze Österreich. Durch uns: Achleitner, Friedrich; Artmann, H. C.; Bauer, Wolfgang; Bisinger, Gerald; Jandl, Ernst; Mayröcker, Friederike; Navratil, Leo; Priesnitz, Reinhard; Rühm, Gerhard; Steiger, Dominik u.a. Berlin: Wagenbach, 1974.

der versteckte hirte. Düsseldorf: Eremiten-Presse, 1975.

alle freut was alle freut. (To pictures by Walter Trier.) Köln: Middelhauve, 1975.

Drei Hörspiele, together with Friedrike Mayröcker. Wien: Thomas Sessler Verlag, 1975.

"Rede zur Verleihung des Georg-Trakl-Preises am 10. Dezember 1974," *Literatur und Kritik,* 1975. Vol. 98, p. 150 f.

"Beitrag zu: Texte von Gästen des Berliner Künstlerprogramms," *10 Jahre Berliner Künstlerprogramm DAAD.* Berlin 1975, p. 46 f.

"Mittel und Bedingungen der schriftstellerischen Arbeit," *Gegenwartsliteratur. Mittel und Bedingungen ihrer Produktion. Eine Dokumentation.* Ed. Peter André Bloch. Bern: A. Francke Verlag, 1975, p. 322 ff.

"Bibliographisches und Theoretisches," *Ausstellungskatalog Kunst aus Sprache (1. und 2. Teil). Museum des 20. Jahrhunderts.* Wien 1975.

"Letter from Austria," *Dimension, Contemporary German Arts and Letters.* Ed. A. Leslie Willson. University of Texas at Austin, 1975. Vol. 1/2, p. 10 ff.

die schöne kunst des schreibens. Darmstadt: Luchterhand Verlag, 1976.

"Dankrede, anläßlich der Verleihung des Preises der Stadt Wien am 15. September 1976," *neue texte.* 1976. Vol. 16.

"Anmerkungen zum Stück 'Die Humanisten' und Meine bisherige Arbeit an Stücken," *Programmheft der Vereinigten Bühnen Graz zu Ernst Jandl: "Die Humanisten" und Reinard P. Gruber/Ernst Wünsch: "Oscar."* 1976/1977.

13 radiophone Texte (1966). Düsseldorf: S-PRESS, 1977. (Tonband.)

Klatschmohn, illustrated by Cristini, E. and Puricelli, L. Köln: Middelhauve, 1977.

"Was ist die Grazer Autorenversammlung?" *manuskripte.* 1977/1978. Vol. 58, p. 117 f.

die bearbeitung der mütze. Darmstadt: Luchterhand, 1978.

"Ein bestes Gedicht" (Zu "ottos mops" u.a. – Text für eine Schulfunksendung des Bayerischen Rundfunks.), *Kinder, Dichter, Interpreten: Zehn Minuten Lyrik.* Ed. Rudolf Riedler. München: R. Oldenbourg, 1979, p. 58 ff.

"Dankrede anläßlich der Verleihung des Würdigungspreises für Literatur"; "Neue Gedichte"; "Anmerkungen zur Dichtkunst," *Literatur und Kritik.* 1979. Vol. 133, p. 158 ff.

Aus der Fremde. Sprechoper in 7 Szenen. Neuwied: Luchterhand, 1980.

der gelbe hund. Gedichte. Neuwied: Luchterhand, 1980.

Secondary Literature

Helmut Heissenbüttel. Postscript to *Laut und Luise* (Olten: Walter, 1966), p. 203 ff.

Walter Höllerer. "Ernst Jandl," *Ein Gedicht und sein Autor. Lyrik und Essay* (Berlin: Literarisches Colloquium, 1967), p. 381.

Michael Hamburger. *The Truth of Poetry. Tensions in Modern Poetry from Baudelaire to the 1960's.* (London: Weidenfels and Nicolson, 1969), p. 308 f.

Karl Riha. *Cross-Reading und Cross-Talking. Zitatcollagen als poetische und satirische Technik* (Stuttgart: Metzler, 1971), p. 70 ff.

Gisela Dischner. "Ernst Jandl und die ästhetische Funktion," *neue texte* (1972), Vol. 8/9, 6 pp., not paginated.

Hans Mayer, Postscript to *dingfest* (Darmstadt and Neuwied: Luchterhand, 1973), p. 187 ff.

Birgit Lermen. "Ernst Jandl – Friederike Mayröcker: 'Fünf Mann Menschen,'" *Das traditionelle und neue Hörspiel im Deutschunterricht* (Paderborn: Schöningh, 1975), pp. 239–254.

Michael Wulff. *Konkrete Poesie und sprachimmanente Lüge. Von Ernst Jandl zu Ansätzen einer Sprachästhetik* (Stuttgarter Arbeiten zur Germanistik No. 44. Stuttgart: Akademischer Verlag Hans-Dieter Heinz, 1978), 407 pp.

Jürgen P. Wallmann. "Ernst Jandl: die bearbeitung der mütze," *Literatur und Kritik* (1979), Vol. 133, p. 180 ff.

An Introduction to the Prose Narratives of Gert Jonke

Johannes W. Vazulik

The response to Gert Friedrich Jonke's first publication, *Geometrischer Heimatroman* (1969, *Geometric Regional Novel*),[1] was one of wide critical acclaim in the German-language press. The author, then just twenty-three years old, was called a spiritual brother of his more famous countryman Peter Handke[2] and was acknowledged to be a significant contributor in his own right to Austria's emergence in contemporary experimental literature.[3] Demonstrating a concern, not unlike Handke's, with the reality inherent in language and the language process, Jonke aimed with this initial publication and other experimental prose that quickly followed to evoke by means of his narrative construction certain alienating, threatening features of modern industrial society. Through a technique of formally and thematically binding together a set of stylistically individual, essentially self-contained texts, he was able to transmit his critical attitude toward conventional language, conventional artistic concepts, and societal conventions. The prose publications since 1977 have been marked by a shift in interest away from examining general social conditions or issues and toward concentrating on the experiences of an individual trying to penetrate reality and the terms of his existence. These texts also indicate that Jonke has developed a command of his material and method that well exceeds the technical accomplishment of his earlier efforts. The narrative refinements evident first in *Schule der Geläufigkeit* (1977, School of Dexterity) have elicited enthusiastic reaction and caused Jonke's writing to be cited for its powerful vision[4] and for achievement that can be categorized with the most memorable of recent literature in the German language.[5]

Jonke was born in Klagenfurt in the southern Austrian province of Kärnten (Carinthia). He was reared there by his mother, a pianist of some accomplishment, under whose instruction he began training in music. After service in the Austrian army, he lived in Vienna, studying for a time at the School for Film and Television of the Academy for Music and Dramatic Arts. His academic preparation focused on philosophy, history, musicology, and Germanistics. Besides residing in Austria he has had relatively long stays in Berlin and London. Since 1969 Jonke has been a free-lance writer best known for his longer prose, although his work both prior and subsequent to 1969 includes poetry, theater pieces, a film script, and radio plays. He has been the recipient of a number of literary prizes and awards, among them the prestigious Ingeborg Bachmann

Prize (1977).

The author has been linked with the Austrian literary avant-garde, which since the early 1960s has had as its nurturing ground the Styrian capital city, Graz, originally in the center known as "Forum Stadtpark Graz," whose benefactors and participants, subsequently allied as the "Graz Authors' Assembly," have sustained a diversity of antitraditional creative impulses.[6] It is also proper to count Jonke among the generation of experimentalist writers emerging from the broader continental base that includes Germany and Switzerland, whose preference for unconventional themes or techniques stands for a general resistance to authoritarianism in all its guises. The tendency of the experimentalists' art has been to instigate a critical awareness of an extremely complex literary as well as social reality. In Jonke's treatment reality appears menacing and ultimately incomprehensible. His writing is difficult, perplexing, defying easy classification. To call his major works novels, even to speak of them as prose, seems in a strict sense not accurate, poetic and musical terms being especially germane to their discussion; but a close examination of certain key works in their larger context does identify the hallmarks of his writing, whereby one can begin to establish its significance.

Geometrischer Heimatroman was the first of several narrative prose publications dating from 1969 to 1971 that reflected on the social ills that inevitably attend industrial-bureaucratic growth, most prominently loss of freedom in the subjugation of the individual to the system, the supplanting of altruistic motivations by materialistic philosophies, and despoliation of the environment. The socially critical messages in Jonke's texts can be deciphered, however, only by a concerted effort on the part of the reader to follow the many strands of narration that are continually weaving forward, backward, under, and over each other. In these beginning works Jonke relates his concerns through a complicated, episodic structure that sets brief sketches of daily work activities alongside excerpts from historical resources; aphoristic entries; reproductions of legal documents, song sheets, and diagrams; and fantastic apocalyptic interludes. Chronological and spatial dimensions are indeterminate; and the narrator, who would ordinarily function to orient the reader to the contents, is relentlessly tentative. The unmitigated provocation of the reader by Jonke's self-conscious, unusual narrative method and the manner in which all social implications can readily become lost in the method lead to recognition of his overriding thematic interest, that is, the literary medium itself, and above all the tenuous connections between language and the real world or the aesthetic construct it wants to convey.

Jonke's antiauthoritarian posture is evident at once in the title of the 1969 book. The incompatibility of the description "geometric" with conceptions of the regional novel as it had been popularized in the nineteenth century alludes to his repudiation of the assumptions upon which that literary form was based.[7] Conspicuously missing are the idyllic settings, the romantically portrayed country folk, the predictable, melodramatic plot, and the benign interventions of a majestically depicted nature. In their place one finds sterile, mathematically plotted landscapes, caricatures or anonymous figures, a seemingly arbitrary sequence of events, and a nature that behaves capriciously and demonically. Jonke's critical attitude suggested in the title applies to both societal custom and literary practice, and equally to idealized rural conditions or modern technological development.

Geometrischer Heimatroman presents an agrarian village on the verge of pernicious industrialization. The abundance of posted warnings, official notices, and ordinances in the village exposes it as a highly structured, inflexible community, wherein power is initially vested in the teacher, priest, and mayor. The objective of the teacher's pedantic, moralistic instruction is to produce model citizens who live according to societal prescriptions. Thus educated, the villagers, like Pavlovian dogs, can only respond to the events around them with conditioned patterns of behavior. Their every move is methodically repetitive, whether they are visiting each other, lining up on the square, carrying out their work, or observing the many rituals that have been imposed on them. Formulas and truncated, wooden sentence structures in the prose suggest the mechanistic character of the villagers' lives. The mayor and priest connive in perpetuating this situation by occupying themselves with ceremony and record keeping but remaining indifferent to constructive social involvement. When the village is confronted with the experience of technological development, and power shifts from familiar, paternalistic local figures to an anonymous authority, the people find themselves defenseless against further encroachments on their already limited freedom. The omnipotence of the new government is conveyed by the inclusion in the text of a lengthy, barely intelligible legalistic document. By drawing attention to the "New Law's" self-serving rhetoric Jonke is revealing his wariness of the capacity of language impinging on the individual from outside sources to dictate the individual's actions. The author is fundamentally opposed to usurping the means of self-determination and expresses that attitude primarily as an obsession for narrative equivocation.

The narrator, in addition to being intimately knowledgeable of the village's institutions, rules, and laws, is endowed with supranormal perceptual powers enabling him to overhear conversations and to discern minute visual details of occurrences and objects in and beyond the village square. However, the indication that he and an anonymous companion are in hiding and must make their observations in secret casts suspicion on his credibility, as does the continual contradiction between the two observers; and for these reasons the customary bond between reader and narrator cannot be formed. Furthermore, instead of affording the reader a ready-made perspective on the events of the novel, the narrator offers multiple points of view, and each of them only provisionally. His extensive use of indirect discourse and subjunctive constructions, while ostensibly for the purpose of relating unbiased reportage, actually contributes to a pervasive element of uncertainty.

By means of an aperspective narrative technique the crucial topic of *Geometrischer Heimatroman* emerges. What is under investigation is the power of language to define or distort perceptions of what exists and thereby to determine the limits of thinking and being. In one section of the text a performance by a tightrope walker in the village square is recounted by quoting fragments of overheard conversations. The highly discrepant opinions of the bystanders have the effect of invalidating each other. They imply the arbitrary relationship between what people say and think they see and what really happens. Along with the villagers' spontaneous reactions to the act the local art critic provides the media version. This, although the only apparently comprehensive account, is at the same time blatantly subjective and stands in vivid contrast to the narrator's attempts to be totally detached and noncommittal. Each cliché in the critic's review seems to beget another, overwhelming the reader with narrow, stereotyped notions. The reviewer's exaggerated praise is a clear demonstration that language, rather than expressing reality, is born of predispositions toward particular attitudes or beliefs.

Striving for linguistic integrity and insinuating that no word and its commonly accepted meaning are to be taken at face value, Jonke resorts to using series of related or nearly synonymous words, the intention being that such accumulation should help to restore the lost scope of the individual elements. He would strip language of outmoded prejudicial connotations, and it is to this end that mathematical terminology and constructs predominate as the means for describing natural phenomena, as in this reference to the mountainous landscape: "The silhouetted margin of the mountain range north of the village has the shape of four curves that lead into one another: a sine curve, a cosine curve, and a sine and a cosine curve, each displaced by one and three-quarter phases."[8] An emphasis on outlines and surfaces and the preeminence of the physical sensations of sight and sound are part of an effort to mediate a physiologically discerned reality without regard for feelings or opinions, but the result is far from satisfactory. For in order to precisely designate items in the environment the author may extend the instant of their perception to supply painstaking detail that would otherwise be ignored or telescoped. The unwieldy sentences and labyrinthine aggregations of phrases that result from this description make it more difficult to ascertain the essence of an object because the broad delineations deprive the reader of the customary and anticipated guidance. In the extreme the monotonous superfluity of a passage may be almost mesmerizing, leaving the reader virtually helpless to disengage from the syntactical maze.

His concern about the attenuated relationship between exterior reality and the words used to convey perceptions of it aligns Jonke with the concrete poets, and he participates in that group's endeavor to create by linguistic manipulation an aesthetic reality that stands apart from, instead of parallel to, the nature world.[9] Exhibiting a concretist preference for linguistic condensation and asyntactical structure, he at times dismantles conventional language and reassembles the components into a design that carries its own meaning, a practice illustrated in the following passage, where the lines render visually the gradually diminishing audibility of the hissing sound:

> . . . then i believed having heard another hissing in the
> air
>   fur
>   button
>   wedge
>   which rolled down the other side of the
> hill behind us
>   hair
>   window
>   wood
>   moving farther and farther
> away . . .[10]

Concrete poetic theory would assert that when language is thus released from longstanding grammatic and syntactic constrictions and all the existing possibilities for combining its basic ingredients are acknowledged, language is free to manifest its rich verbal, visual, and acoustic potential.[11] The concrete text then becomes an object for contemplation. Although Jonke's confidence in concrete poetry as the means to achieve his linguistic aims appears undermined when he allows it to become a subject for parody, he suggests in the totality of his method that he is seeking to construct a narrative whose significance lies primarily in its form.

Each of the various stylistic elements incorporated into the text experimentally is eventually rejected as unsound. Besides referring to concrete poetry, the author tests cinematic and *nouveau roman* devices, among others; but no matter how convincing or appropriate a specific artistic convention may at first seem, Jonke effectively cancels every one either through parody or by including a comparably strong opposing tendency. The fantastic and comic aspects of his prose, for example, counter its *nouveau roman* inclination to register accurately dimensions of shadows and reflections. And in addition to unflattering imitations of provincial journalism and bureaucratic cant, Jonke treats parodistically even those literary forms for which he shows the greatest affinity.

By flaunting stylistic excesses and steadfastly avoiding unequivocalness Jonke repulses any contention of certainty in his art. He discourages complacent acceptance of literary illusion by deliberately exposing all pretense to a destructive scrutiny. This practice creates constant irritation for the reader, irritation that would no doubt be intolerable were Jonke's unrestrained imagination not fortified by trenchant observation and keen wit. As it is, his writing annoys amusingly. And while the comic elements sometimes add to the enormous tension in the prose, by turning macabre, for example, they more often serve as releases. In general the incidents of parody, a clever vocabulary of outrageously long compound nouns, the preposterous logic offered to justify oppression, and the satirical sketches of authority figures prevent the serious and frightening implications of the contents from overpowering the reader.

Glashausbesichtigung (1970, Hothouse Tour) continues in the same vein as *Geometrischer Heimatroman* to conjure images of modern industrial society's malignant increase of products and bureaucratic mechanisms, suggesting that once the machinery has been set in motion, it is beyond human regulation and can eventually annihilate its progenitors. Here, too, the changes emerge from a rural-natural context. Again they are reported by a narrator who, with a companion, is observing the landscape and also participating in its transformation. The narrator at one point declares that he does not believe in normal narratives but only in those wherein each segment is separated from its continuation by the introduction of second and third narratives, resulting in many simultaneous narrations. This principle of continually interrupting the narrative is relayed by the presentation of numerous short sections with recurring titles, each of which is individual in style and readable as a self-contained text with no direct connection to the one immediately preceding or following it. Such superficially haphazard organization is intended to arouse a fascination that causes the reader to concentrate on textual form and to look for opportunities to systematize the components.[12] Under these circumstances an uncommon relationship is forged between the writer and reader; for, being free to reconstruct the text and establish networks of associations, the reader in essence becomes a collaborator in creating the literary work. Furthermore, whatever compulsion the reader senses to decipher a pattern demonstrates Jonke's point about the manipulative force of the language, and thus his ideas on that subject may be said to be rendered concretely. Insofar as Jonke's narrative develops according to an idiosyncratic set of rules and his gigantic word assemblages expand in response to a self-generated momentum, his language constructions reflect conditions in contemporary society; namely, technological advancement and social change occur with a speed, complexity, and impact that put the phenomena beyond the comprehension and control of the individual and, therefore, cause them to appear irrational.[13] If one sees the drive toward narrative precision as an effort to regain control in the face of awesome growth and expansion, it is an unsuccessful attempt that itself dissolves into unreal appearances which blend with the text's other fantastic ingredients.

The notion that nothing can be perceived with certainty is reinforced by the portrayal of objects as being in perpetual flux. The narrator's house, for instance, is described once as standing near a building lot, at another time as being next to a river then again at the side of a canal or by a bridge. And the actuality of the landmarks that are supposed to help designate the house is also questionable. It is stated that the building site, which originated as rumor, exists only because it has been discussed for so long. Language creates the reality, and language can also destroy it. Building sites begin to multiply inexplicably and to bury each other and the landscape. An economic planning commission is claimed to be behind the changes that take place. It turns out, however, that human beings are not imposing designs on the environment but the reverse: building lots are engineering the inhumane course of history. Like the intertwining threads of the narrative fabric the socio-economic and linguistic restrictions governing individuals are not easily unraveled. The fact of their potency is paramount and is clearly referred to at the end of *Glashausbesichtigung*. The narrator is finally overrun by his narration in the form of a horde of rampaging hothouses.

The volume, *Die Vermehrung der Leuchttürme* (1971, Proliferation of Lighthouses), also treats the subject of construction gone out of control and functioning independently of the builders. That Jonke should be so intent on developing the same fundamental ideas with very similar means betrays a considerable cynicism, and one particularly dismaying aspect of the author's vision is that the human beings he depicts allow themselves to become accessories to their own exploitation. In this case they will cooperate in building lighthouses, even working overtime to insure uninterrupted production, as the grass turns black around them, the sun is cut into pieces, and a coughing epidemic sweeps the land. The lighthouses become the basis for political organization, but both the pro-lighthouse forces and the anti-lighthouse party are manufacturing the beacons. Nevertheless, the circumstances of place and event visible at the surface of these complicated narratives remain secondary in importance to the underlying pattern of indefinitely recurring menace.[14] Jonke's inveterate repetition of images, while furthering his purpose of casting doubt on every given perspective by also admitting alternatives, strongly suggests a chronic, pervasive condition of societal inertia and resignation.

The three narrative prose pieces, *Geometrischer Heimatroman, Glashaus-besichtigung,* and *Die Vermehrung der Leuchttürme,* were subsequently revised for publication in *Die erste Reise zum unerforschten Grund des stillen Horizonts* (1980, First Journey to the Unexplored Bottom of the Silent Horizon), a collection of a number of texts written over a fifteen-year period that appear here with deletions, additions, and reworked passages. The most significantly altered of the entries is "Die Hinterhältigkeit der Windmaschinen" ("The Treach-ery of the Wind Machines"), which had originally been written as a play but was never performed.[15] In recasting the work, Jonke judged prose to be more appropriate. The principals in this narrative are continuously threatened by winds and storms emanating from a landscape of thousands of immense concrete buttocks. Scatological humor is couched in elaborately devised, serious-sounding setups which make the nature of these monstrous structures immediately ob-vious to the reader while requiring that the narrator conduct an exhaustive investigation into their identity. Ridicule directed evenly toward institutions that oppress the individual and toward individuals who acquiesce in that rela-tionship closely connects this text to others in the collection.

The drive to penetrate reality motivates all Jonke's writing and is the basis for his enduring interest in portraying the danger that adheres to a credulous reliance on appearances. While his first prose narratives evoke that danger within a relatively broad social context, his recent work is inclined to examine the menace in more subjective terms, that is, as insidiously permeating the experi-ence of an individual. The topics explored in the narratives are expressed as longing—privately and collectively known longing for love, for beauty, for artistic integrity, for timelessness—still rooted in the urgent need to apprehend reality and, thereby, to attain a confirmation of self. In addition to this changed thematic emphasis, *Schule der Geläufigkeit* and the two volumes that followed it, *Der ferne Klang* (1979, The Distant Sound) and *Erwachen zum großen*

Schlafkrieg (1982, Awakening to the Great Sleep War), evidence a significant development of Jonke's technique. The principle of endlessly interrupted and interrupting narratives has now evolved into an almost fugally textured narration dominated by the single subject of the problem of discerning reality, which is ever being imitated and expanded to reveal new facets of itself. Through the narrative flow fanciful, satirical, and grotesque passages that relate to the main theme in an organically unified composition.[16] A question central to these three texts is, where does art stand in relation to reality? Jonke has been resolute in exposing the illusions or pretenses of art as deception. Yet he comes very close with this writing to a goal that had been intimated in *Geometrischer Heimatroman,* namely, to create a form that stands for no reality other than itself, in much the same sense that the successful concrete poem would be both object and subject.

The two parts of *Schule der Geläufigkeit* treat separate incidents in the life of a once acclaimed, presently unproductive, composer. The first is based on a sketch in *Beginn einer Verzweiflung* (1970, Beginning of Desperation), a publication whose manuscript predates *Geometrischer Heimatroman,* but whose content, the diary-like documentation of an individual's deepening depression, is much closer to Jonke's recent work. The narrator in *Schule der Geläufigkeit* is no longer the dispassionate observer. Rather, it is the composer's involvement in the world, his puzzling, frightening, exhilarating encounters and circumstances that are offered for the reader to view.

The garden party for artists and art patrons in the first section, subtitled "remembrance of the present," begins on an unexpectedly sinister note. The hosts, a photographer named Diabelli and his sister Johanna, reveal to the narrator their intentions to replicate so exactly a party of one year before that photographs taken of the two affairs will be identical; memory and the present will be one. Thus it is that the problem of differentiating between experience and imagination is introduced. Fantasy, art, and nature blend into, adulterate, and fuse with one another; and the characters in the book are confused and disoriented by misperceptions, rationalizations, and illusions. The narrative makes explicit that one's senses cannot be presumed to correctly apprehend the environment. At one place in the first episode, Johanna and the narrator exchange their senses so that during their lovemaking each might describe what the other feels, but the impressions obtained in this way are distorted. In other instances sensual perception serves to distract attention from true essence instead of clarifying it. Inspiration, however, seems no less flawed, judging by the effectiveness of the various artists at the party, each of whom is a failure in one way or another.

Neither the artists nor their intended audience are treated sympathetically by Jonke. The artist figures are viewed with suspicion by the public, who liken them to vagrants, criminals, or charlatans. A closer look at the figures in *Schule der Geläufigkeit* reveals that these opinions might well be justified. Diabelli, as the name implies, has an ominous presence. His attempt to recreate the past seems hideous and ludicrous at the same time. And the fact that for him the only legitimate experience is the one occurring in the isolation of the darkroom makes him appear narrow and alienated. The painter Waldstein is derided as the kind who lays claim to lofty vision and insight not easily grasped by ordinary people. It is said that no one is to speak to him when his eyes are open because he is making observations which ought not be disturbed. Nor is he to be addressed when his eyes are closed; for, while he may be sleeping, it is equally likely that he is in the middle of his most profound observations, those of his dreams. Another artist, the poet Kalkbrenner, is an obese, beer-guzzling exhibitionist. And the narrator is an ineffectual alcoholic, lacking the acumen and analytical facility to give order to the irrational world around him. Regarding the events at the party, his perspective is no more enlightened than that provided by the others; and in relation to the development of the narrative as an event, his fantasies and hallucinations are lapses that tend to obscure its meaning.

The artists' public also consists of several non-ideal types: those who distrust personal preferences for art and depend totally on the judgments of imperious critics, those who insist upon completely dissecting the work of art to be able to intellectualize its every aspect, and those who feign aesthetic sensibility but can appreciate only the hackneyed and obvious or the sensational. That the most ardent supporters of the arts are represented by an undertaker, a proctologist, and an insane-asylum architect underscores the moribund state of the arts in such a society; and the second part of the book, "gradus ad parnassum," elaborates on the precarious existence of the genuinely creative individual within this community.

Still proposing that all notions about existence or literature are biased by their formulator's frame of reference and debilitated by reiteration, Jonke projects an authorial ambivalence. He resists in this way the facile substitution of jargon and clichés for more incisive but difficult-to-derive ideas. His objection to the mental atrophy, passivity, and stagnation that result from the internalization of formulas has its corollary in Diabelli's antagonism to the repetitiveness of history and his desire to expose it through photographs. Interpreting Diabelli's project in another light, however, which it is entirely possible to do, one has to concede that his success at catching time in a loop would be a highly desirable outcome. For, by doing so, he would be accomplishing what all artists seek to achieve, to capture forever a moment in which there would be no aging, no degeneration, no death. In the end, the question of whether Diabelli's scheme is to be viewed negatively or positively is reduced to irrelevance because Jonke proceeds unremittingly to dash hopes and expectations at their peak and, with that, to cancel his scrupulously constructed narrative. Therefore, at the conclusion of the book's first section, when the original premise of trying to reproduce an earlier party is denied by Diabelli and Johanna—at the very point that the narrator, captivated with the prospect of being able to suspend time, is beginning to come to terms with that possibility—the inference may be drawn that all artistic experiments and linguistic speculations are exercises in futility. Regardless of how stimulating and attainable the composer's aspirations may seem, they cannot ultimately be realized. And not just the narrator is led on in this manner, but also the reader, who is shown to be no less vulnerable to manipulation. For the reader has had to expend substantial effort to follow the meandering course of the prose thus far, only to have Jonke suddenly negate the entire passage.

The second episode of *Schule der Geläufigkeit,* also based on an earlier prose version,[17] is set in the attic of the music conservatory where the composer and his piano-mover brother had at one time been students. In the brothers' conversations with their former music professor, now director of the conservatory, are revealed the constraints imposed upon the narrator by a noncomprehending audience, as well as by his own inability to penetrate the mundane characteristics of his experience in order to realize creative expression. He has come into conflict with the forms of thought and behavior required by society: his mentor's insistence on orthodoxy in style, his brother's advocacy of regular work, and his public's rejection of difficult compositions. The pursuit of unique, direct experience in a temporally, spatially, and logically constricted universe is alluded to frequently, in Kalkbrenner's goal, for example, of being able to consume a bottle of beer in a span of time that is finished at the very start, and again in the pianist Schleifer's desire to produce pure music in the absence of instruments, indeed, in the absence of audible sound.

With this work Jonke seems to have abandoned the phenomenological delineations of the world that were conspicuous in the early prose, but the patently subjective descriptions currently favored are still unconvincing, suffused as they are with self-doubt and self-mockery. Their exaggerated proportions appear comic and very often lead to shocking revelations. The attention lavished upon a topic as trivial as piano shipping in a discourse replete with technical piano-crate terminology, delivered by the composer's brother, has an immediate humorous effect. When this passage is succeeded by one in which the fatal fall of a roofer is related with offhand indifference the juxtaposition is un-settling. Ironic contrasts provide a large measure of the overt absurdity and im-plicit terror in Jonke's work, an especially noteworthy illustration being the secret tragedy of the music conservatory. Locked away and deteriorating in the building's attic are one hundred eleven never-used pianos, which are irreparably unplayable but cannot be disposed of without publicizing the shamefulness of their waste and which, rather than serving as sources of beauty and inspiration, hold the conservatory director in the grip of constant fear that his mismanage-ment of the institution's assets will be discovered. The arrival of a second dona-tion of one hundred eleven pianos amplifies his helplessness in this situation and duplicates the cynical repetition motif of the first part of the book.

It follows from the author's preoccupation with language's effectiveness as a medium of expression that he would fully exploit its comic potential, and puns are part of the result. When in "remembrance of the present" the music critic Pfeifer says that the audience was moved by Schleifer's playing, he means that they literally changed shape, growing fatter then thinner in response to the music. Peculiar word coinages, oblique musicological references, inverted logic, and satirical sketches serve as diverting but crucial narrative components. The comic elements of the prose retain the dual functions of offsetting and em-bellishing the technically complicated development of serious themes.

The title of the book and the subtitle of the second episode, "gradus ad parnassum," seem to be an ironic commentary on the form and substance of the text. The pedagogical piano pieces of the same names by Czerny and Cle-menti, respectively, are studies in technique for its own sake, difficult and frustrating to play but with what some may consider little intrinsic musical value. These familiar exercises are generally known by their undistinguished melodies, predictable modulations and harmonic style, stable rhythms, minimal excitement, and limited possibilities for interpretation or improvisation. At that, they must be regarded as antithetical to what Jonke seeks to accomplish in his prose.

The plight of *Schule der Geläufigkeit*'s stale composer is taken up once more in *Der ferne Klang*. This title, also borrowed from musicology, is the name of an obscure twentieth-century opera by Franz Schreker. The opera, a tale of artistic longing, had been an immediate failure, denounced for its stark realism and vigorous modern style. Considering Jonke's content and technique, this title seems to have a more literal application to his work than other titles he has used. The book begins with a section in which the composer, seeming to be in a state of half-sleep or semiconsciousness, is carrying on a philosophical dialogue with himself, whom he addresses as "you (*du*)" in the familiar form of the

German pronoun appropriate for family members or intimates. The fantastic impressions and musical images that occur to him in this dreamlike state remain even after he awakens to find himself in a psychiatric clinic. He is there because he is said to have attempted to commit suicide the evening before. But he has no recollection of the event, and the hospital report containing the details of his admission is missing. Presumably a nurse at the hospital with whom he has fallen in love could shed some light on his situation, but she too has disappeared. Although the physicians will not release him, the composer manages to escape from the hospital to seek his loved one. The ensuing narrative renders these suppositions dubious; and whether the anonymous woman is real or a dream ideal, whether she is the key to the narrator's identity, and whether he really wants to find her and thus his lost self become matters for conjecture.

As a subterfuge the composer joins an avant-garde theater troupe and travels with them by train, fleeing, searching, and avoiding, all at the same time. Along the way he meets several of the same figures encountered in *Schule der Geläufigkeit*. Comical, beautiful, absurd, and grotesque images materialize, evaporate, and repeat themselves. The narrator sees a tightrope walker who is able to perform without a rope walking across the air by sheer concentration. At the request of the theatrical director the composer attempts to write a violin piece using only the note D-sharp. He is all too easily distracted from his reason for being on the trip. The train finally returns him to the point of his departure, still without his lover and in ignorance of his past. The theme of inexorable circularity surfaces again when the narrator arrives at the city to see the frenzied celebration of a "revolution" taking place. What appears to be snow falling on this hot summer day is, on closer inspection, confetti, as the ecstatic mass has been ripping to shreds every official document and form that it can find. By evening, however, this jubilant, hopeful vision has deteriorated into a cynical continuation of the prerevolutionary state of misery and oppression.

The composer flees into the country, where he again hears the sound that throughout the course of the narrative has moved and attracted him but kept somehow beyond his apprehension. The wind blowing through cornstalks hollowed out by an infestation produces a never-before-heard music. It is the kind of music he would like to be able to compose, but it cannot be written because it is intrinsic to nature and not extractable. Nature itself creates the music only in the process of self-destructing, a destruction the narrator finds himself almost hoping will occur. The final section, recapitulating the book's beginning, addresses the question of whether the narrator is seeking his own annihilation, for the text ends with the same sounds and images, the same schizophrenic ramblings, with which it began, almost completing another, larger circle, but with one small gap. There is an uncertain expectation that the narrator will yet awaken.

The narrative duality expressed in this volume has its roots in the perceptions and counter-perceptions of the two observers of earlier prose, wherein the proper relationship of subjective interpretation to exterior reality was sought in the method of continuous disputation. The narrative contradictions in *Geometrischer Heimatroman,* for example, were an indication that the viewer's perspective affects experience as unavoidably as experience affects the viewer's perspective, regardless of attempts to maintain objective distance and to describe the world in value-free terms. In the deeply introspective *Der ferne Klang* the narrative "I" and "you" are two aspects of one being. Consequently, any disagreement between "I" and "you" would be devastating, implying the nullification of existence. The disintegration of self is discussed in the book's conclusion, where the narrator claims to be observing himself as a subject from whom he is strangely dissociated. He thinks he might be merely witnessing a memory of himself or a reflection of a memory. He considers the likelihood that his own "you" may be dead from a suicide, dead to the world in the sense of having lost all feeling for it, or in an inebriated stupor. And he wonders whether any such distinction would matter. Perhaps he is so utterly insignificant in this story without beginning and without end that he cannot legitimately refer to himself as "I" but only as a remote "you," and even more accurately as an unfamiliar "you (*Sie*)." He is pondering the imponderable. For, given that consciousness acts like a filter to alter reality, how would it be possible to become aware of oneself? Thinking about the self is analogous to two mirrors reflecting into each other into infinity, an image frequently incorporated into Jonke's prose.

If Jonke gives the impression of teetering on the brink of insanity in his writing, he has reached exactly the destination he once declared for himself.[18] Each time imagination takes him too close to the edge of the abyss, however, wit brings him back a step onto safer footing. He seems compelled to explore this treacherous region and at the same time to be fully aware of the absurdity of his situation. An inventive portrayal of this predicament has been given in *Erwachen zum großen Schlafkrieg,* which is another expedition into the thinking processes of Jonke's narrator-artist. The narrator, Burgmüller, refers to himself as an acoustical interior designer rather than simply as composer. He has an uncommon ability to hear with his eyes, which enables him to communicate with the city's caryatids and atlantes. These telamones confide to Burgmüller their absolute ignorance on the matter of sleep, and he responds by conducting sleep seminars and demonstrations which, in turn, put him in such great demand that he develops his own sleep disorder. Burgmüller's comments about the telamones' circumstances reflect on the artist's. If the stony figures were to go to sleep (an eventuality that would be tantamount to an act of war), the dire result would be the collapse of the city. On the other hand, Burgmüller interprets, if they continue in their sleeplessness, it would be an indication that everything in the world merely goes on repeating itself, proof that all efforts and ambitions are meaningless. This is not just a dilemma for the telamones, but also for Burgmüller, who himself must balance a towering column on his head wherever he goes, except that his is a column of air rather than stone, and who is bound to reexperience events from Jonke's earlier prose: the search for a lost lover, meetings with characters introduced in *Schule der Geläufigkeit*, and the train that carries him nowhere.

The development of Jonke's prose follows no conventional sequence or logic, but it does appear to be shaped according to specific imperatives intrinsic to the subject matter. And it is by virtue of his consistency in responding to these imperatives that Jonke's preoccupations manifest themselves, outstanding among them being the author's skeptical attitude toward language and the notion that the fantastic world of his narration is not necessarily more preposterous than other conceptions of reality. At one time he wanted to eradicate all subjective content from descriptions of nature by means of precise, mathematical designations. In contrast to that his recent work includes attempts to articulate subjective experience with a landscape vocabulary. The following depiction of a sexual encounter relies on the imagery of dynamic geographic entities moving incessantly through horizontal and vertical planes until they conjoin in one final intense heave:

> Rather than perceiving their union as a penetration by him into a female body, as he had up to now been familiar with such intimacies, he suddenly had the sense of being on a bridge with her over which they were rather quickly crossing the Pacific Ocean as though they were going across a relatively wide river, the middle of which was decorated with the equator, while the highest point of the bridge's steel trusses was just arching over the dateline, beyond which a completely new time epoch, emerging from the pools of her eyes into the most hidden recesses of his head, was expanding and coming toward his field of vision until the shores of the converging continents touched, the spring-floodlike towering sea simply being pushed aside, while the coasts, having reached each other, thrust each other upward, unfolded into a mountain range, sank into one another, and fell back onto the floor of the night's darkness rushing by.[19]

The sensuality of the passage is underscored by references to the woman's pool-like eyes and the hidden recesses of the narrator's head, neither of which image fits with the predominant description, but which together anticipate the resolution of the action. The tension in this single long sentence is relieved only when the numerous clauses have completed their inexorable rhythmic movement toward the metaphorical climax.

It remains uncertain, however, whether this technique or some other completely different method of linking words, ideas, and objects is more accurate or more artificially contrived. Jonke seems to be earnestly seeking a prose of meaning, as a conversation between Burgmüller and the actress-writer with whom he becomes involved would suggest. The actress explains that she wants to write a portrayal of the world that will prove that it exists only as an invention, that life does not occur in fact but only in a very convincing description of it. She would reduce reality to letters, words, and sentences but requires a new language in order to attain her goal. The risk to her in this venture is that she might become so enmeshed in her speculations as to disappear in them or be crushed in them, in other words, go insane. Despite the danger of such a project, not to continue probing the nature of existence seems an intolerable proposition. The ambitious and perilous character of this pursuit is alluded to repeatedly in Jonke's references to the tightrope walker whose consummate achievement would be to perform without the rope.

Although he seems to acknowledge the utopian quality of the undertaking, Jonke is striving after a medium of expression so vigorously apt that it reaches directly into the realm of pure contemplation. The continuous resistance of an infinite artistic vision to the limitations of finite form is the substance of an unresolvable opposition that oftentimes can be voiced only ironically; and, while this conflict is one Jonke clearly recognizes, he has been more inclined to react to it with humor and wit than with desperation. His success, of course, would depend on a final determination of an insoluble but fascinating problem: is it art that reflects reality or reality that reflects art? It is in keeping with the principle of inevitable, unending self-reflection adhering to this question that in Jonke's narratives trains should end up at their point of departure, revolutions should leave people in their original conditions, and artists should continue waking up into circumstances that dissolve into dreams from which they may again waken.

Notes

1. Excerpts have been published in translation as G. F. Jonke, *Geometric Regional Novel*/Excerpts, trans. Johannes Vazulik, in *Dimension: Contemporary German Arts and Letters*, 8 (1975), 222-241. An unpublished translation of the complete work is available in Johannes W. Vazulik, "G. F. Jonke's *Geometrischer Heimatroman* – Translation and Critical Introduction," Diss. Case Western Reserve, 1974. Quoted passages are from the unpublished translation.

2. Marianne Kesting, "Abbau einer Idylle: G. F. Jonkes *Geometrischer Heimatroman*," *Die Zeit* (Hamburg), 4 April 1969, p. 6.

3. Hannes Rieser, "Die Grammatik des Dorfes," *Literatur und Kritik* 5 (1970), 560-566.

4. Ulrich Greiner, "Die ferne Blume und der blaue Klang," *Frankfurter Allgemeine Zeitung*, 9 October 1979, not paginated.

5. W. Martin Lüdke, "Wirklichkeit verschwindet," *Frankfurter Rundschau*, 13 August 1977, not paginated.

6. Hilde Spiel, *Austrian Literature after 1945* (New York: Austrian Institute, n.d.), pp. 13-20.

7. Cf. Michael Wegener, "Die Heimat und die Dichtkunst," *Trivialliteratur*, ed. G. Schmidt-Henkel et al. (Berlin: Literarisches Colloquium, 1964), pp. 53-64.

8. Vazulik, p. 25.

9. Liselotte Gumpel, *"Concrete" Poetry from East and West Germany* (New Haven: Yale University Press, 1976), p. 10.

10. Vazulik, p. 47.

11. Gumpel, p. 56.

12. Cf. Max Bense, "Concrete Poetry," *Concrete Poetry: A World View*, ed. Mary Ellen Solt (Bloomington: Indiana University Press, 1968), p. 73.

13. Marianne Kesting, "Der Roman als Baustelle," *Die Zeit* (Hamburg), 10 April 1970, not paginated.

14. Georg F. Schwartzbauer, "Jeden Tag ein kleines Stück weiter," *Frankfurter Rundschau*, 31 December 1971, not paginated.

15. G. F. Jonke, "Die Hinterhältigkeit der Windmaschinen," *Im Inland und im Ausland auch: Prosa. Gedichte. Hörspiel. Theaterstück.* (Frankfurt: Suhrkamp, 1974).

16. Cf. Lüdke.

17. G. F. Jonke, "Schule der Geläufigkeit oder Das Gehirn des Konservatoriums," *Wie die Grazer auszogen, die Literatur zu erobern*, Hrsg. Peter

Laemmle and Jörg Drews (München: edition text & kritik, 1975), pp. 221-268.

18.   Ulrich Greiner, "Gert Jonke," *Der Tod des Nachsommers* (München: Hanser Verlag, 1979), p. 131.

19.   G. F. Jonke, *Erwachen zum großen Schlafkrieg* (Salzburg: Residenz, 1982), p. 39.

Primary Works in German

Geometrischer Heimatroman. Frankfurt: Suhrkamp, 1969.
Glashausbesichtigung. Frankfurt: Suhrkamp, 1970.
Beginn einer Verzweiflung. Salzburg: Residenz, 1970.
Musikgeschichte. Berlin: Literarisches Colloquium, 1970.
Weltbilder: 49 Beschreibungen. Edited with Leo Navratil. München: Hanser, 1970.
Die Vermehrung der Leuchttürme. Frankfurt: Suhrkamp, 1971.
Im Inland und im Ausland auch: Prosa. Gedichte. Hörspiel. Theaterstück. Frankfurt: Suhrkamp, 1974.
Schule der Geläufigkeit. Frankfurt: Suhrkamp, 1977.
Der ferne Klang. Salzburg: Residenz, 1979.
Die erste Reise zum unerforschten Grund des stillen Horizonts. Salzburg: Residenz, 1980.
Erwachen zum großen Schlafkrieg. Salzburg: Residenz, 1982.

Works Translated into English

Vazulik, Johannes W. "G. F. Jonke's *Geometrischer Heimatroman:* Translation and Critical Introduction." Diss. Case Western Reserve, 1974.
Vazulik, Johannes, trans. "Geometric Regional Novel/ Excerpts." *Dimension,* VIII, no. 1-2 (1975), 222-241.

Secondary Works in English

Vazulik, Johannes W. "G. F. Jonke's *Geometrischer Heimatroman.*" *Modern Austrian Literature,* Vol. 10, no. 2 (1977), 1-7.

Selected List of Secondary Works in German

Aue, Maximilian. "Natur und Geometrie: Eine Anmerkung zu Gert Friedrich Jonkes Roman *Geometrischer Heimatroman.*" *Modern Language Notes,* 90 (1975), 696-702.

Beckermann, Thomas. "Kalkül und Melancholie oder Die Vorstellung und die Wirklichkeit. Über Gert Jonke." *Wie die Grazer auszogen, die Literatur zu erobern.* Ed. Peter Laemmle and Jörg Drews. München: edition text + kritik, 1975, pp. 200-220.

Caputo-Mayr, Maria Luise. "Jonkes *Geometrischer Heimatroman:* Will er sich einen Jux machen?" *Modern Austrian Literature,* Vol. 15, no. 2 (1982), 57-63.

Esslin, Martin. "Ein neuer Manierismus? Randbemerkungen zu einigen Werken von Gert F. Jonke und Thomas Bernhard." *Modern Austrian Literature,* Vol. 13, no. 1 (1980), 111-128.

Greiner, Ulrich. "Gert Jonke." In *Der Tod des Nachsommers.* München: Hanser Verlag, 1979, pp. 123-136.

Rieser, Hannes. "Die Grammatik des Dorfes." *Literatur und Kritik,* 49 (1970), 560-566.

The Modern Muse of Friederike Mayröcker's Literary Production

Beth Bjorklund

"I don't see a story anywhere; neither in my own life nor in life in general do I find any story-like phenomena," declared Mayröcker in a radio interview,[1] and there is in fact no "story" in the conventional sense of the term in any of the thirty-some volumes of poetry, prose, and plays that she has produced with phenomenal rapidity, primarily within the past two decades. How much we as readers expect a "story"—a continuity of experience in literature as well as in life—is demonstrated by the bafflement of even the most fascinated admirers and may account for the relative lack of scholarly attention accorded her works,[2] which have however received wide public recognition and numerous literary prizes. The goal of the present study is not to domesticate the texts or to make them understandable as any other literature is understood, but rather to give an overview of the oeuvre with the aim of investigating possible reasons for the renunciation of mimetic intent and, further, to assess what is achieved by a text freed from the constraints of verisimilitude and in which continuities are consequently of a different order.

Friederike Mayröcker was born in 1924 in Vienna, where she has continued to reside, from 1946 to 1969 as a teacher of English and from 1969 to the present as a free-lance writer. As a language teacher she is intimately acquainted with language systems as teachable, learnable structures for purposes of communication, and this forms an interesting backdrop to her literary works, which are often regarded as hermetic and undecipherable. Her familiarity with Anglo-Saxon culture is reflected in frequent English phrases in the texts and explicit references to writers such as Gertrude Stein and e. e. cummings. Of decisive importance has been her friendship and collaboration with Ernst Jandl since 1954. In the 1950s Mayröcker and Jandl were loosely connected with the "Vienna Group," composed initially of Achleitner, Artmann, Bayer, Rühm, and Wiener, and she is presently affiliated with the "Graz Authors' Association" (*GAV*) of the "Forum Stadtpark," a group originally founded in opposition to the more traditional PEN Club in Vienna. Literary production of the group has often been termed "experimental," which is, however, merely a negative epithet expressing contrast to convention and belies the obvious fact that literature is by definition creation and invention, some types of which we are more accustomed to than others. The artistic heritage is often seen in a general-ized variety of dadaism and surrealism, with adaptation of techniques of "automatic writing" and affinities to the "theater of the absurd" as well as to "concrete poetry," particularly because the texts are at times accompanied by drawings, and the visual format often bears semantic significance. Mayröcker is, however, too individual to be classified or encompassed by any particular movement or manifesto, and her development through a variety of styles, as well as the underlying constant concerns, is the topic of this study.

Mayröcker's work has been characterized as "poetic phenomenology,"[3] and indeed she does offer a fresh and highly imaginative mode of perception. Fragments from experience and memory, dream and fantasy, perceptions, reflections, and heterogeneous elements of thought and feeling are brought together in an atemporal amalgam in which time levels of recent and remote pasts are superimposed on present, future, and future perfect possibilities of consciousness. Reality is portrayed as discontinuous, nonchronological, fragmentary, and ambivalent; precisely this open-endedness is more central and significant than anything that can be objectively established. The theme of her works is most basically the sensibility of the writer, and the most persistent motif to emerge is the portrait of an artist, that is, a view of the creative process itself. Autobiographical elements are included but are so transformed that rather than any "confessional," the recovery of the self's own history becomes a fictional documentation of the creative process as a series of imaginative possibilities. The "sea-change" is so thorough that at times the text seems to produce the author rather than the other way around; but the author of course produces both – the text and thereby also the artist-self. Art functions not as a fanciful supplement to the world of practical activity or as an accessory to the "truth" of science or religion but rather as a fundamental mode of apprehending that world, as the container rather than the contained. The organizing sensibility, which is literary and aesthetic, at once involved and dispassionate, is concerned not with the self as such but with the quality of modern life in general and particularly with modes of perceiving it.

It was with *Tod durch Musen* (Death by the Muses) in 1966 that Mayröcker won wide public recognition. As her first major publication it presents the author's selection of poems from the years 1945 to 1965, which has since been expanded and published in a hardback edition of *Ausgewählte Gedichte* (1979, Selected Poetry). The widely acclaimed *Tod durch Musen* receives its title from the opening cycle, which consists of nine "models" addressed to the nine muses and stands as meta-poetic commentary on the creative process, which is conceived as one of devastation. The muses, as the source of art, are also the source of death, for creating a text entails creating also an artist and thus "killing" the person. The totality of destruction wrought by the death gods finds its cultural analogue in the total war of human murder, and Goebbels has a voice in the opening poem addressed to Clio, the muse of history: "(' . . do you want total war . . !' Y E S S)." Goethe speaks in the second poem, as images of art and life, suffering and death recur in crass juxtaposition: "a wasteland full/ and the artificial paradises with the eyes of a lamb." The third "model," addressed to Melpomene, the singing muse of tragedy, illustrates the assembly of disparate elements, as well as the associative chain. It is given below in German and in English translation.

> in rhein-mein-schlinge-gelockt; die tolle
> zugezogen; hochgehalten; gehängt; mit
>   dem bürzel nach oben;
> versenkt -
> ausruf totalen schmerzes (mit zusammengepreszten lippen
>   hervorgebrachter laut)
>
> (poet.) knallen; schnuppe am lampendocht / gebrüll
> weintoll
> entfesselte dame!
> und schon sind wir mitten drin in der suspekten abstraktion

> enticed into rhine-mine-snare; the raging one
> drawn in; held high; hanged; with
>   her hind end up;
> sunk -
> outcry of total pain (sound brought forth with lips
>   pressed together)
>
> (poet.) explosion; snuff of the lampwick / roar
> raging with wine
> unchained woman!
> and already we are in the midst of the suspicious abstraction

The allegory of the muse is here combined with the myth of the Lorelei to set the scene for artistic creation, a construct the validity of which is, however, ironically undercut by the illusion-breaking final line. The muse is invoked by the siren, but creativity reveals itself as sexuality in the service of death, and total song and total silence ensue simultaneously; only, however, to emerge again as the sound of metamorphosis into poetry, that is, as this poem, which then asserts its own incapacity to capture adequately the creative process. Although the poem as a whole can be read as a metaphor or almost an allegory, the basic principle on which it and many others operate is metonymy, that is, a linear progression of associative elements on various levels. Progression here is initially and passim by phonetic similarity, followed by a series of perfect participles, culminating in semantic reference to sound; this serves as transition and transformation into images of poetry, whereby the raging force of the first line is resurrected in incarnated form, only to be questioned by cognitive categories of abstraction and realization. Metaphor thus extended to contiguous relations becomes metonymy and represents a central principle in experimental texts. The arsenal of punctuating symbols, an alienating device present throughout, acquires significance by blocking passage through the poem, and the typographical sign *sz* for *ß* (an idiosyncrasy the author attributes to her typewriter keyboard) is further indication that one is drawn into the world of writing.

The collection *Tod durch Musen* originated largely during the period in which the author adopted the form of the so-called "long poem," a conscious "countermovement to confinement."[4] Titles often bear generic reference, such as "Ode" or "Romanze," but most pieces are entitled simply "Text . . . ," revealing that none of the above refers to traditional forms but rather that the poems establish their own conventions, often with illustrative titles such as "Text mit dynamischen Mähnen und anderen Relationen" (Text with Dynamic Manes and Other Relations). The long poem, extending at times for several pages, displays an irregular line length and stanza length without rhyme or fixed rhythmic scheme. Normal sentence syntax of subject-predicate is dissolved, and the noun phrase becomes the primary structural element in this process of naming; verbs, insofar as they occur, are often in nonfinite form, thus serving to increase the rich supply of modifiers. Gone is any trace of superficial sentiment or inflated emotion, as experience is transformed into, indeed, is created by, language, whereby the "I" appears only occasionally and as quotation. As indicated by *mit* or *zu* (with/to) of the titles, many of the poems are set in a dialogue framework, which, given the fragmentary form, may not otherwise be readily apparent. Although the various personal voices are created mainly for self-enactment, they serve to facilitate the presentation of multiple perspectives, and thus the effect is the preclusion of any privileged position — a concern which becomes increasingly important in Mayröcker's works, as remains to be demonstrated.

Since poetry is intricately related to linguistic expression, it is difficult to discuss without referring to the German, and the interested reader is advised to look elsewhere for commentary.[5] This survey would not be complete, however, without mention of Mayröcker's recent volume of poems entitled *Gute Nacht, guten Morgen* (1982, Good Night, Good Morning), which she produced after nearly a decade of focus on prose works. "Snapshots" or, better, "close-ups" might be a proper term for the new volume of ostensibly "occasional" poetry, whereby she radically alters the notions of that genre as well. Although these short poems are furnished with concrete particulars such as dedications, proper names, and "occasions" of origin, reality is nevertheless portrayed as fragmentary and ambivalent. Evocation is achieved initially simply by the titles – "Hellish February," "Paper Landscape," "Double Scene" – and the motif of photo, image, mirror image and trompe-l'oeil recurs in constant variation on a central theme: art reflecting upon itself. The poem "Cypress" is given here as a "snapshot" in translation: "the wind / blows white, the / bird / clamors in the / wood – / *embracing* / tender strangeness when / the blossom / withers."

Personal experience – a love relationship, mother and father, nature and poetry – is processed and presented with light irony, "as if we lived in the age of sentimentality," and in any case with conscious distancing, denouncing thereby the illusion of inwardness. The resulting network of associations and inventions demonstrates that literature is as formative as it is reproductive: "Now, I think, finally, / without having to make / self-reproach I have stopped / pursuing myself"; but upon another occasion, looking into the mirror, "Is that me? I / ask mutely it rains / on my eyelids." Readers will find this work more accessible than the earlier poetry, and seemingly uninterpretable passages are for that matter the more suggestive ("the silver of the trip / untroubled elliptical"), resulting in a unique amalgam of "naive" experience and "conscious" art. In fresh, unsugared form the wealth and poverty of nature and love are portrayed as stimuli to artistic creation, and thereby also to creation of the self. It is truly a proper sequel to the large prose works of the 1970s.

The late 1960s and early 1970s was a period of change for society in general and for Mayröcker as well, for she began writing texts of a highly experimental – and thus liberating – nature, comparable in some ways to the language experiments of Gertrude Stein and e. e. cummings, which are, again, virtually untranslatable.[6] *Minimonsters Traumlexikon* (1968, Mini-Monster's Dream Dictionary) and *Fantom Fan* (1971) find their culmination in *Arie auf tönernen Füszen. Metaphysisches Theater* (1972, Aria on Feet of Clay: Metaphysical Theater), which is perhaps her most radical work, the heights and depths of which are indicated already by the oxymora of the title and subtitle. The ambitious program of "suspension of the reality of the entire essence of the theater" is realized by an assemblage of ready-mades, found objects, prefabricated banalities, and actual debris taken over from pop and op culture and adapted from such genres as pornography, science fiction, the detective story, and the comics. Protagonists in the short prose or dialogue scenes are artist figures such as Maria Callas in tandem with Snoopy, the Statue of Liberty waving a hand grenade, Shirley Temple's face projected onto a giant screen, and Richard Wagner living in a commune with Lohengrin and other "heroes" (which today would probaly include film star Ronnie Reagan). The theatricality of the Shakespearean motto, "all the world's a stage," stands in contrast to the aesthetic withdrawal of "Catatonic Theater," and the author is implicated along with a group of contemporary artists in the architecture of the [Adolf] Loos Bar in Vienna. Bizarre happenings and disruptive techniques effect a derangement of the senses, as art is separated from its "functional" reality and re-converted into an art-like equivalent of itself, achieving at once a metaphor and a parody of mimesis. As with all process art, tension is textural rather than temporal, but the tedium of psychological superficiality is effectively counteracted by the sophistication of the imaginative focus, and an energetic tempo is sustained by linguistic surprises that the author seems to hold in unlimited reserve.

If theater is traditionally understood to be an artful imitation of life, and if Wagnerian theater is the totalized epitome of this conception, "masterpiece theater" is here divested of its aesthetic illusion by a de-aestheticized construction which attempts to rid literature of its atavistic assumptions and to purge art of the vestiges of artifice. Fortuity and (im-)probability are pitted against the limitations of preconceived patterns, and the stakes are offered as extreme alternatives: to find art in culture is to make art superfluous, whereas to do away with art is to make culture perfect. Whatever meaning our inherited culture may have had for its originators, it has become sterile and stifling through our drawing-room notions of suitability and decorum, which serve more to satisfy a nostalgia than to challenge sensibilities. Guardians of the status quo may be alarmed to learn that creativity is more likely to develop from chaos and confusion than from conformity to convention, whereby the true aim of art is shown to be subversive. In contrast to a rhetorical voice, which directs its audience, this type of guerrilla theater draws the observer in by requiring interpretation, and the participatory poetic reveals the intent to be a communicative one, pledged to human values. Thus the nonsense of comedy combined with criticism, of funniness together with "metaphysical" searching, is nonsense of the most responsible kind, and pressure is exerted by the most effective means possible — not by negation of content but by inversion of form.

This was also the period of Mayröcker's collaboration with Ernst Jandl on the *Hörspiel* (radio play), and their award-winning "fünf mann menschen"

(1967, five men people) innovatively redefined the genre. If the radio play is by definition an acoustic phenomenon, how much more essentially is this true of the so-called "new" radio play in the hands of experimental writers. Gone is the traditional dialogue and monologue form, and speech takes on an entirely different function in combination with other sound effects, whereby the script often resembles a musical score with notations for performance. Decisive was the invention of stereophonic and electronic techniques, which allow for super-imposition of sound levels and thus for simultaneous presentation of different, often widely discrepant, phenomena. The resulting acoustic collage stands as metaphor in itself for the inadequacy of any one-dimensional approach to reality.

Although Mayröcker and Jandl each wrote radio plays individually as well as collectively, "Gemeinsame Kindheit" (Shared Childhood) stands out as a product of true collaboration, the Q.E.D. of this piece. It consists of ten scenes from the childhood of the two authors, whereby various realities are created: recalled individual childhoods, a relationship between two adults, and a colla-boration of artists. Autobiographical elements receive fictional presentation and attain an additional level of fictionality in that they are declared, from the present perspective, to have been "shared"; the work however becomes auto-biographical again in the reality of two adults retrospectively sharing their earlier experiences in a present friendship and in the act of creating this very work of art through the process of this real-life experience.

The "destructive" phase of experimentation in the 1960s led to a "con-structive" period of synthesis in the 1970s, as the author states in an interview: "In retrospect I realize that synthesis would not have been possible without my having gone through the experimental phase."[7] "Synthesis" is attained in her larger prose works, to which we now turn our attention. If the narrative (je ein umwölkter gipfel (1973, each a cloud-covered summit) denotes a de-parture from the radical experimentation with sound and sense, it by no means entails a reversion to conventional form. The work consists of episodes loosely held together more by structural relations than by any consistency of plot or continuity of character. Autobiographical elements are present but inter-spersed with fictional and imaginative possibilities and dispersed among the various speakers so that no unified perspective is discernible. The work deals in part with the author's (actual) trip to the USA, and there are many references in this regard; it is, however, presented as a "trip broken down into many tiny pieces" which enter into relation with other seemingly extraneous events. Temporal and spatial categories are distorted, and fiction is interwoven with fact to give a picture of the potentiality and the fragility of the human condition. These themes recur in her major works of the 1970s, *Das Licht in der Landschaft* and *Die Abschiede*, which merit detailed investigation.

Das Licht in der Landschaft (1978, The Light in the Landscape) was the author's first publication with the prestigious Suhrkamp firm, and it indeed remains one of her major prose works. In characteristic Mayröcker fashion, the text represents a distillation of approximately 1000 pages to 140, and as such it demonstrates a compression comparable to that of poetry, with images operating incrementally to form chains of allusions resulting in a text extraordinarily rich in cross-references. Experiences from recent and remote pasts are interspersed with conversations, letters, dreams, and fantasies, whereby time levels are so distinctly nonlinear that the book can be read backward as well as forward (the reader is advised to try the experiment!). This kaleidoscopic constellation is held together by a central consciousness functioning as both generator and nucleus of the forces that seem designed to break it apart. Rather than any personalized form, however, it represents the narrative device that consists of referring to the leading character as "I." Focus is on perception and consciousness, and the relativity of cognitive categories leads to an ambivalence in interpretation of empirical events. The subjectivity of content is coupled with a tightly controlled form of composition; the work paradoxically elucidates the all-pervasive nature of ambiguity.

The human faculty of memory is what enables the simultaneous presence of past events, and the text on one level stands as demonstration of the nature and functioning of recollection, with fragmentation functioning mimetically to evince a psychological likeness of the discontinuous process of memory. The imminence of the past energizes the present, as impressions, reflections, and sensations from various time periods are presented in the poetic expression of a vivid inner world: the dazzling yellow of the forsythia bush, the first snowflakes, the northern coast, grandparents, war, cherries, birds, dance, Mozart, and Satie. The power is in the concretion, and any analytic abstraction would constitute falsification, for it is truly a phenomenally experienced world, "a breeze of smells, colors, and sounds, to which I want to open my senses even further." Images are evoked, developed, and dropped, only to recur with accrued implications in similar or expanded contexts. Clusters form, regroup, and join in networks of association resembling, in the visual arts, a mobile with planes of interrelations suspended in a space held together by its own inner forces. Only upon rereading does one realize that the central grid is a triadic love relationship. To reconstruct it systematically, however, would be to impose a coherence not present in the text, for this "story," like any other material, is presented in bits and pieces of recurring phrases and motifs.

The immanence enabling phenomenological perception on the part of the first-person narrator also thereby precludes any omniscient point of view, and second- and third-persons are sketchily portrayed mainly in their relation to the protagonist. The only major figure identified by name is "Agnes," which voice at times seems to be identical with that of the protagonist, at times, antithetical, a point to which we shall return, for similarity-identity-assimilation is indeed a central theme. Functioning as an ironic reversal of an omniscient narrator is the "World Biographer," a type of alter ego, who, as the rationalist, is the only one to make direct statements, whose attempts at generalization and explanation result however only in banalities and cliché. The counterpart in the self is the "White Gardener," who says nothing but appears and gestures at significant points. There is thus no preferred position, and the traditional conception of character is rendered inoperative as figures are used mainly as instruments for conveying thoughts, feelings, and memories of the self.

The text begins and ends with the motif of letter-writing, which is picked up also intermittently but by no means constitutes the structural form, as in the traditional epistolary novel. Its function, in addition to the performative aspect, is to break the circularity of the nonlinear chain of associations, as demonstrated by the final letter, which closes the work with the message that the writer is leaving to go on a trip, a trip which, however, in time predates other episodes, since it had already been mentioned early in the text. A climax, if such indeed occurs, may be seen in the center of the work with the "anecdote" of farewell and departure, which represents the most continuously narrated episode, but again its place in the overall structure is spatial rather than temporal, for the fact of "separation" had been mentioned early in the text, and any kind of elucidation comes only later upon accretion of images. Initiation and dissolution of the love affair are throughout inextricably intertwined and accompanied by reflections on the nature and experience of human relationships. Explicit mention is made only very late in the text with the sentence, "It wouldn't have to be a triangular relationship, screamed Agnes," which forces the reader to go back to the beginning and reinterpret events in a new light. Temporal categories are thus flattened out and recast in spatial form as "the internal processes so interpenetrated one another that everything seemed to stand still."

Simultaneity leads to superimposition and to identification in the mind of the narrator, who in and by the presentation establishes relationships among people, places, and things far removed in space and time. The writer of the letter and its recipient (formal pronoun *Sie*) at times merge into one in a "double lighting." As the World Biographer brashly summarizes, "it has recurring character";

and *déjà vu* scenes of "strange coincidence," "confusing similarity," and "inter-
changeability" are frequent in both actuality and in recall: "He didn't like it
when I referred to similarities between this place and that, between this face
and that, between parallel connections, conditions, forms of appearance. It
would otherwise be imitable, at many places the same thing, and one could
no longer see what was real." Most often he, the beloved, "does not come
himself but rather someone who looks very similar." "I am startled each time I
see someone similar to him, it seems that I continually meet people who bear a
resemblance to him until finally I see him himself coming toward me." An
identity is established between the protagonist and Agnes: "We use, it seems,
a very similar vocabulary, screamed Agnes," and, "superfluously enough, she
looked like me. Thus I could relate the entire scene to myself, I could put
myself in her place." Through a type of "negative capability" the persona
identifies with and assimilates herself to other figures and particularly to the
beloved to the point of a desire "to receive the world only through him."
This fluctuation in the borders of the ego represents the central characteristic
which, on the one hand, enables the receptivity and transformability, while
entailing the attendant instability and ambiguity in the concept of the self
and thus of all else as well.

The underlying question is one of cognition, whether and how reality can
be known, and dynamic imagination is here coupled with language experimentation to yield a picture of complete ambivalence. Whereas it is the World-
Biographer side of the self who "would like to make emphatically clear the
all-pervasive ambivalence," the narrator finds that "it is hardly comprehensible.
When one believes to have it in hand, it has long since dissolved again." This
mode of experiencing reality is reflected in language and in the numerous
references to writing: "An interpenetration of situations, of realities has as a
consequence an interpenetration of language." Whereas the World Biographer
advocates a "strategy of encirclement," the text itself deals more subtly with
problems of interpretation (of books and letters, music and myth) and thus
vitiates any conception of a "correct" reading. The absence of narrative cohesion
is compensated for by a tightly woven web of words, whereby "even the smallest
movement of the body transformed itself immediately into language." The
image of a prism, "namely the decomposition of light into various colors in
different directions, as abundance and superabundance," from another prose
piece "Frühstücksgespräche" (Breakfast Conversations) could also serve here
as representative for the nature of the undertaking, as indeed indicated also
by the reference of the title to a "clearing." Lack of coherence in the outside
world is represented in poetically structured language that creates a new and

unified whole—as open-ended as its empirical counterpart.

Fast ein Frühling des Markus M. (1976, Almost a Springtime of Markus M.'s) bears similarities in theme and technique to *Das Licht in der Landschaft*. It is, however, almost alone in the author's oeuvre by possessing—or pretending to possess—a structure not predominantly textural. Thus, because of its purported "story," it has been regarded as more accessible. The semi-autobiographical framework[8] is a commune of artists, writers, and musicians living together in Berlin, in itself an anti-conventional, idealistic undertaking. Sexual and erotic relationships are at the center—as is the garden with its lurid imagery—and serve as occasion for investigating questions of personal identity and interpersonal relations, as well as differing male/female sensibilities. The emotional effect is however controlled through the abstractness of presentation, and character is used mainly instrumentally to focus on the central themes of the interpenetration of temporal categories, the inscrutability of consciousness, and the ambivalence of values.

Mayröcker's most recent prose work, *Die Abschiede* (1980, The Farewells), which was on the "Best-Seller List" in Germany, bears similarities to the previously discussed works, beginning with *je ein umwölkter gipfel*, through *Das Licht in der Landschaft* and *Fast ein Frühling des Markus M.* An artist, however, never duplicates an effort, and the earlier works serve as formal presuppositions for this narrative, which is indeed the author's most ambitious undertaking to date. The dominant metaphor is one of closure, and the valedictory suggested by the title finds expression on many levels: evening, autumn, departure, dissolution, decay, and death. The paradox of life as a process of death, yet life nevertheless as ultimate riches—evanescence and fullness—sets the basic tone of bittersweetness. The most apparent level of farewell is the dissolution of a love relationship, as in previous works, but the "story" is even more summarily absolved by two prefatory statements, "Introitus" and "Exodus," whereupon the remaining two hundred fifty pages are devoted to the all-encompassing implications of the experience of "deaths"—and life. Formal progression is by association in loose paragraph structure, similar to *Das Licht in der Landschaft,* on, however, an intensified level, for which the text offers the metaphor of "Aufflammen und Erlöschen" (flaring up and expiration): a motif may be initiated seemingly unobtrusively; it recurs in various contexts, each time with accrued implications; after having amassed a chain of associations it at some point goes spiraling to a climax; the narrative breaks off, and the motif reverts to dormancy; it may, however, spark off other motifs, or may itself be reactivated to participate in some larger complex.

The narrator, as in the previous works, is represented by a first-person female consciousness, and it is only through her eyes that one sees the female antagonist, Giselle, as well as the male protagonist, Valerian. The name is, of course, derived from the Latin *Valeriānus* (root: *valēre,* "to be strong"), which is from "Valeria," the name of a Roman province whence originated a plant by the same name, more commonly known today as the "garden heliotrope," which bears small white and pink flowers that turn toward the sun and from whose roots is distilled an essence used as a sedative. This excursus into philology and botany was intended to suggest some of the implications entailed in the author's choice of a level of abstraction that may initially appear estranging, as represented by the dust jacket illustration of a "romantic" artist in an idyllic landscape; or by passages reading like allegory, with nymphs and shepherds, animals resembling flowers and flowers that want to talk, observations to which we shall return. The flower-based pink-and-white occurs as leitmotif throughout — together or in various combinations, such as the purity of white and yellow, the sensuality of red and blue, or the absence of color in black — and the colors, whether attached or unattached to objects, are in either case equally nonreferential. The earlier object-oriented focus gives way here to perception of properties, which, dissociated from their base, are free to serve as metaphors for temporal experiences, which "flow together like watercolors," evoking their color complement and calling forth also the corresponding auditory sensation in a synesthetic "series of echos." The use of floral associations and an effeminate name to characterize a male figure is representative of an androgynous motif running throughout Mayröcker's works, simply as another instance of the larger complex of process and change.[9]

Allegory is by definition a construct, which in this case, as the reader learns later, has its basis in memories of travel experiences, for example, at Nîmes, home of a temple to Diana, or Naples, locus of Roman mythology. The naturalistic counterpart to allegory is photographic likeness, and photographs of the trip are periodically brought forth to settle trivial questions on a trivial positivistic basis, e.g., whether or not there were mountains there. At stake, basically, are questions of epistemology: to what could the phrase "things as they are" meaningfully refer, apart from our discredited perceptions, to which everything is so inextricably tied; the "camera eye" scans the face, "as if you wanted to press the truth out of me." The pinnacle of empirical reality is, directly upon attestation, withdrawn again: "We are here on the heights of Naples, but topography and geography are never real." The pilgrims and other figures in the landscape are thus projections of the self — products of memory, vision, and writing — but they regain allegorical significance as representative of the writer's search for clarity of the "confusing paradox" and the unity of "two ideas, which should have been mutually exclusive."

The heritage of German Romanticism is evident in these self-styled, so-designated "Caspar David Friedrich landscapes," which include a "landscape room (place of invention)" where one writes. Parallels can be drawn particularly to Novalis's "Märchen von Hyazinth und Rosenblüte" (Fairy Tale of Hyazinth and Rosenblüte), whereby the hyacinth appears as one of the many floral motifs in the text, coupled with the quest, which culminates at the point when "it seemed to him as if he had arrived at the end of a strenuous pilgrimage." The motif of "keine Räder mehr" (no more wheels) possibly refers to Wackenroder's "Wunderbares morgenländisches Märchen von einem nackten Heiligen" (Wondrous Oriental Fairy Tale of a Naked Saint). This work contains a figure obsessed with the "wheel of time" until he is finally released from time and transformed into a heavenly body, a fate paralleled by that of Valerian, who is also caught up in the temporal flux until finally "he, Valerian, has for us become a star," symbol of the desired permanence.

Only a writer highly aware of the present age and of what can or cannot be said any longer could allow such conscious stylization, and if timelessness is so strongly expressed, it is because the opposing forces are so all-powerful. The sweetness of Arcadia is juxtaposed with surrealistic, fetishistic images of decay, excrement, wounds, dismemberment, reptiles, and Kafkaesque nightmares of terror, guilt, anxiety, and anguish. Both sides—the effects of time and its envisioned suspension—are seen as "variations on one single theme," in which "everything lies as close together as love and damnation," and love is lasting, "if only for hours or days." The tension between mutually inclusive, mirror-image polar forces is topicalized as a recurring motif: "a laughing-crying and vice versa, as children so easily switch from one to the other." The birth of a child is celebrated as occasion for seeing things afresh, as if for the first time: "the fabulous experience of the rejuvenation of this world," a capacity that is retainable or regainable also in adult life as eager appetite for full and vivid experience. This is juxtaposed with the awareness of mutability and the finality of death, which means "that nothing more can be revised," and the text returns to the dominant theme of finale.

Change, as a type of death and transformation, entails both negative and positive features and constitutes a central aspect of Mayröcker's works. Everything that was said earlier to the topic is applicable here as well, on, however, again, an intensified level, for the network of relations is drawn more tightly in proportion to the increased threat of the disintegrative forces. Transformation is basically a consequence of a "process" view of life. Everything is seen as caught up in change, and perception includes a view of things in relation to earlier and later possibilities of themselves, as well as in relation to the other objects. This process is frequently expressed by use of the present participle, which entails the past and future of every object it describes: e.g., "Expansionary images, eyes of ivory, *mocking* every visual experience" (emphasis added). Images range from Hindi transmigration to Christian transubstantiation, from sexual union to unification through imbibing, "as if you wanted to eat the world," and the feast at which "you [the beloved] are yourself the food." Objects too elicit this kind of identification, and paintings or books become real as the observer becomes absorbed. The implication is that to know something truly one must share in its identity; one must become that thing in consciousness and experience it from the inside out.

Experience elicits a sympathetic participation so strong that the self loses all sense of distinct identity and becomes totally merged with the object, whereby consciousness is of nothing other than the object of identification. The result is analogous to what T. S. Eliot presents as a state in which "You are the music / While the music lasts."[10] This pitch of intensity has the effect of "annihilating" time while holding it in an "eternal present," although time is of course the continuum in which the process takes place and which also causes its dissolution. The sheer intensity entails a partial loss of consciousness, and the text contains numerous references to a hypnotic, hallucinatory, delirious, opium-induced, dream- and trance-like state. That condition activates the creative powers, and although the object remains the stimulus, it serves to stimulate the imagination more than the senses; empirical phenomena function as "emblems" or "heralds" of something else, and consciousness may embark on a visionary flight. This transformational capacity is seen as central to the poetic process: "Namely, to live in such a tension, I cry, simultaneously to keep an eye on the nearby and to look into the hemispheric far and wide: is the (fateful) presupposition for poetic experience and insight in general; as it, transmitted through the consuming perception of the outer world, transformed from original form into final form in the cold fire of a mad and sweet obsession, finally appears resurrected in an other, new (reflected) reality." The conception is "classical," with obvious parallels to Schillerian aesthetics and the dialectic of the Romantic-idealistic tradition ("transmitted-transformed-resurrected"). That authentication takes place in the realm of myth, where vision and reality are one, indicates that the dimensions of true reality are aesthetic and serves to legitimate a visionary view of art.

Tradition, however, is radically reinterpreted, and one could also draw parallels to modern writers such as Paul Celan: "Who / says that everything died for us / when our eye broke? / Everything awakened, everything began."[11]

The "eye," as a central image in the works of both Celan and Mayröcker, is the perceptual organ mediating between object and consciousness, sight and "insight," and it thus serves as vehicle for the transformational power that converts the phenomenal world into noumenal vision, a vision that may initially present itself as open, strange, or even empty; "utopia," literally, as *ou topos*, no place. That the vision is not only aesthetic but also existential is indicated by the fact that transformation is not always possible: "when . . . every attempt at approximation failed," reminiscent of a Blakean situation: what, when the vision fails. Whether or not the poet is successful, the aloneness remains absolute; the well-nigh ineffability of experience precludes community, and the sole apparent exception, namely communication with the beloved, entails its own closure. This leads to "silence," which, as another manifestation of "separation," becomes an important motif in the work. Whatever else the narrative may be about, it represents also an exploration of the nature and consequences of commitment to poetic vision.

Time is throughout the work recognized as the medium in which things develop and fulfill their latent potentialities. There is thus no striving to hold on to time or to regain or replace a past; awareness of time arouses a desire to participate, not to withdraw, and this serves as a springboard for other desires, revealing a self-corrective that is part of its own energy. The centrality of this position precludes emotions of nostalgia or sentimentality (if it is sentimental to wish an impossibility), and like any good literature, it often acknowledges as interior appeals the regions it eventually dismisses. Consciousness of the paradox stands at the center, a stance aptly characterized by Keats's now-classic formulation of the notion of "negative capability": "That is, when a man is capable of being in uncertainties, mysteries, doubts, without any irritable reaching after fact and reason."[12] The uncertainty experienced in every human endeavor is prized as a source of creative incentive.

What has here, for purposes of exposition, been categorized as abstract polarities, is presented in the text as a pattern of relational motifs, demonstrating a wide range of awareness and a refusal to compartmentalize experiences, which are woven together in a network of language. The pattern becomes evident only gradually, and reading thus becomes a process of fitting fragments together and keeping allusions in mind until, by reflexive reference, they can be linked to their complement. The above-cited birth and death passages occur near the structural center of the narrative, and the beginning and end could be viewed as an "Aufflammen und Erlöschen," with a visionary view throughout. The narrator often appears not as manipulator of the metaphors but as accomplice in a dynamic relationship to them, reacting differently as the fuller significance of the controlling images is gradually disclosed. Form as well as theme exists in contrast and contradiction, and the formal counterpart to the immanence of the narrator is a deliberate and highly self-conscious mode of narration, one which labels its own techniques: "serial succession," "elisions," "anachronisms," "the copulation of words," "sentences, seamless and seemingly self-generating," "the course through a motif," "a polyphonic mesh," "a vertical text," and the desire "on one single day to write everything, a whole book."

There are also many references to forms of genre, but since all events, conversations, letters, journals, and footnotes take place in the past, the writing of this narrative casts all previous forms and temporal zones of whatever shape onto one flat plane, namely the present page. Thereby, however, all foregoing occasions are included also within the present instance of writing, to which there are numerous allusions: "to bite into the flesh of language," with obvious sexual overtones; "to work almost without a net" below to catch the fall; "with all locks open," and "directed to the most boundless and most disciplined form of writing." The willingness to submit to "self-destructive vision" may be part of what the author had in mind with the conception of "Tod durch Musen," and many of the above-cited statements concerning writing occur also in authorial self-characterizations in regard to the creative process, e.g., in *rot ist unten* (red is below). The result is a linguistic reality, consciously and intentionally distinct from empirical reality: "As soon as one stands up from the typewriter or lays down the book, one becomes all the more aware of the beautiful illusion." By conceding its fictionality, the work paradoxically gains authenticity in its claim to a visionary totality, and a new order of reality is therein created by human consciousness as expressed in language.

One of the figures in the text is reading a book, it is narrated, which another figure, presumably Valerian, conjectures to be a novel by Robbe-Grillet. Whereas a superficial parallel to *La Jalousie* (Jealousy) could be drawn on the thematic basis of a triangular relationship, comparisons are more fruitful on a formal level; for, "to tell a story has become strictly impossible," says Robbe-Grillet,[13] and there are indeed similarities—as well as differences—between Mayröcker's prose and the French *nouveau roman* (new novel). Comparisons could also be made with the novels of Nathalie Sarraute, in their constant verbalization and interplay of dialogue, monologue, and preconscious "subconversations" expressing internal "tropisms," whereby "psychology" becomes an embarrassment, since all that emerges from the deep dark depths is an uninterrupted flow of words. Mayröcker's work could be placed in the context of a general development in modern fiction characterized by dissolution of plot and decomposition of character and thus absence of anecdotal interest; noncausal and nonteleological structures, whereby "time" itself becomes the chief protagonist; mistrust of metaphor as a mask for phony metaphysics, in reaction to which self-referential surface structures flout their own fictionality; a general experimentation with form, conducted perhaps most radically by Latin American writers such as Jorge Luis Borges and Carlos Fuentes. Questions of influence, however, are delicate and dangerous, and in any case remain to be investigated. The unity and consistency of Mayröcker's literary production over a long period of time lead one to view it primarily as an instance of individual development, with, undoubtedly, secondary stimuli from other literary and nonliterary sources.

The theme of creativity is the absolute center of *Heiligenanstalt* (1978, Saints' Asylum), where it is presented with the precision, objectivity, and authority of art, making the text in my opinion one of the most successful of Mayröcker's works. If one were to inquire what conventions are invoked to explain and legitimate the nonreferentiality of theme and discontinuity of form, certainly a musical analogy would come to mind; for, although visual analogies have been used in the preceding discussion for purposes of concretizing (as justified also by the texts), the imagination revealed is captured more by events in time than by objects in space, and literature of this type thus approaches the abstractness of musical composition. Music stands at the center — both as technique and as topic — of this work, which consists of the "biographies" of four musicians: Chopin, Schumann, Bruckner, and Schubert. An accompanying list of records and books indicates the sources used, but, since documentation would be foolhardy (not to say, uninteresting) within the short space, the author abandoned conventional notions of biography, and, thus freed from the facticity of time and place, used history in order to transcend it. The great originality here as well as elsewhere lies in the separation of the materials from their sources, the dissociation of language from its "story," and the result is a characterization of the creative process with a concentration and reduction that reveals more than it conceals. It is art metamorphosed into art, whereby every sentence seems to say that there is nothing but the abilities and appetencies of life and what it means to be alive, namely to create — and this in full awareness of the awful backdrop of isolation, insanity, and death.

The virtuoso brilliance of Chopin's romanticism, "I have looked in the eye of the hurricane," introduces the dichotomous themes of creativity and suffering; sexuality and death; the heights of vision and imagination with their attendant depths of depression and despair. Part One, entitled "Table of material, or the completely lost letters of Frédéric Chopin to his friend Titus Wojciechowski," ostensibly represents a collection of letters, but the first-person

form does not preclude conversational presentation: "As Mendelssohn said:
'... apparently he is (I am!) greatly troubled ...' Lamentation and obstinacy /
as if he (I) had lain on the naked ground and upon awakening felt the urge,
seizing the entire universe like a child by its shoulders, to whirl it high into
the tough atmospheres, yes, high into the incomprehensible atmospheric regions." Chopin's contemporaries thus play a role, as do modern artists such as
Artaud, Magritte, and Duchamp, in an interpenetration of the author's age
and experience with that of the narrator-protagonist. A flashback to the narrator's childhood includes also the childhood of his lover, revealing diverse pasts
that are fictively united, and memory is metaphorically motivated as an attempt
to photograph a person through to his "future age" and thus to achieve a "feeling of simultaneity." Sensitivity and creativity are displayed in a flow of verbal
rhetoric, and "thus we hold ourselves to the strict firmness of form (and pour
into it the boiling life, whose diversity exceeds our knowledge)."

Fictive relationships among the triad Robert and Clara Schumann and Brahms
constitute Part Two, which gives its title to the entire work. The impact of
the piece lies in the contrast between the animated conversations of Clara and
Brahms, on the one hand, in which she sees in him an "inclination to the idyllic"
and he in her the "nature child," and in the background, the silence of Robert
Schumann in a state of depressive isolation with apprehensions of approaching
insanity and death. The silence also of the authorial voice in this section, in
contrast to the others, adds to the tension, with speechlessness pointing to a
realm beyond human comprehension. Part Three, "Odéon Bruckner's Wasteland," presents the figure as an awkward anachronistic outsider engrossed in
a series of monologues/dialogues with himself and a first-person interlocutor,
who is identified with both the character and the author Bruckner and Mayröcker. Relationship is established on the basis of their centenary birth years—
1824 and 1924, respectively—1924 also being the year of Breton's First Sur-
realist Manifesto, which is seen as the common meeting ground of their artistic
impulses. Fatigue and despair follow the death of the child, and the elusiveness
of character is conveyed by obscurity of metaphor. As in music, there is
throughout a precarious equilibrium between theme and development, between
an ever richer expression of the subjective feeling and its objective working out
in the form itself. Form corresponds exactly to both content and intent, as the
subject is revealed to be not starting point but destination, and in the dialectical
interaction of forces the tension is so exact that it paradoxically appears as
peace.

Since Schubert's position at the culmination of the series is not chronological, motivation must be sought elsewhere, and one looks to form. The literal

and metaphorical "Weather Notations" record purely phenomenological experiences, reflecting the same artistic impulse and displaying the same spontaneous improvisation as his warm and open melodies, which unify the arts of poetry and music. Schubert, more than any other, put his entire existence into the creative process; musical life is presented as synonymous with personal life and both are interwoven in expressions of unrequited love: "Excuse me when I write so unreservedly–but the cherry trees." It is a creative vision which sees things ever more simply and ever more clearly, through to "here, here is my end." Closure, which is otherwise formally avoided in Mayröcker's texts, is here effected by a heart-rending statement, which, in its daring proximity to intolerable cliché, appropriately expresses the depth of emotion of the artist Schubert-Mayröcker: "Then one had to stop because all the women were crying."[14] There has been a progressive shift through the four sections of the work from a desire to speak to the fall of silence: Chopin's communicative, loquacious letters, Clara Schumann's easy conversations with Brahms, Bruckner's reluctant dialogue with a partner masking as alter ego, and Schubert's minimal verbalization, at once superfluous and inefficacious, even if only to the self, which expresses itself so much more completely in music. In such abbreviated form, silence is as significant as sound, and language transcends its limitations of referentiality to approach the purer expression of music.

Authorial identification with the artist figures in this work is characteristic of Mayröcker's stance in general, for whether the form be "biography" or prose fiction, poetry or radio play, the texts basically concern one central question, namely that of artistic creativity. An authorial statement in the epilogue of *Heisze Hunde* (Hot Hounds) appears almost verbatim in *Heiligenanstalt* as the words of Chopin, which a loose translation might render as follows: "It is less a question of being inspired than of maintaining a continual openness (non-suspendable vulnerability) to the world." The muse of modern art is revealed, not as an external power transmitting inspiration from on high, but as a personal, internal capacity–cognitive, emotive, volitional–to live and to experience life to the fullest. Art is part of life, and artistic creation ultimately has its source in what it means to be most human.

Mayröcker and Jandl, in a discussion of poetic technique, consider the question of how "to avoid perfection."[15] Whereas that problem does not arise for most of us, what is meant here by "perfection" is over-determination; a formulation so complete that nothing remains to be said; a fixity of any kind that would prevent further change and thus result in closure. In a process view, such as Mayröcker's, life and art are regarded as dynamic movement; immobility is inimical to development, and the arrestment present in a "still life" is tantamount to death, as expressed by the French *nature morte.* "Imperfection" is therefore valued for its provocative effect and indeterminate result. Whereas this has led some artists to sabotage their own work (e.g., mutilation of the painterly canvas, technically impossible musical scores), indeterminacy is here achieved by open-ended structures, intentionally displaying unresolved tension and thus promoting further activity. The centrality of process and change is also part of the reason for the focus on relations rather than objects, for relations are generated by the confrontation of diverse fields of energy and are further perpetuated by their own inner dynamics; they are hence involved in constant change: a *perpetuum mobile.*

That term could serve to describe Mayröcker's entire literary production, which, over the past three decades, demonstrates change and development while maintaining an essential continuity and unity. The author's variable course through diverse genre represents an exploration of linguistic media and a testing of the limits of form, for a writer is first and foremost an artisan of language who aspires to consummate mastery of the means. From the intense encounter with art in *Tod durch Musen* to the richness of poetic perception in *Das Licht in der Landschaft,* from the materialistic reduction of culture in *Metaphysisches Theater* to the visionary expansion of language in *Die Abschiede,* the texts are implicated one in another, evolving from and revolving around one central theme: perception-transformation-creation. It is a phoenix-like death and resurrection of the work of art (and the artist) out of the ashes of life, and it could be viewed as a dialectic, were not the term preempted by causal and teleological systems of thought. What appears as dialectic might be better described as reciprocal interaction of forces, an activity which rejects the limitations entailed in categorization and abstraction. Transformation is, of course, the crux of the matter, and the creative process will probably always remain the mystery it is portrayed to be in the prototypical instance of music and silence in *Heiligenanstalt.*

Art is not a theory but rather continual exploration, and one would "explain" it only in order not to have to experience it, whereby a critical notion is inserted, or rather, built in, by scrupulous self-regulatory powers. Art is experience — certainly for the creator, but also for the receiver, who is an accomplice in the discovery and invention of meanings. If a reader occasionally loses his/her bearings in a text, that is not so different from his/her encounters in the world, and an artist exploits the uncertainty of the situation as a source of creative strength. Reality inheres not in a counterfeit integration of life but in a scattering of random souvenirs, whose charm derives from the inviting spaces between them. Valorization is by experience, not by institutional analysis, and the critic can only hope that the "imperfections" of the present study will direct the reader to the greater freedom and vitality of art.*

Notes

1. 1975; cited by Gisela Lindemann, "Friederike Mayröcker," in *Kritisches Lexikon zur deutschsprachigen Gegenwartsliteratur: KLG,* ed. Heinz Ludwig Arnold (München: edition text + kritik, 197f.), 3 Nlg., p. 5. Translations throughout are my own unless otherwise noted.

2. The monograph *jardin pour friederike mayröcker* (Linz: neue texte 20/21, 1978) presents an interesting collection of material by, for, and about Mayröcker. *Protokolle* (1980/1982) devoted an entire volume to the publication of literary and critical texts in her honor. See also the essays by Viktor Suchy, "Poesie und Poiesis, dargestellt am Werke Friederike Mayröckers," in *Die Andere Welt. Festschrift für Hellmuth Himmel* (Bern: Francke, 1979, pp. 341-358; Gisela Lindemann, "Einleitung," in *Friederike Mayröcker, Ein Lesebuch* (Frankfurt: Suhrkamp, 1979), pp. 7-17. Numerous reviews and isolated commentaries on her works have appeared, but scholarly investigation largely remains to be done.

3. Kurt Klinger, "Poetische Phänomenologie: Friederike Mayröcker," in *Kindlers Literaturgeschichte der Gegenwart. Die zeitgenössische Literatur Österreichs,* ed. Hilde Spiel (Zürich: Kindler, 1976), pp. 436-441.

4. Walter Höllerer, "Thesen zum langen Gedicht," *Akzente,* 2 (1965), 128-130; Gerald Bisinger, "Eine österreichische Variante des 'langen Gedichts,'" *Sprache im technischen Zeitalter,* 17/18 (1966), 137-139.

5. Ernst Jandl, "Die poetische Syntax in den Gedichten von Friederike Mayröcker," and "Versuch, zu einem Gedicht von Friederike Mayröcker etwas zu sagen," *Modern Austrian Literature,* 12 (1979), 237-265 and 267-271; Gisela Lindemann, "'. . . und um mich zu lindern . . . ein Frühlingsgrab,'" *Literatur und Kritik,* 165-166 (1982), 64-73; Beth Bjorklund, "The Austrian Avant-garde as Represented by Friederike Mayröcker," *poesis,* 5 (1984), 48-67.

6. See Ernst Jandl, "Ein neuer poetischer Raum. Zur Prosa von Friederike Mayröcker," in *Festschrift für Adolf D. Klarmann,* ed. Karl S. Weimar (München: Delp, 1974), pp. 285-290; "On the Alleged Incomprehensibility of Modern Poetry: Friederike Mayröcker's Experimental Forms," *Österreich in amerikanischer Sicht,* 2 (1981), 1-9.

7. "Radical Transformation and Magical Synthesis: Interview with Friederike

Mayröcker," by Beth Bjorklund, *The Literary Review,* 25 (1982), 223. Further statements by the author have appeared in the following volumes: *Ein Gedicht und sein Autor,* ed. Walter Höllerer (Berlin: Literarisches Colloguium, 1967), pp. 363-371; *Grenzverschiebungen,* ed. Renate Matthaei (Köln: Kiepenheuer und Witsch, 1970), pp. 237-242; "DADA," *Sprache im technischen Zeitalter,* 55 (1975), 230-231.

8.   In an authorial comment on this text Mayröcker mentions as motivating factors events that have little or nothing to do with the "events" in the text; see "Zu 'Fast ein Frühling des Markus M.,'" *manuskripte,* 52 (1976), 58-59. For interpretation see Lisa Kahn, "Ein Fall von Wahlverwandt-schaft: Kandinsky-Mayröcker," *Literatur und Kritik,* 142 (1980), 106–110; Lisa Kahn, "Mayröckers Markus M.: Welt steter Wandlungen," *Literatur und Kritik,* 165-166 (1982), 73-78.

9.   The following passage represents one of numerous instances: "Almost asexual, even if born female" (from the radio play "Ein Schatten am Weg zur Erde" in *rot ist unten).* Sexuality is indeed an important theme in Mayröcker's works, but activists will look in vain for a "feminist" stance, for male/female sensibilities are seen as subsumed under the common, higher denominator of human existence. The author has addressed herself to this currently topical question in "Über meine Arbeit mich zu äußern," *Protokolle* (1980/1982), 49.

10. T. S. Eliot, "The Dry Salvages," *Four Quartets,* in *The Complete Poems and Plays 1909-1950* (New York: Harcourt, Brace & Co., 1958), p. 136.

11. Paul Celan, *Die Niemandsrose* (Frankfurt: Fischer, 1963), p. 19.

12. John Keats, "Letter to his Brothers," 22 December 1817, in *Poems and Letters of John Keats* (Boston: Houghton Mifflin, 1925), p. 277.

13. Alain Robbe-Grillet, *For a New Novel: Essays on Fiction,* trans. Richard Howard (Freeport, NY: Books for Libraries Press, 1965), p. 33; see also Nathalie Sarraute, *The Age of Suspicion: Essays on the Novel,* trans. Maria Jolas (New York: George Braziller, 1963).

14. Theodor W. Adorno comments similarly on the effects of Schubert's music in *Moments musicaux* (Frankfurt: Suhrkamp, 1964), pp. 18-36.

15. Ernst Jandl/Friederike Mayröcker, "Anmerkungen zum Hörspiel," in *Neues Hörspiel. Essays, Analysen, Gespräche,* ed. Klaus Schöning (Frankfurt: Suhrkamp, 1970), p. 90.

*This project was supported in part by a grant from the National Endowment for the Humanities, to whom I would like to express my gratitude.

Primary Texts

Larifari. Wien: Bergland Verlag, 1956.

metaphorisch. Stuttgart: rot-reihe, 1965.

texte. Innsbruck: Allerheiligenpresse, 1966.

* *Tod durch Musen. Poetische Texte.* Reinbek: Rowohlt Verlag, 1966; rpt. Darmstadt: Luchterhand Verlag, 1973.

Sägespäne für mein Herzbluten. Berlin: rainer-verlag, 1967; rpt. 1973.

* *Minimonsters Traumlexikon. Texte in Prosa.* Reinbek: Rowohlt Verlag, 1968.

* *Fantom Fan.* Reinbek: Rowohlt Verlag, 1971.

* *Fünf Mann Menschen,* with Ernst Jandl. Darmstadt: Luchterhand Verlag, 1971.

Sinclair Sofokles der Babysaurier, illus. Angelika Kaufmann. Wien: Verlag Jugend und Volk, 1971; trans. Moore/Hayward. New York: Random House, 1974.

* *Arie auf tönernen Füszen. Metaphysisches Theater.* Darmstadt: Luchterhand Verlag, 1972.

Blaue Erleuchtungen. Erste Gedichte. Düsseldorf: Verlag Eremiten Presse, 1972.

TRAUBE, with Ernst Jandl and Heinz von Cramer. (TV film) Westdeutscher Rundfunk; rpt. in *Protokolle* (1972/2).

* *je ein umwölkter gipfel. erzählung.* Darmstadt: Luchterhand Verlag, 1973.

Augen wie Schaljapin bevor er starb. Dornbirn: Vorarlberger Verlagsanstalt, 1974.

In langsamen Blitzen. Berlin: Literarisches Colloquium Berlin, 1974.

meine träume ein flügelkleid. Düsseldorf: Verlag Eremiten Presse, 1974.

* *Das Licht in der Landschaft.* Frankfurt: Suhrkamp Verlag, 1975.

schriftungen oder gerüchte aus dem jenseits. Pfaffenweiler: Pfaffenweiler Presse, 1975.

Drei Hörspiele. Wien: Thomas Sessler Verlag, 1975.

SPRECHKLAVIER (stereo record) Wien: preiser-records, 1975.

* *Fast ein Frühling des Markus M.* Frankfurt: Suhrkamp Verlag, 1976.

Heisze Hunde. Pfaffenweiler: Pfaffenweiler Presse, 1977.

lütt' koch. Wien: herbst presse, 1977.

rot ist unten. Wien: Verlag Jugend und Volk, 1977.

* *Heiligenanstalt.* Frankfurt: Suhrkamp Verlag, 1978.

Schwarmgesang—Szenen für die poetische Bühne. Berlin: rainer verlag, 1978.

* *Ausgewählte Gedichte. 1944-1978.* Frankfurt: Suhrkamp Verlag, 1979.

* *Friederike Mayröcker. Ein Lesebuch,* ed. Gisela Lindemann. Frankfurt:

Suhrkamp Verlag, 1979.
Tochter der Bahn. Düsseldorf: Verlag Ermiten Presse, 1979.
Pegas, das Pferd. Salzburg: Verlag Neugebauer, 1980.
* *Die Abschiede.* Frankfurt: Suhrkamp Verlag, 1980.
* *Gute Nacht, guten Morgen.* Frankfurt: Suhrkamp Verlag, 1982.
* *Magische Blätter.* Frankfurt: Suhrkamp Verlag, 1983.
Im Nervensaal, Himmel am zwölften Mai. Wien: Herbstpresse, 1983.
Das Anheben der Arme bei Feuersglut. Stuttgart: Reclam, 1984.
* *Reise durch die Nacht.* Frankfurt: Suhrkamp, 1984.
Rosengarten. Pfaffenweiler: Pfaffenweiler Presse, 1984.

(An asterisk marks the most important works, in my estimation.)

English Translations of Selected Prose and Poetry

Bjorklund, Beth. *The Literary Review,* 25 (1982), 222-231.
Elzay, Michael P. *Dimension,* 4 (1971), 178-191; 6 (1973), 100-105 and 522-529; 8 (1975), 252-265.
Hamburger, Michael. *German Poetry 1910-1975,* ed. M. Hamburger. New York: Persea Books, 1977, pp. 344-345.
Middleton, Christopher. *Modern Poetry in Translation,* 40 (1980), 5-8.
Watts, Harriett. *The Malahat Review,* 37 (1976), 18-19.
Willson, A. Leslie. *Dimension,* 7 (1974), 214-247.
Wynand, Derk. *The Malahat Review,* 37 (1976), 17; *The Chicago Review,* 29 (1978), 132-135.

Selected List of Secondary Literature

Friederike Mayröcker, ed. Siegfried J. Schmidt. Frankfurt: Suhrkamp, 1984.
jardin pour friederike mayröcker. Linz: neue texte, 1978.
Protokolle, 2 (1980).
text + kritik, 84 (1984).

Gerhard Roth

Sigrid Bauschinger

Gerhard Roth's beginnings as an author are closely connected to the artists' association Forum Stadtpark in the city of Graz, the capital of the southeastern Austrian province of Styria. The peace of Graz was somewhat disturbed when in 1960 a group of writers, painters, photographers, film-makers, musicians, and architects overcame the obstacles put in their way by a conservative city administration and opened the Forum Stadtpark as a place to exhibit, perform, and discuss their art. At the same time the first issue of the literary magazine *manuskripte* was published, changing the course of contemporary Austrian literature.

The members of Forum Stadtpark were to a certain extent rebels. In the fourth issue of *manuskripte* (1962) we find a youthfully aggressive text that attacks the Austrian cultural establishment in forceful language:

> What is going on around us? There are people who believe they can gouge the eyes out of the face of our time . . . without knowing that somewhere behind the doors . . . a new place, a different life has been created and that the language of elementary schools spoken by the barbarians of tradition has become consumptive. Whoever is still talking of eternal values, unchangeable norms of art, infallible truths and forms, of wise harmony with nature, . . . is lying. If he is a believer, he is selling his faith to that saturated certainty; if he is an artist, he loses his expression. . . . Those who fight the nihilism of the western world are the true nihilists, because they cannot create life anymore but only open graves. . . .[1]

Gerhard Roth, born in 1942 in Graz as the son of a physician, was too young to belong to the founding fathers of Forum Stadtpark. For the medical student, however, this meeting place, where very different but also like-minded spirits agreed to occupy themselves with the "most recent forms of literary and artistic representation,"[2] became a place of great importance. Several of his earliest publications appeared in *manuskripte*.

Roth did not finish his medical studies. Instead, he joined the Graz Center for Statistics in 1966 and later became its manager. Since 1978 he has been living as an independent writer in Graz and in a small Styrian village. He has been awarded several prizes and fellowships in Austria and in the Federal Republic of Germany, most notably the prize of the Southwestern Broadcasting System (Preis des Literaturmagazins des Südwestfunks) in 1978, a fellowship of the City of Hamburg in 1979, and in 1983 the very prestigious Alfred Döblin Prize, which was established by Günter Grass and is awarded each year to the most promising younger German writer.

Gerhard Roth was recognized as some sort of a literary genius as soon as his first book was published in 1972. *die autobiographie des albert einstein* (the autobiography of albert einstein), identified by the author as a novel, opened his literary career with a considerable bang. During the next three years Roth published texts of a highly experimental nature. However, he captured the attention of readers and critics with his artistic constructions of scientific data, parody, elements of detective stories, criticisms of language and rationalism, and an impressive talent for transposing observations into descriptions: "Instead of psychology and plot: language and observation."[3] In *albert einstein* he observes an Austrian "technical expert, 3rd class" who imagines himself to be Albert Einstein and who suffers from hypersensitivity as an observer. He is unable to select from the impressions gained through the fifteen billion nerve cells in the brain or the four hundred thousand scanning elements in the eyes in order to perceive a "normal" view of the world. This einstein is an obsessed observer of details; his author's main task is to recreate the growing mania of observation in a language that parallels in its development that of einstein's illness, schizophrenia.

This *tour de force* passes through three stages. In the first part of the novel "the voyeur" einstein is unable to stay in his room. He walks the streets of a big city, presumably Vienna, following passersby, observing and imitating them. Soon he feels that he is being observed as a suspicious person. His schizophrenic condition becomes apparent by such behavior as relating every observation to Nietzsche or by attempting to see everything in the color blue. In the second part, "walks through the cerebrum," einstein directs his attention toward himself. His destructive impulses turn self-destructive. Every positive aspect of his life is changed into something negative. ("health is a fart," "work is a torture," "justice is an execution.") Proverbs are turned into their opposites and become self-accusations. His self-observations, such as his description of getting up in the morning, are of minute intensity. In this stage einstein rebels not only against the limitations of his life, but also against the limitations of conventional structures of thinking and writing. Finally, in the third part, "the observateur," einstein not only observes, but also describes himself as an object with scientific accuracy. His illness, his anatomy, his entire body are the source of ever more minute details, which in the end can no longer be captured by language: it disintegrates like einstein's mind. The novel ends with the report of an autopsy performed on a male corpse who died of hemorrhaging.

The basic elements of Roth's first novel reappear in the remaining works during his experimental phase, and, as we shall see, also in his later and apparently different books. In 1975 he published another volume with three texts. *Künstel* (1975) a fragment, presents the reader with a relative of einstein. *Künstel*—his name reminds one of something artificial ("gekünstelt")—who lives alone in a rented room in Vienna, is also an obsessive observer of himself and his environment. This time Roth chooses short passages, sometimes no more than three sentences, to demonstrate Künstel's mania. Again this mania leads to disaster: because many observations, be they of the afflictions of his own body or of the wall of a men's room, are of a most irritating nature. Künstel is finally also driven to madness. At the end of the fragment he kills his landlady.

The two parodies published together with the *Künstel* fragment, *Der Ausbruch des Ersten Weltkriegs* (*The Outbreak of World War I: A Spy Novel*) and *How to Be a Detective: A Crime Novel*, are closely related. We do not learn anything about the beginnings of World War I in this book except that we are becoming aware of impending disaster and a sick society. Instead, we are led onto a surrealistic stageset with an early nineteenth-century cast. Here Roth makes use of a montage technique, incorporating names of characters and entire phrases from Joseph Roth's novel *Der stumme Prophet* (The Mute Prophet) and Giuseppe Tomasi de Lampedusa's *Il Gattopardo*. A close analysis of this "spy novel" would show the strong influence of early film techniques, especially surrealistic movies by Hans Richter and Luis Buñuel. Fast cuts, abrupt movements, unexpected developments in every passage give this kaleidoscope of miniplots a quite witty air. Roth's technique has also been compared to that of the surrealistic painter Max Ernst.[4]

The same techniques are employed in *How to Be a Detective: A Crime Novel*. Roth uses this English title for a story in sixty-nine installments, acknowledging for the first time his predilection for that genre. His earlier protagonists einstein and Künstel had been observers and thus detectives of some kind. In *How to Be a Detective*, however, the detective story is parodied. Kommissar Potter behaves more like the hunted criminal than the hunting detective. In dadaistic short scenes and remarkably brief paratactic sentences he is described as literally throwing evidence out of the window; in the last installment he is shot dead before solving his non-case. The influence of surrealistic movies is again evident. Animals, mostly vermin, crawl all over, reminding the reader of films like Salvador Dali's and Luis Buñuel's *Chien Andalou*. Objects fly in and out of windows, flowers explode, and everything happens with incredible speed.

With the novel *Der Wille zur Krankheit* (1973, The Will for Illness) Roth's first experimental phase comes to an end. It is at the same time a summing up of his previous work and a pointing forward to his later development. The common denominator of both, the earlier as well as the later narratives, is the importance of observation, which determines their language and their themes.

In *Der Wille zur Krankheit* a young man named Kalb, probably a student of medicine and definitely a brother of einstein and Künstel, collects observations even through a magnifying glass, such as examining how his thumb squashes a fly. He is especially fascinated by unexpected observations ("the unexpected always spits out new images"[5]) and every image, even one as unpleasant as the symptom of an illness, has an aesthetic value.

Like albert einstein and Künstel, Kalb suffers from the supersensitivity of the manic observer, which leads to a veritable intoxication. However, unlike his two schizophrenic predecessors, who are destroyed by their illness, Kalb neither gets killed like einstein nor kills like Künstel. Rather he accepts his illness: "When he thought to recognize the feeling of illness in himself, he felt a strange satisfaction."[6] The author uses his own medical knowledge to develop his protagonist's gift for observation. The motif of seeing and the eye as metaphor predominate throughout the text. Also evident is Roth's pleasure in letting his character play the role of detective. Kalb occasionally imagines himself to be a private eye; when he sees a movie about a photographer who becomes entangled in a murder case, this little episode points already to Roth's novel, *Ein neuer Morgen* (1979, A New Morning), where it becomes the main plot.

Der Wille zur Krankheit gives proof of Roth's development within six years. Between 1967, when he began to write *die autobiographie des albert einstein*, and 1973, with *der Wille zur Krankheit*, his language becomes more economical, the observations of his characters more realistic, and his descriptions more impressive.

Gerhard Roth also ventured into the dramatic genre. His play *Lichtenberg*, first performed in 1973, belongs to the group of experimental works. Combining elements of the Viennese theater tradition (Nestroy) with circus elements and motifs of Georg Büchner's *Woyzeck*, it depicts a slick, eloquent professor who tries to prove that a young feeble-minded man, called "the object," has murdered a woman. In the end the object strikes back and shoots the professor. This play is not, however, a surrealistic "comedy of errors." Like Peter Handke's plays *Das Mündel will Vormund sein* (*My Foot, My Tutor*) and *Kaspar*, *Lichtenberg* is about language: power and language are identical, until a speechless and powerless "object" reveals his force.

Sehnsucht (Desire) was first performed in 1977, both in Graz during the "Styrian Fall" Festival, directed by Wolfgang Bauer, and in Basel. In this play Roth has left his experimental phase behind, just as in his prose writing. Here an egocentric writer is shown amidst his family and friends in his summer house gradually talking himself into "a crisis of guilt and damaged feelings." Finally, in *Dämmerung* (Dusk), first performed in Graz in 1978, the family and employees of a mine director assemble in the garden of a country inn after his funeral. Again Roth makes use of techniques and motifs of the southern German theater tradition — Brecht's *Die Kleinbürgerhochzeit* (1919, Wedding of the Petit Bourgeois), Horváth's cruelty of the lower middle class, and the great Munich comic Karl Valentin — all have contributed to this unpleasant portrait of a group of people who are finally blown apart by an approaching thunderstorm.

Gerhard Roth seems to have lost his interest in the drama, having realized that his strength lies in prose writing, especially prose of a descriptive nature. This talent also becomes very obvious in the volume *Menschen, Bilder, Marionetten* (1979, People, Pictures, Marionettes), a collection of his early short novels, three plays, and short texts written between 1972 and 1978. Roth always prefers to write about an event or an experience that produces pictures, be it the studio of a painter friend in Graz, a soccer match in Paris, or a dogcart race. Many first impressions later incorporated into his novels are to be found in this collection. As in his longer works the analytical texts are in the minority and are less convincing. If one applies Georg Lukács's categories of narration and description to Roth's works, they definitely belong to the latter. Their author is thus to be seen in the Austrian literary tradition of great descriptive writers from Adalbert Stifter to Peter Handke.

This fact, however, also caused problems for Roth. After he had finished *Der Wille zur Krankheit,* he must have realized that he could not go on indefinitely describing schizophrenic characters, even if with every new book he further perfected his methods. At the same time he became overwhelmed by his desire to get away from describing the observations of his characters and to make them act, so that he as their author could at last narrate a plot. In this crisis Gerhard Roth made a fateful decision, which influenced his writing more than anything else so far: he visited the United States.

In the spring of 1973 Roth and his Austrian writer colleague Wolfgang Bauer took a trip to America, visiting San Francisco, Los Angeles, Las Vegas, and New York. These cities in this sequence provide the background for Roth's new novel, which in many respects gives proof of the author's remarkable development. *Der große Horizont* (The Great Horizon) was published in 1974, only one year after Roth's journey. Although there is a continuation in the use of topics, motifs, and themes from his earlier period, the change in Roth's writing, especially in his language, is obvious. America taught him a new way of seeing—and consequently of describing—and it intensified his desire to narrate. "I want to be a narrator," Roth told Ulrich Greiner in an interview,[7] showing him a trunk full of plastic bags filled with notebooks and photographs taken during the trip to the United States, material for descriptions which, as we will see, continued to be the substance of Roth's works even after he passed the watershed of his American experience.

Der große Horizont is a much more traditional novel than any of Roth's previous experimental works. It tells the story of the Viennese book dealer Daniel Haid, a thirty-eight-year-old man "with poetic and hypochondriac feelings," who after a painful divorce from his wife travels to the United States to see several friends. In San Francisco, where during the first leg of his journey he visits his friend Mehring, a university professor, disaster strikes. The female student Carson, who rents a room from Mehring and with whom Haid spends two nights, dies in her sleep while Haid is still with her. From this moment on he becomes a fugitive, bringing every passerby, every event into relation with Carson's death. He is convinced that the police are conducting a carefully concealed manhunt for him. Whether he spends a few days with an architect friend in Santa Monica or goes to Las Vegas with a new acquaintance (a Los Angeles police reporter, of all people) or roams the streets of New York City, by then really sick, he is constantly trying to find out who is watching him and where the next stakeout is.

In New York he stays first with Christine, a friend from his university days, who is now married to a wealthy banker. After renewing their former brief relationship he moves to a hotel, where suddenly the Los Angeles police reporter appears. Haid, afraid of being detected as Carson's murderer, knocks him out, but O'Malley only wants to return the money he had borrowed in Las Vegas. Just as this error of Haid's is clarified, his weeks of fear come to an end in a fast and rather incredible development. O'Malley drives Haid through the cemetery landscape of Long Island, where the view of the Manhattan skyline becomes a vision: a city of paradise rises behind the tombstones standing on both sides of the highway. This experience has a liberating effect on Haid. He is now able to call his friend in San Francisco and he learns that Carson had been suffering from a heart ailment, and nobody had ever suspected him of having killed her. The next morning Haid watches a little boy on sunny Washington Square. He recalls his own childhood and the only person he ever truly loved, his grandfather, and feels this love, "as if nothing could ever happen to him."[8]

Up to the last pages of the novel Haid's obsessions are so strong because he is still a relative of his predecessors, einstein, Künstel, and Kalb. Although more of a hypochondriac than a schizophrenic, he is nevertheless also an observer, not so much of scientific details in his environment or of his own body but of himself as another person, his own double. This double even has a name: he is Philip Marlowe, the private eye from Raymond Chandler's detective stories. Even before Carson's death Haid has been playing Marlowe's role, walking through San Francisco, following people at random, once even entering an apartment house to ring at the door behind which, he is convinced by observation from his hotel room opposite the apartment, a man has just strangled a woman. The woman, however, opens the door and Haid realizes he must have witnessed a rather passionate love scene.

Just as *Der große Horizont* is not a novel about America, Daniel Haid's Philip Marlowe is not Raymond Chandler's character. One could find such parallels between Chandler and Roth as the development from scene to scene and the relative unimportance of plot as well as the rather unsatisfactory endings of their novels. There are also such similarities as the attention given to cars: never is a car mentioned by either Chandler or Roth without its make and possibly its color. This stylistic element points toward the preoccupation of both authors with observation and descriptions. But as far as Philip Marlowe and Daniel Haid are concerned, they are literally characters from two different worlds. Marlowe has been described as an angry and bitter man, melancholic but with gallows humor and a definite private code of humanitas.[9] He is a man with strong social concerns, detesting those who enrich themselves through exploitation of others, be it by criminal or so-called legal means. He instinctively sides with the weak and defenseless. His relationships with his fellow human beings are far different from those of the hypochondriac Daniel Haid, as can be seen in their feelings toward women. Marlowe is susceptible to female beauty but at the same time able to control himself heroically; Haid, however, always had "to give himself up," to lose his identity, and play the role of the intelligent, witty man in love in order to win a woman, even if it was only to spend one night with her. All his relationships so far had been dominated by fear of refusal, as had happened with his wife; only after he got used to a woman and a little bored with her could he behave in a more relaxed manner.

Daniel Haid's inability to form a spontaneous, uninhibited relationship extends to his social behavior in general. He seems to attract the hatred and inimical feelings of others, just as he is obsessed by his criticism and aversion that extends to self-hatred. In San Francisco when he watches, without helping, an epileptic having a seizure, Haid hates himself for it. But much more numerous

are the incidents in which he displays disdain for people and events around him.
Hardly anyone who spends a lifetime in New York City or San Francisco would
have as many opportunities to observe repulsive scenes as does this Viennese
book dealer in a few days. Riding in an airport limousine toward Manhattan,
he watches a black couple have sexual intercourse in a passing Buick. This
highly improbable episode sets the tone for innumerable other occurrences,
in many of which Haid is not only the observer but the victim. Passersby whom
he asks for directions don't reply but give him hateful glances as they cross
the street. When he checks out of his San Francisco hotel, the angry old woman
at the desk curses him, refusing to accept his check. As soon as he steps out
of the building, a drunken black man hits him, demanding money. In Las Vegas
he is knocked down by a Filipino whom he has seen "intentionally kicking
the shoe off a white man's heel," while the doorman of the hotel watches
"coldly and full of contempt."[10]

Nearly every person is characterized by race. When Haid visits a university
in New York with his friend Christine, he sees her talking to a "fat Jewish
German scholar." Soon after he watches a black woman dressed in white pushing
a cart with urine samples across the street, a sight "which had something strangely surrealistic."[11] His mounting paranoia makes him allergic to individuals and
crowds like that in a Times Square restaurant, where he feels himself observed
by policemen among "pensioners with prostate ailments, Jewish bank tellers,
blacks with venereal diseases, prostitutes . . . feeble-minded nannies and run-
down actors."[12] It is obvious that Haid's reactions toward others are actually
reactions toward himself. He should be able to avoid situations and places that
arouse his hatred so easily, but he is a character without much—or sometimes
any—willpower. He cannot say no. Thus he follows a drunk into a Times Square
movie theater as if he were pulled into it. There he sits among a "colored stink-
ing audience with screaming children, chatting women, and hostile staring
blacks."[13]

Roth also attempts to discuss his views of America in more theoretical
terms. Periodically we find short passages in which his protagonist contemplates
the American system. As can be expected, Haid's thoughts are not very friendly,
for they are always prompted by his unpleasant observations. In San Francisco
a disheveled man without socks bumps into people, while a black pushes an
aluminum cup into Haid's stomach shouting "CASH!" "He hated America
at this moment. A society with the wealth and greatness of America lived
undisturbed with the big mass of beggars, alcoholics, and despairing, as if they
were necessary for the society or as if one knew that all this was totally natural
according to the plan of creation and would exist in all eternity."[14] Such rather

unoriginal remarks alternate with such a reflection as: "What mechanisms are at work in this country that romanticism constantly breaks into civilization?"[15] Perhaps even crime is a romantic protest in America? Any kind of refusal to adapt to this civilization is welcome. "At this moment Haid understood and loved those young Americans who, dressed as Buddhist monks, offered their leaflets."[16] But even with the help of quotations from Max Horkheimer, the philosopher, sociologist, and authority on mass culture and mass society, these sparse theoretical observations are of a superficial kind. They disappear entirely from the novel after Haid realizes that—whatever he feels while watching an epileptic or an old man from Chinatown who appears to him to be the wise old Hermann Hesse—he always feels personally "with unbearable intensity."[17]

This is also why Haid walks through American cities thinking of his grandfather, who wanted to go to America but had stowed away on the wrong ship and ended up in Cardiff instead. What would have happened to this man had he reached his American destination? What and who would Haid be? Roth does not explore this possibility of Haid's American identity much further, but it is one of the more interesting ideas in the entire novel.

Daniel Haid belongs to the growing cast of characters in contemporary German literature whose creators, beginning in the fifties, have traveled to the United States and have incorporated their impressions in their writings. They all brought their image of America with them, and it was their task to transform their vision into something new after it had met with the American reality. In many instances they succumbed to the lures of sensationalism or were unable to overcome their own narrow ideological limits. In some cases, such as Ingeborg Bachmann's radio play *Der gute Gott von Manhattan* (1963, The Good God of Manhattan), truly great works of twentieth-century German literature were created.

Gerhard Roth's first novel incorporating his American experience is remarkably free of factual errors (except that in one instance Haid buys the *New York Times* to read the comics!). On the other hand, he has certainly not reached the poetic objectivity of a work like that of Bachmann. Daniel Haid's view is still too provincial, owing to the personal crisis that he is trying to overcome. Roth lets him achieve his goal in the end, but the author is unable to prepare the reader for the unexpected conclusion. It seems like a superficial attachment to the book. Nevertheless, Roth gives an idea of the true literary possibilities that the topos of America always has to offer, as in the grandiose vision of the Manhattan skyline rising behind the cemeteries of Long Island, "as if there lay a no-man's land between the living and the dead in which Haid found himself at that moment,"[18] looking toward the great horizon into paradise.

This episode is followed immediately by a visit to the Museum of Modern Art, where Haid sees an exhibition of photojournalism from New York tabloids, pictures of murder victims, criminals, and suicides. These two experiences express the two faces of the city and the entire country, which Roth was not quite able to unite into a single vision. The experience of America, however, greatly enriched his language, which gained a new poetic quality. Sitting in a New York taxicab, "Haid felt how the view of the street captivated his attention more and more, how it had become poetic for him, and he asked himself whether this form of the poetic was not connected to something poetic that had its roots in crime. It was certainly this form of the poetic which Philip Marlowe had created in Chandler's mind."[19] Gerhard Roth had become a different writer because of his American experience.

Roth incorporated his American impressions into a second novel that was generally not well received. Compared to *Der große Horizont, Ein neuer Morgen* (1976, A New Morning) is a smoother, more polished work, but it also lacks the emotional strength of the previous novel, thanks to the passive nature of one of the two main characters, whose story is told in the much longer first part of the book. Weininger, a thirty-three-year-old Austrian photographer, is working on a pictorial book about New York. He meets an American, Norman Dalton, and his girlfriend, Patricia, with whom he begins an affair. On his first outing with Dalton to the New York Stock Exchange Weininger realizes that his friend is being followed; soon afterward he finds the corpse of this pursuer in Dalton's slum quarters in the Bowery. The rest of Weininger's story is a sequence of strange events experienced by the Austrian photographer, who is constantly taking pictures, and by Patricia, who also turns out to know very little about Dalton. The plot culminates at the New York Easter Parade, when a private detective named Olson, whom Weininger has met in the meantime, kills the miraculously resurrected man whose corpse Weininger had found in Dalton's room. Olson in turn is killed by a policeman. Before he dies he is able to hand to Patricia an envelope from Dalton containing airplane tickets to Genoa and Cannes. She and Weininger depart immediately and meet Dalton on the Riviera where, in the short second part of the novel, he tells them his story.

Norman Dalton, actually Robert Fin, was a very ordinary person, a bank teller in Minneapolis, working at the same bank for thirty years and raising a family. He always felt that he was denied his own identity, exploited by his work as well as by his family. When he realizes how many hours of his life he has already sold by leading a proper professional and family life, which he hates, he undertakes an embezzling scheme. After all, the bank could never repay him for all of his lost time. One night he tells his wife that he is going out to get cigarettes and simply walks away.

After having lived an orderly life for so long, he now lives in disorder in Chicago and New York. His wife hires a private detective, Olson, who eventually finds Dalton. Olson in turn is followed by two shady characters, the twins Douglas and Emil Knight, who want to rob him of his reward. Olson kills one of them in Dalton's room and the other one during the Easter Parade.

After telling his entire story for the first time, Dalton admits that he has told it only that he might know who he really is, and that while telling it he has already transformed. As a changed man he apparently does not need to continue his life with Patricia; he disappears in a department store in Nice. Patricia decides to return to New York, and Weininger looks out of his Cannes hotel room on a bright new morning, just as he had looked out of his room at the Hotel Wellington on Seventh Avenue in New York at the beginning of the novel, feeling closer to Dalton than ever.

Weininger and Dalton are complementary figures. One is the passive European observer, the pale intellectual influenced by the events around him but without compassion. In contrast, the American Dalton acts and reacts; he is the master of his fate and does not shy away from guilt. The weaker of the two imitates the stronger. Weininger buys himself a shirt like Dalton's. He falls in love with Dalton's girl. He develops an interest in antique glass, such as Dalton used to give Patricia. And in the end, he, just like Dalton, has to live without her.

Ein neuer Morgen is told in a very detached language, as Weininger takes his New York pictures in a detached manner. His volume of photographs will not be a very original collection, but rather a typical series of sightseeing pictures of Chinatown, the Jewish quarter, Harlem, and shots taken on a boat cruising around Manhattan Island. It is therefore not so much the specific pictures Weininger is taking, but that he is recording random observations compassion-lessly, that characterizes his—as well as Roth's—new way of looking at New York. The author lets chance determine Weininger's fate, and Weininger even enjoys it. Weininger wants his pictures to be accidental, just as Dalton and Patricia had entered his life "by accident without cause and context like characters of film clippings; each of them had a story and he suddenly felt impelled to get entangled in it."[20] Photography as the medium of the observer and describer is the foremost stylistic determinant in this book. Weininger sees endless series of pictures coming to life. When he watches the poster for the movie "The Great Gatsby" being removed from a wall on Times Square, the black silver-edged nylon screen covering the bricks reminds him of a grotesque death announcement. But already another picture catches his eye; it is a gigantic poster of a man with a bare chest, "which extended over fifteen stories, an advertisement of *manman.*" The face of the man is just being painted by a black who climbs toward it on a fragile ladder, looking like nothing in front of the powerful, triumphant face. Weininger has the impression that the black painter could be blown from his ladder by a gust of wind at any moment, and he imagines the naturalistically painted body on the wall beginning to bleed: "a mighty red stream of color running from the wall over the sidewalk down the street into a gully, and the body, limp and colorless would slide off the wall like thin paper."[21] Such episodes confirm that Roth remains the describer rather than becoming a narrator. The improbable plot of *Ein neuer Morgen* is an appendage to the descriptions. While the descriptions are forceful and in some instances quite unforgettable, while they capture the mood of New York and add considerable poetic value to the novel, they are not integrated into the plot, which the reader is apt to forget after a short time.

With his two American novels Roth even more than earlier challenged his critics to compare his writings to those of his fellow countryman Peter Handke. Handke's novel *Der kurze Brief zum langen Abschied* (1972, *Long Farewell*) elicited the remark that Roth consciously continued Handke's book with his own *Der große Horizont.* There are definite similarities and parallels beyond the reference to Raymond Chandler, whose *Long Goodbye* is echoed in Handke's title. Both novels are transcontinental travel accounts, both heroes are in flight, trying to escape a similar personal crisis caused by the breakup of their marriages, and in both cases the American experience eventually has a healing effect on the protagonists.

Although Handke is criticized by many for the narcissistic reflections of his principal character in *Der kurze Brief zum langen Abschied,* his much more economical language is by far the more powerful compared with Roth's occasional use of loquacious idiom. The poetic intensity of Handke's novel is much greater for precisely that reason. Whereas Roth is rightly accused of lacking analytical qualities compared to his epic talents, Handke is capable of integrating both. His analysis is always descriptive and his description always analytical.

Gerhard Roth ended his phase of experimental writing after a few years, but he again tried something new after having incorporated his American experiences into two novels. With *Winterreise* (1977, Winter Journey) the only one of his books so far translated into English, Roth can be compared to many German exile authors who were led by their American experiences to a new perspective toward Europe. America not only enabled them to write some of the most important works of twentieth-century German literature by allowing them to survive, it also gave them a new perspective, allowing them to discover new literary possibilities. In *Winterreise* Roth applied his newly won techniques of observation and description to a novel that takes place in some of the oldest places of the old world.

A young village teacher from Austria named Nagl decides on the last day of the year "that the most normal thing in the world is to surrender yourself."[22] He abruptly ends his affair with the wife of the village policeman, calls on a former lover, Anna, who has been unfaithful to him, and easily persuades her to accompany him on a trip to Italy. They travel to Naples, where Nagl had always wanted to see Vesuvius, to Rome, and to Venice, where Anna leaves him because Nagl is "unable to come to his senses" while she is with him. After a brief encounter with an older woman he leaves the Italian winter for even colder regions. He goes to the next airport and buys a ticket for Fairbanks, Alaska.

This brief summary shows that Roth avoided furnishing his new book with one of those artificially constructed detective story plots that he employed in his two American novels. It is much to his advantage, because it allows the author to concentrate on his essential qualities, the creation of his principal character and the description of the different environments. (As if he wanted to parody his two previous novels, however, Roth lets the jealous village policeman appear at Nagl's house just as the teacher is about to leave and in utter frustration shoot himself in the hand.)

The school teacher Nagl is, like all of Roth's protagonists, a driven man. He is a fugitive not from the scene of a crime in which he imagines himself to be the suspect but from an intolerably empty life. Roth describes Nagl's feeling of emptiness by letting him look at the image of the earth as it hovers, a lonely sapphire blue and white ball in the black universe. But the routine of everyday life, the endless repetition of the most common and normal activities, dissolves the wonderful vision of the universe. Just like Dalton in *Ein neuer Morgen,* but much more convincingly, Nagl suffers from the alienation caused by his work, which forces him to suppress his thoughts and even his political convictions and to pretend to teach the village children "a life with values." He knows that this kind of life would have to be something radical, however, "a life with truth," and such a life he cannot bring himself to teach.

To demonstrate Nagl's loss of his sense of work, Roth lets his teacher be accompanied in his thoughts by his grandfather, a character who has already appeared in *Der große Horizont.* This son of a Bohemian glassblower, who was born abroad on the Bosporus and returned to Austria as a child, had believed in the myth of work. He could survive only through work. Being without work meant having a slow, deadly illness: "For his grandfather survival had been the meaning of life, while for him the meaning was a question of survival."[23] His grandfather had once been without work for five years, but he had always been longing for work. Earlier in his life he had wanted to emigrate to America; in America there was work. But as in *Der große Horizont* he stowed away on the wrong ship, one that went to Cardiff, "and the sun went down on the prairie without his grandfather ever seeing it."[24]

Nothing turns one's thoughts more toward death than a meaningless life. This is why Nagl is constantly confronted with death. Just before he leaves his village he watches the funeral procession of the veterinarian. In Nagl's sleeping compartment on the train to Naples a death figure appears, searching his clothes. Death is omnipresent at the Naples market in the cadavers of animals, in offal and organs. The pictures of the Madonna in little niches of the houses give proof that religion was nothing "but an artistic handiwork from the hands of death,"[25] and in the Villa dei Misteri outside of Naples the murals appear as the Fata Morgana of death. In small Italian churches Nagl remembers the dead of his family, especially his grandfather, whose death he was unable to believe. In Venice he encouters a black boat carrying a wreath, and he visits the island of San Michele where the Venetians bury their dead. There is also a confrontation with death in Rome, where Nagl witnesses a demonstration during which a young girl is killed.

As if he has to prove to himself that he is alive although surrounded by death and memories of death, Nagl escapes with Anna into the most unrestrained, desperate sexual encounters. The love scenes in *Winterreise* are of an ice-cold passion, and it is unavoidable that Nagl and Anna have to part. While he was aroused primarily by her faithlessness, she had always loved him and still does when she leaves him in Venice. Her explanation for her departure is actually a declaration of love. Nagl also loves Anna, but because he is unable to communicate with her except sexually, the reader does not learn anything about her. All the decisions during their trip are made by Nagl; Anna is only fleetingly mentioned, and in many instances we forget entirely that she came along at all.

Winterreise gives its author ample opportunity to demonstrate his talents for description. Nagl is—what else could he be?—an observer of sorts. However, compared to the photographer Weininger, the pseudo-detective Haid, the schizophrenics einstein and Künstel, or the hypochondriac Kalb, he internalizes the images he sees and changes them into memories. This process is most obvious when certain objects remind him of his grandfather, such as the statues on the Bridge of Angels in Rome. When his grandfather was a child, his younger brother died and his mother had shown him a picture of an angel and told him his brother had also become one. After the dead boy had been put into a coffin and taken by boat across the Bosporus, his grandfather noticed something flying away from the windowsill in the evening and thought it had been his little brother.

Roth began taking pictures on his first trip to the United States. These photographs of cities, landscapes, people, houses, and streets were never intended to be used for a book. While planning *Winterreise,* however, Roth wanted to record in pictures "the estrangement, the growing alienation of perception."[26] These pictures, which are reproduced in the volume *Menschen, Bilder, Marionetten,* were taken with a rather simple camera without a wide-angle lens or similar sophisticated gear. They show statues in Rome, Palazzi in Venice, market scenes in Naples, the fuming earth near the crater of Vesuvius, and unidentified streets. These small black and white reproductions are not especially impressive, but they convey the importance that visual impression has for Gerhard Roth. He seems to become more and more susceptible to beauty. The descriptions of various views of the volcanic mountain near Naples at different times of the day and in different atmospheric conditions are of great intensity, as are many descriptions of the Italian winter skies. The picture finally gains a redeeming power when Nagl decides not to stay in Venice:

> . . . the figure of a golden angel glowed in the setting sunlight; the angel was small and bright, while the heavens turned violet and tinged into green away from the houses. The angel glowed supernaturally bright, and the heavens passed into white-blue and gradually shaded into night darkness. From the vaporetto, Nagl saw the last piece of the sky deep violet, covered more and more by the blackness of night. But the radiated angel went on glowing, brighter and clearer. They were moving toward it, and Nagl thought: "It's finally like life and not like a dream."[27]

Gerhard Roth's development as a writer up to this point has been like coming home from a long journey. When he set out, he left behind a cerebral Vienna and Austria filled with schizophrenic characters. In America he learned to look at a new world in a new way, exchanging the cerebral environment for a more realistic one. With this new perception he returned to Europe, and via Italy he finally came back to his homeland where his latest novel takes place, *Der stille Ozean* (1980, *The Quiet Ocean*).

It is the story of Dr. Ascher, a physician who, after having gone through the travails of a malpractice suit, follows the advice of his wife and moves to a small village in the Styrian countryside to recover from the haunting experience. He pretends to be a biologist who has to regain his health after a severe illness; like the villagers the reader for the greater part of the book does not know of Ascher's past. In the course of several weeks Ascher not only gets to know the population of this remote region near the Austrian-Yugoslav border, their customs and many of their life stories, but also experiences unusual events. An outbreak of rabies precipitates intensified hunting activity, which spreads from the animal to the human world when a man who feels unjustly treated by his business associates kills three people and is himself hunted and returned to the authorities. Ascher, the quiet observer in this rural world, is more and more drawn into it; he finally decides to bring his family and to stay as a country doctor.

Der stille Ozean is Roth's best book to date. Without pretension he unfolds a picture of truly epic proportions and, despite the many cruel events, deep compassion. Roth is able to do so by carefully selecting a few themes that he treats very extensively in the course of the narrative, one growing out of and complementing the other.

The first theme is that of the hunt. Ascher moves to the village in fall, hunting season, and he accepts an invitation from his landlord to join the villagers for a pheasant hunt. Ascher, the observer, does not hunt himself, but he takes part in several hunting excursions during which the villagers kill a great number of rabbits and birds. The death of a pheasant and a fox are described with the same objective attention to detail with which Ascher looks at bird feathers and snow crystals under his microscope. A high point of these hunting scenes is the shooting of pigeons at a farm. They are flushed from the roof and before they can land—for the peasants don't shoot them while they are perching—they are killed in great numbers, falling to the ground, into trees, and in the gutter of the barn.

Death is not only ever-present in the animal world but is also the foremost theme of the entire novel. One of the first experiences Ascher has in his immediate neighborhood is that of a dying old man, who is later laid out in an empty house where people pray for him. The interrelation of the fear of death, as it appears in the rampant rabies and the killings of three people, and the instinct to survive, as shown in the hunting down of animals and of the killer, contribute to the density of the narrative.

Roth avoids any accusatory gesture in his description of these hunting scenes. Rather, he uses another prominent theme in his novel to explain the behavior of people who might otherwise appear to be brutal and barbaric. He describes a rural society and its unsentimental realtionship with nature. These peasants live like their ancestors a hundred years ago, Ascher thinks, watching a toothless old woman who cuts the seeds out of pumpkins she is holding between her naked feet. Their life is filled with hard numbing work. Whether Ascher observes people in the fields or talks to them in the village inn about working conditions in the town, he always encounters the same realistic type of people who do their work in order to survive and sometimes even work fanatically. These rural people are free of nostalgic feeling of any kind. They do not perceive natural beauty—a field is a plot of land for growing potatoes—nor do they harbor a sense of historic values. When a family plans to build a new house and to tear down the old one, the woman responds to Ascher's remark that this is sad: "Sad? What's sad? Why should we let the house stand? What should we remember? What should we be proud of?"[28]

Many people tell Ascher about their life, the poverty of their childhood, the hardships of the work in the coal mines. The attentive observer Ascher collects additional anthropological material by observing the customs with which people try to protect themselves in a thunderstorm or during an illness. He notices their bad teeth and cheap dentures and the eyeglasses that they sometimes buy at flea markets. He meets the poorest of them as well as a rather eccentric funeral director who is also a botanist, historian, musicologist, restorer, inventor, composer, painter, gardener, farmer, and merchant. The latter also runs a museum with forty thousand objects, a feast for Roth the describer. In conversations with the strange, withdrawn village priest, the doctor, and an intelligent widow who cooks for him, Ascher learns how this society is held together. It is a network of interdependence in which everyone knows everything about everyone else; but people like to live like this because they cannot live in anonymity. This is also why they always come back to the village, whether from the army, from prison, or from the insane asylum, to do the only thing that counts: their work.

There is nobody in this novel who is resented by all. The village priest tells Ascher that the people have preserved a remnant of faith and that he has never encountered any hostility. It is astonishing how they react when it becomes known that a man has sexually abused a girl. "He is not a bad person," a woman tells Ascher. "He had an accident once and hurt his head; after that he became weird, put on women's clothes, and pretended to be a priest." Another one adds, "Who knows what happened? We weren't there."[29]

Even when the small farmer kills three people and the village is in panic because everyone fears he might come back and kill more or take the schoolchildren hostage, there are attempts made to explain his actions. The mayor confirms that he was an orderly man. "'He is a loner,' the old man said. . . . 'For him the world was in order, only in his case it did not work. This is why he put it back in order for himself."[30]

Like this old man Roth looks at the people of the village with deep understanding. He shows their faults, but he never condemns them. In no other
book is he as close to his great Austrian master, Adalbert Stifter. He had paid
homage to Stifter before in *Der große Horizont,* when Daniel Haid, euphoric
at having arrived in New York, sits in his airport limousine with the comfortable
feeling he used to have while reading Stifter, whose books radiate so much
familiarity. In the "American novels" of Roth, Stifter is an exotic element.
Haid reads him as an author of an utopian world, a science fiction writer.
Stifter's idyll is a social utopia. In the novel *Der Nachsommer (Indian Summer)*
people had the feeling of doing the right thing, and they felt that their doings
were creative. Roth even lets Haid talk about Stifter's style, as if Haid were
giving a seminar paper, stressing the interrelationship of the poetic and the
realistic in his novels. In *Der stille Ozean,* Roth neither imitates nor emulates
Stifter, but he comes much closer to his humanity.

A comparison between *Der stille Ozean* and *Winterreise* shows great differences. Whereas Nagl leaves his village and later even Europe, Ascher decides
to stay. Work for Nagl is intolerable and annihilating, while Ascher realizes
the enormous force contained in work, which forms and preserves society.
He returns to the world and to his work.

In his next short novel, *Circus Saluti,* published in 1981, Gerhard Roth
remained within the familiar surroundings of southwestern Austria, focusing
on one peculiar aspect, the world of a circus traveling through the countryside.
In the brief text *Circus Maus*[31] a young Swiss named Gugelmann travels with
his small animals, a pigeon, a rat, a rooster, a Siamese cat, a pig, and a dog.
He is full of concern for them — if a woman appeared in the audience wearing
a fur coat, Gugelmann would stop the performance, because the animals could
become afraid. The director of Circus Saluti, by contrast, is an altogether evil
man. He exploits his animals, his workers, and his audience with the best of
consciences because "They get what they want." The animals get rewards, the
workers, usually poor, get a job, and the spectators get their illusions by means
of elaborate tricks and other machinations.

The reader meets the circus director through a young mute who has lost
his voice in an accident. He visits the circus with a friend who serves as sort
of an interpreter, although the mute communicates with the circus director
by way of short messages scribbled on pieces of paper. These notes are desperate
cries of protest against the circus and its system which, it soon becomes evident,
serves as a metaphor of the world, with the young mute representing the poet.
The director, a successful, even powerful man who can fulfill his every wish,

sees only a totally powerless person in the young man who cannot change anything with his scribbled notes. This is why he wants to take him into his circus, too: "With your silence and my questions we can make the audience cry with laughter." When the mute writes the question, "And the end?" the director answers, "In the end you will be right, what do I care?"[32] Seldom has there been found a better definition for the role of the poet in society.

Although *Circus Saluti* is a morality tale, it is far from devoid of intriguing, amusing, but also horrifying descriptions. Roth lets us partake of his detailed knowledge of circus work. We see an entire performance, culminating in the hypnotism act in which a number of chickens as well as a poor member of the audience fall prey to the evil powers of the director, who assumes demonic traits like Thomas Mann's Cipolla in *Mario und der Zauberer* (*Mario and the Magician*).

Roth's next prose text, *Das Töten des Bussards* (1982, The Killing of the Buzzard) demonstrates that he is still attracted to experimental forms. The twenty-one brief episodes depicting extreme violence, killings, and murders committed by a creature that appears to be both man and bird, offers a phantasmagoric landscape of death.

Death has been Gerhard Roth's preoccupation ever since he wrote *Der stille Ozean*. In his next and longest novel, his magnum opus to date, the title itself reveals the importance of this all-encompassing theme for him. *Landläufiger Tod* (1984, Common Death) offers a confluence of the two main streams of Roth's writing, i.e., his experiments in the tradition of surrealism and his descriptive prose in the tradition of Stifter's realism. *Landläufiger Tod* tells the story of Franz Lindner, the mute young man from the short narrative *Circus Saluti*. The nearly eight-hundred-page novel is divided into six books with the first entitled "Dark Remembrance" and starting off with "Circus Saluti," connecting the work with the rural world of *Der stille Ozean*. The landscape here is, if anything, even quieter, darker, and more filled with foreboding.

"Totenstill" (deathly quiet) is the title of the second sequence of short texts following "Circus Saluti." Here Lindner travels by car with his friend, the young law student, to the penitentiary where the man who killed three people in *Der stille Ozean* is now incarcerated. "Killing," they agree, "is nothing extraordinary. It is part of human nature. The history of mankind is nothing but a history of criminals and murderers."[33] The gloomy descriptions in "Totenstill" are interspersed with highly inventive episodes drawn from the circus environment. The mean director of the miserable little Circus Saluti is still engaged in his dark machinations. He sends a strange fellow through the countryside as a "herald" or "announcer," literally a walking death figure. ("Durch das Land laufen": "landläufig," = walking through the land.) This former policeman, an epileptic, walks silently and mechanically like an automaton, carrying an old sprayer with enormous propellers on his back, past the farms and through the villages, his white face a mask of omnipresent death.

Lindner sees and hears nothing but manifestations of death. His father, a beekeeper, and an aunt tell him stories about their lives and their village. Having experienced the two World Wars at the Yugoslav border, where Austro-Hungarian troops, Russian soldiers, and prisoners mingled in 1918 and where SS storm-troopers and Yugoslav partisans both preyed upon the villagers in 1945, their accounts of death are innumerable. Even when Lindner meets someone like Doctor Ascher, who is not a villager and who leads the solitary life of an alcoholic, he has to listen to his complaints about the unbearable existence of a country physician. Ascher also relates tales about all of the suicides he has witnessed there; it comes as no surprise when he eventually takes his own life.

In the second book, "Reports from the Labyrinth," Franz Lindner is in an insane asylum. There he occupies himself by writing letters he never sends off and texts with sweeping themes like "The Creation," "The Frozen Paradise," and "The Age of Time." Here Roth returns to the surrealistic mood of his earliest writings, adopting the point of view of his schizophrenic protagonist. "The Creation" consists of unconnected sentences describing natural phenomena in the stream of Lindner's consciousness; e.g., "The talking comets slowly began to change into mushrooms that looked like small dogs"; or "One has to close one's eyes in order not to hear the noise of the plants," or "The wasps' nests ring like church bells."[34] "The Age of Time" is a sequence of six hundred seventy-nine such sentences, consecutively numbered, using the world of the village as their material, such as "Only he who brushes his cow's coat long enough will find gold in his sieve."[35]

If one considers the realistic descriptions of Book One the "thesis," and the surrealistic visions of Book Two the "antithesis" of the novel, the "synthesis" can be found in Book Three, entitled "Microcosm." The longest section, constituting nearly one-half of the text, it consists of a variety of narrative modes, describing the death of the owner of the village sawmill and the life experiences of older villagers along with technical phenomena such as the way a bee sees, the tools a beekeeper needs, and the work at the sawmill. In between these descriptions there is a large number of dreamlike, grotesque texts concerning a one-hundred-and-seven-year-old general who plays a domineering role in the village, the flea master of the circus, and the staff and inmates of the asylum. Birds engage in dialogues, a chorus of the village dead is sung by children, and in the "Metamorphosis of a Breakfast," a knife changes into the skeleton of a bird, the breadbasket is a frozen rabbit, and the radishes purr like cats.

The longer, more realistic narratives remain, however, the more substantial part of the book. They consist of independent stories, whose sequence is interchangeable, and their common denominator is, as the title of the entire novel indicates, death. Whether death occurs in the private sphere of the family, as a jealous husband kills his wife's lover, or whether it results from a strike among the miners or from atrocities perpetrated by soldiers and partisans at the end of the war, death has these villagers constantly in its grip.

While the young, mute protagonist records these stories other deaths occur. The longest of these narratives, "The Youth Falls Silent in the Fiery Furnace" concerns the experiences of his father as a young boy, who in 1918 was also struck mute by witnessing the atrocities of war. The son describes this in writing while an aunt is dying in the next room. Lindner feels these stories growing in him and asks: "Who will tell us those stories that flow through our body as the inheritance from our ancestors? Did they give them to us to take along in order to heal us? To make us insane or to remind us that we are mortal?"[36]

In Book Four, "Departure into the Unknown," the undertaker's assistant experiences fantastic voyages into subterranean realms as if to counterbalance the atrocities that happen on earth. In Book Five the sixty-six "Fairy Tales" created by asylum inmates and "recorded by the brothers Franz and Franz Lindner," bear testimony to the double personality of Lindner, even after his release.

In *Landläufiger Tod* Roth stretches the form of the novel to its limits and beyond. He not only combines his two previous modes of narration in this work, but also returns to his previous themes. Lindner, by being mute, is destined to play the role of an observer like the earlier figures einstein and Künstel. The theme of work, so prominent in *Der stille Ozean* and in the earlier *Winterreise,* is represented here in the activity of the beekeeper. Finally, the theme of death, already so powerful in *Der stille Ozean,* is carried to the limits of the reader's endurance. The shorter, surrealistic texts and disjunctive sentences, however, transcend the limits of the reader's sympathy — for which reason the novel fails. In the most negative response Fritz J. Raddatz accuses Roth of presenting topics of great import without adding anything significant to the understanding of them.[37] Author and publisher must have expected reactions like this one. Roth put together a hundred-page book, *Dorfchronik zum "Landläufigen Tod"* (1984, Village Chronicle for "Common Death") a "convergence" of the themes in the novel. It describes one day in the life of the village, when the "Sunday organ player" has died, a woman who is mentioned in the novel as possibly having been the mother Lindner never knew. In fifty brief paragraphs the villagers and their intrinsic patterns of coexistence parade once more before the reader's eyes. It can be read independently of the novel and might induce some to undertake the enormous task of reading the other eight hundred pages.

This astonishingly prolific author has gone through a remarkable development. Beginning with the highly artificial language constructions of his early phase, which are intended to break with a tradition that had become all too self-complacent, Roth discovered a new way of seeing on his first trip to the United States. He subsequently employed this new mode of observing reality and using it as a vehicle to describe his memories and inner visions in the novels that are again set in Europe. The closer Roth gets to his place of origin, the more convincing he is in his writings. They are not flawless. The fast output of four novels within six years is the reason for a number of faults, including stylistic carelessness. These problems are minor, however, in view of his complete lack of pretension and his obvious striving for perfection. What he once said about Hermann Hesse also holds true for himself: "Hesse's quality consists of sympathy and bringing about sympathy, of patiently feeling for an idea, developing and producing it in a simple perfect German."[38]

Roth is deeply rooted in the Austrian literary tradition. Together with Thomas Bernhard and Peter Handke he belongs among the descendants of Adalbert Stifter who are creating a literature that is antirealistic and apolitical. At the same time it also presents a paradigm for the human predicament of not being able to act and yet capable of transforming this paralysis into a realm of desire and hope.[39]

But this pronouncement on Austrian literature after Stifter nevertheless requires careful modification if it is to be applied to Gerhard Roth. His novel, *Der stille Ozean,* is a book in the tradition of Stifter's *Nachsommer* with its minute descriptions and recordings of nature, but the contemporary observer has to go beyond Stifter in also recording the cruelty of human behavior and nature. Roth looks for the source of this disharmony and exposes society and ultimately human nature itself as the originator of all the pain inflicted upon both nature and humanity. By having his protagonist, a doctor, turn to his fellow men in *Der stille Ozean,* administer to their wounds, and console them in their distress, Roth showed a way out of the old dilemma of Austrian literature. It seems, however, as if this way out was actually a dead-end street. In *Landläufiger Tod* there is no reconciliation among humans nor between them and nature. The doctor takes his own life amid all of the misery that surrounds him. On the last pages of *Dorfchronik zum "Landläufigen Tod"* we see a certain

L. sitting in a meadow among the flowers counting their stamens. He does not sit there as a human being, as the beekeeper, but rather "as a bee." In this state of the world hovering somewhere "between creation and chaos," which Walter Hinck calls "the actual topic of the novel,"[40] such contentment, not to mention happiness, is possible only in madness.

Notes

1. Manfred Mixner, "Ausbruch aus der Provinz. Zur Entstehung des 'Forums Stadtpark' und der Zeitschrift *manuskripte*." Peter Laemmle, Jörg Drews, eds., *Wie die Grazer auszogen, die Literatur zu erobern*. Texte, Portraits, Analysen und Dokumente junger österreichischer Autoren (München: dtv sr 5465, 1979), pp. 17-18.
2. Ibid., p. 15.
3. Gerhard Roth, *albert einstein, Künstel, Der Wille zur Krankheit*. Drei Romane. (Frankfurt: Suhrkamp Taschenbuch 230, 1975), p. 51.
4. Jörg Drews, "'Haid setzte die Brille wieder auf . . .' Über Gerhard Roths Bücher." Peter Laemmle, *Wie die Grazer auszogen, die Literatur zu erobern*, pp. 29-51.
5. Gerhard Roth, *albert einstein, Künstel, Der Wille zur Krankheit*, p. 150.
6. Ibid., p. 160.
7. Ulrich Greiner: "Ich will ein Erzähler sein." Portrait. *Der Tod des Nachsommers:* Aufsätze, Portraits, Kritiken zur österreichischen Gegenwartsliteratur. (München: Hanser, 1979), pp. 158-172.
8. Gerhard Roth, *Der große Horizont*. Roman. (Frankfurt: Suhrkamp Taschenbuch 327, 1976), p. 221.
9. E. M. Beekman, "Raymond Chandler and an American Genre." *Massachusetts Review*, Vol. XIV (1972), no. 1, pp. 149-173.
10. Gerhard Roth, *Der große Horizont*, pp. 132-133.
11. Ibid., p. 147.
12. Ibid., p. 149.
13 Ibid., p. 196.
14. Ibid., p. 18.
15. Ibid., p. 30.
16. Ibid., p. 32.
17. Ibid., pp. 70-71.
18. Ibid., p. 200.
19. Ibid., p. 188.

20. Gerhard Roth, *Ein neuer Morgen.* (Frankfurt: Fischer Bücherei 2107, 1980), p. 23.

21. Ibid., p. 56.

22. Gerhard Roth, *Winterreise.* Translated by Joachim Neugroschl. (New York: Farrar Straus Giroux, 1980), p. 3.

23. Ibid., p. 12.

24. Ibid., p. 81.

25. Ibid., p. 25.

26. Gerhard Roth, "Fotografien zur 'Winterreise,'" in *Menschen, Bilder, Marionetten.* Prosa, Kurzromane, Stücke. (Frankfurt: S. Fischer, 1979), pp. 138-151.

27. *Winterreise*, p. 131.

28. Gerhard Roth, *Der stille Ozean.* (Frankfurt: Fischer Bücherei 5413, 1983), p. 168.

29. Ibid., pp. 76-78.

30 Ibid., p. 205.

31. Gerhard Roth, "Circus Maus," in *Die schönen Bilder beim Trabrennen.* (Frankfurt: Fischer Bücherei 5400, 1982), pp. 156-167.

32. Gerhard Roth, *Circus Saluti.* (Frankfurt: Collection S. Fischer, 1981), pp. 126-127.

33. Gerhard Roth, *Landläufiger Tod.* Roman. (Frankfurt am Main: S. Fischer, 1984), pp. 136-137.

34. Ibid., pp. 136-145.

35. Ibid., p. 154.

36. Ibid., p. 312.

37. Fritz J. Raddatz, "Epische Geisterbahn." Gerhard Roths Roman *Landläufiger Tod* und *Dorfchronik* zu diesem Buch. In *Die Zeit,* nr. 46 (16. November 1984), 23.

38. Gerhard Roth, "Hermann Hesse. 'Kleine Freuden,'" in *Menschen, Bilder, Marionetten,* pp. 122-25.

39. Ulrich Greiner, *Der Tod des Nachsommers,* p. 13.

40. Walter Hinck, "Die aus den Fugen gehende Welt des Dorfes. *Landläufiger Tod* – Gerhard Roths Roman und seine Chronik," in *Frankfurter Allgemeine Zeitung,* nr. 263 (20. November 1984), B3.

Primary Works

die autobiographie des albert einstein. Roman. Frankfurt: Suhrkamp, 1972.

Der Ausbruch des Ersten Weltkriegs und andere Romane. Frankfurt: Suhrkamp, 1972.

Der Wille zur Krankheit. Roman. Frankfurt: Suhrkamp, 1973.

Herr Mantel und Herr Hemd. Text von Gerhard Roth. Bilder von Ida Szigethy. Ein Insel-Bilderbuch. Frankfurt: Insel, 1974.

Der große Horizont. Roman. Frankfurt: Suhrkamp, 1974. (Taschenbuchausgabe, Frankfurt: S. Fischer, 1978, Fischer Taschenbuch 2082).

die autobiographie des albert einstein. Künstel. Der Wille zur Krankheit. Frankfurt: Suhrkamp, 1975. (suhrkamp taschenbuch 230).

Ein neuer Morgen. Roman. Frankfurt: Suhrkamp, 1976. Neuausgabe: Frankfurt: S. Fischer, 1979. (Taschenbuchausgabe, Frankfurt: Fischer, 1980, Fischer Taschenbuch 2107).

Winterreise. Frankfurt: S. Fischer, 1978. (Taschenbuchausgabe, Frankfurt: Fischer, 1979, Fischer Taschenbuch 2094).

Menschen, Bilder, Marionetten. Prosa, Kurzromane, Stücke. Frankfurt: S. Fischer, 1979.

Der stille Ozean. Frankfurt: S. Fischer, 1980.

Das Töten des Bussards. Graz: Verlag Froschl, 1982.

Circus Saluti. Frankfurt: S. Fischer, 1981.

Die schönen Bilder beim Trabrennen. Frankfurt: Fischer Bücherei 5400, 1982.

Landläufiger Tod. Roman. Umschlagzeichnung und Illustrationen von Günter Brus. Frankfurt am Main: S. Fischer, 1984.

Dorfchronik zum "Landläufigen Tod." Frankfurt: S. Fischer, 1984.

Works in English Translation

Winter Journey (Winterreise), translated by Joachim Neugroschl. New York: Farrar Straus Giroux, 1980.

Secondary Sources

Peter von Becker, "Gewalt als Idylle," *Theater heute* Vol. 11 (1977). 40-45. (On "Sehnsucht").

Jörg Drews, "'Haid setzte die Brille wieder auf . . .' Über Gerhard Roths Bücher," in Peter Laemmle, Jörg Drews, *Wie die Grazer auszogen, die Literatur zu erobern* (München: dtv Sonderreihe 5465, 1979), pp. 29-51.

Ulrich Greiner, "Gerhard Roth," *Der Tod des Nachsommers* (München: Hanser, 1979), pp. 155-172.

Gerhard Melzer, "Dieselben Dinge täglich bringen langsam um. Die Reisemodelle in Peter Handkes 'Der kurze Brief zum langen Abschied' und Gerhard Roths 'Winterreise,' in *Die andere Welt,* ed. Kurt Bartsch. Festschrift für Hellmuth Himmel (Bern, München: Francke, 1979), pp. 373-393.

Martin Swales, "Gerhard Roth: Der stille Ozean," *World Literature Today,* Vol. 55 (Spring 1981), 305.

John Updike, "Disaffection in Deutsch," in *Hugging the Shore.* Essays in Criticism. New York: Knopf, 1983, pp. 448-452 (On *Winterreise*).

Harry Zohn, "Gerhard Roth: Winterreise," *World Literature Today,* Vol. 53 (Autumn 1979), 682.

Peter Turrini

Margarita Pazi

There seems to be little if anything left of the proverbial Austrian "Gemütlich-keit," that syndrome of an easygoing nature, inborn cheerfulness, and the capability of overlooking those things that could lessen enjoyment of life, in the drama of modern Austrian playwrights. Only five years after his com-patriot Peter Handke had outraged the audience with the insults leveled against it in his *Publikumsbeschimpfung* (Offending the Audience),[1] Peter Turrini's play *Rozznjogd* (1971, Shooting Rats) caused a scandal at the first performance in the Wiener Volkstheater. Like Handke, Turrini achieved a certain notoriety with his first play, but apparently the audience had become used to this new form by 1971, because the positive reviews about this willfully and intentionally challenging drama of a totally unknown writer equaled the negative and damning reviews. The Viennese performance was quickly followed by others in Wuppertal and in Pforzheim, where, in October 1971, the play was put on the stage for the first time in a High German version under the title *Rattenjagd*. By that time the author, the actors, and the stage manager could count on an audience prepared and willing to understand the acts of aggression in the play as Turrini wanted them to be understood: as the result of the difficulties encountered by the dramatic persons in their endeavor to make contact with each other, to achieve a "human" relationship, to find the human warmth they so patheticly craved. Before turning to the play itself, the reasons for the protest, dispute, and the acclaim it aroused, let us meet the author of this drama, which since its première has been shown on dozens of European and transcontinental stages, an author whose second play *Sauschlachten* met with even more opposition, almost with repulsion, but who is now counted among the Austrian playwrights whose plays are an important feature on the contemporary stage.

Peter Turrini was born in 1944 in Carinthia, the most southern of the nine provinces within the federation of the Austrian Republic. The village of St. Margarethen in the Lavan valley, where Turrini was born to an Italian cabinet-maker and a farmer's daughter from neighboring Styria, was just as set in its narrow, preconceived ideas and its rigid way of life as the other villages in this area and just as unwilling to accept any "outsider," even one married to a local girl. To a great extent, the life of Turrini's father was identical to the way of life of thousands of foreign workers in Austria and other Western Euro-pean countries in the past decades. They always remain – partly by their own choice—on the periphery of the social and cultural life of the communities within which they live. Unlike the *Gastarbeiter* (guest-workers), as they are euphemistically termed, Turrini's father had the advantage of being a highly skilled worker, but on the other hand he lacked the comfort of his countrymen's company. The loneliness of the father, the fact that he was ostracized by the village population and forced into an isolation from which he did not find relief even in his family, influenced decisively the son's attitude toward society. These childhood memories of not belonging are very probably the source of the protest Peter Turrini voiced in his first plays.

He finished commercial high school at Klagenfurt, the capital of Carinthia, and dutifully passed the *Matura,* the examinations enabling him to continue his studies at the university, but that was not his aim. In the four years that followed he worked in a variety of jobs. He was a laborer in several factories, a handyman in a warehouse, and later a successful writer of commercial ads. By 1967 he was earning a good salary at an American commercial advertising agency, when he suddenly could no longer stand the "state of schizophrenia, the mixture of postponed hopes and self-deception."[2] Overnight he gave up everything, left his job, boarded the next Balkan Express, and "landed" on a Greek island. Within a few weeks he wrote his first play, *Rozznjogd.*[3] In 1977 Turrini explained retrospectively: "It was a desperate cleansing process. I wanted to get rid of all the pressure that during the last years had been accumulating within me. It was a project of total freedom, beneath which I can feel even today the anguish of that time. Under no circumstances did I want to return to a 'bourgeois' profession, but I had no idea of how to go on, because even on the most beautiful island one needs money to live . . ." (71). That Turrini did not remain "on the beach" and already in 1968 was looking for work on the Italian Adriatic probably reveals more about his basic attitude to life than research into his writings could ever disclose.

In 1969, while working in West Germany as a handyman, he met Hans Carl Artmann, the Austrian poet, at the book fair in Frankfurt. Artmann had published a book of Viennese dialect poetry, *med ana schwoazzen dintn,* (written in black ink) in 1958, which had met with general acclaim.[4] Turrini showed Artmann his play, which had also been written in Viennese dialect although interspersed with Carinthian dialect forms. Artmann read the play and gave Turrini the name of a Viennese theater agency. Only two weeks later Turrini was informed by the agency that the Wiener Volkstheater had accepted his play and was going to perform it at an early date. Without disparaging the quality of the play, one can surmise that its being written in dialect had hastened the decision of the agency, because of the success of Artmann's poems.

Quite a number of writers had followed Artmann's example and had started to write in dialect although not all for the same reason. The progressive authors wanted to stress the recent changes in the rural surrounding and style of life, and for that purpose the vernacular provided a suitable vehicle. Traditionalists, who considered language an appropriate means to revive "folklore" (*Heimatkunst*) and with it the romantic idyll of country life and society given to healthy, uncomplicated behavior, used dialect as a weapon in their fight against the various forms of standardization, against the destruction of the country environment and commercialized tourism. Neither group showed much desire to idealize regional idiosyncrasies or to gloss over them; In German literature regional literature has always played an important role, from the sometimes rather romantic *Dorfgeschichten* (village tales) in the nineteenth century to the *Volksstücke*, plays written usually in the vernacular and depicting problems within the rural communities. The degeneration of this type of literature into the "blood-and-soil" literature produced during the Nazi period with the intention of extolling and magnifying nationalistic characteristics discredited it after 1945. But in the middle sixties a new interest in these plays could be discerned.

Turrini joined the ranks of these *Volksstück* authors with only his second play. His first drama can in no way be considered a rural play; its scenery is typical of city life and so is the whole trend of the actions. But the use of dialect was the feature Turrini stressed. The original version stipulates that performances outside Austria have to utilize the local vernacular. The version of 1971 in High German is intended only to serve as the model for local dialect versions. Its aim is solely to expound the intention of the play to Austrians "who have become alienated from their mother tongue, and to non-Austrians, Germans, Swiss, etc." (17).

Turrini is often mentioned together with the group of younger German dramatists like Martin Sperr, Rainer Werner Fassbinder, and Franz Xaver Kroetz, who are known as the dramatists of the new folk theater. However, the new folk theater had no intention of creating plays that could be termed *volkstümlich*, that is, popular or almost commonplace, requiring neither an intellectual approach nor a discerning attitude from the audience. The contents and the language of the new folk theater are intended to be understood by the general public, but the author's approach to the audience carries an appeal for understanding without even a hint of condescension. The aim is not to amuse but to rouse the onlooker into awareness of life and into an interest in the happenings around him. Turrini's first play went farther than many in demonstrating the pressure that society exerts on the hapless individual. It shows the prison created by the desire to adjust and to meet the required "standard"; it also points out the futility of any attempt to break out of this prison, constructed by the conceptions and notions of a consumer society.

According to Turrini's stage instructions, the opening scene shows a stage under a dark, starless sky, illuminated only by isolated lights from the distant city. In the foreground is an enormous heap of refuse: the public dump of the city. The two actors of the play, "she" and "he," arrive on the scene. Their having no names symbolizes, just as does the stage setting, the obscurity and dejection of their lives. They are fairly young, ordinary people. Everything about this is commonplace; only the car in which they arrive looks odd, for "he" has painstakingly assembled the car from parts found in the junkyard. During the weeks and months he had worked on it even his dreams had centered on the car. He tells her he had seen himself flying over the rooftops in it. Then the work was finished, and the feeling of freedom, of elevation, was gone. Still the car retained one major importance for him: it is the only thing he can really be sure of because he "knows" it: "Because I have put it together myself . . . taken everything apart, put everything together again . . . each part I held in my hands . . . and because I can't do that with people, I never will get to know anybody" (29).

Not "knowing" a person means not to be able to be close to him or her. But the symbolic meaning beneath the action and the dialogue is sometimes twofold. For instance, the car is a status symbol of society, but also a means to sublimate the age-old desire to fly. In this play it also represents a means to elevate oneself above the others. The reasons for his special attachment to the car are also manifold: his loneliness, uncertainty, and inability to communicate with people. According to his understanding, the refusal of the "others" to be taken apart, to let themselves be known, stems from their fear to show what is hidden beneath the "body"; the rubbish, litter, refuse. Provoked by the woman's protest, he bursts into a violent tirade proclaiming that from the day of his birth man is filled with drugs and goes on absorbing rubbish and assembling odds and ends until there is nothing "true or real" either inside or outside himself: ". . . Your face is a battlefield for cosmetics! Not even your hair is genuine, you have horsehair or some other kind of bristle on your head . . ." (29).

The reason why he has brought her to the dump is also twofold: it is the only place where one can be unobserved, and he likes the place, for there are no other people, no police. And the rats, which heighten her unwillingness to remain there, are for him the essential attraction. He has come well prepared to meet them; he carries a shotgun which he now eagerly aims at the rats —

at the audience. Turrini is not trying to anger or abuse the audience by identifying it with rats. But rats are a part of each of us, he explains on the title page of the stage text: "Don't we try to love the rat in us in order to be able to view with more pleasure our reflection from the beer in our glass" (16). That is not meant as an accusation directed by one part of the society against another; it is more or less the damning of everyone. After the euphoria he had experienced while assembling the car, the man on stage has only one thing left from which he can derive pleasure: shooting rats.

Turrini operates skillfully; he presents the two actors neither as victims nor aggressors. The "rats" are not the "audience," they are in and among the audience. Turrini lessens the aversion the man on the stage would normally evoke in the audience by stressing the fact that though he has a maniacal urge to "kill,"[5] what he is out to kill is "vermin," something foul and disgusting, which people loathe anyway. What we are to see on the stage is the *Kleinbürger*, the little man of the late sixties, trapped by norms and demands of a surrounding world he has neither the mental capacity nor the inner strength to disregard or control. He is shown not as a victim of social injustice, but as the product of a society that dictates what one should feel and how one should look and behave. Every impulse of "truth"—which here stands also for "freedom"—is stifled under these circumstances. Turrini once called the play "a great project of freedom" (72), and the action on the stage is the desperate attempt of the man and the woman to get "free," to rid themselves of the trappings of "beautifying" aids and accessories. His teasing at her hair reveals the artificial parts of it, part of his rather brutal attempt to "get to know her," is reciprocated by her pointing to his dentures. The scene quickly escalates into a crude plucking and tearing out of the artificial "embellishments" both of them carry on their bodies. The frenzied woman urges him on and they now also delve into pockets and purses, snatch at the masses of cosmetics, pills, photographs, and letters produced by this search. Everything is smashed and thrown on the rubbish pile; at the end even the car is demolished.

To a large degree these acts of violent protest are also meant as acts of expiation: the man and the woman sinned by wanting to conform, by aspiring to appear to be better, bigger, and nicer than they really are. The vile language accompanying their actions, the obscene remarks about their bodily functions while they undress, the way in which they claw and paw at each other, caress and kiss, only stress the futility of their endeavors to redeem their previous faults and errors by giving in to the cheap enticements offered by society; thus they fail to achieve their "freedom" by destroying the litter they had accumulated.

Shrill music and glaring light, which the stage directions demand, grow progressively louder and harsher, in the same measure as the actions and words of the couple become more and more frantic. Then a shot sounds and everything stops. The woman, apparently hit by the shot, drops on the rubbish pile, and only now at the point of death does the couple on stage become "human" enough to have names: "What's your name actually?" the man softly asks as he bends over the dying woman. Then he too is struck by a bullet. Two men with shotguns, obviously intent on killing the rats on the site, come on the stage. One of them remarks that the two rats he just killed had such a "human manner," the other only jeers: "People like rats . . . rats like people . . . are you drunk?" (67). Then he "discovers" a whole group of rats in the audience, and both men start furiously shooting into the audience.

In 1971 Turrini employed the same provocative style and language of the play in a Letter to the Editor, in which he announced the end of the language of ideologies and programs: ". . . FINISHED the words of love, those crapulous and prompted EKG-tones of language. FINISHED with this letter. IN THE BEGINNING was the grunt. And thus it shall be. And thus it shall remain . . ." (68).

In this letter to the "customer of culture" (69f.), which the audience was to read before seeing the play, Turrini quotes a number of opinions about his drama, with the aim of stressing the divergent, even contradictory viewpoints of the critics. But, as he writes in the letter, he as the playwright is not interested in the critics, only in the audience: ". . . my plays do not proclaim eternal values, they pose actual questions. . . ." Therefore his reaction to the attacks launched against him by some newspapers after the première of the play is simply: ". . . the word 'arise' has surely sent fewer people to death than 'forward march.' Thus I consider 'forward march' 'pornographic.' A naked bosom is more beautiful than a soldier torn to pieces. I consider war a blasphemy, and I prefer an orgy to the entry of the Russians into Prague. That was really something 'degenerate'. . ." (69).[6]

One reviewer of the first performance of *Rozznjogd* came to the conclusion that the more fervently the Austrian authors wish to distance themselves from the past, the closer they get to the conceptions of their predecessors. The baroque loathing of life lies at the source of Turrini's play, in which according to his critic people do not get closer to their intellectual sources but to their "animal origins" (73). Another critic wrote that the play intends to prove that the average citizen is at the same time the rat and the rat-killer, and consequently he refutes the author's attitude, which he finds untrue, dangerous, and overladen with symbolical implications (75). However, in 1974 a Hanoverian newspaper praised Turrini's skill as a dramatist and saw in him a moralist: "But it may well be that Turrini neither recognizes nor wants this" (77). Also, the success of the play was mentioned in this paper: "The audience was led from initial laughter through fright and shock to a grateful applause at the end" (77).

A point of interest is Turrini's conception of the end of this play: time and again the conclusion has been changed by stage managers and actors. Turrini agreed to having the dialogue shortened or left out completely at the end and also to the couple killing themselves on the stage or being killed by an actor sitting in the audience. He himself would prefer an ending where a truck carrying rubble dumps an avalanche of rubbish on the rubbish pile, burying the couple beneath it; but he is aware of the difficulties this ending would pose to a stage manager (71). As he said on another occasion in 1977: ". . . the theaters, . . . can stage the end in a way they consider right. Only one thing seems important to me: every attempt to gain freedom is destroyed the moment it starts to threaten the powerful people of this society . . ." (72). However, this statement could be countered by the play itself: the man and the woman are shot by mistake, because in a place people usually do not frequent they are believed to be rats and not because they themselves or the rats constitute a danger to the "powerful people."

In 1977 Turrini recalled with satisfaction the many occasions on which he had given readings of the play and talked about it to students, apprentices, and factory workers. He considers *Rozznjogd* a play to be "used" (*Gebrauchs-stück*). By relating it to the individual experiences of his listerners the play became "a part of the means for freedom." Nevertheless he came to the conclusion: ". . . were I to write this play today, it would be different. I would try to show an alternative. I believe it is uselsss to lead a fight for a freer and more just way of life alone. I believe that those who are in an identical or similar situation can only defend themselves when acting together. I believe in solidarity." (72).

"AT THE BEGINNING was the grunt . . ." Turrini had written in 1971, the year in which he wrote the folk play *Sauschlachten* (Pig-Killing), a play in which "grunting" is the main theme. Turrini follows the course set in 1966 with Martin Sperr's *Jagdszenen aus Niederbayern* (Hunting Scenes from Lower Bavaria), where Sperr demonstrates the unbroken continuity of fascistic be-havior among the rural population. In the introduction to his play Turrini states: "The language of this play is Austrian, approaching Carinthian. The happenings of the play are a series of physical and mental brutalities. Of course we Austrians didn't invent violence, we only inflict it more amusingly. And we are therefore justly called an extremely easygoing little nation" (83).

Quite a number of plays produced by the playwrights of the "new folk plays" hinge on the "little man's" diminishing ability to express himself. Loss of language is shown as the result of the unbearable pressure put upon him by the problems he has to face. That also happens to Valentin, or Volte, as he is called in Turrini's play. A grunt is the only form of expression he is willing or able to use. In the introduction, dedicated ironically to "my all too beloved country," Turrini at the first performance in Linz in 1972 stressed: "The son of the farmer Valentin, the grunter, is not an intellectual refusing to speak, the grunting does not express a conception, a *Weltanschauung,* here a person reacts out of his physical and psychic distress. The soul of this man had been destroyed before the same was done to his body" (126). And in the "actual edition" of 1977 Turrini expounded that the play simply represents the story of a man who does not fit into his surroundings: "I identify myself with the central figure of this play. My father was an Italian. I grew up in a Carinthian village. I always felt rejected by the rural surroundings, though I wanted so eagerly to belong . . ." (126).

Turrini blames the population and the newspapers for the things said and written about "guest-laborers," about people who for some reason are different and think differently: ". . . what shall we do with these people . . . pig killing? In my play words become deeds, murder of reputation becomes murder. Of late I have the feeling that reality is beginning to catch up with the play, with the theater" (127). The second play by far surpasses the first in brutality; not only verbal abuse, but also bodily harm is inflicted on Valentin – by his own father, by his half-brother, and by servants, before he is finally slaughtered like a pig.

In *Sauschlachten* Turrini depicts the dire picture of a farmer's household, in which each person has to be ashamed about something in his past. The famer's wife, Volte's mother, presented her husband, after his return fom the war, with a bastard, the son of a Russian prisoner of war; the farmer sleeps with the hired help; the farmhand recalls without compunction or shame his cruelties to the prisoners of war; and the bastard, Franz, revels in his hate. He hates everybody but above all his half-brother Volte, who is the rightful heir to the farm. And it is Franz who sets out to prove that Volte, because he refuses to speak, is no longer a human being. United by the hatred for the "creature Volte" – the farmer even forgets for the moment his aversion to his wife's bastard – they both attack Volte and force his head into a bucket filled with garbage, swine's food now suitable for Volte. The mother's halfhearted attempts to protect Volte cannot deter the other people on the farm from heaping abuse of the most despicable kind on Volte, and the horror becomes almost frenetic when the family in a united effort tries to make Volte talk with the help of "spiritual" encouragement: the father is certain that "his" son, unlike the bastard Franz, cannot fail to respond to the "song of the homeland," the hymn of the province. The farmhand wants Volte to pronounce the name of "our homeland" and does not mean by homeland "Austria" but the term *Großdeutschland* (Greater Germany) used during the Nazi reign. The fatal flaw in each of them is revealed in their sanctimonious patriotism: the pride and pleasure they take in remembering the "glorious" Nazi past, the tortures they inflicted on the "lesser people," the "others." Even the mother bemoans the callousness of Volte, who now refuses to join in the hymn, although as a two-year-old his picture had been in the local paper showing him saluting the District Commissioner.

As in the first play, here too the crux of the matter lies as much in what is implied as in what is actually said and done, in the readiness of each member of the household to agree to any suggestion about how to inflict pain and humiliation on Volte. And beneath the talk the tacit agreement between them to get rid of Volte is felt. Turrini skillfully discloses the workings of their minds, warped by fascistic conceptions, in the malicious misinterpretation of Volte's intention in cherishing some small possessions: a letter written to him by a sick girl, a book by Selma Lagerlöf, and paper flowers made by him all objects showing him to be far more "human" than his tormentors, who in their hatred for everything different from their own taste and sphere of interest and in their evil hypocrisy, find in these pitiful "treasures" only additional proof of Volte's not being "human."

Turrini leaves no doubt that Volte's family, under the pretext of imploring him to speak, gets a sadistic enjoyment from tormenting him. But it is only with the arrival of the "intelligentsia" of the village – the priest, the doctor, the teacher, and the lawyer – who are called in to help "convince" Volte to speak, that the moral depravity of the community is laid bare. Each of the four guests is in reality a distortion of what he ought to be: the lawyer who would have known very well what to do with Volte thirty years ago, when "our dear family physician was in charge of things like that" (116), a thinly veiled allusion to the practice of euthanasia during the Nazi regime. The doctor can only state that Valentin is just as healthy as the pigs and other farm animals, thus guiding the thoughts of the family to the "killing." The teacher matches the mental savagery of the lawyer and doctor by violating the language, "the highest accomplishment of heart and mind," into a muddle of misquotations, all aimed to prove that Volte's refusal to speak, his grunts are signs of not being "human." Finally, in the priest's "advice" all Turrini's sarcasm comes to the surface: the priest's quotations from the scripture refer solely to animals, creatures, and the like, and he does not even spare a thought for solving the problem of how Volte, the "human being," could be saved. He is far more concerned with the church tax the farmers have to pay (117). Finllly the doctor's taunting remark to the farmer: "Show us what you understand about farming, farmer Tonhof. Not every farmer is a good butcher . . ." (118), shows the family the path they are only too willing to follow: "If it pleases the gentlemen, I can give them a first-class example of pig-killing!" (118). Left to themselves the members of the household might eventually have brought about Volte's death by their cruel attempts to make him behave like "a human being." But now they have the "blessing" of the authorities and talk without restraint about killing the "animal" and about the meat and the sausages they will get from "it."

According to the stage instructions, the actual slaughter scene is enacted off stage; but the noises of the slaughtering, accompanied by music, form the aural background to the words and phrases which, although not connected, become sentences and evoke mental pictures of the lies, cruelty, and inhuman behavior witnessed on the stage. Turrini achieves this effect by pun-like genitive phrases which alliterate in German:

> The oath of the physician
> The suffering of men.
> The dash of the physician.
> The cutting up of men . . .

> > Tolerance
> > Total tolerance
> > Totalitarian tolerance
> > Dance of death . . . (122)

Turrini added to the program of the play a detailed description of pig-killing as "information for those who have not had the opportunity to attend a rural pig-killing . . .!" (122). The final scene is an exact repetition of the initial scene. The farmer's wife calls out: "The pork-roast is ready" (123) and the same people as in the first scene are seated around the table and start to eat—only Volte is missing.

Audiences and critics alike were shocked by the play. There was almost unanimous rejection of the drama and the accusations implied in it. Few were those who discerned "a deep, strong pity for animals, a hurt humanity" (137) beneath the gruesome actions on the stage, although many remarked on Turrini's talent, "perhaps the greatest talent among all the young theater-poachers from Sperr to Bauer" (132). The renowned György Sebestyén in the Viennese *Kronen-Zeitung* of 31 March 1972, however, deemed Turrini's situation a "tragic" one: "Here somebody wants to fight brutality—and preaches brutality." Sebestyén grants that Turrini is a "sensitive person and a militant moralist" but somewhat surprisingly reproaches him with advocating an attitude that "confuses sincerity with truthfulness" (136).

Clearly the play has to be understood as a parable, even though it differs from the parable plays of contemporary dramatists who also construct their plays around the problem of the outsider. All those dramatists, like Turrini, follow to a certain degree in the footsteps of Ödön von Horváth and Marieluise Fleißer, who in the 1920s exposed in their critical folk plays the stifling, sometimes even lethal coercion of the individual by circumstances and surroundings, which leave him little choice: if he wanted to live he had to conform. The "new folk plays" show the perfection of the ways and means by which pressure is applied; but they also strive to disclose the root of the matter. The roots grew out of the recent past and its ideology. The actions and reactions in their plays indicate an unregenerated society, which still unquestioningly believes in evil notions and nourishes blind prejudices. The playwrights of the "new folk plays" aim to denounce a generation that has forfeited every sense of personal responsibility and has subordinated itself to a state authority without questioning its moral validity. Turrini is perhaps the most outspoken in his criticism. He puts on stage the paradigm of rural parochialism, sustained by a still powerful adherence to fascist ideology and filled with the impenitent certainty that the community is competent to answer every question. His drama also differs from the "new folk play" in that the contingent aspects of personality are totally absorbed by the collective mentality. The "pig-killing" divests the executioners of the last shreds of human compassion. Just as Turrini exposed the dichotomy between appearance and reality in his first play, here in the second play the gulf between the surface and the scoundrel hidden beneath it is pointed out with a special twist by the patriotic songs and the use of slogans. They hark back to a past in which one part of the population usurped the right to decide who is "human" and had the power to kill and torture those judged by them to be "inferior."[8]

Turrini's next play, *Kindsmord* (*Infanticide*), was first performed in March 1973 in Klagenfurt and in Darmstadt. As some critics were quick to point out, Turrini here is primarily concerned with woman's emancipation or rather with the oppression of women, which, as he says, has become "in an infamous way 'bourgeois' . . . ." In the short notes about the play, written for the performance at Klagenfurt, Turrini points out that he is interested in the everyday occurrence of oppression, in the "normal" catastrophe of it: ". . . to show this, I can choose a proletarian setting, but I don't have to. I have written a play about the middle-class madness, about relations and circumstances that are all right, up to the time they end in murder" (155).

The play hinges on the personal relationship of the young woman with her father and her lover. Again the dichotomy between the visible and the hidden is the crucial point: "The brutal father, who thrashes his daughter, has turned into the loving father who blackmails his daughter with kindness. The husbands no longer command, they persuade. They are concerned about the whims of their wives and keep them pregnant to keep them busy. This open-minded middle class, a saurian reading 'Jasmin,' has sympathy for the suffering of those it misuses" (155).[9]

The play recalls "Outsiders of Society," a series of publications written by well-known writers of the early 1920s, each describing a crime actually committed. Turrini's play is preceded by a newspaper notice: "A twenty-six-year-old mother killed her ten-day-old child in he home of her well-to-do parents. The details and motive are not yet known. It is assumed that the act was committed in a state of emotional confusion" (142). The text is more or less a dramatic monologue by the accused young woman. The functions of the men – the judge, the father, the lover – are limited to steering the monologue along. The daughter-lover-accused perceives everything in emotional terms. There is no rational cause for her behavior neither before nor during the "infanticide": "I was bathing my daughter. Then I closed my hands around her throat. I held her under the water for a long time. Then she came up, and she looked like my doll . . ." (143 and 153).

This description of the murder is given twice: at the beginning and at the end of her monologue. It is not supposed to be an explanation for the deed, because the protagonist is not capable of giving an explanation for the deed, not having been brought up to consider either the cause or the result of her actions. The male domination in her life prevented her from developing her personality: "What is a woman after all? Every answer to that is masculine. My father always spoke of the mystery of woman. Men attribute what they want to us. A puzzle. A whore. A child. A lady. If you hear it often enough, you believe it. It gives you fulfillment. Being a daughter. Being a woman. Being a mother. I'm like moss. Frogs lay eggs in my hair. Snow covers everything." (152).

She knows that there must be more, that something must bring "her to life."

It is not enough to get free of the protective, smothering care that made her afraid and unsure. To "become alive" she would have had to erase everything that made up her life; but she had never succeeded in doing that, and so all her attempts to break away had resulted only in exchanging old chains for new ones. The lover plays the same role in her life as the father before him. Standing before the judge she recollects, bit by bit, the stages of her oppression, the means by which the suppression of her free will was achieved. Turrini lays bare the constraint and the coercion of her sexual needs, the fear of doctors during her pregnancy, the whole disaster of the twenty-six years of her life. The monologue divulges the repeated moral and spiritual violation of the girl's personality, the moral guilt and complicity of middle-class society.

There are some weak spots in the play, and the critics have been eager to point them out: the willingness of the young woman to follow the line of least resistance and the presentation of the "story" from one perspective only, because the remarks of the father and the lover only strengthen the young woman's version. Turrini here took up the trend of the socioliterary conceptions of the early 1970s by encapsulating the failure of the woman to avail herself of the possibilities for her personal development within the male-dominated atmosphere which was ignorant of her needs. However, despite the potential sentimentality in the presentation of the monologue, Turrini does not belabor the tragedy of the situation nor does he show the father or the lover as enjoying the girl's passivity and immaturity. Still, the interaction between overprotection and impairment of will power and ability to act, sets the tone for the play.

The reception of this play was rather tepid. Perhaps it follows from the theme of the drama that the bigger and more important newspapers were almost all in favor of Turrini's conception and treatment of the questions of woman's emancipation. *Kindsmord* was also the first of Turrini's plays to be screened by the Austrian Television ORF as well as aired by Austrian radio stations.

Only a few months after the première of *Kindsmord* there was a première of Turrini's *Die Wirtin* (1978, *The Landlady*), an adaptation of Goldoni's *La Locandiera*. It was commissioned by the municipal theaters of Nürnberg and was performed there in November 1973. In this play Turrini once more takes up the theme of woman's life in a society ruled by men. But in the eighteenth century this rule was neither disguised as protection nor clothed in flattery and caresses; it comprised all forms of life, every level of society. Turrini surprised quite a few of his critics and audiences by using Goldoni's *commedia dell'arte*. One must recall, however, that it had been Goldoni who struck the mortal blow to this kind of comedy, which by his time had become vulgarized and its inspiration had been replaced by exaggeration. It had also been Goldoni who two hundred years before Turrini and his contemporaries used the dialect of Venice in his comedies instead of the customary literary Italian spoken on the stage until then. Goldoni is often likened to Molière, but he is a Molière without the latter's cutting edge of wit. Although Goldoni enriched the *commedia dell'arte* with elements of the comedy of character, his plays lack bite; they are supposed to amuse, not to incite. The figures are for the most part likable, and the appeal of the comedies lies in their gentle humor. Turrini, of course, was quite aware of this, and he also knew that for Goldoni a woman's position in society depended largely on her individual skill and adaptability. In the introduction to his version of the play he points out:

> In Goldoni's comedy about Mirandolina everything is possible . . . For Goldoni woman's independence is a question of character. I love comedy, but there is quite a lot I do not consider possible. Certainly not then and not yet today. In my version a woman slaves and demeans herself for years, before she can get the lease of a tavern. The waiter loves "the innkeeper," because he wants to get hold of the tavern. The lord allows the emancipated Mirandolina to dupe him, only to hit back the harder. He who has the power has the means. In short, my play shows the connection between love and economic conditions (295).

As was to be expected, the critics did not like the reversal of the original play. Regrets were voiced that Turrini, by changing the comedy's ending, had ruined it and reduced Goldoni's polished play to the level of the "landlady couplets."[10] There were also some others who welcomed Turrini's message. He was praised for successfully transforming the comedy of character into a comedy of society, laying bare the selfish interest of this society, interests which ultimately determine the character of the individual. Those critics who found fault with the sometimes outspoken language used in Turrini's version had apparently overlooked the fact that Goldoni in his later plays, when he used the Venetian vernacular, paid little attention to the daintiness of language. At a later performance, in 1975, however, critics already recognized that Turrini had turned the *commedia dell'arte* into a tragic farce, into a folk play.

Just as in Turrini's *Der tollste Tag* (1973, *The Follies of a Day*), an adaptation of Beaumarchais's play, here too the most important changes are put into the last act. In effect Turrini presents a Goldoni "upside down." The action, which takes place about 1749 at a tavern in Florence, calls for three types of female roles: Mirandolina, the "landlady," and two "actresses," who are introduced as ladies of the aristocracy. Their only function is to show up the undiscerning personal reaction of two aristocrats who believe them to be a "baroness" and a "countess"; but when their "mistake" is pointed out to them, their flattery speedily turns into scorn and disdain. The deception as well as its disclosure was devised and carried out by the waiter Fabrizio with the aim of luring the two nobles away from Mirandolina. The sententiousness with which Mirandolina comes to the aid of her two female "guests" is motivated by more than personal feelings alone. When after the disclosure of the women's true identity she demands that they be treated with respect, she meets with the indignation of the two nobles. It is then that Mirandolina calls them to account: ". . . For you women are goods and love is a marketplace. You pay according to the size of the bosom and the importance of the title. This time you were mistaken, Earl. You invested unwisely . . ." She bids the two women good-bye with the exhortation: ". . . keep in mind: we women must stand by one another!" (290).

All the men in the play, the rich Earl and the poor Marquis, the Cavalier and the waiter, are after Mirandolina. She is beautiful, witty, and charming, and Goldoni lets her get the better of the men because of her wit, her "character." Turrini in his version of the play follows this course: even the avowed hater of women, the Cavalier, cannot resist her. At first impressed only by her witty conversation interspersed with clever flattery, he becomes enthralled by her high-spirited repartees as well as by her womanly charms. Finally he gives up all pretense and openly shows his infatuation with her. Even after Fabrizio in his jealousy has grossly slandered her and tried to convince the Cavalier that she is nothing but a strumpet indiscriminately squandering her favors, she finds the ways and means to persuade the Cavalier of the falsity of these accusations and has him again on his knees, imploring her to be his love.

Turrini's version runs close to its model, but it suddenly changes course when Mirandolina sends the Cavalier away after she pities him for his incapability of understanding woman: "For you a woman is a piece of dirt or a saint, a goddess. I can't help you there. I am neither the one nor the other. I am just a completely normal woman with good qualities and bad ones. A human being, do you understand? I am afraid, you don't . . . ." To his question about the meaning of her words, comes her halting answer: "I am sorry for you, Cavalier" (290-291).

The "proletarian" Fabrizio is chided for the lies he spreads about her, but after a short intermezzo, in which they try to get to understand each other, first by flattery then by rudeness, they agree upon "mutuality" in everything. The play approaches its "happy end"—apparently. Mirandolina recites the couplets that were meant to sum up the action at the end. Turrini also added

some barbed hints at the critics in these lines, and at the close of the play
Mirandolina explains the "aim" of this play:

> Honored audience. We wanted to show you to
> what, among other things, men are inclined,
> if they do not understand us women
> and only see our bosom or something.
> Yet, praised be God, at the finish
> of this play a beautiful ending was achieved.
> True love conquers.
> It is the best of everything and everyone.
> Now the curtain should come down . . . (293).

But the curtain does not come down. While Mirandolina speaks the last
lines, the Cavalier has come on the stage with a couple of policemen. They
arrest Fabrizio, and then the Cavalier cautiously taps Mirandolina on the shoulder and informs her about a few facts that are not "without importance" to
her: The man from whom she had rented the tavern is no longer its owner.
He, the Cavalier, had bought it four months ago and only the "somewhat
comedy-like happenings of the last few hours" had prevented him from telling
her sooner. He continues:

> As the responsible owner, I see myself forced to
> have a few personnel changes made.
> You, Mirandolina, shall in the future work in the kitchen.
> As to the waiter we'll hand him over to the military
> authorities now. Concerning the punishment for his
> other crimes, about which you so kindly have informed
> me, I'll abstain from it as long as you behave to my
> satisfaction.
> I believe that's all.
> How do you say it so beautifully?
> True love conquers.
> It is the best of everything and everyone.
> He who thinks so, will quickly come to his downfall.
> What counts is money.
> See you again (294).

The perspective of *Kindsmord* has been widened here. Again a woman is being manipulated, but she also manipulates others. However, Turrini leaves no doubt that by doing so she only avails herself of the sole way open to her. That she is nevertheless the loser at the end is a criticism of a society in which men are prepared to court a woman but refuse to let her succeed in her "practical" plans because she is not willing to play the part allocated to her. Turrini does not want to blur the issue: our society has an increased awareness of the possibility of such situations, and thus the sensitivity of the audience to the problem inherent in the theme is sharpened. The playwright operates at the close of the play on two levels: the audience witnesses a twofold humiliation of Mirandolina. It is not only the actual downfall, the drop from "innkeeper" to kitchen maid; she is also forced to acknowledge that her sway over men cannot be relied upon. The Cavalier's sudden switch from admirer to spiteful master has taught her that even her charms come second to money.

The objections of some critics to the atavism of showing the aristocracy as representatives of a degenerated stratum of society has also been raised at Turrini's version of Beaumarchais's *Der tollste Tag*. But Turrini in his endeavor to activate the audience's conscience was more concerned with the theme than with the dramatic figures. In the selection of the classical plays for his adaptation he has a clear-cut guiding principle: their suitability for demonstrating, first in the play itself and secondly in the deviation from the original, the significance of political and social aspects. The audience's reception of his first three plays had convinced Turrini that untrammeled aggression might force the author into the role of a court jester, a role he considered not only undignified but also unsuited to sociopolitical reality. In the remarks about the play published on the occasion of the first performance of *Der tollste Tag* in Darmstadt in February 1975 Turrini explained: "Of course, I didn't want to meddle with the master Beaumarchais's so very famous topic. I borrowed the theme to try out something: the relation between wit and power. Or: between language and facts" (22).

P. A. Baron de Beaumarchais's two comedies *Le Barbier de Séville* (1775) and *Le Mariage de Figaro* (1778, banned until 1784) were throwbacks to the old comedy of intrigue. With these two plays, Beaumarchais created comedies that were to convey, alongside the laughter, criticism of the ruling class, of society as such. Figaro's lines: ". . . Because you are a great lord you think you have a great talent . . . What have you done to deserve all these things? You took the trouble to get born, nothing more," gave the play a burning topicality and made Beaumarchais the bravest author of the century, despite the fact that Molière had nurtured conceptions far more revolutionary, and the Jacobins had cause to mistrust this "auteur-citoyen Beaumarchais," who had bought himself an aristocratic title. The philosophy of Beaumarchais's figures is not the philosophy of revolutionaries. In his plays one does not want to overthrow, only to correct, and the "corrections" sought are middle-class reforms. Thus in spite of the topical stirring speeches Beaumarchais puts into his Figaro's mouth, his comedy is not a political comedy. But it becomes one in Turrini's version. Still, one must concede in fairness that the impact of Beaumarchais's comedies was enormous; Danton is quoted as having said that Beaumarchais's Figaro killed the aristocracy, and Napoleon, according to some sources, saw beneath the hilarity of the play "the revolution in its approach."

Turrini objected to the happy ending of the play, to the illogical conciliatory spirit manifested at the end. Most importantly, he knew what had been Beaumarchais's real intention in writing the play, and he, Turrini, now could model his version according to it. Beaumarchais's own words had been: "Oh, how I regret not having made a tragedy of this moral theme. I would have put a dagger into the hand of the offended husband—whom I would not have called Figaro—and in his wrathful jealousy would have had him stab with a noble gesture that powerful seducer" (167). Turrini set out to do what Beaumarchais had not dared to do. In the third act, when Beaumarchais so brilliantly lets wit conquer force and power (because the possibilities and the power of speech are stronger than sheer might), Turrini turns the tables on this conception and puts the scales of history into their proper position. Figaro is sentenced to marry the elderly Marcelline. His beloved Susanne will have to submit to the count's will—Figaro's wit and resourcefulness have come to nought—and he too will have to submit to the count's decision. Both Beaumarchais and Turrini have the count say to the desperate Susanne: "What I like so much about Figaro is his wit. I'll think of some witty punishment for him" (222).

As Edmund Gleede has pointed out, Figaro is no better off than Rigoletto; both are but court jesters, and their wit is suffered by the ruler only as long as it is not directed against him (228-229). Also Susanne can only strike back verbally when the count, taunting her, considers the marriage to Marcelline not "witty" enough: "Thirty inspiring lashes on the back of the bridegroom are still lacking" (222). She can only retort: "Your wit is so powerful that the power smothers the wit" (222). But Susanne, when the count in distrust of her sudden meekness lashes out at her with the whip, discovers in her pain and anger the extent of her hate: not only the count, but everything he represents is vile and has to be deprived of power: "I hate you. Your blood is like filthy dregs. You are already dead even if you kill me. Dust seeps from your trousers. You are a generation that carries its entrails in its hands . . ." (222). Figaro, arriving on the scene, strangles the count with the same whip that a moment ago had cut Susanne's back.

Though on the surface Figaro's reaction is entirely personal in its motivation and his strangling the count an act of individual vengeance, his action is to be understood as the response of a whole class of society. The count's death, therefore, is the punishment not only for his intentions and actions, but also for those of the society to which he belonged. The dichotomy here is not the fundamental one between good and evil but between the powerful and their victims.

In his remarks "To this Play" Turrini stressed: "When power creates the facts, wit is no longer a weapon. Circumstances are stronger than language, power is stronger than wit: that is the theme of my play. Whether under these conditions a comedy can be maintained? Why not? I only hope people will understand what they are laughing about" (227). In the laughter, however, lies also the weakness of the play, and the success of Turrini's version of Beaumarchais's original cannot blur the discrepancy between the overtly expressed intention – the revolt against corrupt power – and the means, that is, the persons in the play who achieve that intention. The complacency of the underlings – of Bazillus, the judge Don Guzman, his servant Marcelline, even Cherubino – their readiness to adjust to the wish of their masters, flaws the implied revolutionary symbolism. They are not less corrupt than the count and they use all their cunning to harm those in lower social categories in order to please those of higher status. At the end Bazillus, when he finds the strangled count, rejoices in his death, robs him, and then bursts out: "Murder! Manslaughter! Revolution! Revolution!" Turrini concludes his version of Beaumarchais's incisive comedy in a way that the author of the original was afraid to adopt – with the "proclamation" of the revolution – by a subservient lackey who could well have served as a foil to the rebel Figaro.

That these disparities do not detract from the audience's pleasure and the play's success proves the skill with which Turrini builds up the climax-anticlimax of the drama and his mastery in handling the language. Klaus Colber has rightly pointed out that Turrini succeeds in getting the audience's attention with a pun taken from the original play, or at least reminiscent of it, and almost imperceptibly entices the public to accept a conclusion quite different from the one expected: in place of restored order the audience suddenly faces only the shambles of an illusion (238).

There were many speculations about the reasons that had caused Turrini to turn from the contentious folk play to the "tamer" adaptation of classical plays. In September 1975 in a *Werkstättengespräch* (workshop discussion) with Günther Nenning, Turrini explained his change of genre. The conviction had grown within him that in his plays he approaches the public with great vehemence and purpose only to learn "that his concern trickles away before a freshly dressed and perfumed audience" (343). He had learned also that with his plays written in dialect he would not be able to achieve what he had set out to do: "I found out that I crash through doors made of cotton wool. I shout or have people shout on the stage, pray for redemption, and there sits an audience applauding, pleased that for once it is not forced to sleep through a performance . . ." (249).

There was an additional reason: plays like *Rozenjogd* and *Sauschlachten* were usually shown as "special performances" of the big theaters, which thereby proclaimed their open-mindedness, their readiness to support new trends. At the same time they take good care not to shock their "regulars." As a result the "modern" plays are shown either at a very late hour or under a special heading: confrontation, experiment, etc. Therefore Turrini tried to find a way to reach the "regular" audience with plays they were used to but remodeled to show that the illusion created in these plays cannot be right. That beneath it are quite real social problems. The point of departure was *Der tollste Tag:* "Of course, it is a social parable, one that shows that wit leveled against great power is but a form of helplessness and that is, especially for Austria, something of great relevance. In Austria time and again political resistance has expressed itself in a very witty way. At every corner of a pub there the wittiest remarks are made about our politicians. But beyond that wit very little happens here . . ." (349).

In 1972, in the remarks in this adaptation, Turrini had pointed out that the theme of his version was to shatter the illusion that power could be overcome by wit; but two years later, after the demonstrated success of the play, Turrini was still dissatisfied. He did not believe he had achieved his goal because he had not really "succeeded in differentiating politically" (350) in his plays. To some extent at least he believed this failure to be the critics' fault too, because the crux of the matter was not the acuteness or differentiation of the political or sociopolitical message he wanted to convey but whether the message on reaching the public still carried the implication and signification that he, the author, had intended. Turrini was painfully aware of the danger of being misinterpreted by the critics and other literary specialists. He was afraid of being turned into a literary figure, an author writing for art's sake: "All of a sudden you find out that you wanted to convey something to the audience but the critic or the learned literary historian or Adabeis[11] intervened and started in a very learned way to qualify and quantify. That means one sets out with a question and ends up as a literary showpiece which is viewed by people from the other side of the glass. That is the harshest form of 'deprivation of love' . . ." (350). This "deprivation of love," or rather the deprivation of the author's right to communicate with the public without an intermediary, is deplored by a number of authors. Still, the failure to transmit the point of concern straight to the public without having it blurred by explanations and attempts at literary definitions cannot be put solely at the critics' door. It is the inertia that Turrini and others would like to put to an end with all means, dramatic and literary, to activate people to fight for a better life. The inertia of the audience gives the critics their power. Turrini believes that concentrating on television plays would free him from this circulus vitiosus. Through this medium he hopes to reach the public directly, to get the direct response that he received from his public readings and that gave him the feeling of being useful and needed.

During a conversation with Günther Nenning, Turrini protested against the "romantic conception" that in a society of contradiction and contention one could produce pure art. The imputation of "standing aside" is usually raised against the generation of these authors' fathers,[12] whereas the engagement and involvement of the generation of sons in the sociopolitical scene is hardly to be questioned. But here again Turrini is asking for more—for inside knowledge. When he turned to regional literature in his television scripts, he did not, as in *Sauschlachten*, intend to draw the attention to the aftereffects of a past remembered without compunction. In *Alpensaga* (1980, Tale of the Alps) the potential reality of the situations and happenings shown was the author's prime concern. Therefore the background of the scenes shown had to be historically as well as economically and socially correct.

A case in point is the importance Turrini attached to the research that preceded work on the script *Der Bauer und der Millionär* (1975, The Farmer and the Millionaire).[13] "When I write a book with Pevny, like The Farmer and the Millionaire, we go to Upper Austria for three months. We painstakingly research everything on the spot, from the abbot at the monastery Kremsmünster to the smallest farmer, to find out what has happened in this part of the country" (348).

The preparations for the *Alpensaga* were even more thorough. In January 1973 the head of the Institute for Contemporary History of the University of Vienna informed the relevant department of the Austrian television network that the study of the script for *Alpensaga* had shown it to be a very workable rendering of reality, from the historical as well as from the socioeconomical point of view; that all the social components of Upper Austria, important events, etc., had been duly taken into consideration and that the atmosphere of the time and the persons living in it had been well presented. Furthermore, it was agreed that a specialist for the local history of Upper Austria should supervise the construction of the sets during the shooting of the series, since especially in the twentieth century there had been great changes in the manner of building and furnishing farms.

But in spite of all these precautions, after only three days of work on the film and before the first part of the series was aired, the protests began solely on the basis of a few pages about the *Alpensaga* in an Austrian literary journal. Letters and articles by various rural organizations expressing indignation and wrath arrived at the offices of the ORF television station. Attempts to repudiate the accusations leveled at the authors, whose political allegiance was mentioned as an a priori cause for suspicion, were of little avail. Church authorities joined the protest, and previously granted permission to shoot the scenes for the fourth part of the series in a village church was withdrawn. The farmers' journal exhorted its members and readers to keep in mind that they must unite to prevent the screening of the *Alpensaga*. Individual members of the rural communities voiced their indignation about the speech patterns in the series. Veterans of the First World War felt that some of the scenes showing the farmers' reaction during the last year of the war were a vicious slander of their generation. Some newspapers viewed the attempts to prevent the showing of the series as a return to the methods of the recent past and remonstrated strongly against those interferences. Finally the series was shown in Austria, in West Germany, and in Switzerland and met with considerable success, even in rural communities!

In the Nenning interview Turrini expounded the twofold reasons for his attempt to create "regional Austria culture": to show the communities' roots and to stem the influx of foreign ideological influences as propagated by overseas films and shows. As to the farm milieu he and his co-writer had chosen, there were again two reasons: that Turrini had grown up in such an environment and that Turrini wanted to correct its image: "I believe that of all social strata the rural one has been ridiculed most by the media. Such a twisting of the real situation almost never occurs with other social strata. Here was a concrete possibility to show an alternative . . ." (346).

The first part of the *Alpensaga,* "Liebe im Dorf" (Love in the Village), first televised in October 1976, centers on a love story that mirrors the situation and the atmosphere at the turn of the century. The action of the second part takes place shortly before the outbreak of the First World War, and its main characters are two outsiders—a soldier returning to his native village after many years and a Slovenian woman expecting a child. The third part of the series caused the most violent protests. The time of the story was 1918, and the farmers' wives were shown hiding their few belongings, mostly food, from the soldiers of the Austrian army. The last three parts show situations and life in the thirties and after the Second World War. The interest of the public and the fact that other European television companies also screened the series prove that the intentions and hopes of Turrini and his co-workers in producing the films had been quite justified.

In the mid-seventies Turrini could often be read and heard outside the theatrical scene. In pamphlets and proclamations he protested against the literary situation, and his manifesto of "cultural fog," *Es ist ein gutes Land – Manifest der österreichischen Kulturnebolution* (1972, It Is a Good Land – Manifesto of the Austrian Cultural Nebolution, 367ff.) attracted considerable attention. The manifesto is an attack consisting of a mixture of puns, suggestions, and statements aimed against state authorities, the church, and the malleable public. Turrini must have been well aware of the paradox inherent in the manifesto: the mastery of language in the seventy-five "pronouncements" would let the intellectual "elite" enjoy them but at the same time make them incomprehensible to those he had wanted to reach in order to ridicule the intellectual "elite."

The common denominator of all of Turrini's writings is doubtlessly a desire to inform people, situations, the society, and the world. The way to this goal may well begin by raising doubts, especially since the last generation had to learn that one cannot trust the moral rectitude of its leaders and that there are no guidelines for the individual in a society suffering from moral disorientation. Doubt is an important element in the search for certainty and rectitude. Turrini starts his search by trying to understand the community he comes from, by narrowing the search in his endeavors to get to know his family and by recalling his childhood. In *Ein paar Schritte zurück* (A Few Steps Back), a volume of poems published in 1980, Turrini retraces his steps; he looks closely at the hurt incurred in childhood, at the scars he willfully prevented from healing. The poems help us to find the key to the author's personality. They show the cause for his actions and reactions, illustrate the events and experience that make up his life. Not surprisingly the book starts with a question: "Is this weariness that suddenly overcomes me / the cloak to cover all the tears of my childhood? Is the ache / that racks me / an invitation / to go back once more? . . ." (79).

Childhood is very seldom a time of complete happiness. Turrini's childhood was haunted by fears nurtured by a permanent sense of not belonging; Turrini voices all those fears and sentiments that will probably abound in the next decade in the childhood memories of children of guest workers living in Western

Europe. The language of the poems is simple and adds but little to the stark images involved. It is the simplicity of the language and the short form of the poems that offer Turrini the possibility of divulging so convincingly the cause of a child's anguish, of conveying the bashful experiences of the adolescent, the dejection of the grown-up. Images and memories of the kind most of us want to forget are forced to the surface of Turrini's conscience while he directs his steps backward into his childhood. It is not self-pity that makes him do this, nor self-justification; he simply wants to know, to understand in order to voice a knowledge to be shared by others and thus ease their pain.

The child's halfhearted attempts to reach out to his father were thwarted by fear and by the far stronger presence of his mother. The efforts of the youth to approach his father through poetry were rebuffed by the latter's passivity. Turrini is most eloquent in those poems invoking the image of his father— "That little Italian / for whom the snow came too early / and the German language too late / was afraid "—(82) because he felt that there was no place for "foreigners" among the local people at the pub. "Not to attract attention / he kept silent and worked / assumed the local virtues / until they buried him . . ." (82). Turrini even remembers lovingly the only time his father had hit him: ". . . all the other blows / I invented them / out of a longing / for a repetition of this blow" (80). The reader has to identify with the expectation and frustration in the stanza of the poem describing the day on which Turrini's first poems were aired in Klagenfurt: "Friday at half past two. / Five minutes after half past two / my father came into the kitchen / my mother put his tea before him / and he ate. / It was impossible / to find out from the looks of his / whether he was listening / or not."[14] There is an almost exaggerated lack of attempt to embellish the images and thoughts by poetic language; in the love poems too, the uncertainty, the dire repetition and disappointment, the failure to reach the "shore" are only recalled, nothing is glossed over.

Turrini's poems have an undeniable affinity with the lyrics of the "New Subjectivity" (*Neue Subjektivität*) in form, content, and in the language bordering on rhythmic prose. The poetry of the *Neue Subjektivität* – just like Turrini's –does not imply or connote, neither does it aspire to esoteric meaning. Still, despite this apparent similarity Turrini does not really belong to this group of writers. To expound the disparity would entail scrutiny of the poetry of the *Neue Subjektivität* and transcend the frame of this essay. But one can point out the main difference which lies in Turrini's approach to the theme and in his continuous questioning of the role of the observer, even of the capacity of this observer, the "I," to understand. There is fear in Turrini's poems, but it never erodes feelings; there is regret for a vacuum that no longer can be filled, for gestures and words omitted. Sad, sometimes even trite as the images presented may be, together they merge into a picture in which there is still hope and belief. The regret in these poems never becomes self-pity, but it approaches compassion and wishful thinking.

Compassion is also the keynote of Turrini's play of 1980 *Josef und Maria.* [15] As in his first play the number of actors is limited to two: Maria, a sixty-five-year-old charwoman, whose daughter-in-law does not want her, does not even agree to her rare visits to see her son and grandchild, and Josef, sixty-eight years old, employed as a security guard. Without family or friends he clings to his party membership, although the "comrades" of the past that he so fondly remembers are all dead, and the younger members no longer want him. In the introduction to the play Turrini writes: "Society's image of old people is least of all determined by the aged themselves. Advertising discovers them as a 'special group of buyers,' television presents them as cheerful 'senior citizens,' and even academic sociology discovers in them only what is presupposed from the beginning: that they are an underprivileged minority" (3).

Still Turrini wrote a play *for* old people rather than one *about* old people. By choosing Christmas Eve as the time of the play's action and giving the figures names evoking the biblical personages connected with the holiday he intentionally and daringly brings the play close to the trivial: the cliché of the Christmas spirit sets the tone for the story. In a consumer society, an image stressed by the choice of the salesrooms of a big department store as stage setting, the individual is motivated mainly by materialistic need, the veneer of brotherhood, love, and compassion has worn thin in the ceaseless strife for possession — those are the impressions Turrini wants to convey to his audience — but nevertheless human warmth and mutual understanding triumph.

Consistent with the decor is the attitude of this society in which people are categorized according to their usefulness; this attitude manifests itself even before the actors appear on the stage: the holiday music suitable for the Christmas atmosphere is interrupted by an announcement — the management is pleased to award to the personnel as a token of appreciation a small bottle of liqueur — "The personnel of the accounting department, those not working on a regular basis, the cleaning women and our foreign co-workers," are not included however. During the announcement an "elderly lady," made-up and well-dressed, comes on the stage. From the first moment of the action Turrini's dramatic strategy of disclosing dichotomy becomes obvious. By shedding the outer garments, rubbing off the makeup and hiding her freshly done hair beneath a handkerchief the lady is transformed into Maria, the charwoman, who does not belong to the "regular workers." The speed and the simple means by which this transformation can be achieved reveals not only the thin line between appearance and reality—the authenticity of everything else becomes questionable. Just as Maria is so easily and quickly able to peel off these layers of a life not really hers, the sentences she shouts into an unconnected microphone—wishes addressed to her son for a nice holiday, health and happiness—are shown up in the following conversation with Josef to be nothing but a substitute for actual human contact, a verbal expression of her own unhappiness and loneliness.

Turrini wants the discrepancy between the visible and the hidden to be understood as something forced on these elderly people, made necessary by the callousness of an environment that no longer has time for understanding and compassion. Therefore the dialogue between Maria and Josef deteriorates quickly into two soliloquies. Each of the two elderly people tells the thoughts uppermost in his or her mind without listening to the words of the other. This "lack of communication" reflects the problems they have to cope with in a society in which youth and health are at a premium, and the elderly are faced with the necessity of continually coming to terms with these facts. They are no longer used to talking to people because they cannot expect anybody to listen to them. The longer the "conversation" between these two people goes on, however, the closer they come to understanding each other.

Gerd Heinz, who staged the first performance of the play in 1980, drew attention to the structure of the dialogue: ". . . a dialogue arrived at through the experience with *Alpensaga,* finally gives the theater in a theatrical form that realism which the film had usurped from reality some time before; a discontinuous dialogue, associative, synoptic. The depth is on the surface (Heraclitus). If one can make the surface as transparent as Turrini is able to . . ." (5). The dialogue is not lacking in humor, sometimes unintentional humor. For example, the offer Josef adds to some long-winded story he has just recounted: "If it is interesting, I can give more details, . . ." (14), while Maria has clearly shown by her remarks that she had not been listening at all to Josef's story. On another occasion Maria interrupts Josef's soliloguy with the speech-gesture: "Don't let me interrupt you . . ." (16).

While recounting their unhappiness, recalling the lost hopes and the highlights of their past, they come closer to each other, more by hearing a human voice actually speaking to them directly than by taking in what is said. In their attempt to reach each other they disclose their bodily pains as well, desiring the other to touch and feel the hurt. But they are still so entangled in their loneliness, imprisoned in the memories of solitude, that they cannot quite span the distance that years of bitter experience had taught them to keep from their fellowmen. However, from the rambling disclosures of their past life it becomes clear that the barrier erected throughout the time of disappointment and rejection has to a certain extent also served as a screen to ward off new injuries and hurts.

Maria and Josef dare to come out of their loneliness and to approach each other; ready to take a fresh lease on life, they risk love. In the notes for the staging of the play Turrini stipulates that the two persons in the play not be presented as scurrilous types: "The ridiculous about them should not be ridiculed. The sad and the tragic should not be acted sadly or tragically. The two old people in the play have lived so long with their peculiarities that they are for them something normal, self-evident. That obviousness and the attempt to overcome it is the theme of the play" (6). Before Turrini published the play, a television version of it had been shown under the same title. The success of both the film and the play seems to suggest that there still is a need for a play with a happy ending.

But the author himself arrived at a different conclusion, and in the fall of 1981 the announcement of the planned performance of his new play *Die Bürger von Wien* (1982, The Citizens of Vienna) created an uproar. Because of the protest of a number of personages belonging to Viennese high society, who believed themselves to be portrayed by some of the dramatic personae of the play, the title of the play had to be shortened to *Die Bürger* and some alterations of text had to be made. But in spite of the rather violent discussions about the play in the local newspapers, which surely heightened the interest of the audience-to-be, the play, when final staged at the *Volkstheater* in Vienna, was far from being a success. There was no doubt about the actuality of the theme and the vehemence with which Turrini castigated the career- and money-minded types in contemporary society. However, the moralist Turrini did not get the help of the dramatist Turrini: the tirades of accusations voiced on the stage and the lack of dramatic action were judged "monotonous and dull." The suicide of the son of the house, the result of his hopeless disgust with the life and society of his parents, came "too late" to save the play.

Perhaps it was the failure of *Die Bürger* which caused Turrini immediately afterward to turn again to Goldoni; his version of *Il Campiello* (The Little Square)—the original play dates back to 1756—divided the critics into Turrini fans and Goldoni defenders. The latter contested Turrini's version because they deemed it too crude and not in accord either with Goldoni's style and intention or with the setting in Venice. But even those who called the version a "romantic changeling" conceded that Turrini had written an amusing play along the lines of a "precious model" constructed by Goldoni. The plot revolves around the lives of four families who live in a little square in Venice. There are street fights and domineering mothers, social ambitions, and young love threatened with being sacrificed to material motives. Turrini, satirizing the social conflict with vigor, achieves a "verbal masterpiece," rich in comical and amusing scenes, as some of his fans among the critics have pointed out. Supported by an excellent staging and acting team, the play right from the first performance was an undisputed success. The love scenes especially were praised as among the best written and staged in our decade.[16]

It seems rather inopportune to arrive at any final evaluation of an author in mid-career. If there is a general impression to be gathered from the trend and tone of Turrini's writings up to now, it is his constant concern for mankind. The prominent position Turrini holds among the playwrights and authors of his generation derives from his brave attempt to find the way back from authenticity to sincerity. The world he depicts is no less cruel and dire than the world we are made to see by Thomas Bernhard or Wolfgang Bauer, Turrini's Austrian colleagues. But the Turrini of the past few years permits a spark of hope. The field of vision he presents opens a gap where a ray of light may come in. He has proved himself to be an eclectic writer, belonging to the rather rare group of Austrians who share with many of their German colleagues the wish to contribute to a purer conception of life by treating themes of *Vergangenheitsbewältigung* (coming to terms with the recent past, i.e. the Nazi period). That stance automatically makes him concerned with the moral obligations to the present and even more to the future. His figures enact this obligation. He does not offer them refuge in a make-believe world and does not encourage attempts to escape into doctrines and political ideologies, because he does not want to lessen the ultimate responsibility for the state of the world, a responsibility that Turrini, as an uncompromising if compassionate moralist, places upon each of us.

Notes

1. Peter Handke, *Publikumsbeschimpfung und andere Sprechstücke* (Frankfurt am Main: Suhrkamp, 1966).
2. Peter Turrini, *Turrini Lesebuch* (Wien: Europaverlag, 1978), p. 71. Unless otherwise stated all quotations are taken from this book and will be cited in the text by page number.
3. The full title of the play is *Rozznjogd*, from motifs by Willard Manus. Manus belonged to the group of young people with whom Turrini lived on Rhodos.

4. See Peter Pabisch, "Sensitivität und Kalkül in der jüngsten Prosa Hans Carl Artmanns," in *Modern Austrian Literature*, Vol. 13, no. 1 (1980), 129–147.

5. In the dialect as well as in the High-German version the word "kill" is used, with the letter 'n' or 'en' added to give it the standard German verb ending.

6. Turrini deviates here from the German grammatical rules of writing and does not use capitals for nouns or at the beginning of a sentence. This form of "language protest" was in vogue for a short time around 1917 and again fifty years later.

7. The Nazis had brought into the language "German notions" like *Gau* for "county" etc. A Gauleiter was the man put in charge of the county, almost always an all-powerful member of the NS-party.

8. Both Martin Sperr in *Jagdszenen aus Niederbayern* (1971) and Franz Xaver Kroetz in *Wildwechsel* (1971) have persons in their plays utter sentiments stemming from the time and ideology of the Nazi regime.

9. *Jasmin* is an Austrian woman's journal.

10. An allusion to the rather bawdy songs about *Die Wirtin von der Lahn* and her sexual escapades.

11. *Adabei* is an Austriacism, mainly used in Vienna, stemming from the fusion of "a dabai" (auch dabei—"been there too"). It is used to define a person who wants to belong, to have been there too. The English equivalent would be a "name dropper." The expression is listed by Heinz Küpper in *Wörterbuch der deutschen Umgangssprache II* (Hamburg: Classen Verlag, 1966).

12. See also the essay about Peter Henisch (a friend of Turrini's in an accompanying volume as well as Joseph P. Strelka, "Eine Phänomenologie des Mitmachens: Zur frühen, autobiographischen Erzählprosa von Peter Henisch," in *Modern Austrian Literature*, Vol. 13, no. 1 (1980), 149–161.

13. The series *Alpensaga* is also a co-production of Peter Turrini and Wilhelm Pevny.

14. The poems are quoted from Peter Turrini: *Ein paar Schritte zurück. Gedichte,* in *Literatur und Kritik,* Tag der Lyrik, Vol. 142 (1980), 79ff.

15. Peter Turrini, *Josef und Maria* (Wien: Thomas Sessler-Verlag, 1980).

16. In *Bühne. Das österreichische Theatermagazin* (November 1982), 29f.

Primary Works

Erlebnisse in der Mundhöhle. Roman. Reinbek: Rowohlt, 1972.
Der tollste Tag. Frei nach Beaumarchais. Wollerau, Wien, München: Georg Lentz, 1973.
Rozznjogd. Wollerau, Wien, München: Georg Lentz, 1973.
Sauschlachten. Wollerau, Wien, München: George Lentz, 1973.
Der Dorfschullehrer. Zusammen mit Wilhelm Pevny. Eisenstadt: Edition Roetzer, Wien, München: Sessler, 1975.
Der Bauer und der Millionär. Eine Filmerzählung. Zusammen mit Wilhelm Pevny. Salzburg, Wien: Residenz Verlag, 1978.
Die Wirtin. Frei nach Goldoni. Wien, München: Sessler, 1978.
Turrini Lesebuch. Stücke, Pamphlete, Filme, Reaktionen etc. Ausgewählt und bearbeitet von Ulf Birbaumer. Wien, München, Zürich: Europaverlag, 1978.
Alpensaga. Zusammen mit Wilhelm Pevny. Salzburg, Wien: Residenz Verlag, 1980.
In meinem Kopf schreit es. Gedichte. München: Autoren Edition, 1980.
Josef und Maria. Wien: Frischfleisch & Löwenmaul, 1980.
Ein paar Schritte zurück. Gedichte. München: Autoren Edition, 1980.
Turrini Lesebuch zwei. Stücke, Film, Gedichte, Reaktionen etc. Ausgewählt und bearbeitet von Ulf Birbaumer. Wien, München, Zürich: Europaverlag, 1983.

Works in English Translation

Infanticide (Kindsmord), translated by Herbert Kuhner. *Dimension,* Vol. 11, no. 2 (1978).

Selected Secondary Works

Ulf Birbaumer, ed., *Turrini Lesebuch.* Wien: Europaverlag, 1978. Contains various reviews and critiques.
Johann Drumbl, "Die falschen Sätze. Annäherung an eine Poetik," in *Annali dell'Istituto di lingue e letterature germanische della Facoltà di magistero dell'università di Parma,* Vol. 5 (1978-1979), 207-230.
Jean-Claude François. "De Ödön von Horváth à Peter Turrini. Aspects du "Volksstück" dans le theâtre autrichien de 1918 à nos jours," in: *Austriaca,* Heft 5 (1979), Sonderheft "Deux fois l'Autriche," pp. 61-77, 149-161.

Brigitte Hofer, "Peter Turrini, Schriftsteller (Gespräch)," in *Antworten: Gespräche mit Wiener Künstlern.* Wien: Edition Tusch, 1980.

Elfriede Jelinek, "Der Turrini-Peter," in *Österreich zum Beispiel.* Salzburg, Wien, 1982, pp. 335-336.

Name and Title Index

Brigitte L. Schneider-Halvorson

The Late Dramatic Works of Arthur Schnitzler

American University Studies: Series I
(Germanic Languages and Literature). Vol. 10
ISBN 0-8204-0009-2   174 pp.   paperback US $ 18.40

Recommended price – alterations reserved

A thorough interpretation of Schnitzler's dramas, published after World War I, shows a distinct development toward maturity. This can be seen in the complexity of his characters, especially women who manifest personal freedom of choice in their lives. The idea of equating "home or returning home" with "love" is new an indicative of the maturing process. The theme of age or aging is interpreted differently. Recurring "Leitgestalten" and "Leitmotive" emphasize Schnitzler's process of ethical and moral revaluation in his late dramatic works. Contrary to common assumptions, these dramas continue to demonstrate the importance Schnitzler's as a dramatist.

Contents: The key issues raised in *Die Schwestern oder Casanova in Spa* concern the principle of polarity in both characters and incidents in their lives, complexity of human nature, question of fidelity in terms of "Heimkehr" or "Wiederkehr", acceptance of individual responsibility. The constellation of *Eros-Krieg-Märchen/Imagination* and its various triangular combinations seen in *Komödie der Verführung* crystallize Schnitzler's key ideas and concerns. The idea of freedom forms an important aspect in *Der Gang zum Weiher*. It is connected to the question of responsibility and commitment, and willingness to accept these premises. It is in light of a person's inner search that Schnitzler's latest drama *Im Spiel der Sommerlüfte* gains in value and deserves more recognition. The answer to the question: "Sind wir ein Spiel von jedem Druck der Luft?" depends upon strength of character to maintain its identity and govern the intensity of one's life experience.

PETER LANG PUBLISHING, INC.
62 West 45th Street
USA – New York, NY 10036

Donna C. Van Handle

Das Spiel vor der Menge

Hugo von Hofmannsthals Bemühungen um Bühnenwirksamkeit am Beispiel
ausgewählter Dramen

American University Studies: Series I
(Germanic Languages and Literature). Vol. 44
ISBN 0-8204-0260-5   172 pp.   hardcover US $ 24.50

Recommended price – alterations reserved

Dieses Buch befaßt sich mit der Entwicklung des österreichischen Dichters
Hugo von Hofmannsthal als Theaterdichter, der der Rolle der Bühne in seinem
Werk eine immer größere Bedeutung zuschrieb. Durch eine Untersuchung ausgewählter Dramen aus den von Hofmannsthal selber definierten drei Epochen
seines dramatischen Schaffens wird gezeigt, wie der Dichter sich immer mehr
um die Bühnenwirksamkeit seiner Werke bemühte. Neben den lyrischen Dramen und „Alkestis" werden einige spätere Werke des Dichters behandelt: den
Publikumserfolg „Jedermann" sowie die verschiedenen Fassungen der miß-
glückten Komödie „Cristinas Heimreise" und des mehrmals revidierten Libret-
tos „Ariadne auf Naxos". Mit den Revisionen und Umarbeitungen der Texte
wollte Hofmannsthal Stücke schaffen, die dem Zuschauer seine Ideen am wir-
kungsvollsten offenbaren, während sie ihn zugleich unterhalten.
Aus dem Inhalt: Hugo von Hofmannsthal: seine Bemühungen um Bühnenwirksamkeit in seinen frühen lyrischen Dramen, „Jedermann", „Cristinas
Heimreise", „Adriadne auf Naxos", „Der Bürger als Edelmann".

PETER LANG PUBLISHING, INC.
62 West 45th Street
USA – New York, NY 10036